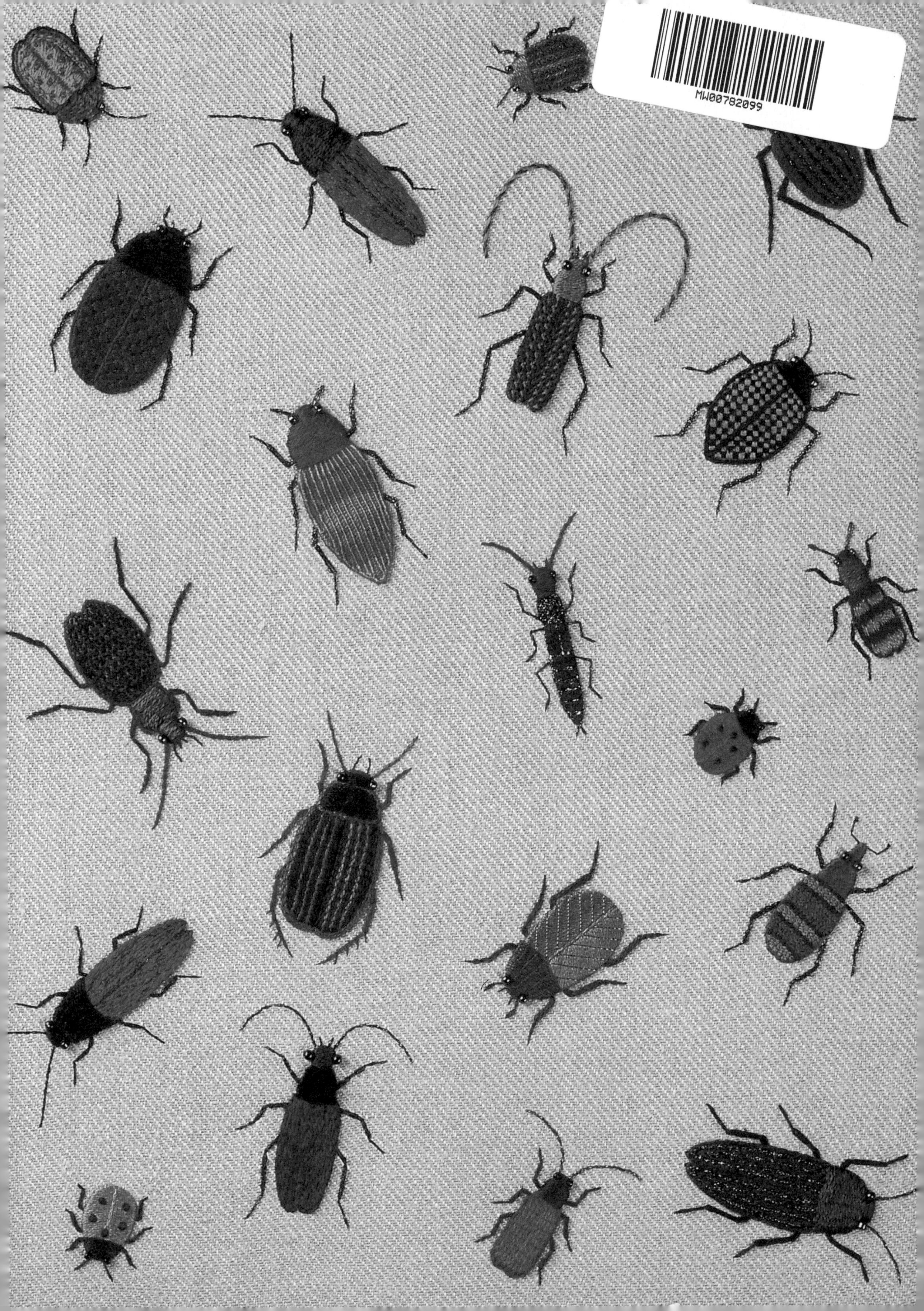
MW00782099

The Stumpwork, Goldwork and Surface Embroidery Beetle Collection

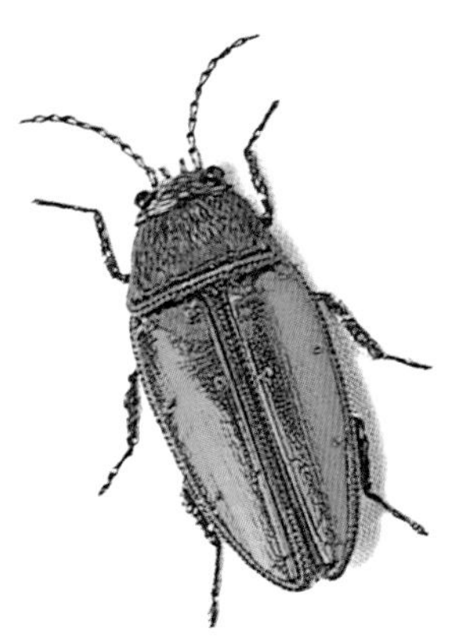

The Stumpwork, Goldwork and Surface Embroidery Beetle Collection

Jane Nicholas

First published in 2004 by
Sally Milner Publishing Pty Ltd
PO Box 2104
Bowral NSW 2576
AUSTRALIA

Reprinted 2004

Design: Anna Warren, Warren Ventures Pty Ltd
Editing: Anne Savage
Photography: Tim Connolly

Printed in China

National Library of Australia Cataloguing-in-Publication data:

Nicholas, Jane.
The stumpwork, goldwork and surface embroidery beetle collection.

Bibliography.
Includes index.
ISBN 1 86351 318 3.

1. Stump work. 2. Embroidery. I. Title. (Series : Milner craft series).

746.44

10 9 8 7 6 5 4 3 2

Contents

Introduction 9

Part 1: The Beetle 11

Natural History 12

Anatomy of a Beetle 15

Part 2: The Beetle as Embellishment 19

The Scarab Beetle 20

The Beetle as Design Source 22

The Beetle and Jewellery 27

Beetle Buttons 32

Beaded Beetles 36

Red-orange Beaded Beetle 37

Blue-green Beaded Beetle 41

The Medallion Borders 43

Part 3: Beetle Wing Embroidery 47

Beetle Wings as Adornment 49

A Victorian Dress 54

Victorian Jewel Embroidery 59

Working with Beetle Wings 64

Beetle Wing Evening Bag 67

Part 4: Stumpwork Beetles 73

How to Embroider a Stumpwork Beetle 74

The Beetle Specimen Box 83

Stumpwork Projects 177

Peacock, Grapevine and Beetle 178

Crocus, Clover and Jewel Beetle 193

Fritillary, Fennel and Scarab Beetle 206

Beetle and Boysenberries 219

Scarab Beetle Brooch 223

Part 5: Goldwork Beetles 227

How to Embroider a Goldwork Beetle 230

Goldwork Beetle Sampler 237

Pomegranates, Snail and Gold Beetle 249

Gold Violin Beetle 262

Or Nué Beetle 271

Gold Stumpwork Beetles 275

How to Embroider a Gold Stumpwork Beetle 276

Embroidered Initial and Beetle 284

Part 6: Beetles in Surface Embroidery 291

How to Work a Beetle in Surface Embroidery 294

The Ladybird Notebook Cover 338

Redwork Beetles 339

How to Embroider Redwork Beetles 341

Redwork Beetle Bag 341

Part 7: Appliqué Beetles 345
How to Appliqué a Beetle 347
Appliqué Beetles in Fabric 348
Appliqué Beetle in Felt 356
Part 8: Beetle Bags 361
The Beetle Shape as Inspiration 362
Scarab Beetle Pouch 363
Beetle Evening Bag 369
Part 9: Techniques and Equipment 377
Transferring a Design to Fabric 378
Working with Vliesofix 381
Working with Wire 382
Working with Leather 384
To Mount Stumpwork into a Paperweight 386
Equipment 388
Needles 389
Thread Conversion Chart 391
Part 10: Stitch Glossary 395
Bibliography and Further Reading 412
Stumpwork Supplies and Kit Information 414
Picture Credits 415
Index 417
Acknowledgements 424

Introduction

'Why beetles?', I am often asked. What started as a fascination with beetles became an absolute passion when I discovered Evans and Bellamy's book, *An Inordinate Fondness for Beetles*, at a bookstore in Indianapolis in 1998, the title being a reference to scientist J.B.S. Haldane's response when asked 'What could be inferred about the Creator from a study of His works?' As I turned the pages of this wonderful book, my imagination was captured, visualising the stumpwork beetles that could be stitched, using the stunning photographs for inspiration. The idea of the stumpwork beetle specimen box was born! From then on, whenever time allowed, my destination was the entomology department of many museums, observing and drawing actual beetle specimens to my heart's delight.

I have always recorded ideas and drawn sketches in a notebook, and as the months went by the entries burgeoned to interpret the beetle not only in stumpwork, but in many other forms of embroidery. Glittering goldwork beetles, inspired by Art Nouveau jewellery; beaded beetles, from mosaic buttons; redwork beetles, first seen on an antique quilt on display in Omaha, Nebraska; and beetles in surface stitchery, using lustrous silk and metallic threads (what started out as a few beetles for the endpapers ended up being 39!).

An even more tenuous link with embroidered beetles was the discovery of beetle wings for use in embroidery. Whilst teaching near San Francisco, a friend had taken me to a curious shop where, amongst many intriguing items, iridescent green beetle elytra (singular elytron: the hard outer wing case) were for sale. I had to have some! This lead to research about beetle wings as embellishment, from their use by remote tribes in isolated regions of the world to Europe and the decorated embroideries of the late nineteenth century.

Still the notebook entries continued—the beetles getting larger, with simplified versions in appliqué; and finally the beetle shape itself, manifested as a handbag.

The journey has been fascinating and compelling, with invaluable contributions from many interesting people. Having a theme to explore has given direction and purpose to research, and a great excuse to purchase 'just one more book'! On looking back over the pages of my notebooks, I came across a scrawled note—'we must keep adding to our store of things that delight and inspire us'. My hope is that this book will 'delight and inspire', and that you may find an idea that you just have to stitch!

Part 1:
The Beetle

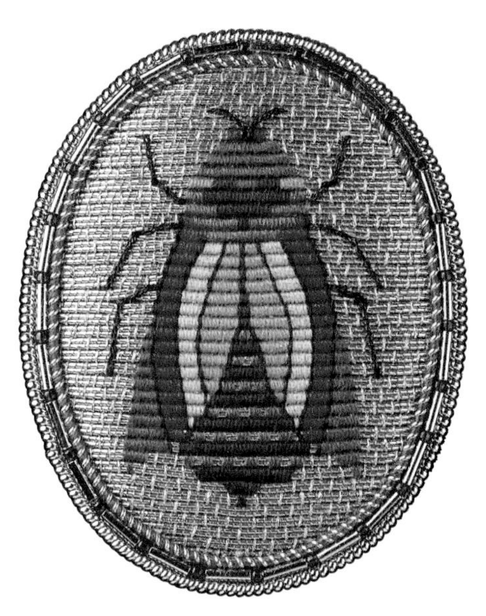

Natural History

Beetles, probably the most successful form of all animal life, have a history going back over 240 million years to the lower Permian period. With more than 350 000 identified species (a number which could, in fact, rise to more than 10 million), beetles represent one in four of all animal species on earth. The scientific term used to classify beetles is Coleoptera, named in the fourth century BC by Aristotle, who described beetles as 'insects that have wing cases' (from the Greek *koleon*, 'sheath', and *pteron*, 'wing'). For ease of study, the order Coleoptera has been divided into 166 families according to distinguishing body features such as the shape of the elytra and its connection to the thorax, and antennae and leg structure. The families vary in size, with the largest being the weevils, with more than 50 000 named species.

Beetles inhabit every climate and landscape on Earth: from tropical, temperate and subarctic forests to grassy plains, deserts and muddy ponds, suburban backyards and kitchens. Many beetles are serious pests, feeding on crops, food stores, domesticated animals and timber; many are valuable allies of man, consuming dead plants and animals and returning them to the soil as valuable nutrients; all insects, however, contribute to the health of the biosphere.

Beetles display incredible diversity in size, shape, colour, pattern and texture. Their size can vary from the tiny feather-winged beetle, smaller than the head of a pin, to *Titanus giganteus*, a longhorn beetle, which can grow to 20 centimetres

(8 inches) in length. In the beetle's natural environment, its 'decoration' is the camouflage that allows it to blend into the leaf litter of the forest floor, or the shiny foliage of the rainforest canopy. A variety of colours and textures contributes to the beetle's camouflage—iridescent and metallic colours (caused by optical interference) predominate in the tropical rainforests, whilst the pigment colours of earthy red, orange, brown and black protect the grassland beetles.

Most beetles have a fairly regular life cycle, varying in length from a few weeks to several years, depending on the species and climatic conditions. Some species of wood borer have a life cycle of seven or eight years, with many instances recorded of wood borers emerging after the wood has been made into furniture!

All beetles undergo complete metamorphosis with four main life stages—egg, larva, pupa and adult—each with distinctive characteristics. Beetle eggs are usually small, soft and smooth, with a shell permeable by water and, in some cases, oxygen. From as few as four eggs to many hundreds are laid, either scattered haphazardly or carefully placed on or near a suitable food supply for the larvae.

The beetle larva (a term derived from the Latin for 'ghost' or 'mask') usually looks like a grub or worm, with a well-developed head capsule with chewing mouthparts. Upon hatching, the first aim of the larva is to eat, feeding on roots, leaves, dead wood or carrion. They grow rapidly, shedding their exoskeleton (moulting) at least three times before reaching the pupal stage, which can take from a few weeks to several years.

The pupa (derived from the Latin for 'little girl' or 'little doll') serves as the vessel for the dramatic transformation from larva to adult beetle. The pupa, located either within the host plant or in the soil, remains at that stage (usually over winter) until the adult beetle, signalled by the right combination of warmth and moisture, emerges from it, ready to find a mate and continue the cycle of life.

Beetles vary considerably in shape and form but all share the characteristics that have contributed to their success: a highly specialised body, protected by a tough exoskeleton, and the ability to adapt to a continually changing environment.

Compare this illustration with the labelled diagram of the external anatomy of the beetle.

Anatomy of a Beetle

A typical adult beetle has three distinct body regions—the head, thorax and abdomen. When viewed from above, the prominent features are the head, the pronotum and the elytra.

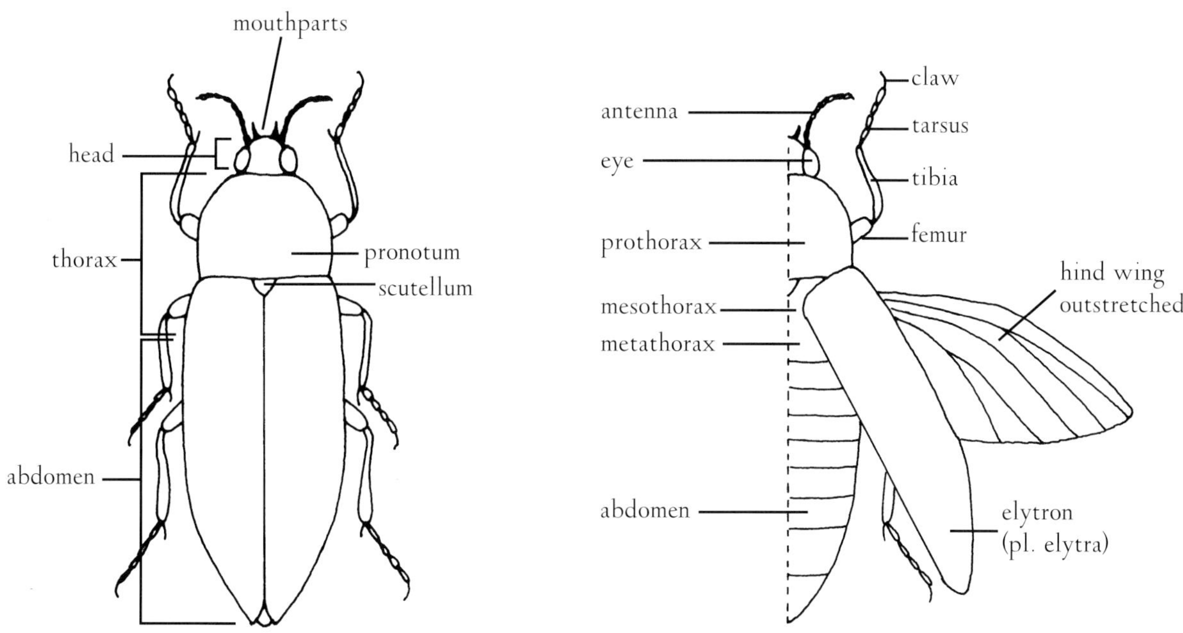

External anatomy of the beetle

The head

The head is a hardened capsule bearing the compound eyes, antennae and chewing mouthparts.

Eyes

Beetles have a pair of separated, hemispherical compound eyes, made up of hundreds of individual facets which enable them to detect movement in almost every direction at once.

Antennae

Two antennae, attached to the head between the mouthparts and the eyes, are equipped with sensors that are able to detect vibrations, air movements, temperature, humidity and smell. Antennae vary greatly in length and shape—they may be long and slender, short and bead-like, serrate, feather-like, or distinctly clubbed.

Mouthparts

The feeding apparatus of the beetle includes mandibles, the upper chewing pair of mouthparts, and palps or feelers, which help give information about the taste and smell of its food.

The thorax

The thorax is made up of three segments—the prothorax, the mesothorax and the metathorax. The second and third segments are closely joined to the abdomen and are covered by the elytra.

Prothorax

The first segment, the prothorax, bears the front pair of legs, and is often clearly separated from the second and third segments. The plate which covers this segment is called the pronotum, below which is often found a small triangular segment, the scutellum.

Mesothorax

The second segment, the mesothorax, bears a pair of legs and a pair of hard wing cases, elytra, which are often brightly coloured. The elytra are held at rest over the abdomen, the edges forming a straight line along the centre, and protect the body and the hind wings. When the beetle flies, the elytra, which do not beat in flight, are held forward.

Metathorax

The third segment, the metathorax, supports the third pair of legs and a pair of wings, with which the beetle flies. In order to fit beneath the wing cases, the larger membranous hind wings are often intricately folded under the elytra.

Legs

Beetles have three pairs of jointed legs which are held below the body. Each leg has four main parts: the coxa, which joins the leg to the thorax; the femur, the most muscular section of the leg; the tibia, which often carries spines for self-defence; and the tarsus, comprising one to five segments and two claws.

The abdomen

The abdomen, usually ten discernible segments, contains most of the digestive organs, breathing apparatus and the reproductive organs. Like the other parts of the beetle body, it is protected by a rigid exoskeleton which is flexible between the segments.

Part 2:

The Beetle as Embellishment

Beetles have inspired artisans for centuries. They have been depicted in burial chambers, paintings, porcelain statuary, precious stones, glass paintings, sculptures, mediaeval illuminated manuscripts, wallpaper, textiles, jewellery, buttons, coins and postage stamps. The following examples are but a glimpse of the beetle as used for embellishment.

The Scarab Beetle

The beetle has been used as a decorative motif since ancient times; ornaments in the shape of beetles have been found which date back 25 000 years. Fashioned from anthracite (a hard form of coal), these highly polished shapes were drilled with a hole, presumably so that they could be strung and worn. In early cultures, everything in nature had a magical purpose and significance—beetles, and the observation of their life cycle (seen as a metaphor for life, death and rebirth), inspired the creation myths and legends in many ancient societies. Nowhere did the beetle play as significant a role as in the civilisation of ancient Egypt, where the sun god was represented as a great scarab, rolling the sun (like a ball of dung) across the heavens of a universe with Earth as its

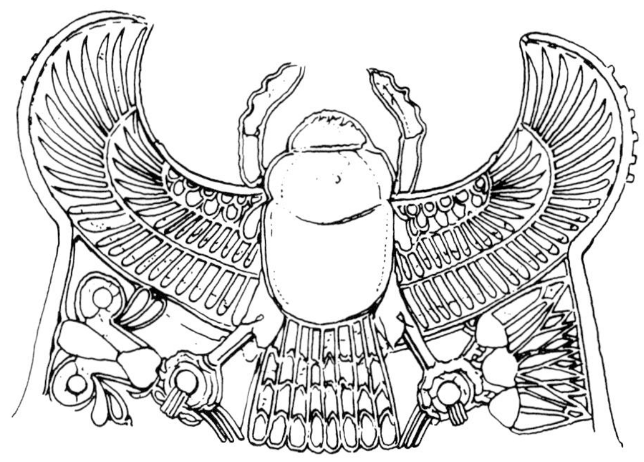

Sun-god, c. 1340 BC.

centre. The Scarab Beetle, *Scarabaeus sacer*, the emblem of the god Khopri (the god of creation), symbolised the sun, life, rebirth and immortality. This sacred scarab was often represented as a scarabaeus with outstretched wings, and raised upper claws holding a disc (the sun).

Egyptian scarabaeus

As a religious motif, scarab ornaments appeared on tombs, mummy cases and ceilings in Egypt as early as 1600 to 1100 BC. For protection in this life, and the life to come, Egyptians wore scarab amulets bearing inscriptions, or having been blessed with powers of good luck, health and life. Made of dried beetles or carved faience, soapstone, ivory, amber, obsidian and a variety of semi-precious stones, scarab amulets were worn by all levels of society. The wealthy and powerful wore them mounted in elaborately worked gold armbands and pectorals; warriors wore a scarab ring as a sign of masculine valour; while a peasant might wear a single scarab strung on a cord. Scarabs, rendered in green stones such as basalt, schist or jade, were placed over the hearts of the mummified dead to ensure safe passage to the next life.

The Beetle as Design Source

Nature has always been a source-book for artists and designers, but never more so than in the nineteenth century, where the fascination for the natural world was evident in all aspects of life. In the 1830s there was an intensified search for new motifs to decorate the products of industrialisation—wallpapers, carpets, fabrics, lace, linoleum, ceramics, furniture, cast iron, silver and silverplate, jewellery and buttons. In response to the ever-increasing demand for ideas for design, George Phillips published *Rudiments of Curvilinear Design* (1838–40), containing a wide variety of design styles. Phillips was one of the first to suggest insects, the feathers of birds, and even sea-urchins as sources of inspiration for the ornamental designer.

George Phillips: insects suggested as sources of design.

Christopher Dresser: decorative composition.

Designer, botanist and writer Christopher Dresser (1834–1904), who had a lifelong enthusiasm for the application of natural science to design, used beetles in some of his designs for wallpapers, carpets and fabrics. His decorative composition, 'intended to give the idea of evening', from *The Art of Decorative Design* (London 1862), features stag beetles, moths, spiders and webs in a stylised floral border design.

During the early 1900s the magazine *Art et Décoration* published many articles on how decoration could be based on living forms. Habert Dys' drawings of the cockchafer beetle, and his subsequent design for a 'repeat pattern based upon the cockchafer' illustrate the possibilities.

The French artist and designer Eugene Seguy created numerous colour portfolios of visual ideas for artists, illustrators and designers in the 1920s. Included in his *Insectes* portfolio are several striking examples of beetles (jewel beetles, glow-worms and scarabs), each species identified with the scientific name and habit and drawn with scrupulous accuracy of form and colour (see page 25). He then provides

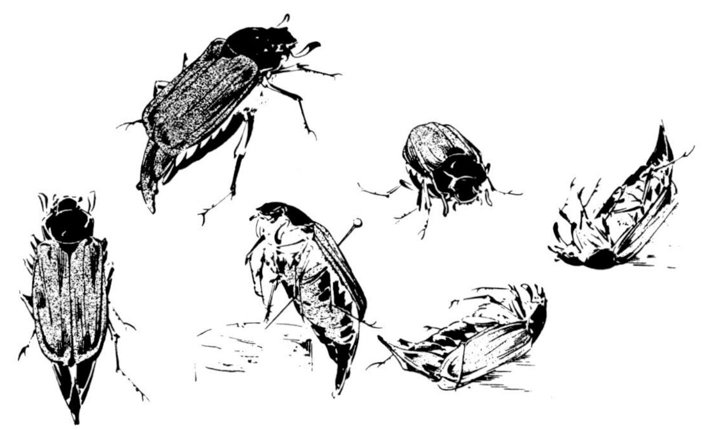

Habert Dys: study of cockchafer beetle.

decorative compositions with these insects as a source of ideas for textiles, wallpapers, mosaics, stained glass and many other areas of design (see page 26).

Countries around the world have celebrated the beauty of beetles by placing their colourful images on postage stamps (269 species of beetles had been featured by 1990). A set of stamps called 'Insect and Spiders', printed in 1998 in the United States, includes seven beetles.

Habert Dys: repeat pattern based upon the cockchafer.

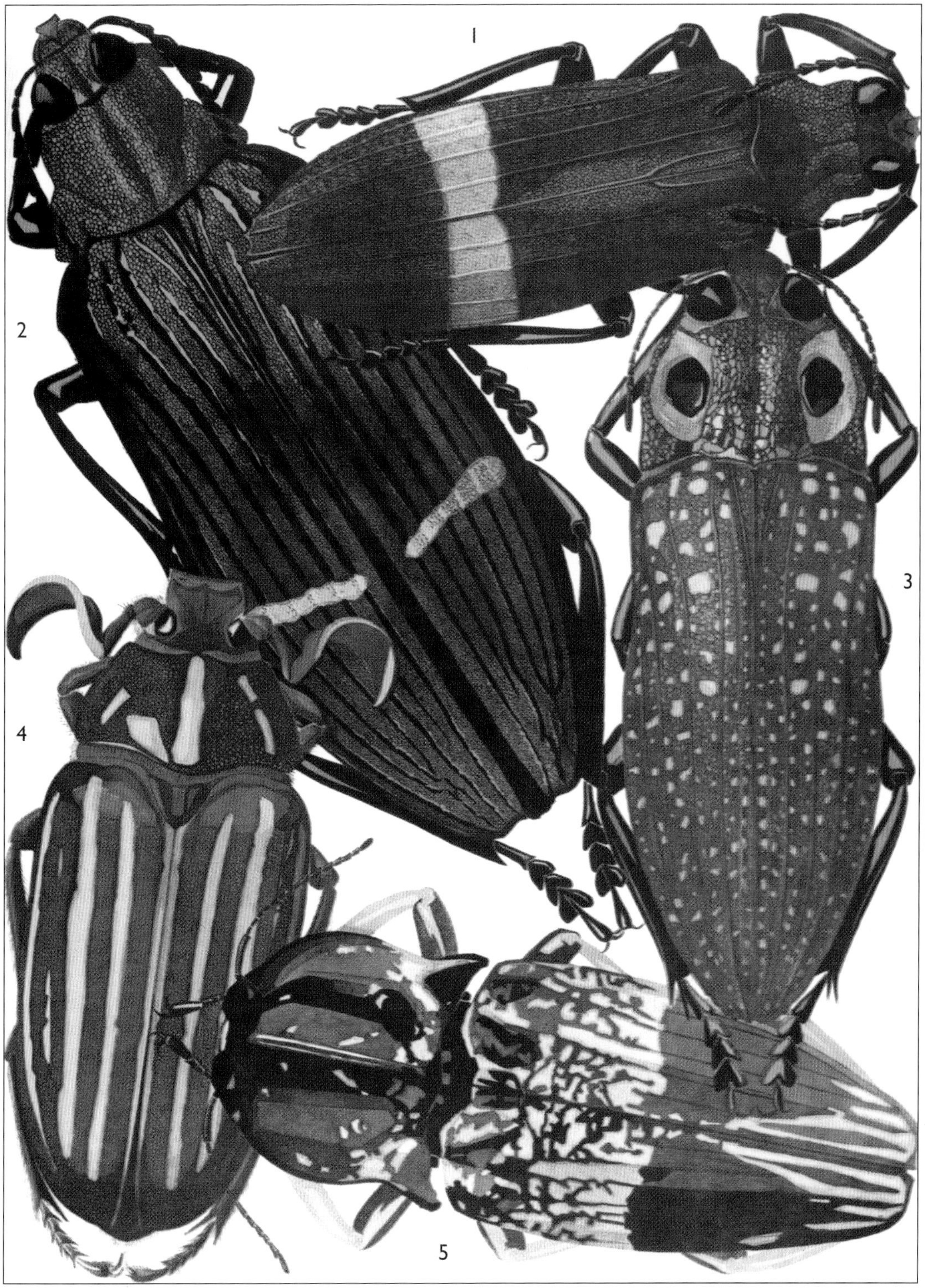

Eugene Seguy — beetles as design sources: 1. Catoxantha gratiosa (*Indochina*); 2. Catoxantha opulenta (*Malacca*); 3. Lampropepla rothschildii (*Madagascar*); 4. Polyphylla petiti (*Mexico*); 5. Lyoreus alluaudi (*Madagascar*).

Eugene Seguy: decorative compositions based on beetles.

The Beetle and Jewellery

The earliest pieces of jewellery may well have played a dual role as both decoration and amulet to ward off evil spirits, but there is no doubt that humans have always experienced the urge for self-adornment—using nature's bounty, from shells and bones to precious stones and gold, and taking inspiration from natural forms. Over the centuries the insect, as a decorative motif, has appeared in many cultures. In ancient Egypt, images of beetles and other insects were carved from stone or fashioned from glass or metal and worn for decoration (and good fortune). The Japanese carved toggles (*netsuke*) in a variety of insect forms, while *tsuba*, the metal guards for the

This black glass beetle brooch, made from Vauxhall mirror glass in the late nineteenth century, is indicative of the Victorian era's obsession with nature.

traditional swords, were decorated with crickets, centipedes, beetles and dragonflies worked in relief.

Realistically rendered insects have been a recurrent theme in all the decorative arts, particularly in the realm of jewellery. Until the nineteenth century, the depiction of insects in jewellery was often symbolic; Napoleon adopted the bee, a symbol of determination and industry, as his emblem. The eighteenth century's obsession with nature encouraged jewellers at the turn of the century to incorporate insects into brooches, lockets and necklaces. 'The next step was a veritable plague of bejeweled wasps, earwigs, flies, stag beetles, and spiders, which began to crawl over bodices, hats, and veils in the 1860s' (Nissenson and Jonas, *Jeweled Bugs and Butterflies*, p. 11).

Lalique Longhorn Beetle ring.

Japanese prints, textiles and ceramics, introduced to Europe late in the century, had a powerful influence on all the decorative arts. The principles of Japanese design—its spareness, asymmetry and flowing lines—fundamentally influenced Art Nouveau, and the many items of jewellery that were designed in that style. Frenchman René Lalique, possibly the finest jeweller of the period, crafted some stunning insect pieces, such as the Blister Beetle corsage

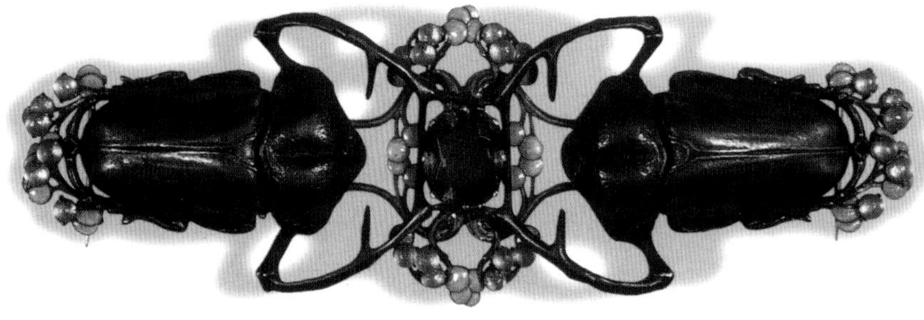

Lalique Blister Beetle corsage ornament.

ornament (c.1903–04), made from gold, glass, enamel, silver and tourmaline, and the gold and foiled enamel ring (c.1900–03), made in the shape of a Longhorn Beetle.

The industrial advances of the era allowed for the mass production of beautifully designed items, stamped from sheets of silver or gilt metal, which became accessible to a widely expanded market. A delightful example is this Art Nouveau buckle, featuring a beetle mounted within a bejewelled floral border—the inspiration for the Art Nouveau beetle brooch on the next page.

Using the outline of the stumpwork Leaf Beetle, *Plagiodera versicolor*, on page 124, the beetle was worked in tiny glass bugle beads and bronze leather. The wrapped-wire legs of the beetle were inserted into the ochre-coloured suede border, embellished with large metal beads, over a background of dark purple silk. The skeleton outline of the design is included

Art Nouveau buckle.

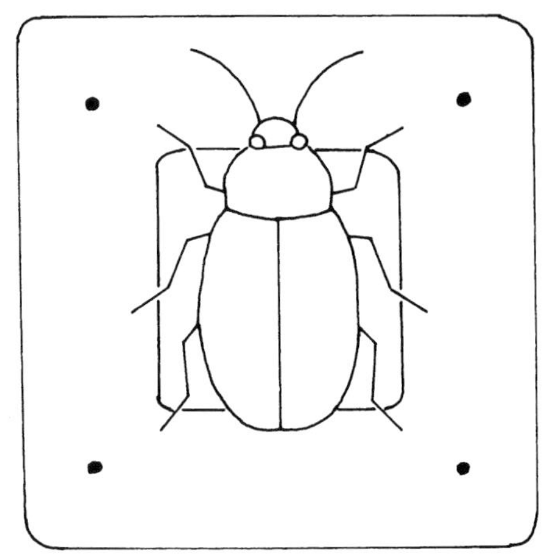

here to facilitate your own interpretation of this lovely buckle.

Art Nouveau beetle brooch.

Various archaeological discoveries in Egypt lead to the scarab being revived as a design motif; rendered in fine gold and precious stones, enamels, art glass and semi-precious stones, by all the major jewellery designers of the nineteenth and twentieth centuries. Cartier's designers, in particular, were inspired by the Egyptian discoveries, and often incorporated an original faience scarab or a portion of ancient carved ivory or wood in their pieces. A beautiful example is this 1924 Cartier brooch and belt ornament featuring an ancient blue faience scarab.

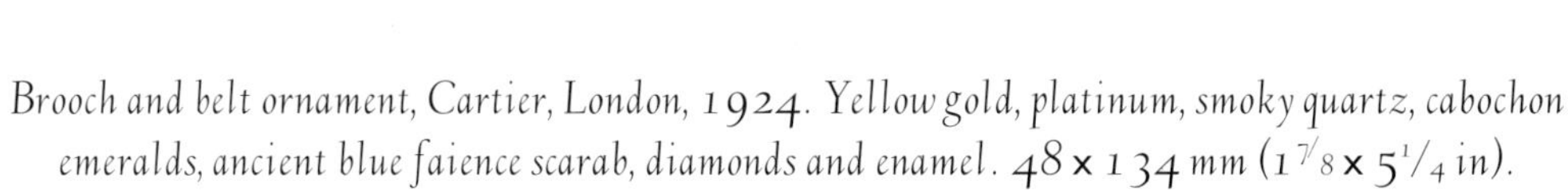

Brooch and belt ornament, Cartier, London, 1924. Yellow gold, platinum, smoky quartz, cabochon emeralds, ancient blue faience scarab, diamonds and enamel. 48 x 134 mm ($1^7/_8$ x $5^1/_4$ in).

The order Coleoptera continues to inspire contemporary designers, with jewelled beetles appearing in a range of materials—from pure gold to the modern plastics. American designer John Paul Miller works exquisitely detailed beetles in gold and enamel. His beetle pendant/brooch, 1995, is 18-carat yellow gold with enamel on pure gold—what an inspiration for goldwork!

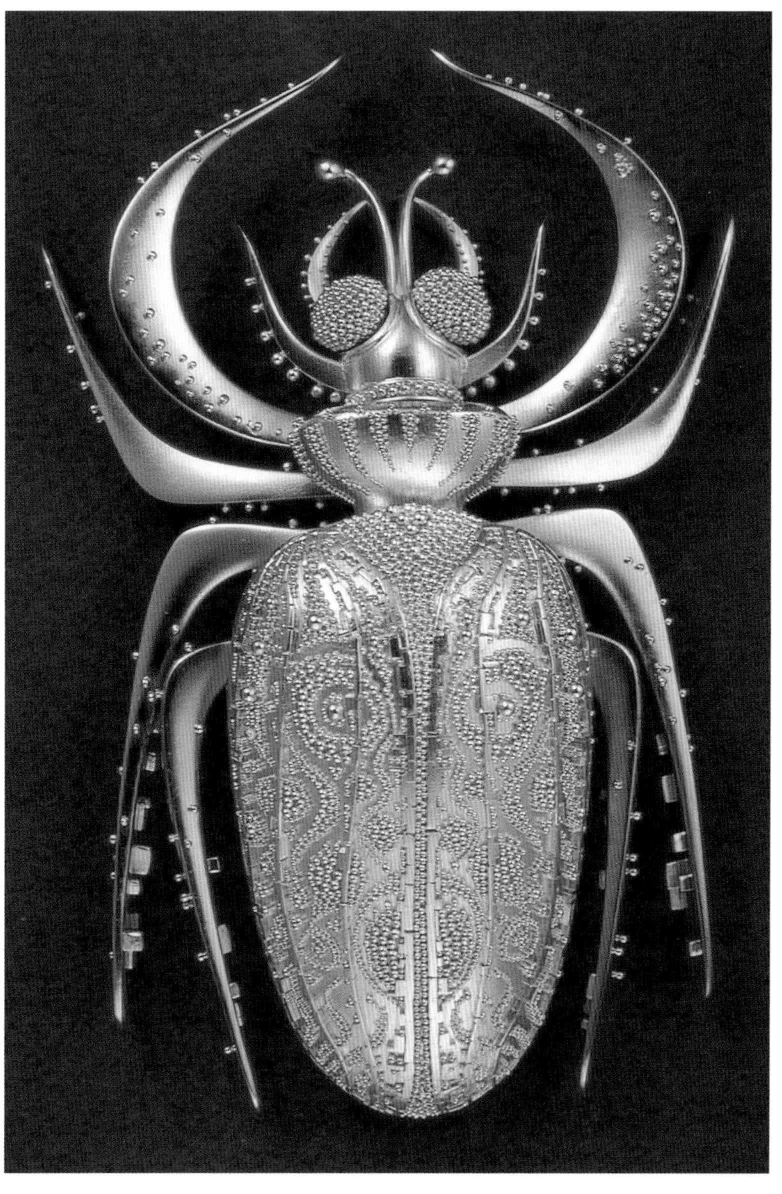

John Paul Miller beetle pendant/brooch, 77 mm (3 in).

Beetle Buttons

The beetle has also found its way into the realm of the button, in images ranging from the Victorian glass 'jewelled' creature surrounded by an ornate gold border to the primitive hand-carved scarab in wood, such as the contemporary buttons from Nepal in my collection.

Specific to the late eighteenth century were buttons depicting minutely observed insects as decorative motifs, reflecting the era's scientific interest in the natural world.

Author's collection of beetle brooches.

Especially interesting is this button depicting a beetle, its elytra raised in flight, displaying the translucent hind wings and segmented abdomen. The button, believed to be Irish, is made from semi-precious stones set on rock crystal, and is one of a large set depicting a variety of insects in catalogue manner.

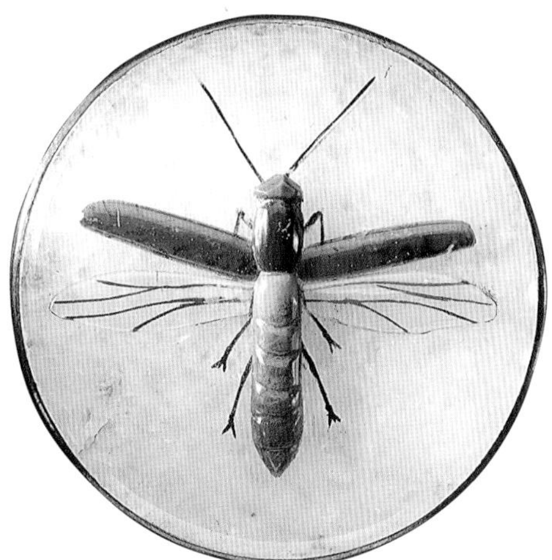

A stylised beetle cut from abalone shell and slivers of metal, was inlaid into tortoiseshell to decorate this mid-nineteenth century English button.

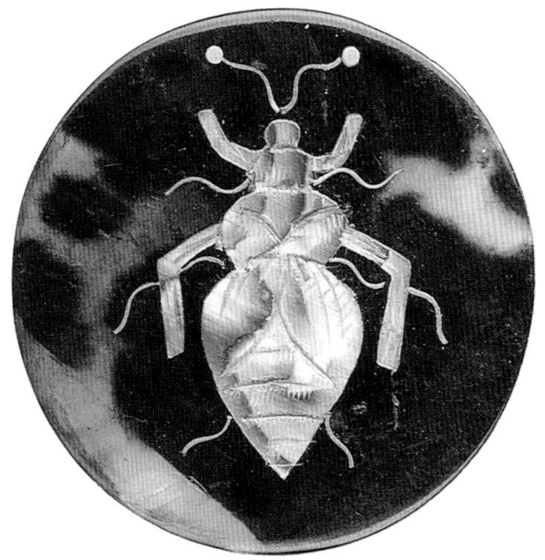

Top: Beetle button set on rock crystal.
Below: Inlaid beetle on tortoiseshell.

The scarab beetle of ancient Egypt is evident as a decorative motif in these Italian glass micromosaic buttons, composed of a mosaic of tiny fragments of coloured glass called 'tesserae', dating from the early twentieth century. The oval button is in gold.

Italian mosaic buttons.

THE BUTTERFLY MAN OF KURANDA

From 1895 until his death in 1937, Queensland entomologist Frederick Parkhurst Dodd applied himself to the exploration of Australia's then unknown tropical insects with a passion. He supplied tens of thousands of perfect specimens to the great museums of the world and to the wealthy private collectors of the Victorian era. Almost one hundred new species that he discovered were named in his honour. In his later years, F.P. Dodd became a personality of national prominence as 'The Butterfly Man of Kuranda' when he toured his spectacular show collection of insects (including 'The Grand Parade') to the southern states in 1918 and 1923.

Monteith, *The Butterfly Man of Kuranda.*

The Grand Parade, c.1917, F.P. Dodd. This case has been so named because of its resemblance to the concentric circles of stud livestock arranged in the centre ring of big agricultural shows in Australia. It features many species of Christmas Beetles, Flower Chafers and Stag Beetles.

Beaded Beetles

The iridescent ribbed surface of a beetle's elytra and its variations in colour—a green surface blending to a pink or magenta edge; deep greens and blues flashing bronze or gold reflections—can be beautifully interpreted with sparkling glass beads. The detached curved elytra of stumpwork beetles look stunning worked with beads; green-bronze faceted beads cover the wing cases of the Pill Beetle, while tiny glittering bugle beads embellish the elegant Ground Beetle. Similar beading techniques could be used to work the elytra of padded surface beetles (such as the goldwork beetles from pages 232–251).

Tiny glass beads and gleaming gold threads combine to work the rich, flat surfaces of my Beaded Beetles, their design inspired by the Italian glass mosaic buttons. The Beaded Beetles, and their oval companion, the Or Nué Beetle (see

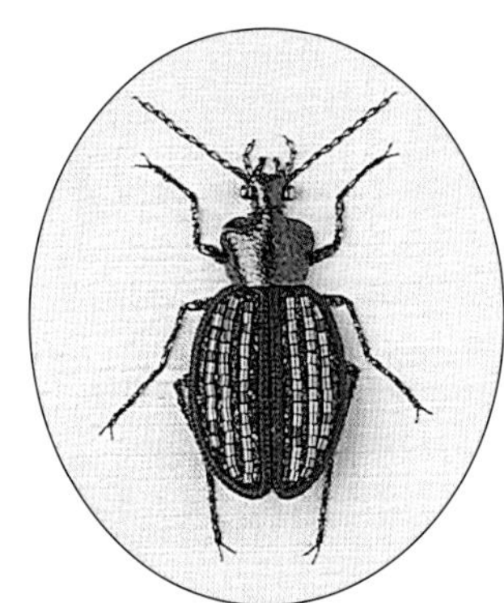

Stumpwork Pill Beetle and Ground Beetle from the Specimen Box.

page 274), have been made into medallions with decorative borders of gold Pearl Purl and beads. I display them together on a midnight blue velvet background. The circular Beaded Beetles can be worked individually and used to decorate the top of a music box, made into a brooch, or inserted into the base of a small glass paperweight.

Red-orange Beaded Beetle

Requirements

Beaded Beetles.

- gold-coloured cotton homespun, 15 cm (6 in) square
- quilter's muslin or fine calico, 15 cm (6 in) square
- 10 cm (4 in) embroidery hoop
- fine marking pen (optional)
- fine silk sewing thread (YLI Silk #100 col. 215 or #50 col. 79), beeswaxed
- fine metallic sewing thread (YLI Metallic Yarn col. Gold), beeswaxed
- beeswax
- gold Super Pearl Purl
- light gold stranded metallic thread (Madeira Metallic Art 9803 col. 3003)
- blue-black metallic thread (Kreinik Fine #8 Metallic Braid col. 202C)
- Mill Hill glass seed beads (2014 black)
- Mill Hill petite glass beads:

  40332 emerald
  40374 rainbow
  42013 red red

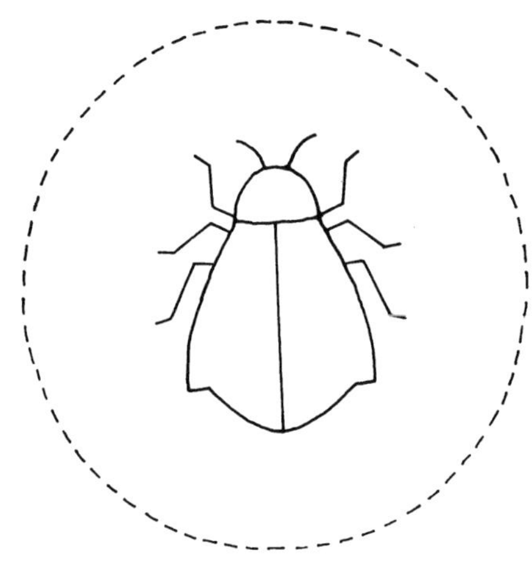

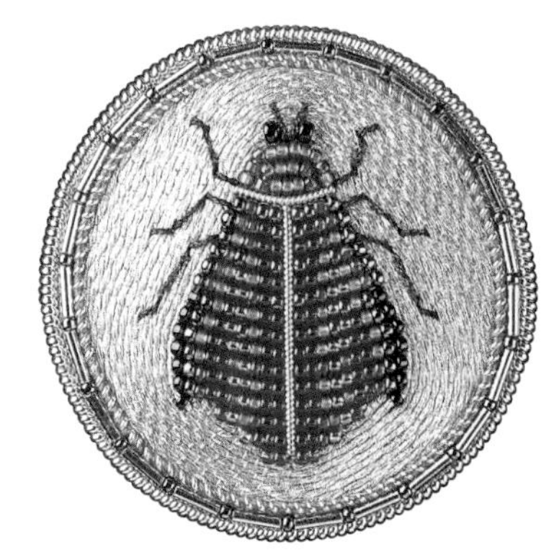

skeleton outline

42014 black
42028 ginger
42033 autumn flame
42034 matt pumpkin
42037 green velvet
42043 rich red

Preparation

1. Mount the gold homespun and the muslin backing into the embroidery hoop, making sure that both fabrics are drum tight.

2. Trace the design onto the background fabric (draw over the pencil outlines with a fine marking pen if desired). Check that the outline circle is an accurate size for the finished object. For the medallions, the edge is turned under; however, the gold background for the music box and the paperweight need to be 1–2 mm smaller than the object's actual outline.

To work the beetle

Elytra

1. Cut a length of Super Pearl Purl the length of the centre line of the elytra. Using beeswaxed silk sewing thread, bring the needle out at the top of the centre line, thread on the

Pearl Purl and insert the needle at the tail end of the line. Couch the Pearl Purl in place with about four stitches.

2. The elytra is filled with rows of beads, threaded on a double strand of gold metallic sewing thread, and couched in place, between every bead, with one strand of silk. Starting at the top corner, bring the needle out 1.5 mm outside the outline, thread on four beads (referring to the diagram for the bead colours), slide the needle and gold thread *under* the Pearl Purl, then thread on four beads (in a mirror image) and insert the needle 1.5 mm outside the opposite outline. Couch between each bead, spreading them a little to fill the space, if necessary, making sure that the inner beads are close to the Pearl Purl, and the outer beads are *on top of the outline*. Continue in this fashion for the remaining 14 rows, leaving the spaces in rows 13, 14 and 15 as indicated in the diagram.

3. Couch a length of Super Pearl Purl, cut to size, along the line between the thorax and the elytra, using beeswaxed silk sewing thread.

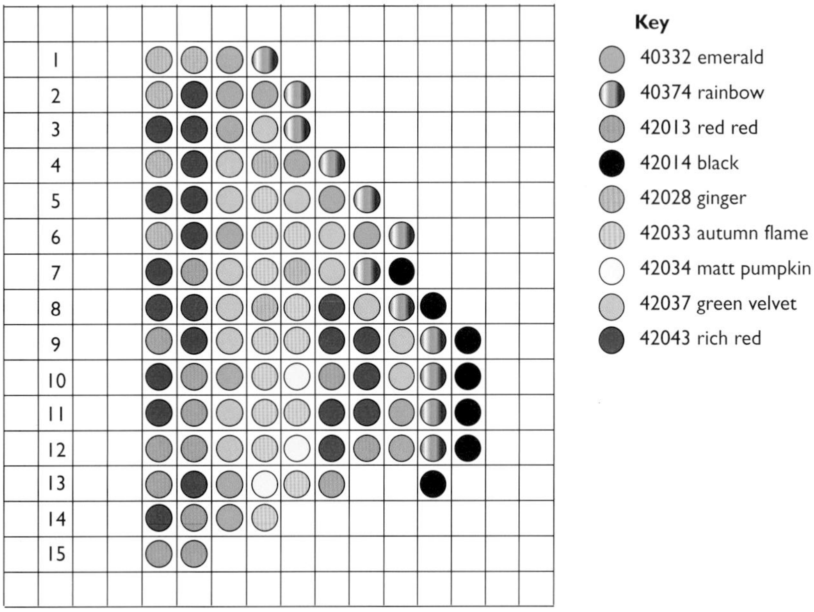

1
2
3
4
5
6
7
8
9
10
11
12
13
14
15

Key

- 40332 emerald
- 40374 rainbow
- 42013 red red
- 42014 black
- 42028 ginger
- 42033 autumn flame
- 42034 matt pumpkin
- 42037 green velvet
- 42043 rich red

Red-orange beetle beading diagram

THORAX

The thorax is filled with three rows of beads, threaded on a double strand of metallic sewing thread, and couched in place, between every bead, with one strand of silk.

1. Couch three beads (42037) in the centre of the thorax, next to the Pearl Purl.

2. The second row of beads curves around the first row, beginning and ending at the Pearl Purl (two 40332, two 42037, two 40332).

3. The third row of beads curves around the second row, beginning and ending at the Pearl Purl (three 40332, four 42037, three 40332).

BACKGROUND

The background is filled with rows of couched light gold metallic thread, using one strand of the same thread (beeswaxed) to work the couching stitches. *Hint*: Cut several lengths of this thread (for couching with) *before* you start, as the couching is worked with a continuous thread from the protective plastic pack.

Thread two black seed beads onto the couching thread, sliding them along the thread until they are required to be stitched into position for the eyes. Insert the tail of the light gold metallic thread at the base of the beetle and secure. Couch a row of gold thread around the beaded beetle outline, working the couching stitches 2–3 mm apart, stitching the black beads into position at the top of the head for the eyes. Continue couching rows of gold thread (in a brick pattern when possible) until the background area is filled, working short rows at the edges, as required, to maintain the circle shape. Hint: work the couching stitches towards the previous row, inserting the needle at a slight angle to help prevent gaps between the rows.

LEGS

Work the legs and antennae with straight stitches using the blue-black metallic thread.

Blue-green Beaded Beetle

The requirements and preparation are the same as for the Red-orange Beetle.

To work the beetle

ELYTRA

1. Couch a length of Super Pearl Purl, cut to size, along the line between the thorax and the elytra, using beeswaxed silk sewing thread.

2. Stitch a row of ginger beads along the centre line of the elytra; this line consists of two beads side by side at the top, then 12 beads stitched individually (with the holes of the beads being horizontal). Work a couching stitch between the two top beads, then thread the needle, in an S fashion, through the remaining beads to the tail, then back again to the top, pulling the row of beads close together.

3. Using beeswaxed silk sewing thread, couch a length of Super Pearl Purl on either side of the centre beads, curving the Purl to the sides at the top, thus forming a double row of Purl between the thorax and the elytra.

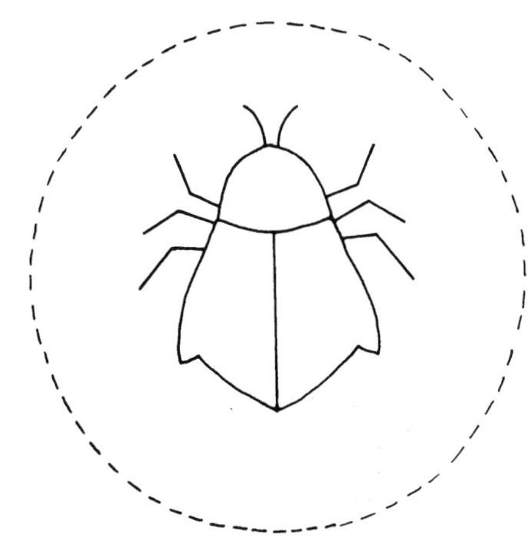

skeleton outline

4. The elytra are filled with rows of beads, worked in the same way as the Red-orange Beetle, following the beading diagram for the bead colours.

THORAX

The thorax is filled with four rows of beads, worked in the same way as the Red-orange Beetle, using the following bead numbers and colours:

1. Couch six beads in the centre of the thorax, next to the Pearl Purl (40374, 40332, two 42037, 40332, 40374).

2. Couch four beads in the centre of the thorax, above the previous row (40374, two 40332, 40374).

3. The third row of beads curves around the first row, beginning and ending at the Pearl Purl (eleven 40332).

4. The fourth row of beads curves around the third row, beginning and ending at the Pearl Purl (six 40374, two 42043, six 40374).

The background and the legs are worked in the same way as for the Red-orange Beaded Beetle.

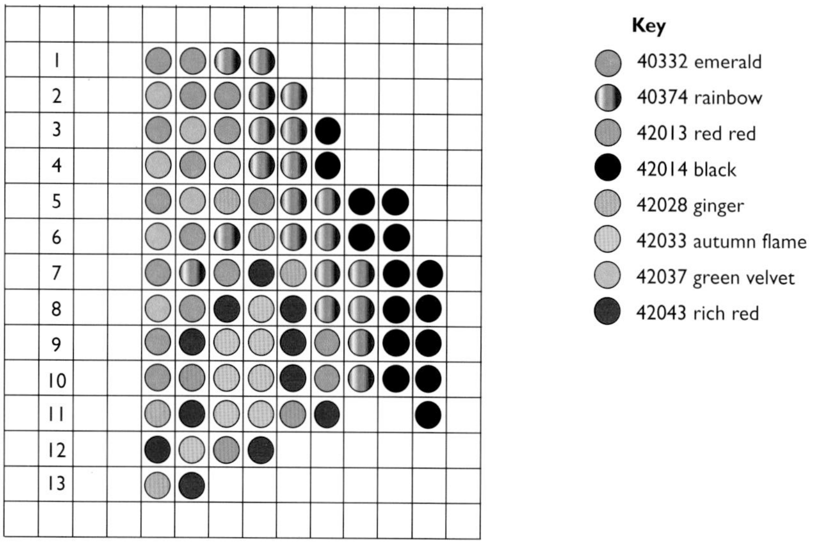

Key

- 40332 emerald
- 40374 rainbow
- 42013 red red
- 42014 black
- 42028 ginger
- 42033 autumn flame
- 42037 green velvet
- 42043 rich red

Blue-green beetle beading diagram

The Medallion Borders

The Beaded Beetles and the oval Or Nué Beetle have been made into medallions, with decorative borders of gold Pearl Purl and beads.

Decorative borders can be worked with rows of couched gold thread (Pearl Purl, Jap gold, gold twists, milliary), coloured pearl thread (DMC Coton Perlé 3), and tiny beads of all shapes. I have used 4 mm gilt metal bugle beads, in combination with glass petite beads, in the second row of the border. These could be replaced with glass bugle beads, or cut pieces of Pearl Purl. Using the borders in the diagram as a guide, feel free to invent your own combination of threads and beads.

Requirements

- thin card for the circle or oval template guides
- Mill Hill petite beads 40374 rainbow (for the Red-orange Beetle)
- Mill Hill petite beads 40332 emerald (for the Blue-green Beetle)
- Mill Hill petite beads 42043 rich red (for the Or Nué Beetle)
- small glass bugle beads in the colour of your choice or gilt metal bugle beads
- white-covered 30-gauge wire
- nylon thread (Madeira Monofil No.60, clear)
- gold No.1 Pearl Purl
- gold No.2 Pearl Purl
- orange stranded thread (DMC 900, for the Red-orange Beetle)
- red stranded thread (DMC 349, for the Blue-green Beetle)

- teal stranded thread (DMC 924, for the Or Nué Beetle)
- cardboard, padding and strong thread to make the medallions

The following instructions apply to the Red-orange Beaded Beetle. Substitute beads, thread colour and oval shape as required to work the other two medallions.

1. Using the outline provided, cut a circle out of the centre of a piece of thin card. Use the remaining card as a template when applying the row of beads for the border. Centre the template over the gold background of the beetle and secure at the edges with masking tape.

2. Thread petite beads (40374) and bugle beads, alternately, onto a piece of white-covered wire to a length sufficient to match the circumference of the paper template. Thread one end of the wire (paper removed) through a bugle bead to form a circle (the tails of wire will be cut away after the beads have been couched in place).

3. Couch the beaded circle to the background of the medallion, using the paper template as a guide. Work the couching stitches with nylon thread. Trim the wire tails.

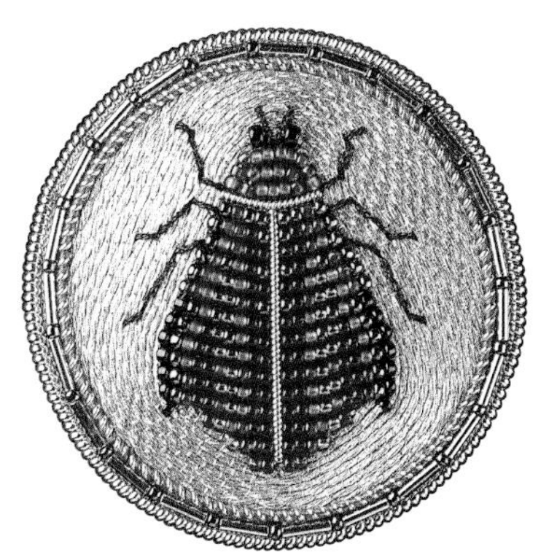

4. Cut a piece of gold No.1 Pearl Purl just over half the length of the circumference of the circle. Stretch the Purl slightly longer than the circumference. Insert a length of wire through the extended Purl and wrap with three strands of orange stranded thread. Using nylon thread, couch the wrapped Purl inside the row of beads, butting the ends to meet, and taking the tails of the wrapping thread through to the back. Remove the paper template.

5. Remove the embroidery from the hoop and cut the muslin backing away close to the background couching stitches. Cut a circle of cardboard the size of the template (check the size with the embroidered border). Cut out the fabric with a 1 cm (3/8 in) turning allowance. Cut several layers of padding to insert between the cardboard and the fabric. Using strong thread, gather the embroidered fabric over the padding and the cardboard circle (checking that the row of beading is just at the edge), forming a 'button' shape, and secure.

6. Using nylon thread, couch a row of gold No.2 Pearl Purl around the outside edge to complete the medallion.

Part 3: Beetle Wing Embroidery

My first encounter with beetle wings for use in embroidery was during a visit to California in 1998. A friend had taken me to The Bone Room, a most extraordinary shop in Berkeley where, amongst many other fascinating items, iridescent green beetle elytra were for sale. Having made my purchase—a handful of sparkling green wings—I began the quest for more information on the use of beetle wings as embellishment. A fascinating journey began: through tropical Amazon regions, where head-hunters in the past used them to ornament ceremonial ear ornaments and head-dresses, via Mughal India, where rich materials such as emerald beetle elytra and gold were used to convey high status and favour, to England, and their use as decoration on the muslin evening dresses of the Victorian era.

While gathering information from many sources, my research was greatly aided by Victoria Rivers' excellent book, The Shining Cloth, published in the United Kingdom in 1999, and her vast knowledge of 'dress and adornment that glitters'.

The high point came in 1999 while exploring the wonderful Heritage Museum, Narryna, in Hobart, Tasmania. There on display was a stunning late-Victorian black silk dress, embellished with beetle wings and gold thread. The best was yet to come. Not only was the dress available for close inspection, but the museum had samples of the trimming fabrics tucked away in tissue paper—every textile researcher's dream come true!

This chapter contains but a glimpse of the fascinating history surrounding embroidery with beetle wings, and concludes with the instructions for an evening bag using my 'treasures' from The Bone Room.

Beetle Wings as Adornment

The brilliantly coloured bodies of beetles, with their hard, durable exoskeletons, have been incorporated into jewellery, or used as embellishment on clothing or objects, for centuries. Some of the more colourful and widely used beetles come from the family Buprestidae, the aptly named jewel beetles, their metallic elytra being most sought after. The iridescent colours of these beetles are most vivid in species found in the tropical

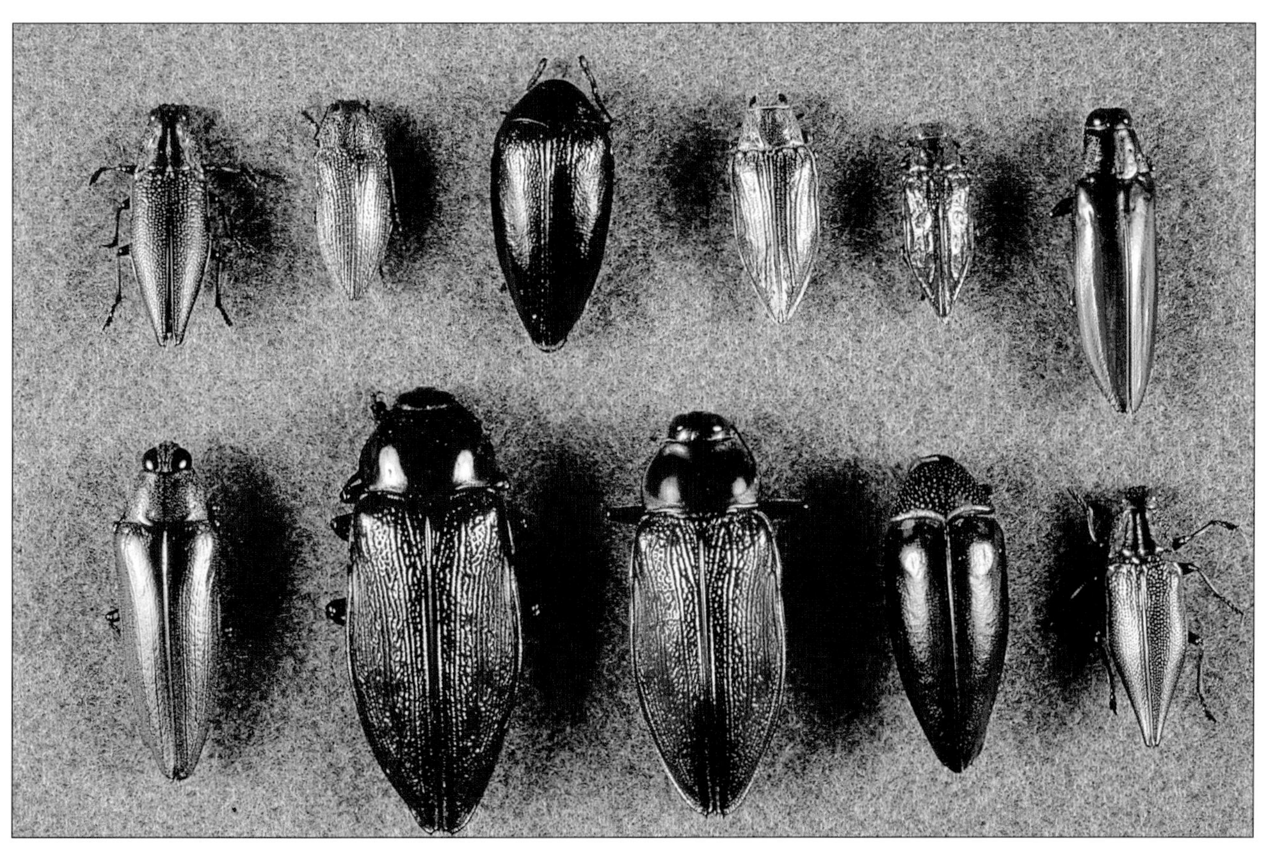

Buprestid beetles.

rainforests of Southeast Asia and South America, some being entirely metallic emerald blue-green in colour, whilst others combine metallic green with a deep plum red or violet.

Objects incorporating beetle elytra, thoraxes and mandibles have been used for decorative and symbolic purposes by numerous cultures, including peoples of the Amazon Basin, highland groups in Papua New Guinea and some of the hill tribes in Burma and northern Thailand. Natural materials such as beetle wings, brilliant orchid straw, feathers, shiny shells, claws and bones, were not only used for personal adornment, they 'were favoured ornaments of traditional head-hunting communities because of the encapsulated life-force and vitality their non-fading colours conveyed' (Rivers, *The Shining Cloth*, p. 158). They often played a magical or protective role (against evil spirits), and in some societies denoted kinship and social standing.

The Shuar and Jivaro peoples of the Amazon region consider adornment essential and decorate necklaces, ear ornaments and head-pieces with toucan feathers, and the iridescent greenish violet elytra of the giant Buprestid *Euchroma gigantea*. Fringes of beetle elytra decorate the skirts and breast cloths worn by the Naga women of northeast India. Often symbolic or indicative of social rank, beetle wings from *Sternocera aquisigmata* also embellish the ear ornaments and cloaks worn by their men on festive occasions. The people of the Waugi Valley, in the highlands of Papua New Guinea, string metallic scarabs together to decorate armbands and headdresses.

In northern Thailand and Burma, the Pwo Karen hill tribe people use beetle elytra to decorate clothing and items for everyday use. At funerals, which are festive occasions, the young unmarried women wear singing shawls made from woven red blankets, embellished with white beads and a fringe of beetles' wings and bells at the hem. 'The tinkling sounds of beetle elytra, coins, and bells on young women's long singing shawl fringes help to send the deceased safely to the afterworld' (Rivers, *The Shining Cloth*, p. 136).

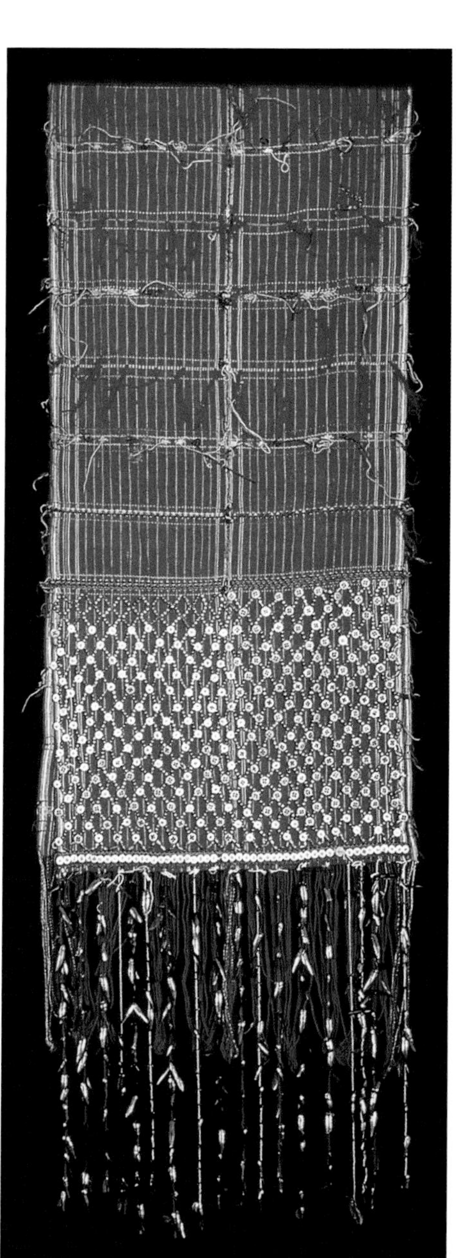

Singing shawl, Pwo Karen people, northern Thailand.

Beetle wing embroidery has always been popular in rural India, where wings and thoraxes decorated such items as camel trappings, clothing, belts and doorway hangings. The most extensive use of beetle elytra in textiles, however, was during the Mughal era (1526–1756), when they were used to embellish the traditional embroideries on silk brocades or cloth of gold used for the ceremonial robes and furnishings of the courts. Some of the finest examples belonged to royalty, such as a turban cloth, richly embroidered in gold in a fish scale pattern, encrusted with glittering beetle elytra; or were treasured gifts, such as sashes awarded for meritorious service. These splendid embroideries with small pieces of iridescent green elytra, perhaps imitating emeralds, were worked on silks, satins, velvets and delicate muslins using precious gold and silver metal threads.

In the nineteenth century, in response to a demand in England for exotic goods from the far-flung corners of the Empire, an industry developed whereby Indian artisans, working from beetle wing embroidery centres set up in Calcutta, Madras and Delhi, produced textiles (silks, white muslin and cotton net), table linens, fans and other decorative accessories for export to England and the rest of Europe. Woollen export shawls, loomed in northern India, were sent to these centres where they also were embellished with beetle sequins and metallic thread. Beetle wings (from dead insects)

were collected from the hardwood forests of Burma and northern Thailand, and exported to Calcutta for distribution.

Beetle wings appear to have been first seen in Europe in the early 1820s as embroidered decoration on the gauzy white cotton muslins from Calcutta and Madras intended for evening dresses for European ladies in India, and exported to Britain and Europe via the East India Company. The green elytra were used to form floral patterns and scalloped edges on the flounces of the full-skirted white dresses, or tiny sections of wing were applied in a decorative all-over pattern. Other items sent from India included woollen shawls, small decorative bags made of silk taffeta or satin, and dazzling fans, embellished with exotic peacock feathers and the emerald-like

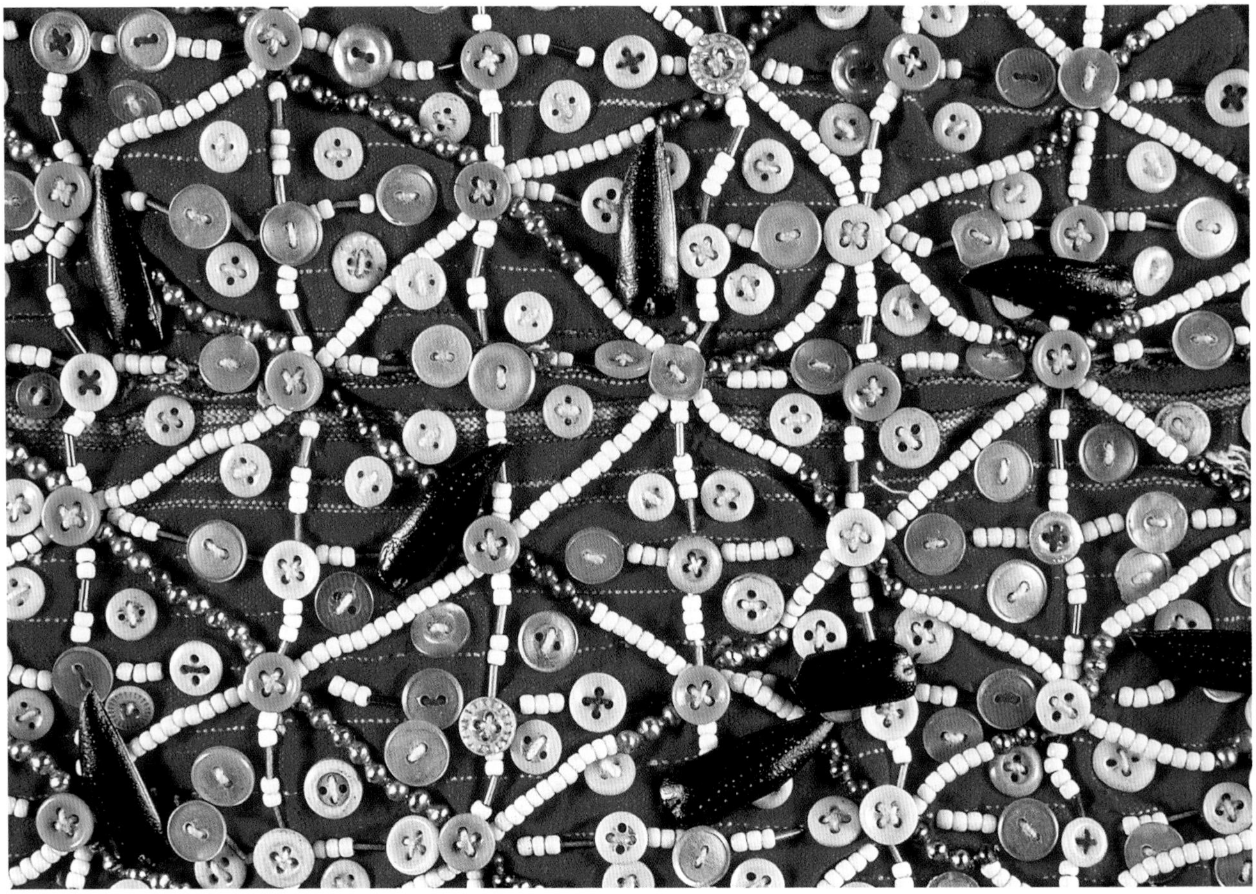

Detail of another singing shawl, Pwo Karen people, northern Thailand.

beetle elytra. The designs, generally of stylised flowers and leaves, were embroidered with coloured silks, spangles and beetle wings, outlined with couched gold or silver threads.

By the 1860s the fashion for the embroidered muslins had declined. However, following Queen Victoria's assumption of the title Empress of India in 1877, a craze for all things Indian caused an upsurge in the popularity of beetles' wings, both for the trimming of dress accessories and the decoration of entire dresses, which continued into the early years of the twentieth century. The backgrounds for the beetle wing embroideries became richer and darker, often dark green satin or black voile, while fine cotton net was the choice for dress and millinery trimmings.

Whatever garment or textile they ornamented, these 'emeralds' of the insect world, with their iridescence, brilliant colour and sparkle, always created a spectacular effect.

For the Delhi Coronation Durbar in 1903, the Vicereine, the Marchioness of Curzon, ordered a dress from Jean-Philippe Worth. She wished it to be a compliment to the Indian people and their traditions and yet be able to hold its own beside the sumptuous clothes and jewels of the Indian princes. Worth made for her the exquisite 'peacock dress', embroidered all over with a pattern of peacock feathers in gold thread, with a beetle wing forming the eye of each feather.

A. Jarvis, 'Beetle Wing Embroidery', in *Embroidery*, Vol. 40, No 3, 1989, p. 135.

A Victorian Dress

Narryna, a Heritage Museum in Hobart, Tasmania, has an extensive costume collection. One of their treasures is a black silk dress, embellished with beetles' wings and gold embroidery. Very little is recorded about this beautiful dress, but the style, colour and decoration are typically late Victorian (1890s), and the label inside the bodice waistband indicates that it was made in England (R.N.D. Mayne & Co, Robes, New Bond St. W.)

The two-piece dress, made from black, finely corded silk, has a close-fitting, front-opening bodice with long sleeves (ruched at the head), and a long skirt pleated into a narrow waistband. The dress is trimmed with black net (embroidered with beetles' wings and couched gold thread), insertions of dark green silk fabric, and a green silk tassel fringe around the hem.

Most fascinating are the remnants of the embroidered net trimming fabrics, amazingly still with the dress after more than one hundred years! All have the same background of black cotton net, embellished with couched gold thread and iridescent green jewel beetle wings. As the embroidery is rather free and fluent, the fabrics were probably worked at one of the beetle wing embroidery centres in Madras or Calcutta. The motifs on these fabrics—stylised leaves, flowers and vines—are traditional Indian designs produced for the European export market. Each trimming fabric is different, although obviously designed to be used together,

Black corded silk two-piece dress, trimmed with gold embroidery and beetles' wings (c.1890).

Detail showing trimming on bodice, sleeves and skirt.

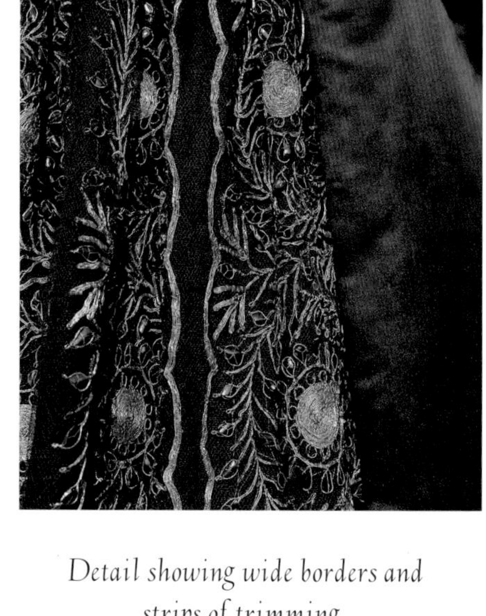

Detail showing wide borders and strips of trimming.

and would have been available by the yard. There is an all-over design, with 16.5 cm ($6^1/_2$ in) medallions repeated across the width of the fabric; several patterned borders, varying in width, with scalloped edges that could be cut away; and panels of embroidered strips that could be cut apart and used where a narrow trimming was required. This stunning outfit has panels of the wide border down the front of the skirt and around the lower edge; a scalloped border decorates the neck and front opening edges; and narrow embroidered strips were used to trim the front panels of the skirt and the sleeves. While the black net shows some signs of age, the wings are still brilliant and sparkling.

Top: Detail of all-over design of 16.5 cm (6½ in) medallions.
Bottom: Trimming fabric—wide border.

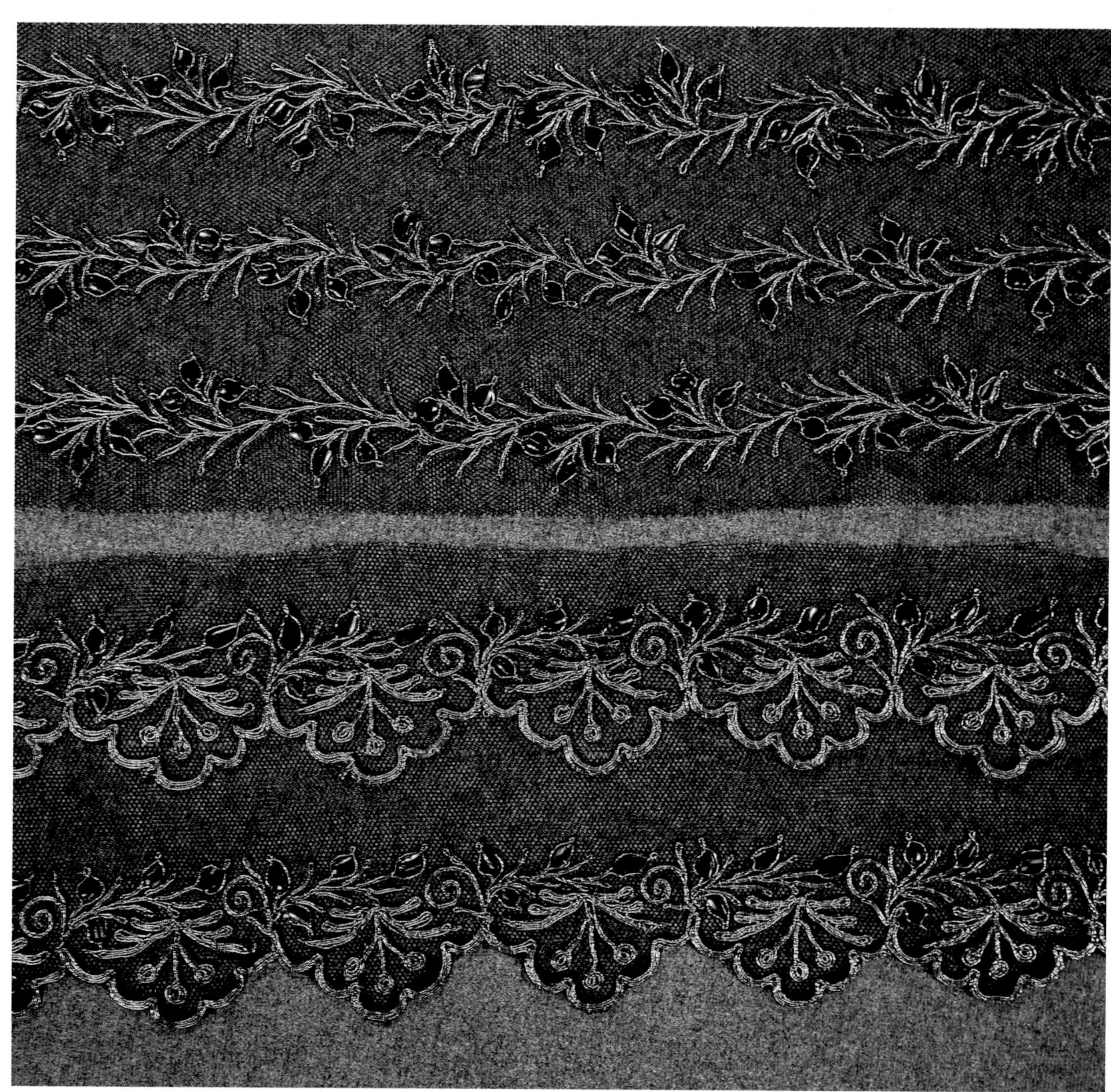

Trimming fabric—narrow embroidered strip (above) and narrow embroidered border (below).

Victorian Jewel Embroidery

All types of glitter contributed to this work; imitation diamonds, rubies, opals, topazes, sapphires, aquamarines and emeralds; imitation pearls and small flat pieces of mother-of-pearl; scraps of coral, iridescent sequins and spangles, beetles' wings and all manner of glass beads. Gold threads in many varieties and shades, metal-wire purl or bullion, gold braid and passementerie all contributed to the rich effect.

Morris, *Victorian Embroidery*, p. 163.

Needlework played an important role in the lives of almost all women of the upper and middle classes during the nineteenth century; the pursuit of higher education and careers was rare and, because plentiful domestic help was available, these women had much time to indulge in the myriad pastimes on offer, including the embroidery of clothes, furnishings, and purely decorative items for their homes.

Victorian England had a fascination for exotic goods from the far-flung corners of the Empire and this was reflected in the unusual array of embroidery materials available; iridescent beetle wings from India, fish scales, feathers, beads and even the dried husks of larval cases. This taste for the exotic coincided with the heightened interest in the natural sciences, inspired by the investigations of men like Charles Darwin. No Victorian parlour was complete without a collection of beautiful tropical beetles, butterflies or moths, mounted under glass.

As the century progressed, interest in needlework was encouraged by the vast quantity of catalogues and booklets available, containing patterns and instructions for the working of pictures, clothes and miscellaneous family items. Magazines and newsletters such as *Weldon's Practical Needlework* were very popular, as was the 'Fashion Notes and Queries' column in *The Queen* (one edition of 1865 offering advice on the removal

of beetle wings from the then unfashionable muslins, and ideas for their re-use!).

Thus, with the introduction in the 1880s of cheap imitation jewels (glass beads moulded into the shapes of precious gems, backed with metal foil to give them a jewel-like glitter), it is no wonder the passion for 'jewel embroidery' developed.

Jewel embroidery and beetle wings were used to decorate a wide range of articles; book-covers, work and opera bags, sachets, pincushions, wall pockets and tea-cosies; for dress trimmings and millinery, and even the fine net grounds of entire dresses. Beetle wings also embellished already decorated fabrics such as brocade.

Another treasure discovered at Narryna is an old catalogue containing three patterns 'For Jewels and Beetles' Wings work'. Sadly, the buff-coloured catalogue with its brown printing no longer has its covers, so the date and source of publication can only be surmised—it appears to slot perfectly into the era of beetle wings and jewel embroidery!

The three designs reproduced here from this catalogue, the Pomegranate and Punica designs measuring about 28 x 26.5 cm (11 x 10½ inches) and the Pamela Spray measuring 29 x 23 cm (11½ x 9 inches), were intended to be worked as piano or mantel slip ends, no doubt using silks, couched gold threads, jewels and beetles' wings.

Pomegranate.—PIANO OR MANTEL SLIP END.
For Jewels and Beetles' Wings work.
No. 4095.
Design 11½ inches by 10½ inches.

Design No. 4095 Pomegranate

No. 4266. **Pamela Spray.**—PIANO OR MANTEL SLIP END.

Design 11½ inches by 9 inches. For Jewels and Beetles' Wings work.

Design No. 4266 Pamela Spray

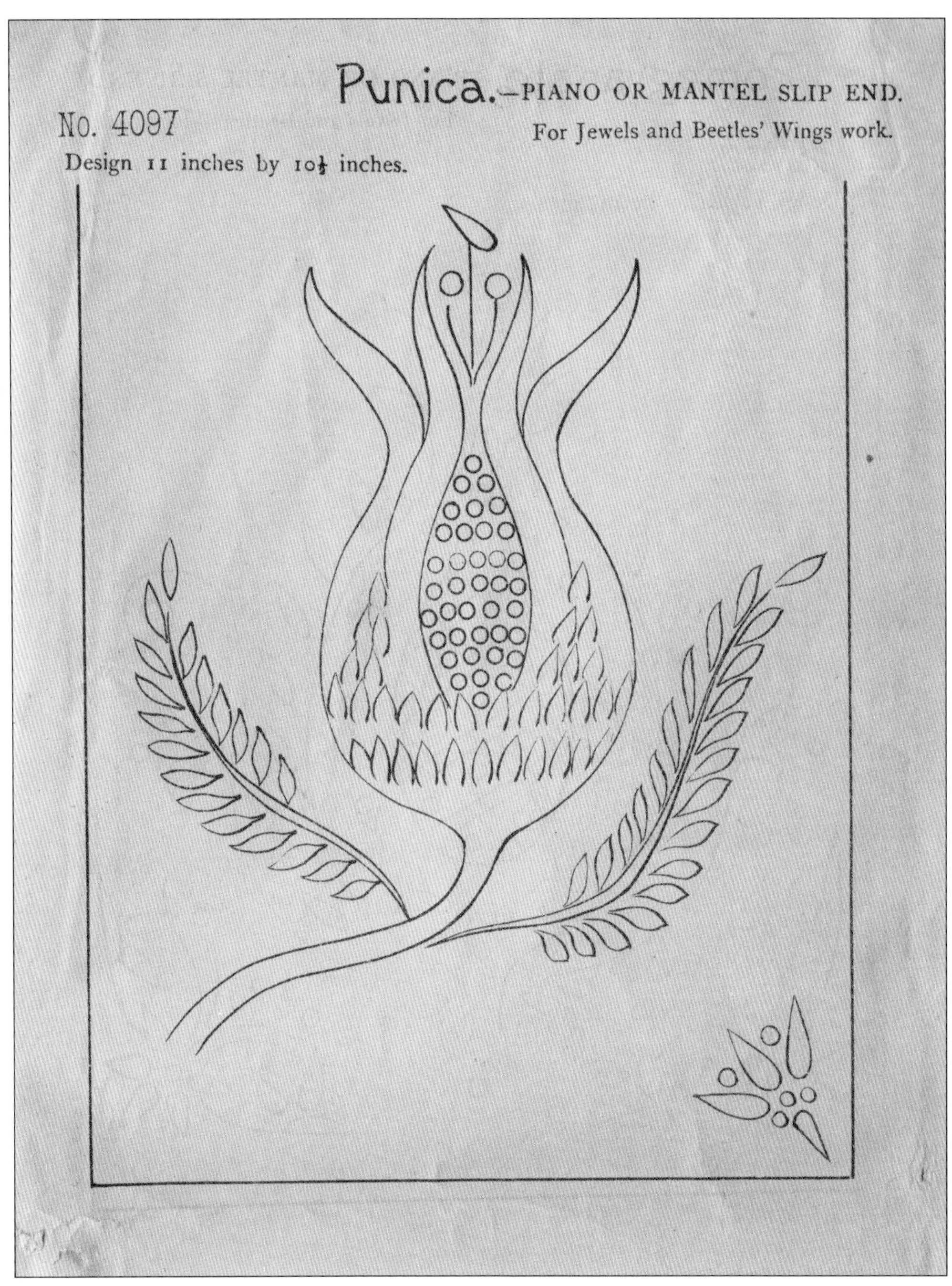

Design No. 4097 Punica

Working with Beetle Wings

The beetle wings that are generally used in embroidery are the hard outer wing cases, or elytra, of the jewel beetles (often the species *Sternocera aquisignata*). These iridescent green 'sequins' are still used to decorate items such as clothing, accessories, cushions and wall hangings, in areas of Southeast Asia and the Indian subcontinent, and are available in centres such as Bangkok. As they are extremely durable, they can also be unpicked from worn items to be re-used, adding a unique colour and sparkle to your work.

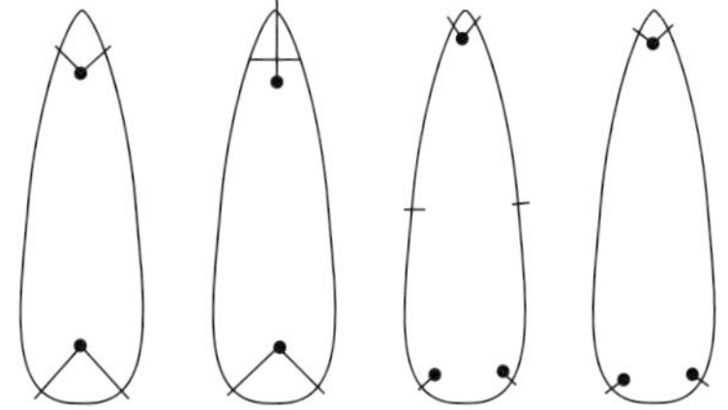

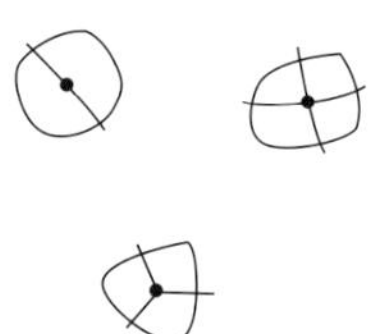

Methods of attaching whole beetle wings and sequin-sized pieces

Varying in size from less than 1 cm to more than 3 cm (about 3/8–1 1/4 in), the whole beetle wing may be applied or may be cut into smaller pieces with sharp nail scissors—narrow, tapered shapes make very elegant dragonfly wings! As the elytra can be quite brittle, the process of cutting and piercing is greatly facilitated by first steaming them to make them more pliable (thanks to Victoria Rivers for this advice).

Whole beetle wings need to be pierced around the edges so that they can be stitched to a background. Make a minimum number of holes with a very fine needle (size 11 or 12 sharps), 1 mm away from the edge (if too close the wing will break away). *Hint*: Steam the wings first and pierce from the front, holding an eraser or cork underneath the wing for support. The nineteenth century embroiderer was advised to make 'four holes—one top and bottom, and one on either

Beetle Wing Evening Bag.

side—about a sixteenth part of an inch from the edge', however, most of the wings I have observed from that era have a hole about 5 mm (3/16 in) from each end, with two stitches through each hole forming a V; or one stitch to the point crossed by a right-angled stitch over the tip of the wing. Another method of attaching the wings is to make 3–5 holes 1 mm from the edge, and apply with small stab stitches.

For the evening bag, I cut large 3–5 cm (1 3/8 in) elytra into teardrop shapes and made three holes—one at the tip and two on either side of each rounded end. Small pieces of beetle wing can be applied as sequins, with two, three or four evenly spaced stitches worked through one central hole. Attach the wings with a fine green sewing thread, or nylon monofilament, using a size 12 sharps needle.

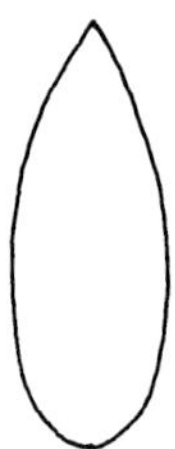

Template for beetle wing and substitute beetle wing

Detail of beetle wings used on evening bag

Beetle Wing Evening Bag

I used beetle wings purchased from The Bone Room to embellish this evening bag. If you do not have a ready supply of wings, there are many alternatives. Iridescent fabrics, cut into teardrop shapes, could be fused or appliquéd to the background. Many goldwork techniques could be employed; couched Japanese gold, Bright Check Purl chips, cut Smooth Purl over padding, applied gold kid, just to name a few. However, the easiest solution would be to fill the shapes with tiny, glittering beads, perhaps worked over padding to give a rounded form to the tear drops.

Requirements

- 45 cm (18 in) square or slate frame dressed with calico; or a 30 cm (12 in) embroidery hoop
- dark navy, purple or black silk dupion, 30 x 75 cm (12 x 30 in)
- black felt, 30 x 75 cm (12 x 30 in)
- Vliesofix, 30 x 75 cm (12 x 30 in)
- lining fabric, 30 x 50 cm (12 x 20 in)
- 16 whole beetle wings (or substitute) and 10 small pieces
- pale gold 3-ply twist
- nylon thread (Madeira Monofil No.60, clear and dark)
- tacking thread
- machine thread to match the silk dupion
- twisted cord for the handles

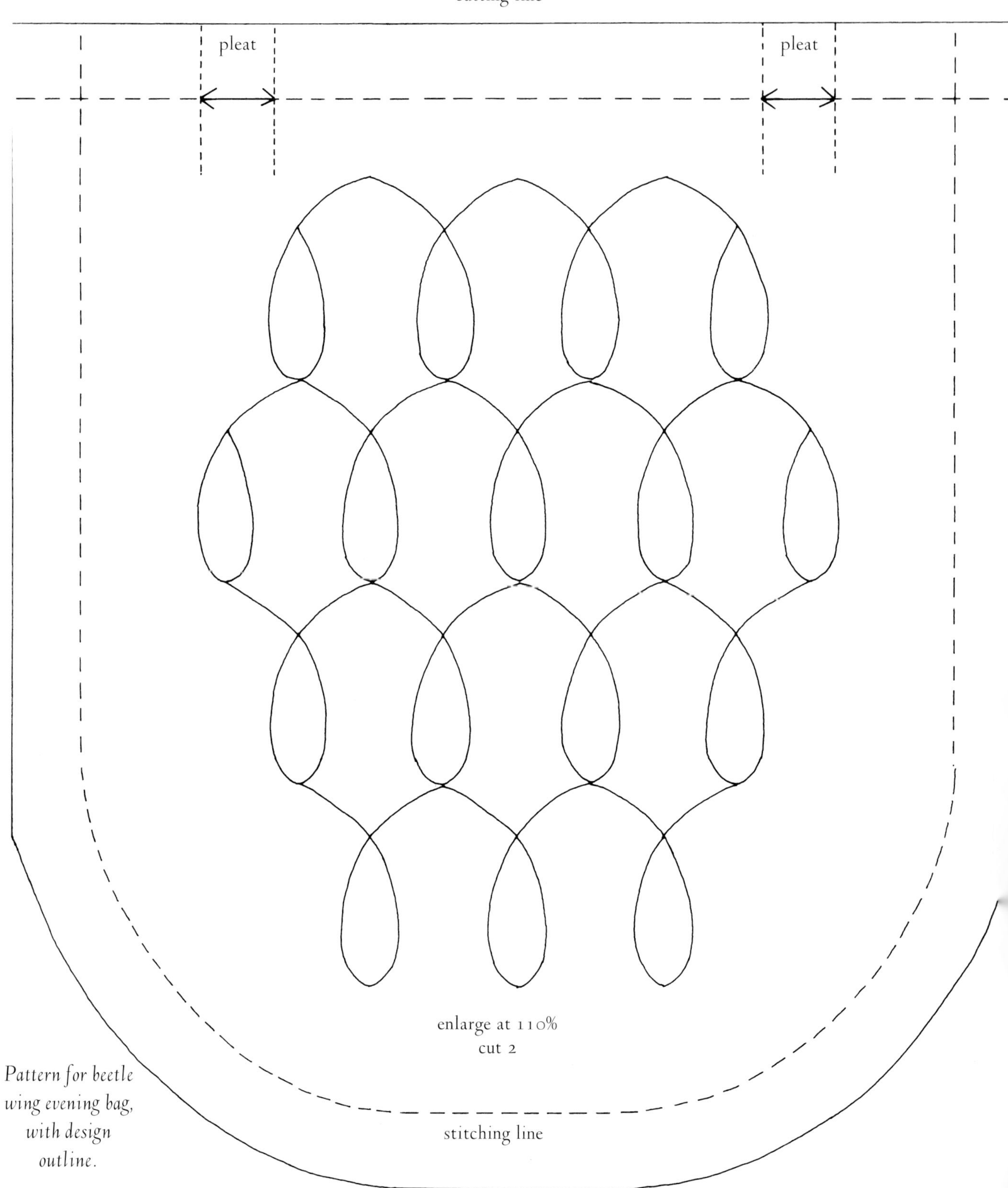

Pattern for beetle wing evening bag, with design outline.

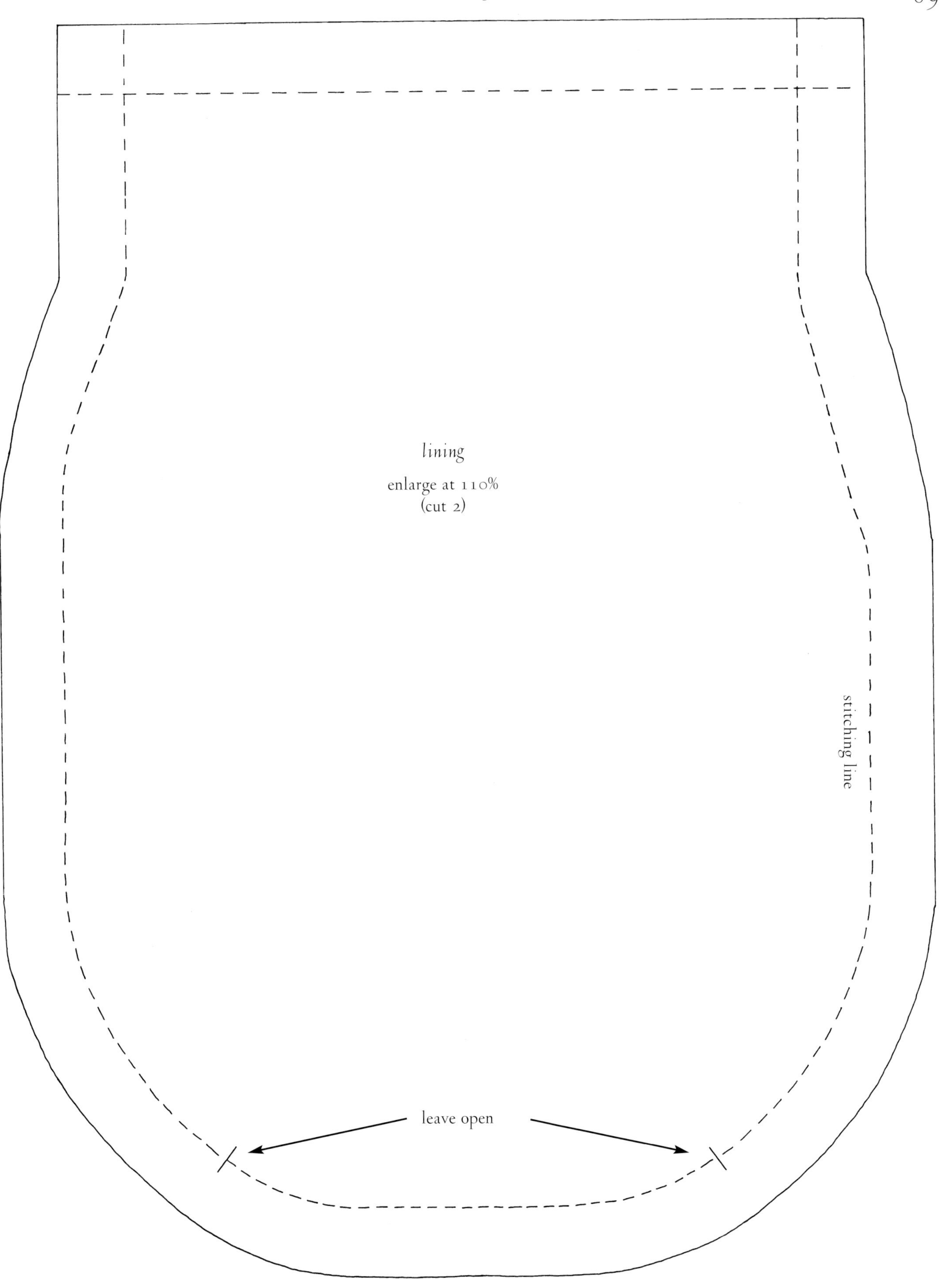
cutting line
lining
enlarge at 110%
(cut 2)
stitching line
leave open

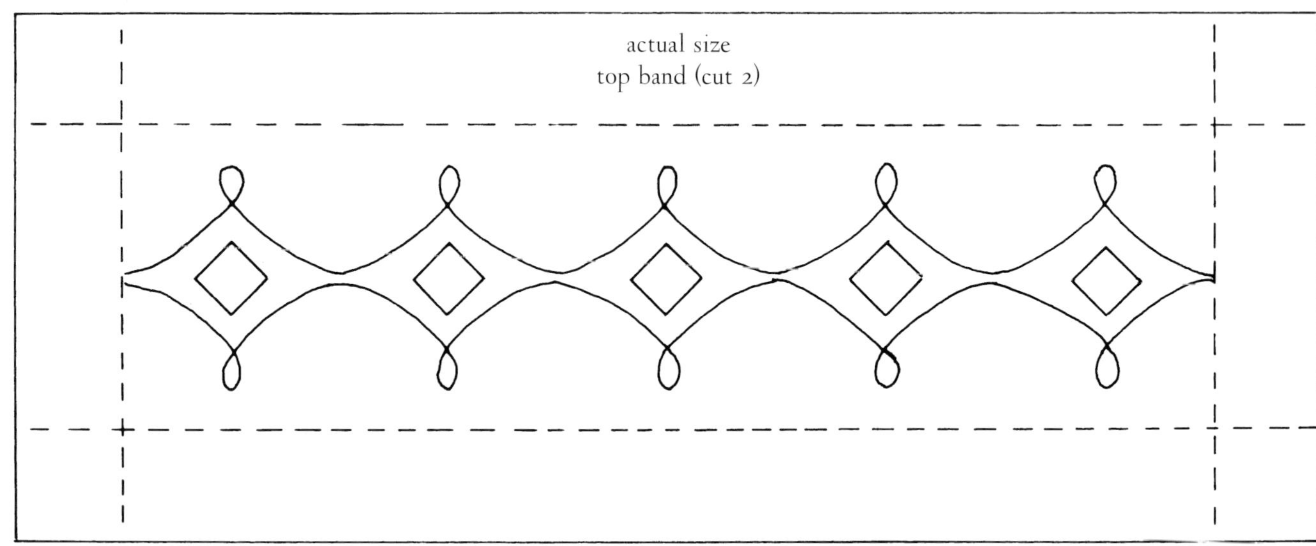

Preparation

1. Cut the silk, felt and Vliesofix as follows: two pieces 27 x 25 cm ($10\frac{5}{8}$ x 10 in) for the bag front and back, and two pieces 10 x 21 cm (4 x $8\frac{1}{4}$ in) for the top band pieces.

2. Using Vliesofix, fuse a layer of felt to the back of each piece of silk, to give support to the embroidery.

3. Mount the bag front and both the top band pieces onto the prepared square frame (the embroidery could be worked in a large round hoop if preferred).

4. Trace the design outlines, stitching lines and cutting lines for the bag front and two band pieces onto tissue paper. Place the tissue paper over the silk in the frame and thread-trace these lines with small running stitches, then tear the paper away. These stitches will be removed as you work.

Bag front

1. Prepare the beetle wings by trimming into teardrop shapes using the template as a guide, if required. Make three holes in the wings; one at the tip and two on either side of the rounded base. Stitch the wings to the silk inside the tacked teardrop shapes, using dark nylon thread in a size 12 sharps needle.

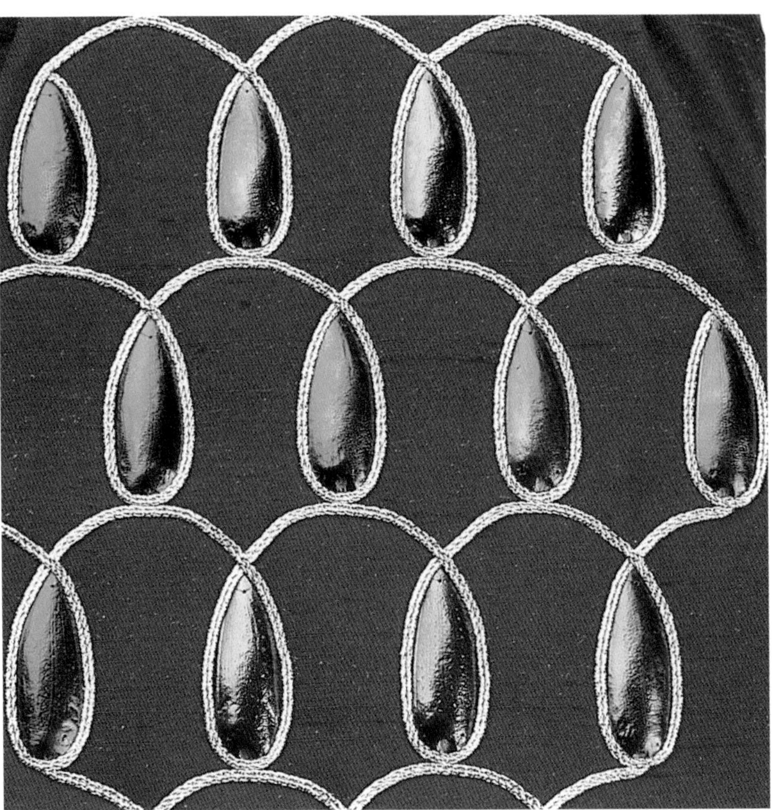

Detail of Beetle Wing Evening Bag.

2. Using clear nylon thread, couch the doubled gold twist over the design outlines, looping around the wings, removing the tacking stitches as you go. Start working at the top, sinking the tails of metal thread through to the back when each row is complete. Secure and trim.

Top bands

1. Using clear nylon thread, couch the doubled gold twist over the design outlines, making a tiny single loop at the points, removing the tacking stitches as you go. Work the top line of the design first, then the bottom line (they just touch), sinking the tails of metal thread through to the back when both lines have been worked. Secure and trim. Repeat for the other band.

2. Cut beetle wings into 10 pieces 7 mm (approx. 1/4 in) square, using a template if required. Make a hole in each corner of the squares. Stitch the square wing shapes to both bands, inside the gold outlines, using dark nylon thread in a size 12 sharps needle.

TO COMPLETE THE BAG

1. Cut out the bag front, and the two top band pieces, along the cutting lines. Mark the pleat lines on the bag front. Trim away most of the calico backing, leaving 1 cm (3/8 in) outside all the stitched areas (take care not to cut any of the couching stitches).

2. Using the patterns, cut out the bag back (marking the pleat lines), and two lining pieces (marking the lower opening).

3. Form two pleats on the bag front where marked, then stitch the front to one band piece, along the stitching line. Repeat for the bag back. Trim the seams.

4. With right sides facing, stitch the front to the back around the outside edge, along the stitching line. Trim the seams and finger-press open.

5. Stitch the two lining pieces together around the outside edge, leaving an opening at the base between the points as marked. Trim the seam, then turn right side out.

6. Cut the twisted cord to the desired length for handles and tack to the top side edges of the bag, raw edges even.

7. Insert the lining inside the bag and stitch around the top edges, catching in the cord handles. Carefully turn the bag the right way out through the opening in the lining. Slip stitch the opening, then ease the lining inside the bag, so that the seam is just inside the top edge. Couch a line of gold twist along the seam line, to keep the lining in place.

Part 4:
Stumpwork Beetles

Stumpwork is the ideal method to choose if you wish to embroider a life-like beetle.

The unique characteristic of stumpwork—embroidered detached shapes with wired edges—is ideal for working the elytra, which can be embellished in a myriad ways; the wired edge allows for the surface of the elytra to be raised and curved. This technique, together with the felt padding used to give a mounded shape to the body of the beetle, and the ability to raise the legs away from the surface with wrapped wire, makes for a very realistic interpretation of this fascinating creature. Using the information contained in this section, work a specimen to mount into a brooch or paperweight as a special gift; nestle a beetle amidst the foliage of an embroidery or stumpwork project, or select your favourite three or nine (or more) to display in a specimen box.

How to Embroider a Stumpwork Beetle

A stumpwork beetle can be embroidered on almost any type of background fabric: silk, satin, linen, cotton, velvet, even suede. Provide support for the beetle with a backing of quilter's muslin or fine calico.

Preparation

1. Mount the background fabric, with a muslin or fine calico backing, into an embroidery hoop or frame. Both fabrics need to be kept very taut.

2. Trace a skeleton outline of the beetle onto the backing fabric. The beetle is worked using the outline on the back as a guide. The outline may be thread-traced (with a line of tacking stitches) if preferred.

Order of work

A stumpwork beetle is usually embroidered in the following order: abdomen, elytra, thorax, head and eyes, antennae and finally the legs. There are several alternative methods provided for each of these. Select the one appropriate for the beetle you are working.

Beetle parts to embroider

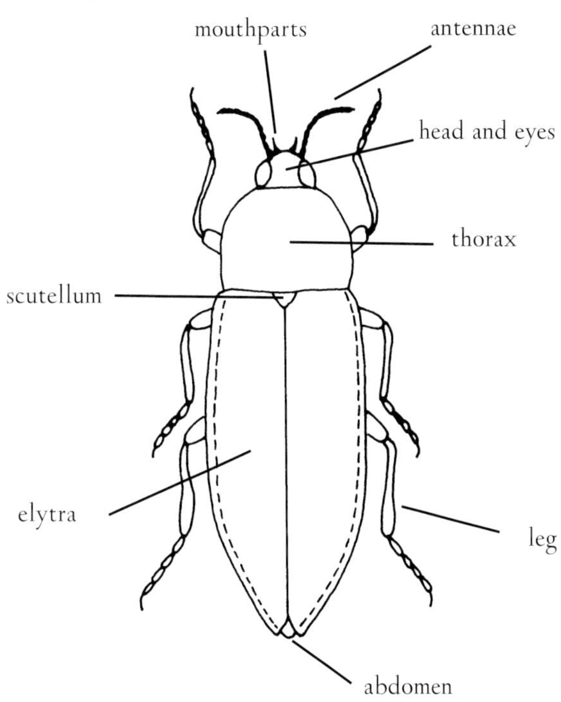

How to work the abdomen

The beetle abdomen is padded with one or more layers of felt, usually covered with satin stitch.

You will need:

- felt of the appropriate colour
- Vliesofix
- stranded thread—one strand in a size 10 crewel/ embroidery needle

1. Trace the abdomen outline (and one or more successively smaller outlines if required) onto Vliesofix and fuse to the felt. Cut out the shapes (remove the paper) and apply to the background fabric with small stab stitches, using the outline on the back as a guide. If applying more than one layer of felt, apply the smallest layer first. Work a row of buttonhole stitches 2 mm (1/16 in) apart around the edge of the felt to give a neat outline.

2. The felt padding (and buttonholed edge) is then covered with satin stitch, worked horizontally to represent segments. My favourite thread for working a beetle abdomen is Soie d'Alger 3326—a beautiful dark purple.

Or:

2. The felt padding may be covered with lengths of metal purl, cut to size, and applied with well-waxed matching thread in a fine needle. Refer to the Rove Beetle (page 173) for detailed instructions.

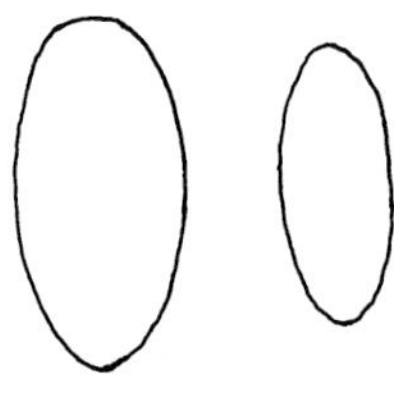

layers of padding

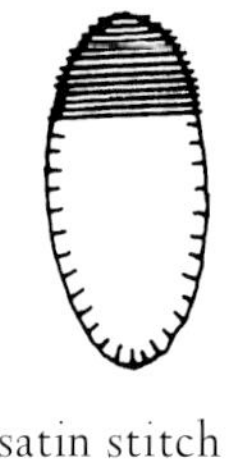

satin stitch

Steps in working the abdomen

How to work the elytra

The elytra, the most decorative element of the beetle, can be worked in many ways; 21 different examples are shown in the Beetle Specimen Box on page 84. The fabrics and methods used for working these elytra fall into six categories. Some require the elytra fabric to be prepared (or embellished) before being mounted into the hoop (categories A and B below), while others work the elytra decoration after wire has been stitched to a background fabric (categories C, D and E). Select the appropriate fabric to mount into the hoop, according to the beetle you are working (see individual beetles for detailed instructions).

A: *Exotic fabric elytra* Use exotic fabric, sometimes with a backing, for the elytra.

- Great Diving Beetle: taffeta (page 144)
- Ruby Longhorn Beetle: velveteen (page 120)
- Rove Beetle: metallic fabric (page 173)
- Soldier Beetle: ribbed ottoman (page 101)

B: *Fused fabric elytra* Fuse and embellish fabric for the elytra.

- Weevil: fused metallic fabric and threads (page 139)

- Green Tortoise Beetle : fused, painted and gilded fabric (page 127)
- Violin Beetle: fused metallic fabric and threads (page 108)

C: *Embroidered elytra* Embroider on quilter's muslin or coloured cotton (homespun).

- Ladybird: worked in satin stitch on red fabric (page 135)
- Checkered Beetle: tent stitch worked on silk gauze over muslin (page 131)
- Longhorn Beetle: long and short stitch worked on muslin (page 115)
- Fungus Beetle: French knots worked on yellow fabric (page 157)

D: *Couched elytra* Couch metallic thread, purl or beads on muslin or coloured fabric.

- Net-winged Beetle: couched metallic thread on muslin (page 160)
- Jewel Beetle: couched metallic thread and or nué on muslin (page 90)
- Metallic Woodboring Beetle: couched metallic thread on muslin (page 93)
- Ground Beetle: couched beads on coloured fabric (page 106)
- Pill Beetle: couched beads on coloured fabric (page 97)
- Leaf Beetle: couched metal purl on coloured fabric (page 124)

E: *Elytra with applied decoration* Apply leather, suede or beetle elytra on muslin.

- Garden Chafer: applied suede on muslin (page 168)
- Click Beetle: applied beetle elytra on muslin (page 149)
- Scarab Beetle: applied leather on muslin (page 165)

F: *Needlelace elytra* These elytra are not worked on fabric. Refer to the instructions for the Skipjack Beetle (page 152).

You will need:

- appropriate fabric, mounted in a 10 cm (4 in) hoop
- wire, either 30-gauge paper-covered, 28-gauge uncovered or fine flower wire
- stranded thread, one strand in a size 10 crewel/embroidery needle
- embellishment—refer to the individual beetles for specific requirements

1. Select or prepare the fabric for your chosen beetle and mount into the hoop, stretching the fabric as tight as a drum.

2. Trace a pair of elytra outlines on to the fabric, making sure that the straight edge of the elytra is on the straight grain of the fabric. If the elytra are joined, place them at right angles on the straight grain. An alternative method is to cut templates of the elytra out of paper, magic tape or 'Post-it' paper to use as outlines. *Only one elytra outline is provided in the instructions. A more accurate pair is obtained if the tracing is flipped over to obtain the mirror image.*

3. Using fine tweezers, shape and couch wire around the elytra outlines, leaving tails of wire about 5 cm (2 in) long either on the front of the fabric or taken through to the back (depending on the beetle being worked). *Use masking tape to keep the wire tails out of the way.*

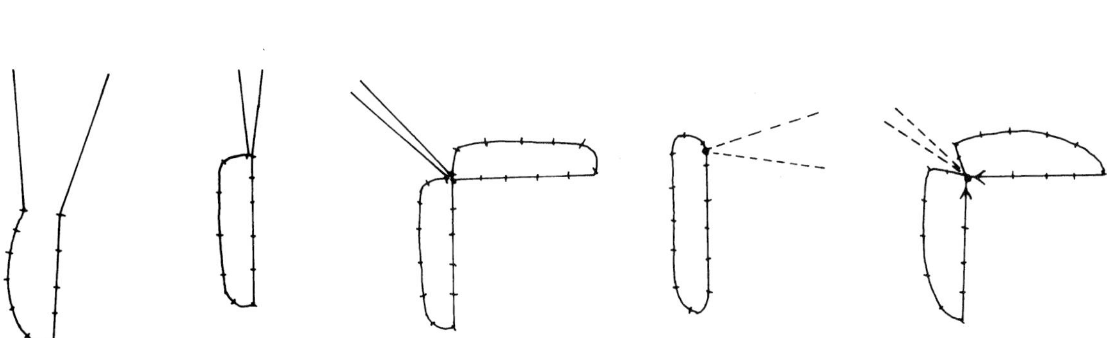

Methods for shaping wire around elytra outlines

4. Stitch the wire to the fabric with buttonhole stitch or overcast stitch, using one strand of thread.

5. Embellish the elytra, inside the wire outline, as required (categories C, D or E).

6. Using very sharp scissors with fine points, cut out the elytra very close to the stitching, taking care not to cut the thread. Do not cut the wire tails.

7. To apply the elytra over the abdomen, insert the wire tails through to the back at the points indicated, using a large, sharp yarn darner (usually size 14). *The wire insertion points are given as a guide only—hold the elytra over the abdomen to check before inserting.* Bend the wires under the abdomen and secure with a few stitches. Trim the wires so that they do not protrude outside the embroidered abdomen. *For small shapes, make a U turn in the wire and stitch again for extra security. Note:* In some beetles the wires are not stitched to the back, but are secured temporarily with masking tape until being brought through to the front for legs (see the Scarab Beetle).

How to work the thorax, head and eyes

The thorax, head and eyes, generally worked after the elytra have been applied, can be worked in several ways (see individual beetles for detailed instructions).

Leather Thorax

Leather, suede or snakeskin, applied over the top of the padded abdomen, is used for the thorax and the head in many of the beetles.

Leather thorax

You will need:

- leather, suede or snakeskin
- nylon thread in a size 12 sharps needle
- beads for eyes

Cut a thorax shape from leather, suede or snakeskin (if the leather is to cover the top of the elytra as well, check that it is wide enough). Apply the leather over the top of the padded abdomen, with small stab stitches, working the first two stitches in the lower corners of the thorax. If the head is included in the shape, work a stitch on either side of the head (in each corner), then stitch a bead on either side of the head for eyes (use tweezers to shape the thorax and the head as you work).

Wired fabric thorax

The thorax can be worked on fabric, in a similar way to the elytra of the beetles.

You will need:

- appropriate fabric, mounted in a 10 cm (4 in) hoop
- wire, either 30-gauge paper-covered, 28-gauge uncovered or fine flower wire
- stranded thread, one strand in a size 10 crewel/embroidery needle
- embellishment—refer to the individual beetles for detailed requirements
- beads for eyes

1. Mount fabric into the hoop and trace thorax outline (or use a paper template). Using fine tweezers, shape and couch wire around the outline, leaving two tails of wire about 5 cm (2 in) long either on the front of the fabric or taken through to the back.

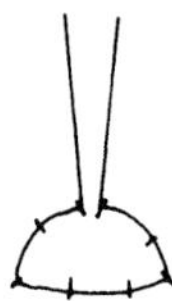

2. Buttonhole stitch the wire to the fabric. If required, embroider the thorax inside the wire outline, or apply leather (refer to the beetle you are working).

Methods for shaping wire around thorax outlines

3. Cut out the thorax and apply at the top of the abdomen, inserting the wire tails through to the back at the points indicated. Bend the wires under the abdomen, secure and

trim. Shape the thorax with tweezers and secure the corners with an invisible stitch (using nylon thread) if necessary.

4. Work the head in satin stitch, covering the wire insertion points. Stitch a bead on either side of the head for eyes.

EMBROIDERED THORAX

The thorax may be worked in satin stitch, using one strand of thread. Apply a bead on either side of the head for eyes.

Work stitches horizontally through the eye beads

EYES

Apply the beads with either stranded thread or nylon thread, working the stitches horizontally through the beads, towards the head, for the most realistic effect.

How to work the antennae

The antennae occur on the head, between the mouthparts and the eyes, and can be stitched in several ways.

Chain stitch antennae

1. With one strand of fine metallic thread in a size 9 straw/milliners needle, work a row of chain stitches for each antenna (often 9, 10 or 11 stitches to represent segments).

2. For short antennae or feelers, work two straight stitches, using one strand of fine metallic thread in a size 9 straw/milliners needle.

Straight stitch antennae

3. Tiny bugle beads can be threaded on to metallic thread and couched in place for antennae (see the Ruby Longhorn Beetle).

4. Separate two plumules from a peacock feather and apply for the antennae (see the Skipjack Beetle).

How to work the legs

The six legs of the beetle can be worked in several ways. Three segments of the leg are shown on stumpwork beetles; the femur (inner segment closest to the abdomen), the tibia and the tarsus (the two outer segments).

Embroidered legs

The legs may be stitched with stranded or metallic thread (use a straw/milliners needle when working with metallic thread), in one of two ways.

Chain stitch leg

1. Work two chain stitches for the two inner leg segments, with a long tie-down stitch forming the outer segment.

2. Work the leg in straight stitches, using two strands of thread for the inner segments, and one strand for the outer segment.

Straight stitch leg

Wrapped wire legs

Wire can be wrapped with stranded or metallic thread and inserted for legs, or the wire tails from the elytra may be used (see the Scarab Beetle).

Secure the thread, wrap closely and firmly to cover the wire (wrap more wire than you will need for the leg), then knot the thread to the wire, leaving a tail of thread. Insert the wrapped wire tails (and the tails of thread) through to the back, using a large sharp yarn darner. Shape the legs with tweezers, then bend the wire back behind the leg and secure 3–4 mm ($^{1}/_{8}$ in) to the muslin backing with a few stitches worked in a pale (ecru) thread. Trim excess wire.

Shaping the beetle

The final and possibly most important stage is to 'fine tune' your beetle. Using fine tweezers, gently shape the elytra into a curved shell over the abdomen. Use a nail file to nudge any leather edges into place, and adjust the position of the beads (eyes) with a needle. Attention to these details makes all the difference!

The Beetle Specimen Box

This section contains the techniques employed to embroider the beetles in the Beetle Specimen Box, the second in my series of stumpwork insect boxes. The first, the Dragonfly Specimen Box, appears in my book *Stumpwork Dragonflies* (Sally Milner Publishing, 2000). The Beetle Specimen Box contains 21 specimens from the order Coleoptera: the selection was no easy task, considering the huge number of beetles that have been described in this really diverse group of insects! The challenge was to interpret each beetle in a different and appropriate way, drawing from the many ideas jotted down in notebooks over the past four years. The beetles in the specimen box were embroidered for pleasure, often using treasures from many years of collecting. For this reason the instructions cannot always identify specific materials, but instead encourage you to indulge in the search for just the right thread, fabric or bead. Most of these beetles are not difficult to work; some are more challenging; all are fun!

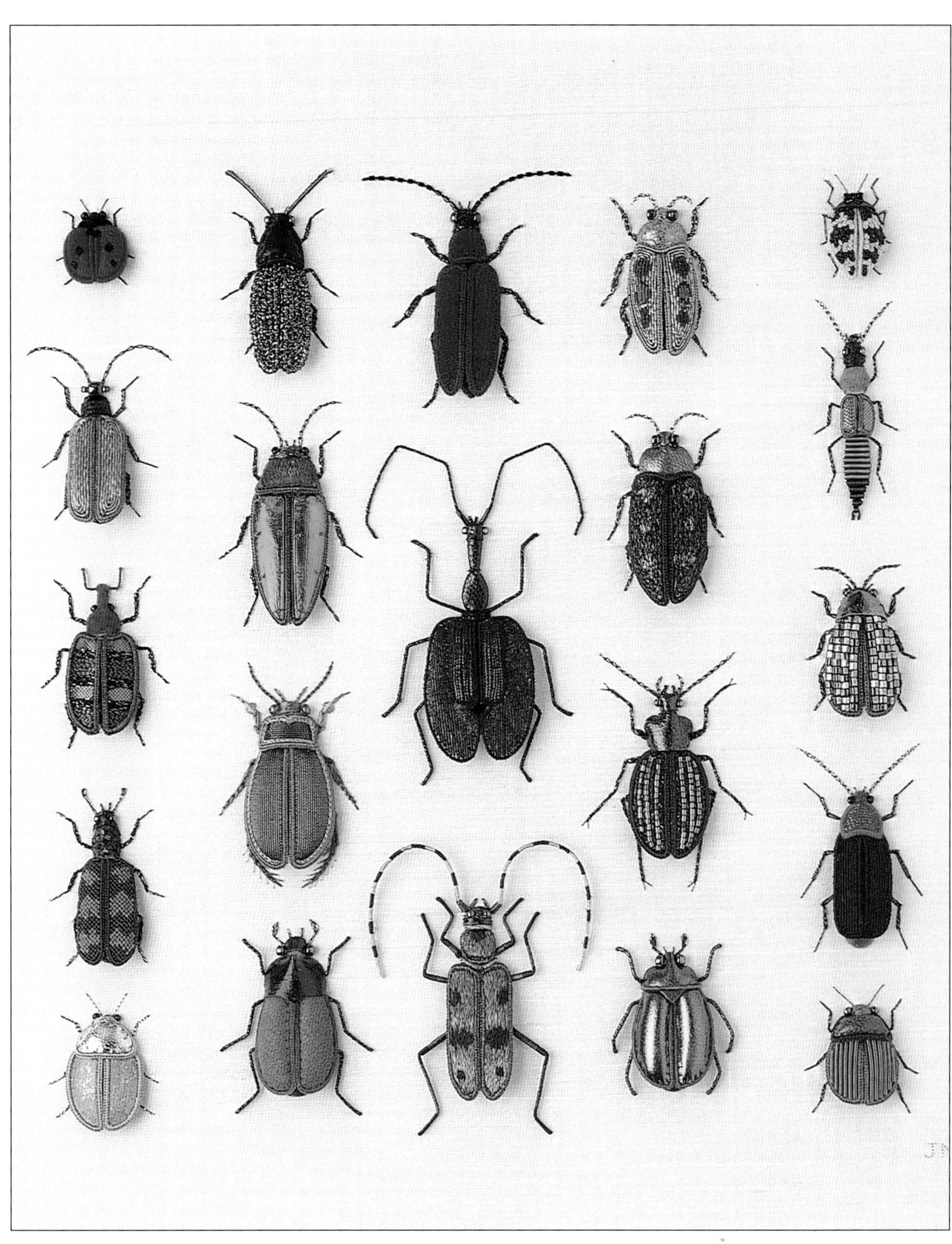

The Beetle Specimen Box.

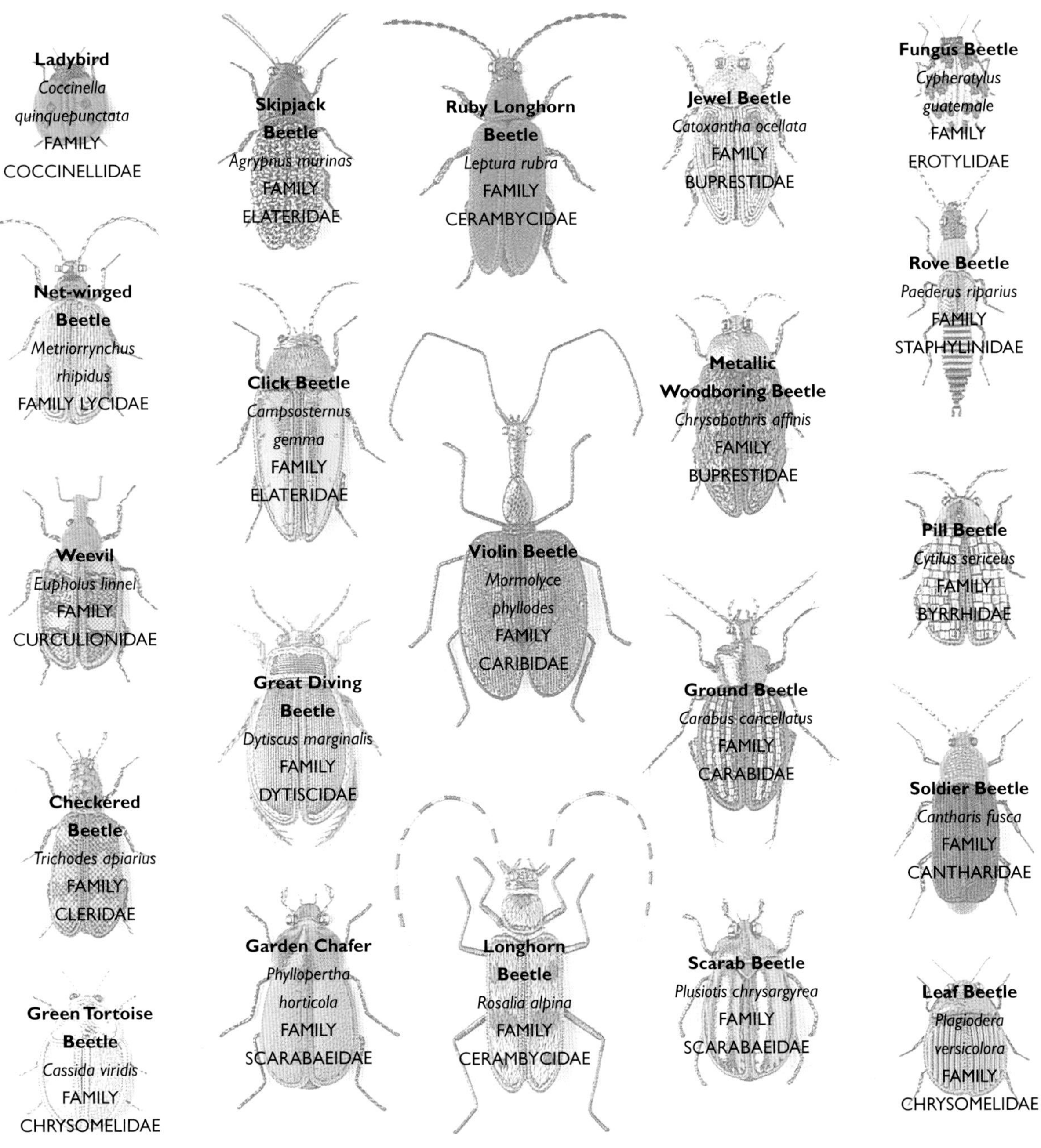

Key to Beetles.

Whether you are working a specimen box of beetles, or just one, the following information may be helpful:

- The background fabric of the specimen box, a very finely textured silk, was chosen to represent parchment. The backing fabric is muslin.
- The beetle diagrams and skeleton outlines are actual working size; the drawings illustrating the instructions may not be.
- The beetles are as 'entomologically accurate' as the limitations of materials will allow. The challenge is to interpret the various parts of the anatomy in fabrics, threads and beads. Feel free to change any part of these beetles—if it works you are allowed to do it!
- The beetles in the specimen box are not true to size; the actual Violin Beetle can be up to 9 cm (3½ in) body length, whilst a Rove Beetle may be only 1 mm.
- All the embroidery is worked with one strand of thread, unless specified otherwise.
- Read Part 9 on general techniques and equipment before you start.

FAMILIES AND SPECIES REPRESENTED IN THE SPECIMEN BOX

The order Coleoptera is made up of many beetle families, 15 of which are represented in this specimen box. The beetle families are set out below in alphabetical order, according to their scientific family name. As some families have two representatives, each beetle is referred to by its common name.

Family Buprestidae: Jewel Beetle, Metallic Woodboring Beetle

Family Byrrhidae: Pill Beetle

Family Cantharidae: Soldier Beetle

Family Carabidae: Ground Beetle, Violin Beetle

Family Cerambycidae: Longhorn Beetle, Ruby Longhorn Beetle

Family Chrysomelidae: Leaf Beetle, Green Tortoise Beetle

Family Cleridae: Checkered Beetle

Family Coccinelidae: Ladybird

Family Curculionidae: Weevil

Family Dytiscidae: Great Diving Beetle

Family Elateridae: Click Beetle, Skipjack Beetle

Family Erotylidae: Fungus Beetle

Family Lycidae: Net-winged Beetle

Family Scarabaeidae: Scarab Beetle, Garden Chafer

Family Staphylinidae: Rove Beetle

Jewel Beetles (Metallic Woodboring Beetles).

Family Buprestidae

The large and distinctive family Buprestidae, the jewel beetles (also known as metallic woodboring beetles), is very popular with collectors. The adults have usually flattened bodies, up to 70 mm ($2^{3}/_{4}$ in) long, with large eyes and short antennae and legs. Most of these beetles are swift flyers, feeding on flower pollen, tree foliage and fruit, whilst their larvae live primarily on plant roots or the organic material of decaying trees. Their feeding habits help speed the decomposition of wood in forests worldwide.

Many members of the Buprestid family are amongst the most brilliantly coloured of all insects, especially those species found in tropical and subtropical parts of the world. They are very hard, compact beetles, with a metallic lustre over the whole body. Some of them resemble polished brass or copper, whilst others are bright green or rusty red. *Catoxantha ocellata* has blotches of purple, golden ochre and coppery red on its iridescent, metallic green elytra. Distinguishing features of *Chrysobothris affinis* are the gold-gleaming spots and faint longitudinal ribs on its burnished amethyst elytra.

Justifiably called jewel beetles (or flying jewels), many tropical species have been used in gold-mounted jewellery by several civilisations since ancient times (notably in India, Southeast Asia and Peru), whilst 'the elytra of Amazonian bupestrids are strung and worn as necklaces and ear pendants, and fashioned into headdresses by indigenous tribes in South America' (Beckmann, *Living Jewels*, p. 8).

In Japan there exists a buprestid beetle shrine, the Tamamushi-no-zushi in the Horiuji temple at Nara. Built in the seventh century AD for the Empress Suiko, it contains sacred Buddhist objects embellished with nine thousand shimmering green elytra of the bupestrid Chrysochroa fulgidissima *set in gilded filigree. An old Japanese legend says that a specimen of* Chrysochroa *placed in a tansu chest will cause clothing to magically accumulate within.*

Beckmann, *Living Jewels*, p. 8.

Jewel Beetle

Catoxantha ocellata

ORDER: COLEOPTERA

SUBORDER: POLYPHAGA

FAMILY: BUPRESTIDAE

Requirements

- quilter's muslin or calico, 15 cm (6 in) square
- 10 cm (4 in) embroidery hoop
- black felt and Vliesofix
- pale gold leather
- green stranded thread (Cifonda 523A or DMC 3346)
- red stranded thread (Cifonda 254A or DMC 349)
- copper stranded thread (Cifonda 64 or DMC 921)
- purple stranded thread (Cifonda 125 or DMC 550)
- dark purple stranded thread (Soie d'Alger 3326) or DMC 310 black
- green metallic thread (Grass Green Metallic Couching Thread 371)

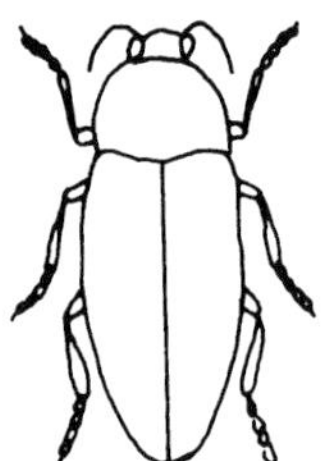

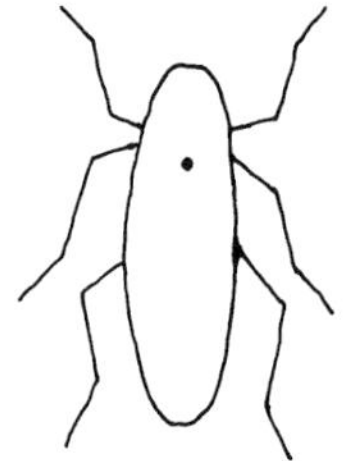

skeleton outline

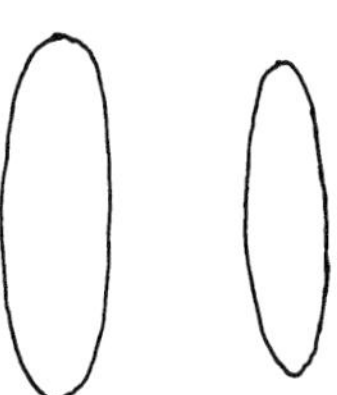

abdomen padding

- fine gold/black metallic thread (Kreinik Cord 205c)
- peacock green metallic thread (Kreinik Fine (#8) Braid 850)
- nylon thread (Madeira Monofil No.60, clear)
- Mill Hill seed beads (374 blue-black)
- fine flower wire (colour green if desired)

Order of work

Trace a skeleton outline of the jewel beetle onto the backing fabric. The abdomen and thorax are worked on the background fabric of the specimen box (silk or the fabric of your choice, backed with muslin or calico).

Abdomen

Apply two layers of felt to pad the abdomen then cover with satin stitch, worked horizontally, with dark purple thread.

thorax

Thorax, head and eyes

It is easier to apply the thorax *before* the elytra for this beetle. Cut the thorax from pale gold leather and apply with nylon thread: work two stitches at each lower corner of the thorax, a stitch on either side of the head (in each corner), then stitch a bead on either side of the head for eyes (use tweezers to shape the thorax and the head as you work). To define the head, work a stitch across the leather (behind the eyes) with two strands of gold/black metallic thread.

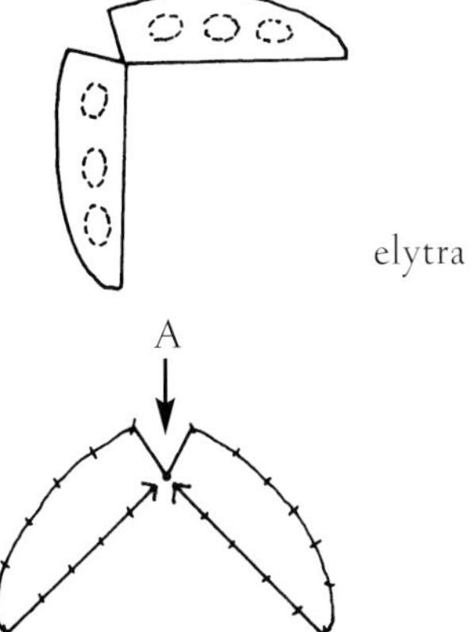

elytra

Elytra

1. Mount the muslin into the hoop and trace the elytra outline (including the blotches). Using green thread to couch the wire, start with a stitch at A (the centre of the wire), couch the wire around each elytra outline, *then* insert the wire tails through to the back at A. Buttonhole stitch the wire to the fabric, keeping the tails of wire free.

Optional Using appropriately coloured marking pens,

colour the blotches in the desired colours and the background of the elytra green (be careful to avoid colouring the buttonhole stitches).

2. The elytra are filled with rows of green metallic thread, couched down in a brick pattern (whenever possible) with one strand of green thread. At the same time, the blotches are embroidered in the goldwork technique of or nué (work close couching stitches, in the appropriate coloured thread, whenever the green metallic thread passes over a coloured blotch). To work one side of the elytra, sink an end of green metallic thread at the top corner, then couch a row close to the inside edge of the wire outline. Continue couching the thread, close to the previous row (working the blotches in or nué), until the elytra is filled. Sink the remaining end, secure at the back and trim. Repeat for the other side.

3. Cut out the elytra and apply over the abdomen, inserting the wire tails close to the lower edge of the thorax. Secure the wires at the back and trim. Use a needle to ease the lower edge of the thorax *under* the top edge of the elytra.

Antennae

With one strand of gold/black metallic thread, work five chain stitches for each antenna.

Legs

Using two strands of peacock green metallic thread, work two straight stitches for the inner segments of each leg. Work the outer segment with one strand of thread.

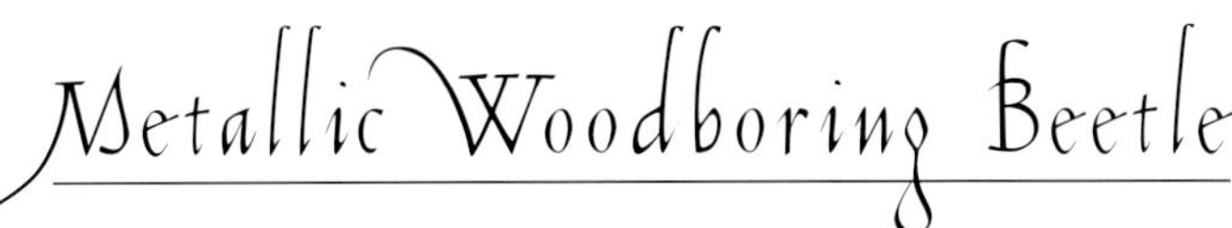

Metallic Woodboring Beetle

Chrysobothris affinis

ORDER: COLEOPTERA

SUBORDER: POLYPHAGA

FAMILY: BUPRESTIDAE

Requirements

- dark brown cotton (homespun), 15 cm (6 in) square
- 10 cm (4 in) embroidery hoop
- black felt and Vliesofix
- bronze leather
- dark purple stranded thread (Soie d'Alger 3326 or DMC 939)
- amethyst metallic thread (Kreinik Very Fine (#4) Braid 026V)
- orange metallic thread (Kreinik Very Fine (#4) Braid 152V)
- bronze metallic thread (Kreinik Very Fine (#4) Braid 154V)
- fine copper/black metallic thread (Kreinik Cord 215c)

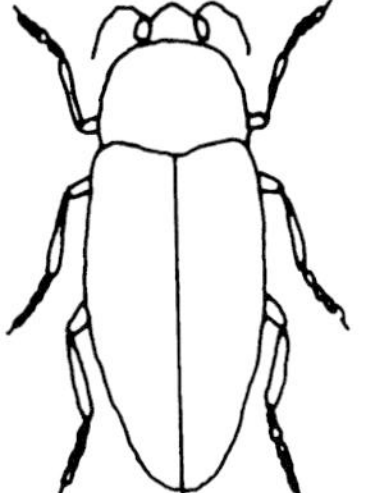

skeleton outline

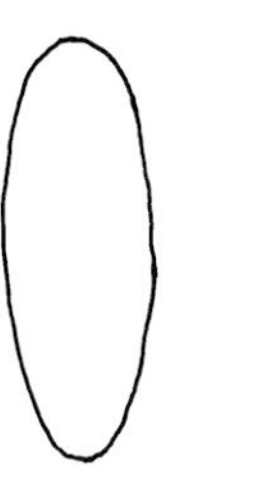

abdomen padding

- nylon thread (Madeira Monofil No.60, dark)
- Mill Hill seed beads (374 blue-black)
- fine flower wire (colour purple if desired)

Order of work

Trace a skeleton outline of the metallic woodboring beetle onto the backing fabric. The abdomen and thorax are worked on the background fabric of the specimen box (silk or the fabric of your choice, backed with muslin or calico).

Abdomen

Apply two layers of felt to pad the abdomen then cover with satin stitch, worked horizontally, with dark purple thread.

Thorax, head and eyes

It is easier to apply the thorax *before* the elytra for this beetle. Cut the thorax from bronze leather and apply with nylon thread: work two stitches at each lower corner of the thorax, a stitch on either side of the head (in each corner), then stitch a bead on either side of the head for eyes (use tweezers to shape the thorax and the head as you work). To define the head, work a stitch across the leather (behind the eyes) with two strands of copper/black metallic thread.

thorax

Elytra

1. Mount the brown fabric into the hoop and trace the elytra outline (or use a paper template). Using dark purple thread to couch the wire, start with a stitch at A (the centre of the wire), couch the wire around each elytra outline, *then* insert the wire tails through to the back at A. Buttonhole stitch the wire to the fabric, keeping the tails of wire free.

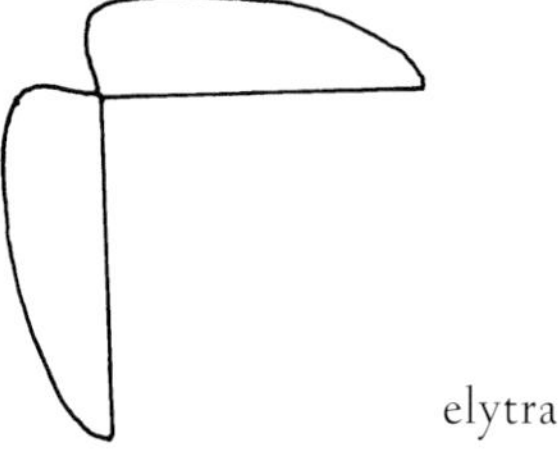

elytra

2. The elytra are filled with rows of amethyst metallic thread (four strands), couched down with dark nylon thread. To work one side of the elytra, couch a row of metallic thread (four strands) close to the inside edge of the wire outline. Continue couching the threads, close to the previous row, until the

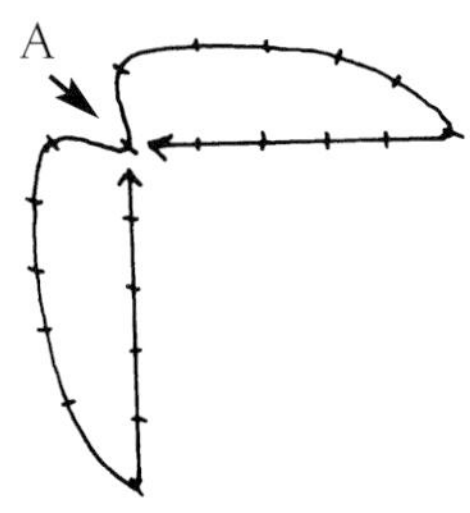

shape is filled. Embroider blotches in satin stitch with one strand of orange metallic thread. Repeat for the other side.

3. Cut out the elytra and apply over the abdomen, inserting the wire tails close to the lower edge of the thorax. Secure the wires at the back and trim. Use a needle to ease the lower edge of the thorax *under* the top edge of the elytra.

Antennae

With one strand of copper/black metallic thread, work 6 chain stitches for each antenna.

Legs

Using two strands of bronze metallic thread, work two straight stitches for the inner segments of each leg. Work the outer segment with one strand of thread.

Family Byrrhidae

The small family Byrrhidae, the pill beetles, is notable for the way the beetles defend themselves—when in danger, the creature tucks its head and legs under the body and turns itself into a little ball. *Cytilus sericeus* and other species are masters at the art. When it has assured itself that the danger has passed, the beetle unrolls and continues on its way.

A typical pill beetle is a small oval insect, with convex wings, often metallic in colour. *Cytilus sericeus,* 4.5–5.5 mm (about 5/32 in) in body length, has metallic bronze and green striped wing cases and a bronze thorax. It inhabits moss in damp, grassy spaces from spring to summer.

Pill Beetle.

Pill Beetle

Cytilus sericeus

ORDER: COLEOPTERA

SUBORDER: POLYPHAGA

FAMILY: BYRRHIDAE

Requirements

- olive green cotton (homespun), 15 cm (6 in) square
- 10 cm (4 in) embroidery hoop
- brown felt and fusible web
- bronze snakeskin
- olive green stranded thread (DMC 936)
- nylon thread (Madeira Monofil No.60, clear)
- Delica Beads DB C24 (green-bronze)
- Mill Hill petite beads (40374 blue-black)
- fine brown/black metallic thread (Kreinik Cord 201c)
- bronze/black metallic thread (Kreinik Very Fine (#4) Braid 154v)
- 30-gauge green covered wire

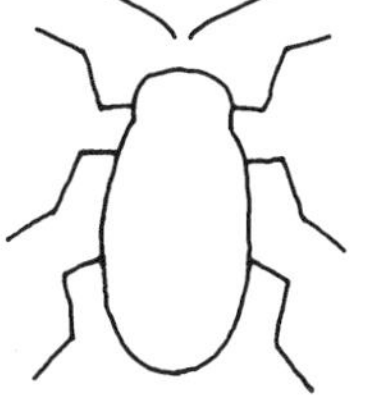

skeleton outline

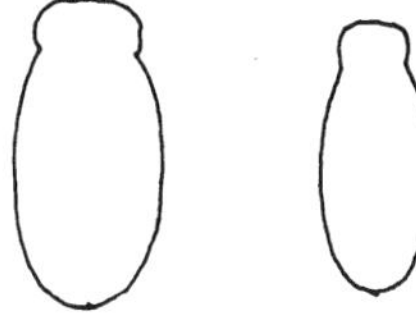

abdomen padding

Order of work

Trace a skeleton outline of the pill beetle onto the backing fabric. The abdomen and thorax are worked on the background fabric of the specimen box (silk or the fabric of your choice, backed with muslin or calico).

Abdomen

Apply two layers of felt to pad the abdomen then cover with satin stitch, worked horizontally, with olive green thread.

Elytra

1. Mount the green fabric into the hoop and trace the elytra. Using olive green thread, couch the wire around the outline, leaving two tails, then buttonhole stitch the wire to the fabric.

elytra

2. Fill the elytra with four rows of couched Delica beads, starting at the inside edge:

Using olive green thread in a 12 sharps needle, come out at 1, thread on 13 beads and insert at 2 (*over* the wire into the buttonholed edge).

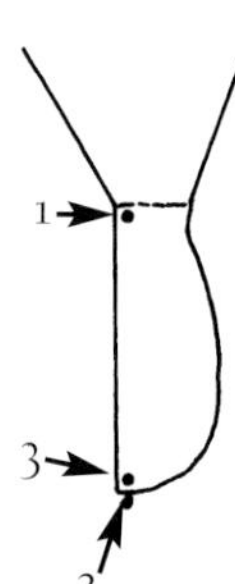

Bring the needle out at 3 (close to inside wire), thread through all beads back to 1, then hold this thread under tension while couching between each bead with nylon thread (start at the lower bead). Insert green thread at 1.

Repeat for three more rows (13/14 beads, 13 beads, 9 beads).

3. Cut out the elytra and apply over the abdomen, inserting the wire tails at the points indicated. Secure the wires at the back and trim.

THORAX

thorax

Draw the beads in at the top of the elytra and stitch to the abdomen. Cut a piece of felt to pad the space between the end of the beads and the top of the abdomen. Using the thorax outline as a guide, cut a piece of bronze snakeskin and apply, using nylon thread, over the drawn-in beads and padding. Stroke the snakeskin in around the edge of the thorax with a blunt needle.

HEAD AND EYES

Apply two petite beads for the eyes. With two strands of brown/black metallic thread, work one stitch behind the beads for the head, and two stitches for the mouthparts.

ANTENNAE

With one strand of brown/black metallic thread, work eight chain stitches for each antenna, using the outline on the back as a guide.

LEGS

With two strands of bronze/black metallic thread, work two straight stitches for the inner segments of each leg. Work the outer segment with one strand of thread.

Family Cantharidae

Members of this small but distinctive family, the soldier beetles, feature an elegant, slender body 3–23 mm (1/8–7/8 in) long, and soft elytra. *Cantharis fusca* is just one of several species known as soldier beetles because of the striking colour combination of black wing cases and bright red-orange thoraxes resemble nineteenth century military uniforms. The cantharids' colours are a warning to birds and other predators that these beetles contain distasteful chemicals and are not edible.

A familiar sight in summer, soldier beetles frequent large flowerheads such as those of cow parsley, and the leaves of herbaceous and woody plants, feeding on soft-bodied insects including aphids, flies and caterpillars.

Soldier Beetle.

Soldier Beetle

Cantharis fusca

Order: Coleoptera

Suborder: Polyphaga

Family: Cantharidae

Requirements

- 10 cm (4 in) embroidery hoop
- black silk ottoman, 15 cm (6 in) square, or any fine-ribbed fabric or grosgrain ribbon
- black organza and Vliesofix, 15 cm (6 in) square
- dark orange-gold fabric or ribbon, small piece
- quilter's muslin or calico, 15 cm (6 in) square
- orange felt and fusible web
- orange stranded thread (DMC 900)
- dark orange stranded thread (DMC 919)
- black stranded thread (DMC 310)
- copper/black metallic thread (Kreinik Cord 215c)
- gold/black metallic thread (Kreinik Cord 205c)

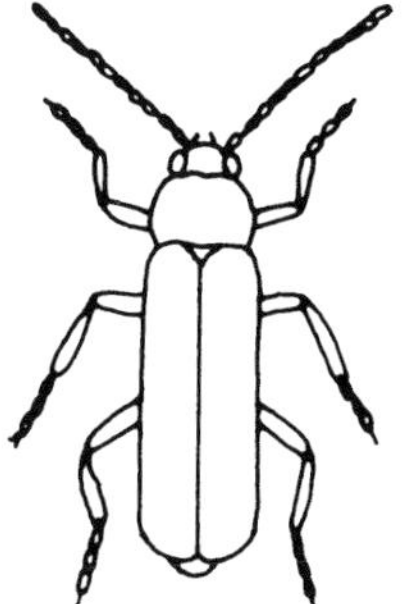

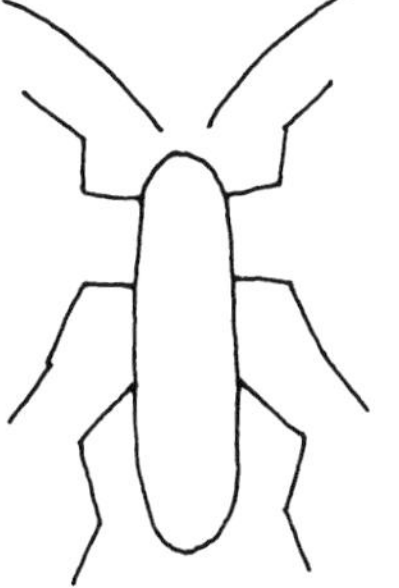

skeleton outline

abdomen padding

- nylon thread (Madeira Monofil No.60, clear)
- Mill Hill petite beads (42014 black)
- 28-gauge uncovered wire

Order of work

Trace a skeleton outline of the soldier beetle onto the backing fabric. The abdomen and thorax are worked on the background fabric of the specimen box (silk or the fabric of your choice, backed with muslin or calico).

Abdomen

Apply one layer of felt to pad the abdomen then cover with satin stitch, worked horizontally, with orange thread.

Elytra

1. Fuse a layer of organza to the back of the black ribbed fabric (for support) and mount into the hoop. Using a paper template for the elytra outline (make sure the straight edges of the elytra are parallel to the ridges of the fabric) and black thread, couch the wire around the outline, leaving two tails, then overcast the wire to the fabric. Work a few diagonal stitches at each upper corner for the scutellum.

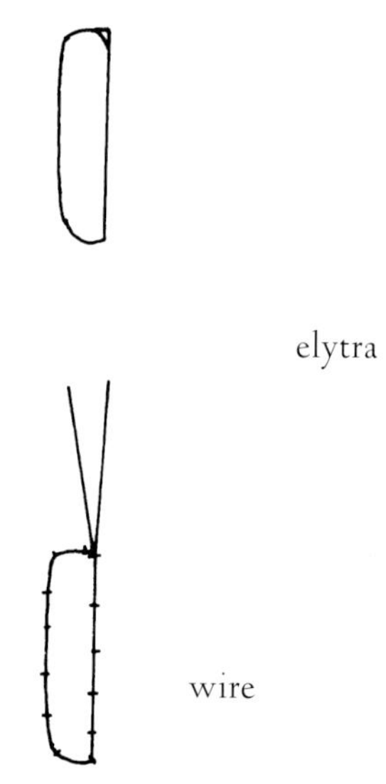

2. Cut out the elytra and catch both inner wires together. Apply over the abdomen, inserting the wire tails at the point indicated. Secure the wires at the back and trim.

Thorax, head and eyes

1. Stitch the orange-gold fabric to the centre of the muslin, mount into the hoop and trace the thorax outline (or use a paper template). Using orange thread, couch the wire around the outline, leaving two tails, then buttonhole stitch the wire to the fabric.

2. Cut out the thorax and apply at the top of abdomen, inserting the wire tails at the points indicated (it slightly overlaps the elytra). Secure the wires at the back and trim.

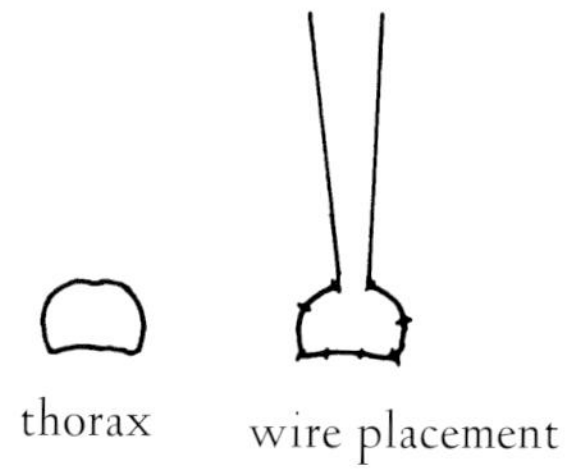

3. Using dark orange thread, work the head in satin stitch, covering the raw edge of the elytra and the wire insertion points.

4. Using nylon thread, apply a petite bead on either side of the head for eyes. Secure the corners of the elytra with two small (invisible) stitches.

Antennae

With one strand of copper/black metallic thread, work 11 chain stitches for each antenna. Use two strands to work two straight stitches for the mouthparts.

Legs

Using two strands of gold/black metallic thread, work two chain stitches and a long tie-down stitch for each leg, following the outline on the back.

Ground Beetles.

Family Carabidae

All members of the major family Carabidae, the ground beetles, are considered beneficial as they feed on other insects. Their distinguishing features include a stout, usually flattened body, from 1 mm to 60 mm (2¼ in), long legs for fast movement and thread-like antennae. As the name implies, most species live on the ground; they are usually nocturnal, hiding under logs, stones and surface litter during the day. Fiercely predacious, ground beetles, using rather pronounced mandibles to capture their prey, consume more than their own weight in food daily, feeding on dead or living insects, rotting fruit and carrion. Their larvae are also predators, catching and eating other soft-bodied insects. Carabids are widespread in distribution, frequenting nearly all climates, from hot dry deserts to cold wet mountain areas.

Although mostly dark brown or black, with little or no ornamentation, the elytra of many ground beetles are characterised by intricate sculpting and ornament: some are pitted by dimples, others have fine grooves. The handsome *Carabus cancellatus* has longitudinal ribs alternating with chains decorating its elytra, which can be bronze, brassy green, coppery or even black in colour.

The elegant violin-shaped ground beetle *Mormolyce phyllodes* (see page 108), with its curiously flattened body and elytra, lives in the forests of Indonesia. The compressed nature of its body allows it to hunt for its insect prey in the narrow space between the bark and the wood of decaying trees. Also known as the Ghost-walker, its colour (dark brown or black) and shape make it almost invisible at night when it is most active. Adult violin beetles grow to a length of about 9 cm (3½ in).

Ground Beetle

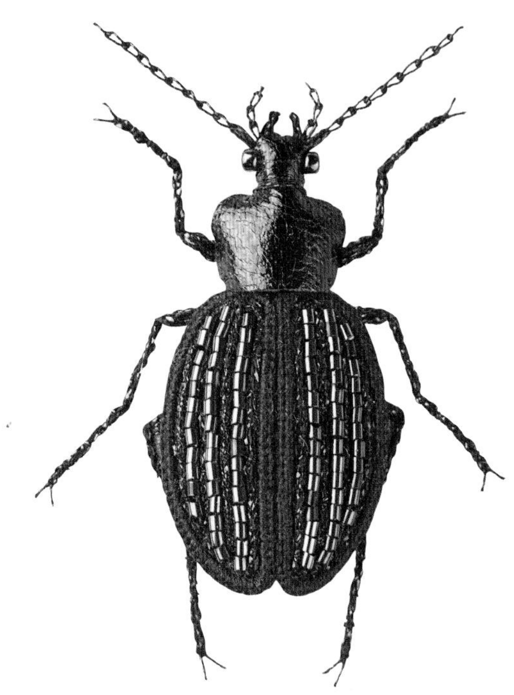

Carabus cancellatus

ORDER: COLEOPTERA

SUBORDER: ADEPHAGA

FAMILY: CARABIDAE

Requirements

- 10 cm (4 in) embroidery hoop
- dark brown cotton (homespun), 15 cm (6 in) square
- brown felt and Vliesofix
- mahogany metallic leather
- dark brown stranded thread (Soie d'Alger 4136 or DMC 3371)
- brown metallic braid (Kreinik Medium (#16) Braid 022)
- brown metallic thread (Kreinik Fine (#8) Braid 022)
- fine bronze/black metallic thread (Kreinik Cord 201c)
- nylon thread (Madeira Monofil No.60, dark)
- tiny bronze bugle beads (see elytra notes, page 107)
- Mill Hill petite beads (40374 blue-black)
- 30-gauge green covered wire

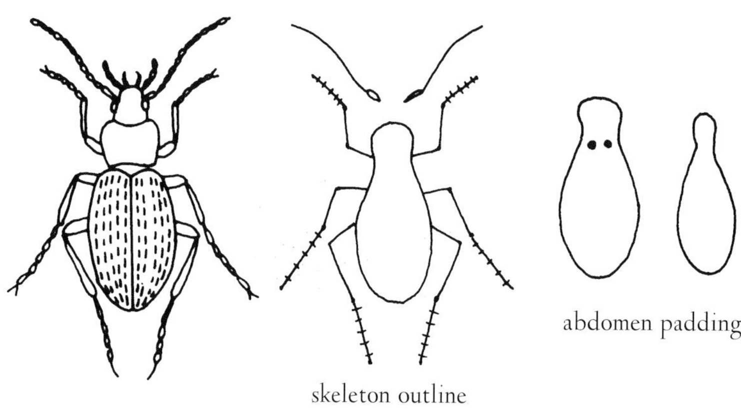

Order of work

Trace a skeleton outline of the ground beetle onto the backing fabric. The abdomen and thorax are worked on the background fabric of the specimen box (silk or the fabric of your choice, backed with muslin or calico).

Abdomen

Apply two layers of felt to pad the abdomen then cover with satin stitch, worked horizontally, with dark brown thread.

Elytra

I used tiny bugle beads, purchased in Vancouver, to work the elytra. With a little adjustment, Mill Hill petite beads 42028 or 40374 could be substituted.

elytra

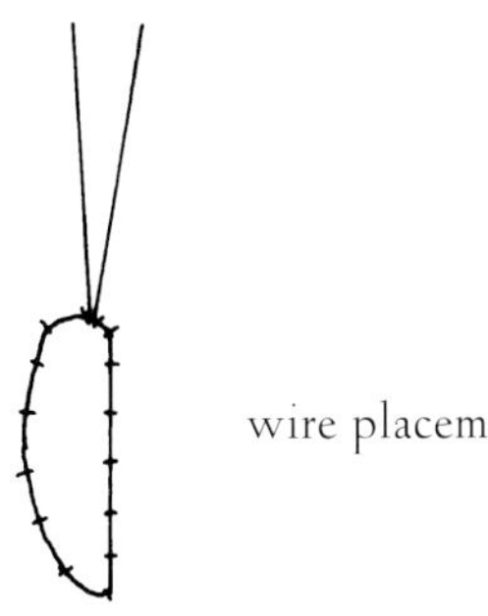

wire placement

1. Mount the brown fabric into the hoop and trace the elytra (or use a paper template). Using dark brown thread, couch the wire around the outline, leaving two tails, then buttonhole stitch the wire to the fabric.

2. To work one side of the elytra, couch a row of brown metallic braid (#16) close to the inside edge of the wire outline, using nylon thread for the couching stitches.

Fill the elytra with alternate rows of couched braid and couched beads (threaded on dark brown thread and couched, between every two beads, with nylon thread). The number of rows depends on the size of the beads used. Repeat for the other side.

3. Cut out the elytra and apply over the abdomen, inserting the wire tails at the points indicated. Secure the wires at the back and trim.

Thorax, head and eyes

Using the thorax outline as a guide cut a piece of mahogany leather and apply with nylon thread, working stitches at each lower corner, sides and on either side of the head (in each corner). Stitch a bead on either side of the head for eyes (use tweezers to shape the thorax and head as you work. To define the head, work a stitch across the leather (behind the eyes) with two strands of fine bronze/black metallic thread.

thorax

ANTENNAE AND MOUTHPARTS

With fine bronze/black metallic thread, work ten chain stitches for each antenna, using one strand, and three chain stitches for each mandible, using two strands. Work two straight stitches for the mouthparts with one strand of brown metallic braid (#16).

LEGS

With two strands of brown metallic thread (#8), work one straight stitch for the inner segment of each leg. Work the outer two segments of each leg with one strand of thread. Couch the long outer stitch in place with fine bronze/black metallic thread, then work a fly stitch at the end of each leg for claws.

Violin Beetle

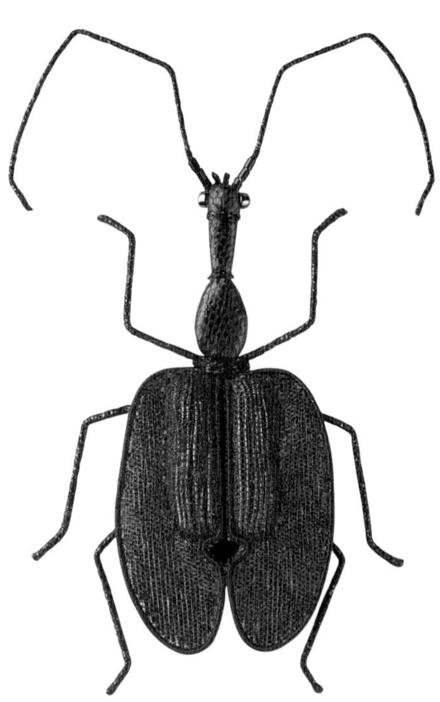

Mormolyce phyllodes

ORDER: COLEOPTERA

SUBORDER: ADEPHAGA

FAMILY: CARABIDAE

Requirements

- 10 cm (4 in) embroidery hoop
- steel black metal organdie, 15 cm (6 in) square
- black sparkle organza, 15 cm (6 in) square (two pieces)
- Vliesofix, 15 cm (6 in) square
- black felt and Vliesofix

Violin Beetle.

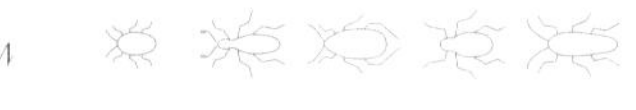

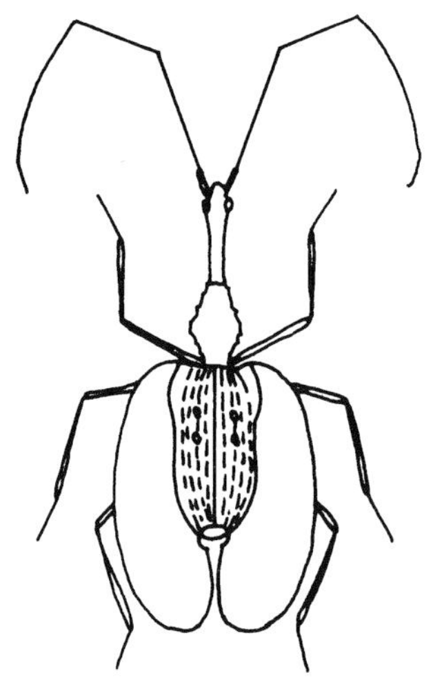

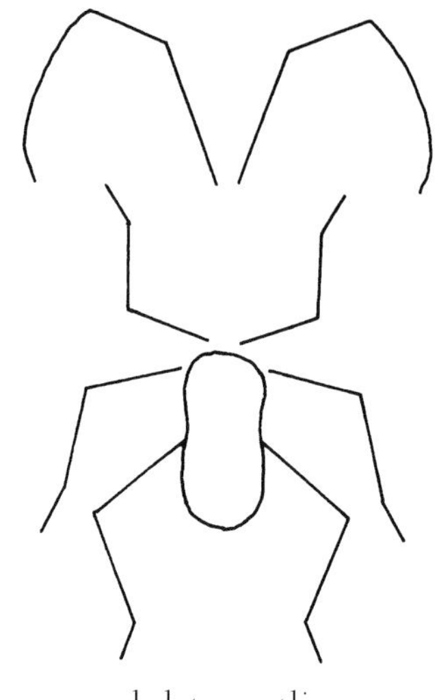

skeleton outline

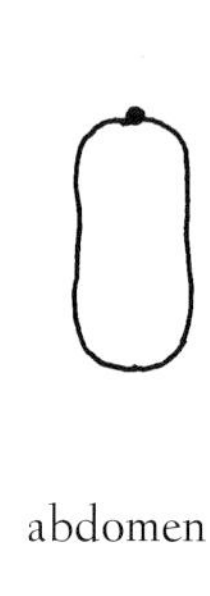

abdomen

- black snakeskin and thin cardboard
- black stranded thread (Cifonda black or DMC 310)
- black machine embroidery thread (Madeira Rayon No.40 colour 1000)
- grey/black metallic couching thread (Black Opal Metallic Couching Thread 371)
- black metallic thread (Kreinik Very Fine (#4) Braid 005)
- nylon thread (Madeira Monofil No.60, dark)
- Mill Hill petite beads (40374 blue-black)
- tiny (1 mm) black bugle beads (optional)
- 28-gauge uncovered wire
- 30-gauge green covered wire

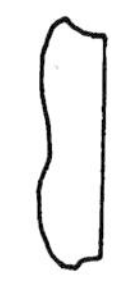

elytra padding

Order of work

Trace a skeleton outline of the violin beetle onto the backing fabric. The abdomen and thorax are worked on the background fabric of the specimen box (silk or the fabric of your choice, backed with muslin or calico).

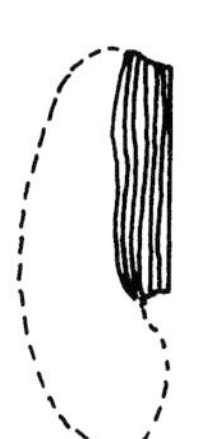

satin stitch

Abdomen

Apply one layer of felt to pad the abdomen then cover with satin stitch, worked horizontally, with black stranded thread.

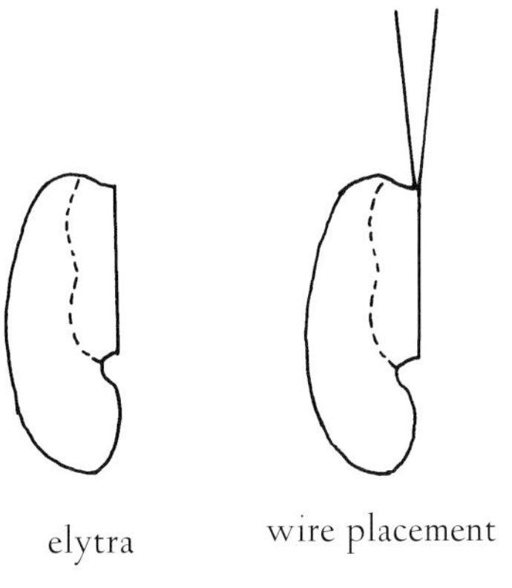

elytra wire placement

Elytra

1. Fuse a layer of organza to the back of the metallic organdie (for support), then mount the 'sandwich' into the hoop. Cut a pair of elytra padding shapes out of black felt and fuse to the organdie (use a small board under the hoop for support and baking parchment to protect the fabrics). To form 'ridges' on the elytra, work six satin stitches over the felt padding with the grey/black metallic thread (secure the thread tails at the back).

2. Remove the organdie 'sandwich' from the hoop, cover with the other piece of black organza, then mount both fabrics back into the hoop. Pull fabrics tight as a drum, taking care not to distort the lower layer.

3. Use tweezers to bend uncovered wire into an elytra shape (with two tails), using the diagram as a guide (or use a paper template). Place shaped wire onto the fabric in the hoop, having the straight edge of the wire next to the straight edge of the elytra padding (hold the wire in place with small pieces of masking tape—do not couch). Using black machine thread, overcast the wire to the fabric. Using the same thread, back stitch an outline around the elytra padding. Repeat for the other side.

4. Cut out the elytra and catch both inner wires together. Apply over the abdomen, inserting all the wire tails at the point indicated. Secure the wires at the back and trim.

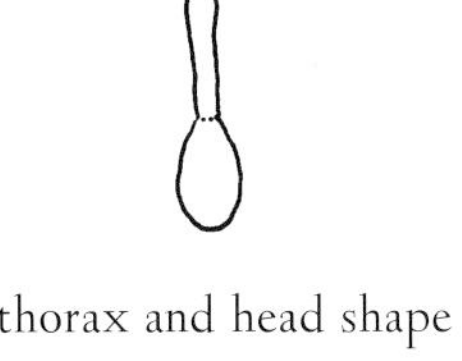

thorax and head shape

Thorax, head and eyes

1. Trace thorax and head shape onto thin card and cut out. Fuse a small oval of black felt to the card to pad the thorax. Cut a thorax and head shape from black snakeskin, using the card shape as a guide, leaving a turning of 3 mm (1/8 in) around the outside edge.

2. Wrap the snakeskin around the cardboard shape and catch the edges together at the back with nylon thread. Squeeze into shape with tweezers. Apply the wrapped shape to the main fabric (with the thorax close to the wire insertion point), working stitches over the head and the neck, and a stitch at the end of the thorax, with nylon thread (leave the tip of the head free for the antennae). Stitch a petite bead on either side of the head for eyes.

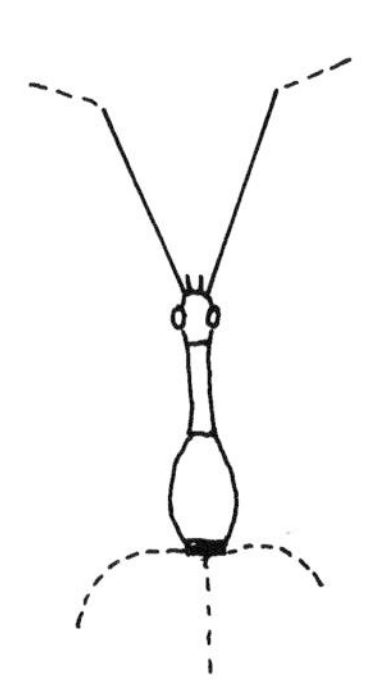
head, neck and antennae

3. Using the black metallic thread, work stitches over the leather to define the head and the neck, then 4–6 stitches to cover the join between the thorax and the elytra.

Antennae

Wrap uncovered wire with black metallic thread. (*Optional*: Thread six tiny bugle beads over the wrapped wire.) Bend into antennae shape (using the diagram as a guide) and insert tails (wire and thread) through to the back. Secure the centre of the wrapped wire under the tip of the head (with three beads on either side), then couch antennae invisibly in place with dark nylon thread. Bend wire tails back under the tips of the antennae, secure and trim. Secure the tip of the head. With black metallic thread, work a fly stitch for the mouthparts at the tip of the head.

Legs

Use the outline on the back of the fabric as a guide to wire insertion points and shape.

To form the front legs, wrap a piece of green covered wire with black metallic thread. Insert the wrapped wire on either side of the thorax and secure the centre of the wire to the muslin backing (under the thorax). Shape the legs with tweezers, insert the wire tails at the end of the legs, bend wire back under the 'foot', secure and trim. Couch legs invisibly in place with dark nylon thread. Repeat for the other two pairs of legs, securing the centres of the wires under the abdomen.

Family Cerambycidae

Members of this large family, with their elongated, flattened bodies, may be readily identified by their exceedingly long antennae, often several body lengths in size, which appear to be mounted within the margins of the large eyes, and the well-developed mandibles with distinct claws.

Longhorn Beetle.

Longhorn beetles vary widely in distribution, colouration, patterning and size, with the tropical cerambycid, *Titanus giganteus*, 12–20 cm (5–8 in) in body length, being one of the largest beetles in the world. Adult longhorns feed on flower pollen, tree foliage and fruit; their larvae, usually white in colour, feed on plant roots and living or decaying trees.

In certain parts of the world, the large, plump-bodied larvae of the longhorn beetle are considered a delicacy. The ancient Romans also consumed the larvae of cerambycids 'after specially fattening them with a spicy meal of flour and wine. The father of the modern study of insect behaviour, Jean-Henri Fabre, once served grubs prepared in this manner to guests, who later reported that the flavour of the meal suggested almonds with the slight aroma of vanilla' (Evans and Bellamy, *An Inordinate Fondness for Beetles*, p. 156).

The rare cerambycid *Rosalia alpina*, with its pretty blue and grey colouring, is a protected species in many countries, inhabiting old beech woods on hills and mountains up to about 1500 m (4900 ft). Indeed, if this longhorn and its habitats are not strictly protected, it will soon disappear altogether. Conversely, the Ruby Longhorn, *Leptura rubra*, is one of the most common longhorns, with widespread distribution. The male and female vary greatly in body form and colour; the female is a rich, velvety red-brown, whilst the male is black and dull yellow. Like other longhorn beetles, this species emits sharp, creaking sounds.

Several families of beetles use sound to locate one another. Passalids, cerambycids, and bark beetles create a shrill noise by rubbing various parts of their bodies together. This behaviour is called stridulation. *Male death watch beetles bang their heads against the walls of their wooden galleries to lure females. South African tok-tokkies march to a different tune: they drum their abdomens against the soil to attract mates.*

Evans and Bellamy,
An Inordinate Fondness for Beetles, p. 98.

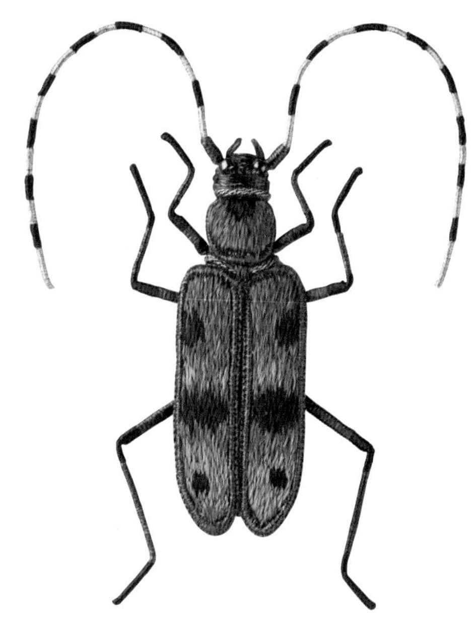

Longhorn Beetle

Rosalia alpina

ORDER: COLEOPTERA

SUBORDER: POLYPHAGA

FAMILY: CERAMBYCIDAE

Requirements

- 10 cm (4 in) hoop
- quilter's muslin, 15 cm (6 in) square
- black felt and Vliesofix
- fine black stranded thread (Cifonda Black)
- dark grey-blue stranded thread (Cifonda 215 or DMC 3750)
- medium grey-blue stranded thread (Cifonda 214 or DMC 930)
- light blue-grey stranded thread (Cifonda 212 or DMC 3752)
- black stranded thread (Soie d'Alger Noir or DMC 310)

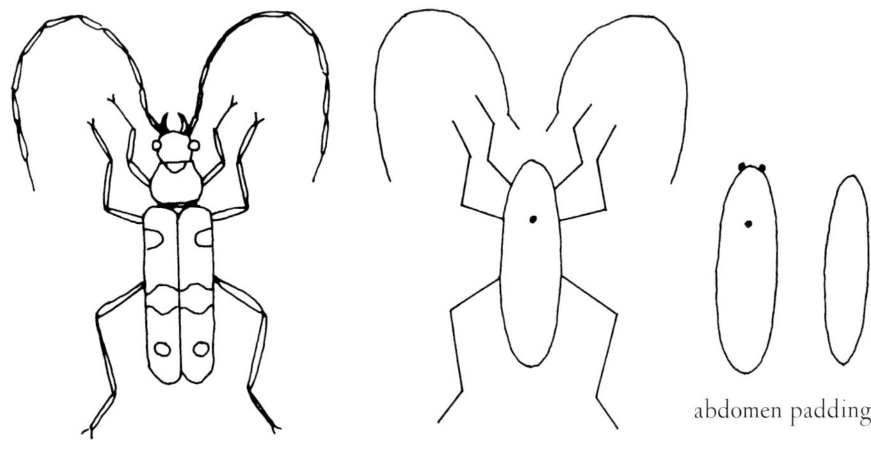

- gold metallic thread (Kreinik Fine #8 Braid 002)
- Mill Hill petite beads (42028 ginger)
- 30-gauge green covered wire

Order of work

Trace a skeleton outline of the longhorn beetle onto the backing fabric. The abdomen and thorax are worked on the background fabric of the specimen box (silk or the fabric of your choice, backed with muslin or calico).

Abdomen

Apply two layers of felt to pad the abdomen then cover with satin stitch, worked horizontally, with either black thread.

Elytra

1. Mount the muslin into the hoop and trace the elytra and thorax outlines (work the elytra and thorax in the same hoop). Using dark blue-grey thread, couch wire around the elytra outline, inserting both wire tails through to the back at A. Buttonhole stitch the wire to the fabric, avoiding the wire tails (stitch over the wire insertion point to make the buttonholing look continuous).

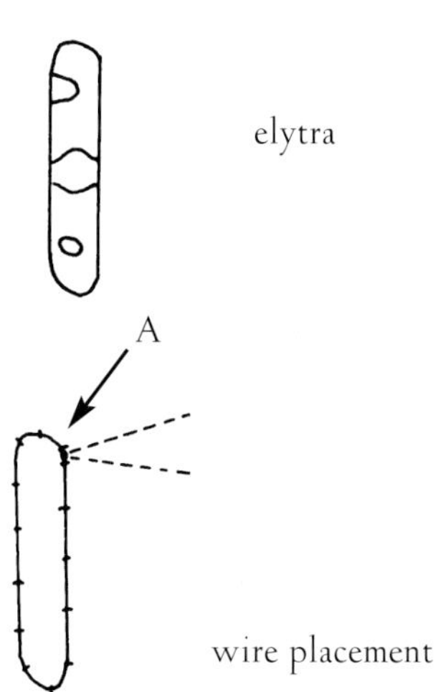

2. Embroider the elytra in long and short stitch, shading the background from dark blue-grey (at the thorax end) to medium blue-grey, and working the blotches in black (I used Cifonda for the fineness and the sheen).

3. Using dark blue-grey thread, couch wire around the thorax outline, leaving two wire tails on the front. Buttonhole stitch the wire to the fabric, then embroider in dark blue-grey thread, working a blotch in black.

4. Cut out the elytra and apply over the abdomen, inserting the wire tails at the point indicated. Secure the wires at the back and trim.

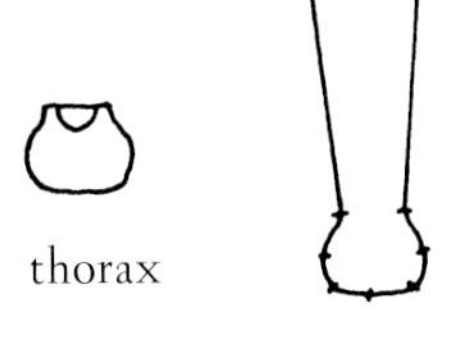

THORAX, HEAD AND EYES

1. Cut out the thorax, leaving a 1.5 mm (1/16 in) tab of muslin between the wires, and apply at the top of the abdomen, inserting the wire tails at the points indicated. Secure the wires at the back and trim.

2. Using dark blue-grey thread, work the head in satin stitch (covering the tab of the thorax and the wire insertion points), then apply a bead on either side of the head for eyes.

3. Make a stitch across the neck with one strand of gold metallic thread. Work a stitch across the body (between the thorax and elytra) with two strands of gold metallic thread. Using dark blue-grey thread, work a triangle of satin stitches (for the scutellum) over the gold thread.

ANTENNAE

1. Using the diagram as a guide, wrap wire with Soie d'Alger black and light blue-grey thread in bands to represent the segments of the antenna (enclose unused thread in the wrapping as you go), leaving unwrapped wire at each end.

2. To form the thicker segment near the head, wrap over the previous wrapping at one end with dark blue-grey thread. Insert this end through to the back near the eyes, and the other at the end of the antenna, forming a nice curve. Bend the wire tail back under antenna. Secure and trim both wire tails. Repeat for the other antenna.

3. Work three satin stitches for each mouthpart in dark blue-grey thread.

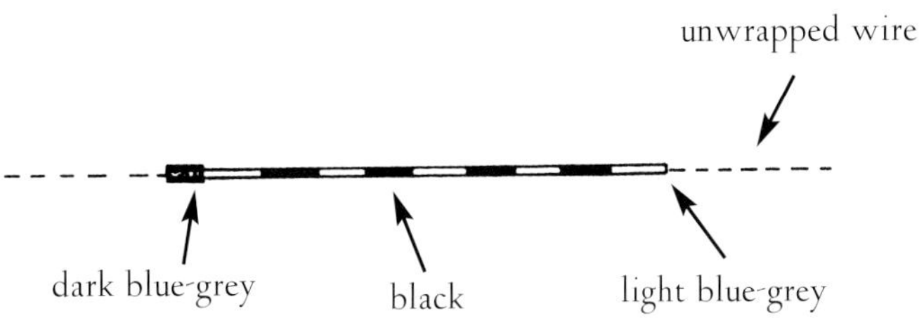

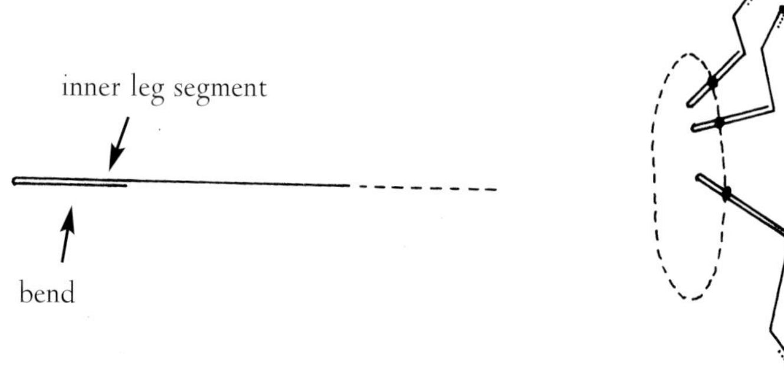

LEGS

The legs are made by wrapping wire (doubled for the thicker, inner leg segment) with Cifonda black and dark blue-grey thread.

1. Make a bend in the wire at one end 5 mm (3/16 in) longer than the inner leg segment. Tie a length of each thread to the bend in the wire. Using the photograph of the beetle as a guide to colour bands (or make up your own), wrap the wire (doubled, then single) with either black or blue-grey thread (enclose unused thread in the wrapping as you go), wrapping a longer length of wire than is needed for the leg. Using the skeleton outline as a guide, bend the wire into a leg shape with tweezers (make the first bend at the end of the doubled wire for the inner leg segment).

2. Insert the doubled end of wire at the body edge, the single wire at the leg end (bend wire back under leg, secure and trim). Secure doubled wire under the body.

Repeat for each leg.

Ruby Longhorn Beetle

Leptura rubra

Order: Coleoptera

Suborder: Polyphaga

Family: Cerambycidae

Ruby Longhorn Beetle.

Requirements

- 10 cm (4 in) embroidery hoop
- quilter's muslin, 15 cm (6 in) square
- red-brown velveteen, 15 cm (6 in) square
- dark brown felt and Vliesofix
- brick red stranded thread (Soie d'Alger 2926 or DMC 3777)
- dark brown stranded thread (Soie d'Alger 4136 or DMC 3371)
- brown metallic thread (Kreinik Fine (#8) Braid 022)
- black metallic thread (Kreinik Very Fine (#4) Braid 005)
- nylon thread (Madeira Monofil No.60, clear)
- Mill Hill antique beads (3033 claret)
- 30-gauge green-covered wire
- (optional) bronze oil paint stick (Shiva Iridescent Paintstick, Iridescent Brown 1)
- (optional) tiny (1.5 mm) black bugle beads

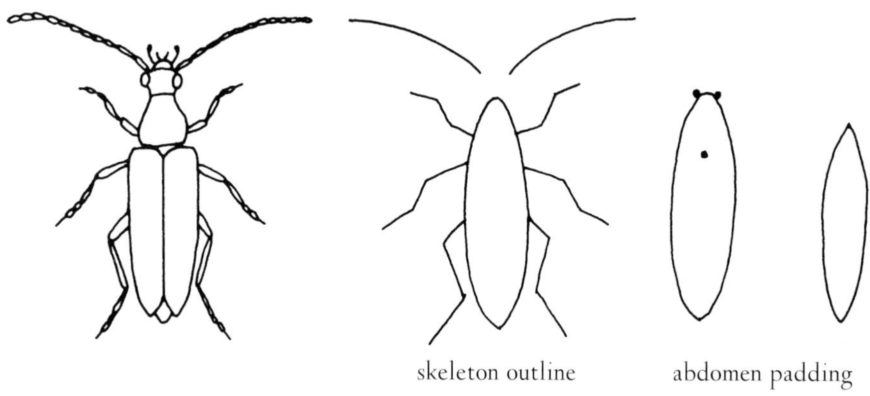

Order of work

Trace a skeleton outline of the ruby longhorn beetle onto the backing fabric. The abdomen and thorax are worked on the background fabric of the specimen box (silk or the fabric of your choice, backed with muslin or calico).

Abdomen

Apply two layers of felt to pad the abdomen then cover with satin stitch, worked horizontally, with dark brown thread.

Elytra

Optional The velveteen can be shaded with the iridescent paintstick. Apply with a small stiff brush in the direction of the pile and allow to dry.

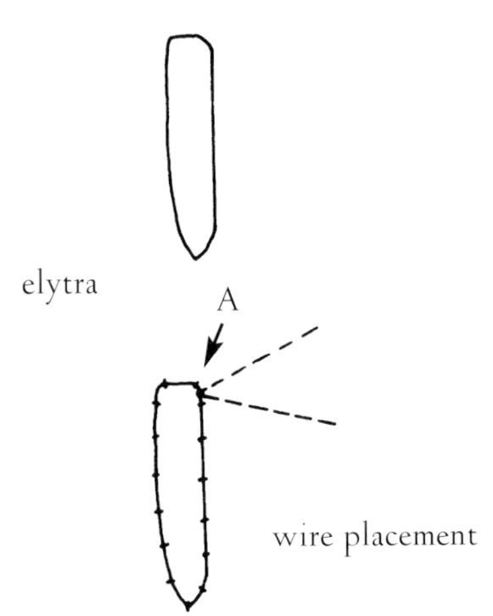

1. Mount the velveteen into the hoop, with the fabric pile running 'up' for the richest colour (work the elytra and thorax in the same hoop). Using a paper template for the elytra outline, and brick red thread, couch the wire around the outline, inserting both wire tails through to the back at A. Buttonhole stitch the wire to the fabric, avoiding the wire tails (stitch over the wire insertion point to make the buttonholing look continuous).

2. Using a paper template for the thorax outline, and brick red thread, couch the wire around the outline, leaving two wire tails on front. Buttonhole stitch the wire to the fabric, working a few back stitches across the gap between the wires. (Shade the shapes around the edges with the paintstick, if desired.)

3. Cut out the elytra and apply over the abdomen, inserting the wire tails at the point indicated. Secure the wires at the back and trim.

Thorax, head and eyes

thorax

wire placement

1. Cut out the thorax, leaving a 1.5 mm (1/16 in) tab between the wires (I applied PVA glue to prevent fraying), and apply at the top of abdomen, inserting the wire tails at the points indicated. Secure the wires at the back and trim.

2. Using dark brown thread, work the head in satin stitch (covering the tab of the thorax and the wire insertion points), then apply a bead on either side of the head for eyes. Make a stitch across the neck with brown metallic thread.

Antennae

Using the skeleton outline as a guide, work the antennae with either of these methods:

- Thread 11 tiny bugle beads on a double strand of black metallic thread. Insert the thread near the head and at the end of the antenna, secure. Couch between every bead with nylon thread.

Or

- With one strand of black metallic thread, work 11 chain stitches for each antenna.

Work two straight stitches for the mouthparts.

Legs

Using two strands of brown/black metallic thread, work two straight stitches for the inner segments of each leg. Work the outer segment with one strand of thread.

FAMILY CHRYSOMELIDAE

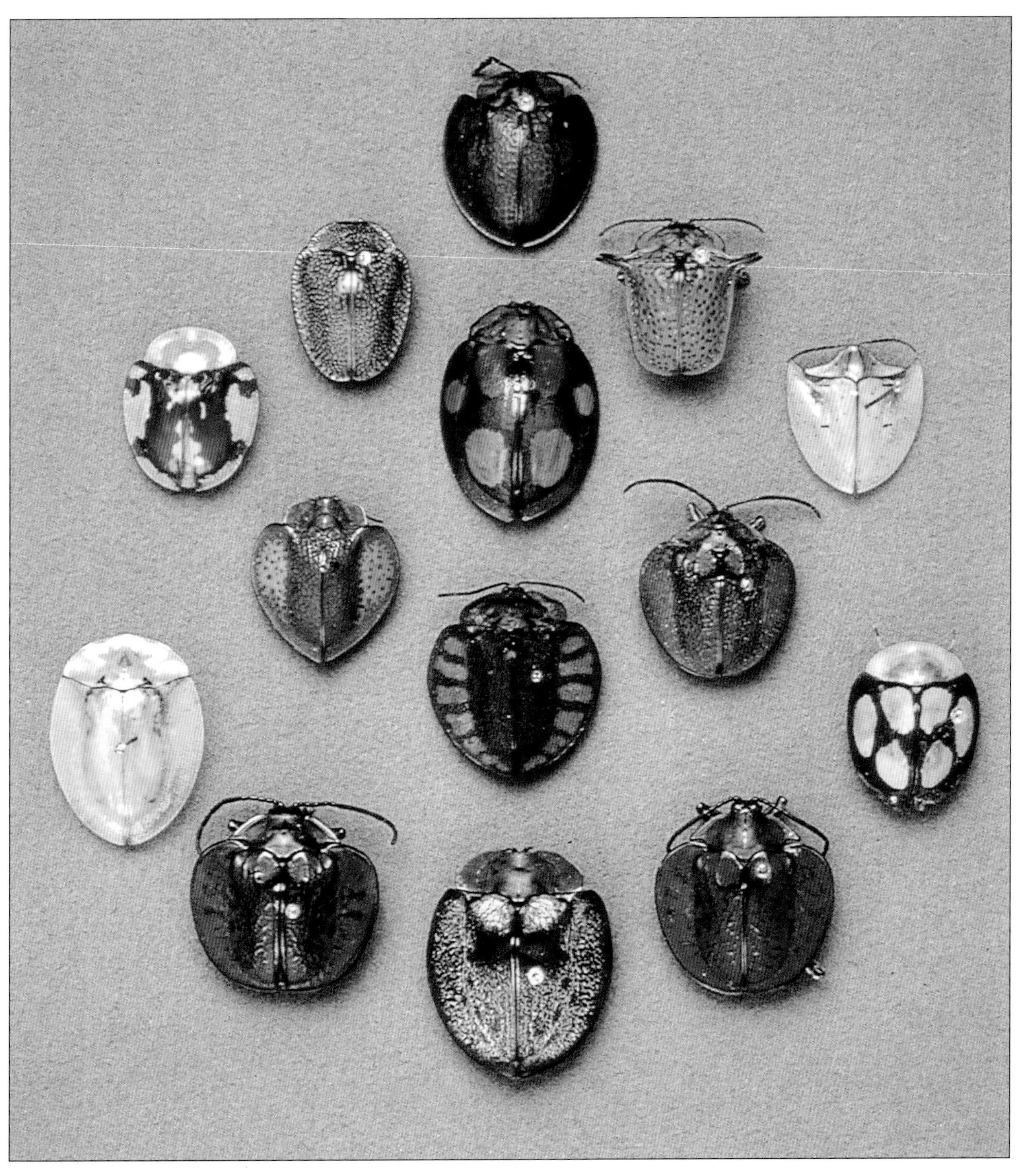

Leaf Beetles.

The family Chrysomelidae is one of the largest families of beetles, with species inhabiting nearly every portion of the earth's surface. Usually small, 5–15 mm (3/16–5/8 in) in body length, chrysomelids exhibit a wide variation in shape (flattened, globular or elongate) and colouration. A pretty example is *Plagiodera versicolora*, a smooth, oval-shaped leaf beetle whose metallic colouring is so variable that some individuals are blue or bluish green while others are green or copper coloured.

A great many leaf-eating beetles belong to this family. Nearly all chrysomelid adults feed on living plant tissue and the female beetle lays her eggs on the underside of leaves. As chrysomelid larvae can completely skeletonise most of the leaves on a plant, they are often considered a serious agricultural pest.

The Green Tortoise Beetle, *Cassida viridis*, is characterised by the nearly circular outline of its thorax and elytra, the edges of which are flared out and flattened, completely covering the head and most of the legs. It is herbivorous, being particularly fond of plants belonging to the mint family, against which background the green beetles are almost invisible.

The dazzling array of colors and forms of beetles have inspired the use of their bodies as jewelery. Some of the species of cassidine chrysomelids are popularly used in necklaces, earrings, pins and other human adornments.

Evans and Bellamy,
An Inordinate Fondness for Beetles,
p. 142.

Leaf Beetle

Plagiodera versicolora

ORDER: COLEOPTERA

SUBORDER: POLYPHAGA

FAMILY: CHRYSOMELIDAE

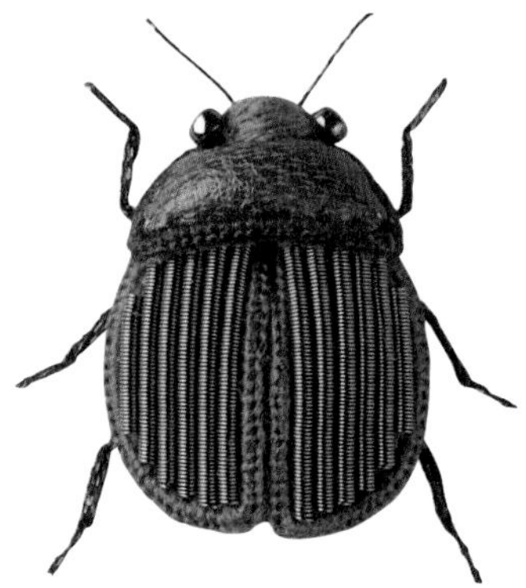

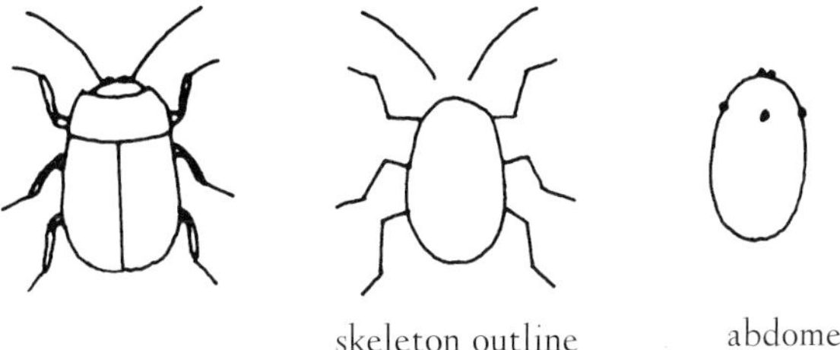

Requirements

- 10 cm (4 in) hoop
- quilter's muslin, 15 cm (6 in) square
- dark green cotton (homespun), 15 cm (6 in) square
- green felt and Vliesofix
- green leather
- green metallic purl (Green No.6 Rough Purl)
- beeswax
- green stranded thread (Soie d'Alger 215 or DMC 3818)
- dark green stranded thread (Soie d'Alger 1846 or DMC 890)
- brown/black metallic thread (Kreinik Cord 201c)
- nylon thread (Madeira Monofil No.60, clear)
- Mill Hill petite beads (40374 blue-black)
- 30-gauge green-covered wire

Order of work

Trace a skeleton outline of the leaf beetle onto the backing fabric. The abdomen and thorax are worked on the background fabric of the specimen box (silk or the fabric of your choice, backed with muslin or calico).

Abdomen

Apply two layers of felt to pad the abdomen then cover with satin stitch, worked horizontally, with dark green thread.

Elytra

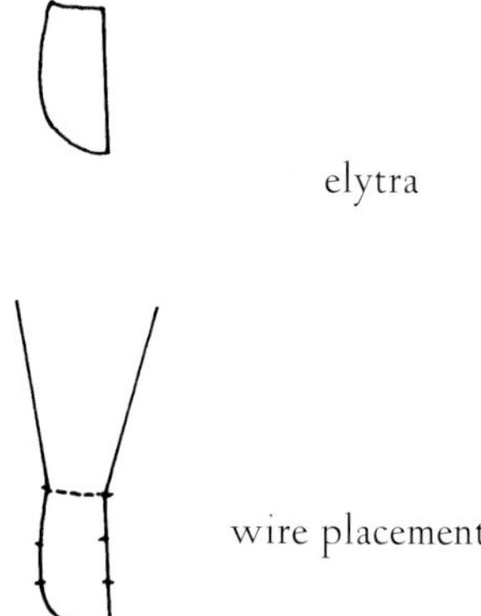

1. Mount green fabric into the hoop and trace the elytra and thorax (it is important that the elytra are traced accurately to allow six lengths of purl to fit into the space—check size before stitching the wire). Using green thread, couch wire around the elytra outline, leaving two tails of wire (work backstitch across the gap), then buttonhole stitch the wire to the fabric.

2. The elytra is filled with lengths of green purl, cut to size, and applied with well-waxed green thread in a fine needle. Starting at the straight inner edge, cut a length of purl to correct size, bring the needle out at the lower corner (inside the wire), thread on the purl, insert the needle just over the row of backstitch (make sure the purl is slightly shorter than the stitch). Repeat for the remaining rows.

3. Using dark green thread, couch wire around the thorax outline, leaving two tails of wire, then buttonhole stitch the wire to the fabric. Cut a smaller thorax shape out of felt for padding, and apply with stab stitches. Cut a thorax shape out of green leather and stitch inside the wire (over the padding) with nylon thread.

4. Cut out the elytra (1 mm away from the purl between the wires), and apply over the abdomen, inserting the wire tails at the points indicated. Secure the wires at the back and trim.

Thorax, head and eyes

1. Cut out the thorax and apply at the top of the abdomen (slightly overlapping the purl), inserting the wire tails at the points indicated. Secure the wires at the back and trim. Work an invisible stitch in each corner with nylon thread, if required.

thorax

wire placement

2. Using green thread, work the head in satin stitch (covering the wire insertion points), then apply a bead on either side of the head for eyes.

Antennae

Work two straight stitches for the antennae using one strand of brown/black metallic thread.

Legs

With four strands of brown/black metallic thread, work two straight stitches for the inner segments of each leg. Work the outer segment with two strands of thread.

Cassida viridis

Order: Coleoptera

Suborder: Polyphaga

Family: Chrysomelidae

Requirements

- 10 cm (4 in) embroidery hoop
- quilter's muslin, 15 cm (6 in) square
- medium green silk, 15 cm (6 in) square
- medium green organza, 15 cm (6 in) square

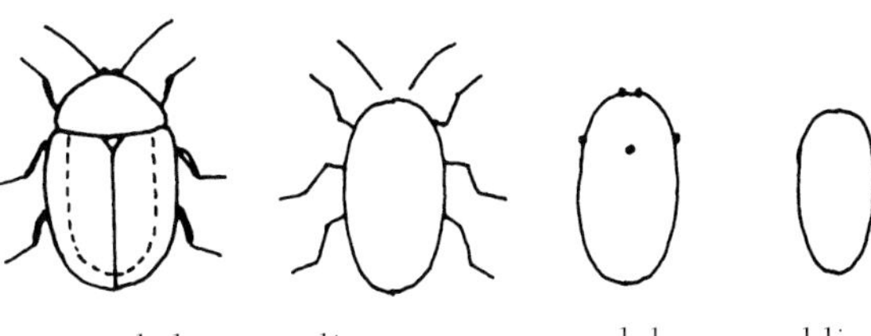

skeleton outline   abdomen padding

- fusible web, paints and gilding medium (see elytra notes, page 75–79)
- green felt and Vliesofix
- light gold leather
- dark green stranded thread (Cifonda 523 or DMC 470)
- medium green stranded thread (Cifonda 522 or DMC 471)
- pale green stranded thread (Cifonda 521 or DMC 472)
- gold/black metallic thread (Kreinik Cord 205c)
- nylon thread (Madeira Monofil No.60, clear)
- Mill Hill petite beads (40374 blue-black)
- fine flower wire (colour green if desired)

Order of work

Trace a skeleton outline of the green tortoise beetle onto the backing fabric. The abdomen and thorax are worked on the background fabric of the specimen box (silk or the fabric of your choice, backed with muslin or calico).

Abdomen

Apply two layers of felt to pad the abdomen then cover with satin stitch, worked horizontally, with dark green thread.

Elytra

I coloured and gilded plain green silk using Beany and Littlejohn's bonding method. Refer to their book *Bonding and Beyond* for detailed instructions. Green silk dupion could be substituted.

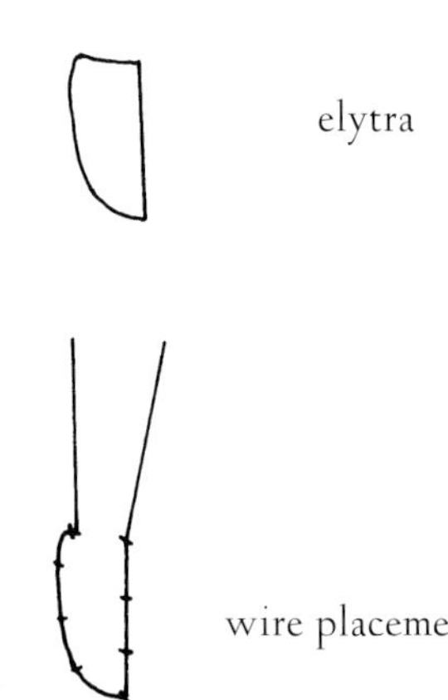

1. Fuse a layer of organza to the back of the green silk (for support). Sponge fusible web with a mixture of gold and green paint, and allow to dry thoroughly. Iron the painted fusible web to the front of the green silk and, while still

warm/hot, apply gilding to the surface (Omnicrom matt gold), rubbed gently with finger.

2. Mount gilded 'sandwich' into the hoop and trace the elytra and thorax outlines (or use paper templates). Using medium green thread, couch wire around the elytra outline, leaving two tails of wire, then buttonhole stitch the wire to the fabric.

3. Using pale green thread, couch wire around the thorax outline, leaving two tails of wire, then buttonhole stitch the wire to the fabric. Cut a smaller thorax shape out of felt for padding, and apply with stab stitches. Cut a thorax shape out of gold leather and stitch inside the wire (over the padding) with nylon thread.

4. Cut out the elytra, leaving a 2 mm (1/8 in) tab of silk between the wires, and apply over the abdomen, inserting the wire tails at the points indicated (the tab will extend *under* the thorax). Secure the wires at the back and trim.

Thorax, head and eyes

1. Cut out the thorax and apply at the top of the abdomen, inserting the wire tails at the points indicated. Secure the wires at the back and trim. Work an invisible stitch in each corner with nylon thread, if required.

thorax

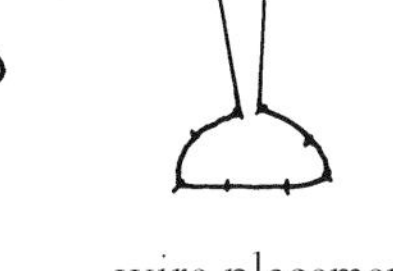
wire placement

2. Using pale green thread, work the head in satin stitch (covering the wire insertion points), then apply a bead on either side of the head for eyes.

Antennae

Work two straight stitches for the antennae using one strand of gold/black metallic thread.

Legs

With two strands of gold/black metallic thread, work two straight stitches for the inner segments of each leg. Work the outer segment with one strand of thread.

Checkered Beetle.

Family Cleridae

The Cleridae (the checkered beetles) are a medium sized family of distinctive beetles, with often hairy bodies, 5–40 mm (3/16–1 1/2 in) long, strong running legs and large eyes. Checkered beetles tend to have an appearance characteristic to their habitat, with the brightly coloured or metallic species common on flowers.

The strikingly coloured species, *Trichodes apiarius*, the Bee-eating Beetle, with its purple and reddish orange checkered elytra, is often seen in spring and summer in areas where there is an abundance of bright flowering plants (a favourite being the flowerheads of the carrot family), where it feeds on pollen and small insects found in the flowerheads.

Most clerids are active predators, both as larvae and adults, with some species known to be parasites of ground-dwelling insects. Sometimes known as bee-wolves, the larvae of *Trichodes apiarius* develop in the nests of several species of solitary bees.

Trichodes apiarius

Order: Coleoptera

Suborder: Polyphaga

Family: Cleridae

Requirements

- 10 cm (4 in) embroidery hoop
- quilter's muslin, 15 cm (6 in) square
- purple organza, 15 cm (6 in) square
- 42-count silk gauze, 7 cm (2 3/4 in) square
- dark blue felt and Vliesofix

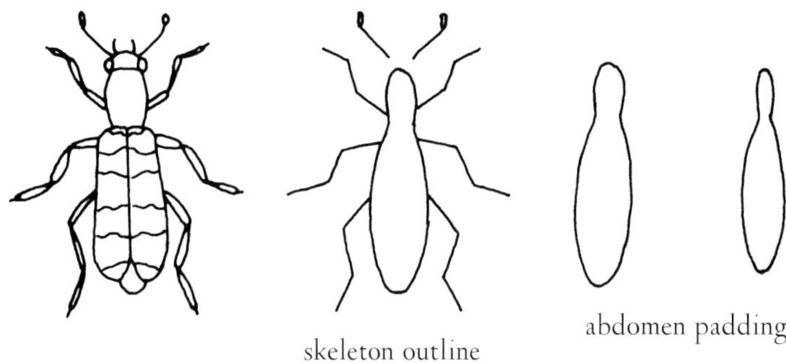

- blue-green snakeskin or leather
- blue-green stranded thread (DMC 500)
- fine purple stranded thread (Rajmahal 115 or DMC 791)
- purple stranded thread (Madeira Decora 1433 or DMC 791)
- orange stranded thread (Madeira Decora 1578 or DMC 606)
- pale copper metallic thread (Kreinik Very Fine (#4) Braid 2122)
- green metallic thread (Kreinik Very Fine (#4) Braid 009)
- nylon thread (Madeira Monofil No.60, clear)
- Mill Hill petite beads (40374 blue-black)
- fine flower wire (colour purple if desired)

Order of work

Trace a skeleton outline of the checkered beetle onto the backing fabric. The abdomen and thorax are worked on the background fabric of the specimen box (silk or the fabric of your choice, backed with muslin or calico).

Abdomen

Apply two layers of felt to pad the abdomen then cover with satin stitch, worked horizontally, with blue-green thread.

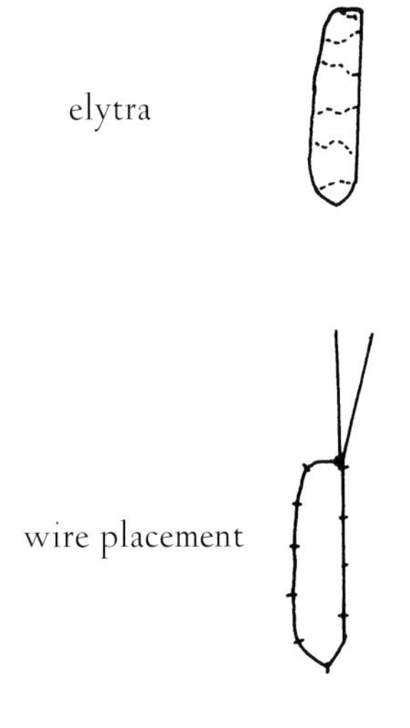

Elytra

The elytra are worked in tent stitch over silk gauze.

1. Stitch the small square of silk gauze in the centre of the organza (grains aligned), then mount into the hoop.

2. Trace the elytra outlines (or use a paper template) onto the gauze, with the centre lines of the elytra on the true diagonal (bias) of the gauze (mark with tacking stitches). Using fine purple thread, couch the wire around the outline, leaving two tails, then buttonhole stitch the wire to the gauze/organza. Work the elytra (inside the wire) in tent stitch, using the purple and orange threads in a checkered pattern (use the diagram as a guide).

3. Cut out the elytra and catch both inner wires together. Apply over the abdomen, inserting all the wire tails at the point indicated. Secure the wires at the back and trim.

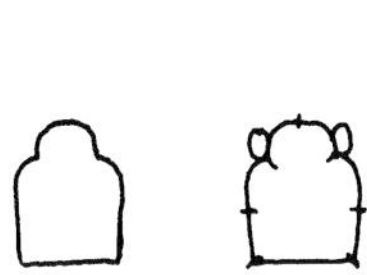

Thorax, head and eyes

Cut the thorax from blue-green snakeskin and apply with nylon thread, working stitches at each lower corner, sides and on either side of the head (in each corner). Stitch a bead on either side of the head for eyes (use tweezers to shape the thorax and head as you work) and a stitch at the top of the head if required. To define the head, work a stitch across the snakeskin (behind the eyes) with blue-green thread.

Antennae

Using pale copper metallic thread, work a chain stitch, with a long tie-down, for each antenna, and two straight stitches for the mouthparts.

Legs

With two strands of green metallic thread, work two straight stitches for the inner segments of each leg. Work the outer segment with one strand of pale copper thread. Use the outline on the back as a guide.

Family Coccinellidae

The family Coccinellidae, the ladybirds, with more than 5200 species known worldwide, is one of the most economically important groups of beetles. Ladybirds, up to 15 mm (5/8 in) in body length, are usually bright reddish orange or yellow in colour, with distinct black spots on their oval, convex wing cases. With their fierce predatory habits, ladybirds are of great value to horticulturalists in combating insect pests such as aphids and scale insects. After hibernating over winter under logs, leaves or surface litter, the female deposits her eggs (about 200) on a plant infested with aphids or scale insects, thus providing a ready source of food for the larvae when they hatch. A ladybird can munch its way through more than 5000 aphids in the course of its short life!

Ladybird.

Ladybird

The ladybird's bright colour is a vivid warning to predators that the insect, containing alkaloid poisons, is unpalatable and poisonous to insects, however, 'in Europe, pulverized carabids, chrysomelids, weevils, and coccinellids, were used to relieve toothaches. Ground ladybirds were sold at the apothecary as Pulvis dentrifricius, or tooth powder. Ladybirds were also recommended as a cure for measles and colic.'

Evans and Bellamy, *An Inordinate Fondness for Beetles*, p. 159.

Coccinella quinquepunctata

ORDER: COLEOPTERA

SUBORDER: POLYPHAGA

FAMILY: COCCINELLIDAE

Requirements

- 10 cm (4 in) embroidery hoop
- quilter's muslin, 15 cm (6 in) square
- red cotton (homespun), 15 cm (6 in) square
- black felt and Vliesofix
- red stranded thread (DMC 817)
- black stranded thread (DMC 310)
- fine black metallic thread (Kreinik Cord 005c)
- Mill Hill petite beads (42014 black)
- fine flower wire (colour red if desired)

Order of work

Trace a skeleton outline of the ladybird onto the backing fabric. The abdomen and thorax are worked on the background fabric of the specimen box (silk or the fabric of your choice, backed with muslin or calico).

skeleton outline

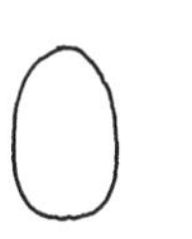

abdomen padding

Abdomen

Apply two layers of felt to pad the abdomen then cover with satin stitch, worked horizontally, with black thread.

Elytra

1. Mount the red fabric into the hoop and trace the elytra outlines. Using red thread, couch the wire around the outline, leaving two tails. Overcast the wire to the fabric, using black thread for the inner spot (five stitches) and red for the remainder of the outline.

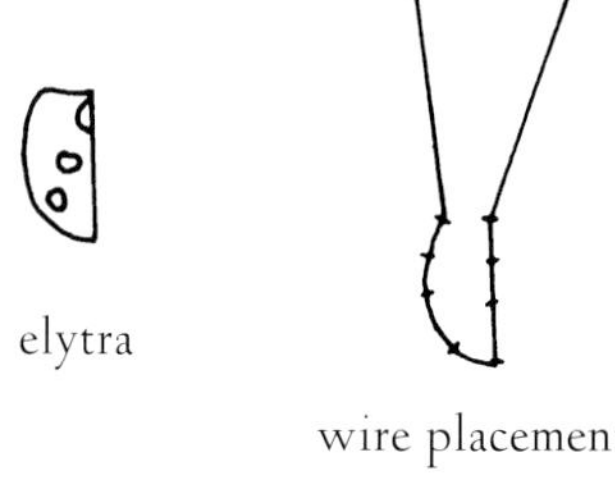

2. Embroider the elytra with red thread, in padded satin stitch, worked diagonally. Work spots over the previous stitches in satin stitch, using black thread.

3. Cut out the elytra and apply over the abdomen, inserting the wire tails at the points indicated. Secure the wires at the back and trim.

Thorax

With black thread, embroider the thorax with long satin stitches, hiding the insertion points of the wire.

Head and eyes

Work the head in satin stitch with black thread, attaching a bead on either side for the eyes.

Legs and antennae

Work the legs in straight stitches with two strands of black metallic thread. Use one strand to work two straight stitches for the antennae.

In the Middle Ages, Coccinella septempunctata, *the seven-spot ladybird, came to be known as 'Our Lady's Bird, after the Virgin Mary. The vivid red wing case is said to represent early depictions of her cloak, while the spots are a reminder of her seven joys and seven sorrows. The family name of ladybird comes from this beetle'.*

D. Tomlinson, 'The Scarlet Lady', in *Country Living*, June 2001.

FAMILY CURCULIONIDAE

With over 50 000 named species, nearly half of all known beetles are weevils. The family Curculionidae is a very diverse family, ranging in length from 1–60 mm (up to 2¼ in). Most weevils share the distinctive characteristic of an elongated snout, or rostrum, in front of the eyes, which in some species is longer than the body. At the end of the snout can be found small biting jaws, and the antennae with their distinct 'elbow' shape. Certain species of weevils are brilliantly coloured (metallic blue or green) and patterned, but the majority are usually grey or brown and hairy. Their movements are very slow and deliberate.

Many weevils are major destroyers of trees, vegetables, grains and ornamentals, using the rostrum and chewing mouthparts to drill into plant stems, roots, seeds and fruits, and sometimes the leaves. One of the world's greatest pests is the Boll Weevil, *Anthonomus grandis*, causing damage to cotton crops estimated in the tens of millions of dollars annually.

Beetles often have a religious or mythological significance. Such is the case of the bizarre Giraffe Beetle, Lasiorrhynchus barbicornis, *'one of the most grotesquely shaped weevils in New Zealand. Because of its striking resemblance to the shape of their canoes, the native Maori dubbed this weevil* Tuwhaipapa, *the god of the new-made canoe'.*

Evans and Bellamy, *An Inordinate Fondness for Beetles*, p. 141.

Weevil.

Weevil

Eupholus linnei

Order: Coleoptera

Suborder: Polyphaga

Family: Curculionidae

Requirements

- 10 cm (4 in) embroidery hoop
- quilter's muslin, 15 cm (6 in) square
- dark aqua metal organdie and organza, 15 cm (6 in) square of each and various metallic threads (see elytra notes, page 75–79)
- dark blue felt and Vliesofix
- bright blue suede
- dark blue stranded thread (DMC 939)
- bright blue stranded thread (Cifonda 989B or DMC 797)
- blue/black metallic thread (Kreinik Very Fine (#4) Braid 060)
- green/black metallic thread (Kreinik Very Fine (#4) Braid 009)

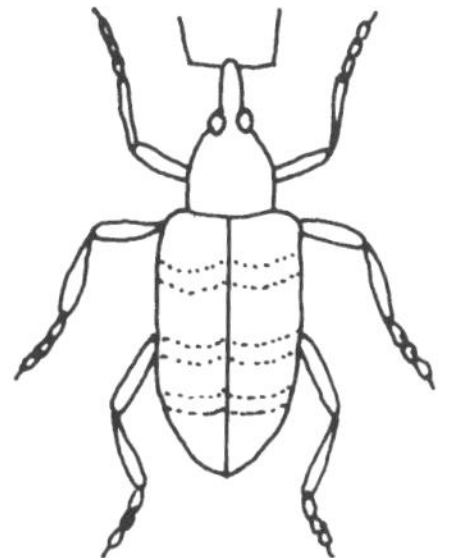

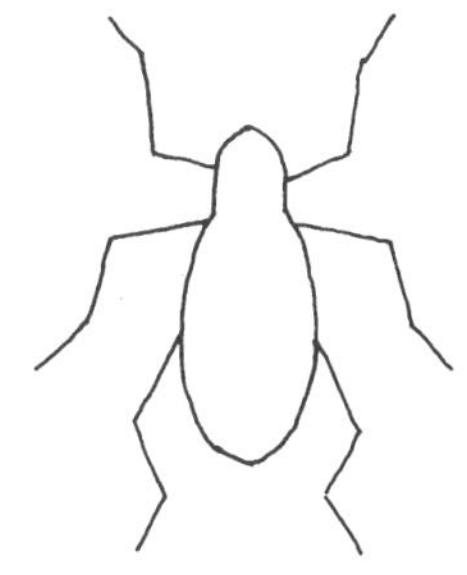

skeleton outline

abdomen padding

- nylon thread (Madeira Monofil No.60, clear)
- Mill Hill petite beads (42014 black)
- fine flower wire (colour blue if desired)
- 28-gauge uncovered wire

Order of work

Trace a skeleton outline of the weevil onto the backing fabric. The abdomen and thorax are worked on the background fabric of the specimen box (silk or the fabric of your choice, backed with muslin or calico).

Abdomen

Apply two layers of felt to pad the abdomen then cover with satin stitch, worked horizontally, with dark blue thread.

Elytra

Any bright metallic fabric can be used for the elytra. Embellish (using fusible web) with metallic threads, as desired.

1. Fuse a layer of organza to the back of the metallic fabric for support, then mount the 'sandwich' into the hoop. Cut fusible web into thin strips and position (and fuse) across fabric sandwich as required (use a small board under the hoop for support).

   Form stripes by laying metallic threads (bright blue and black) over the web, as desired. Fuse to the fabric sandwich (under baking parchment).

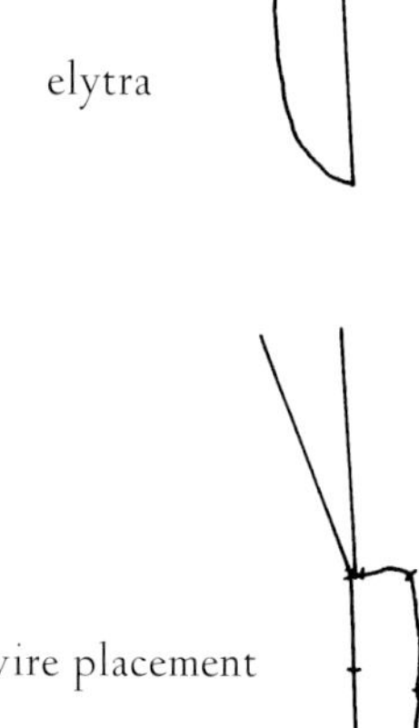

2. Trace the elytra outlines (or use a paper template) onto the fabric sandwich, with due regard to the stripes. Using bright blue thread, couch the flower wire around the outline, leaving two tails, then buttonhole stitch the wire to the fabric.

3. Cut out the elytra and catch both inner wires together. Apply over the abdomen, inserting all the wire tails at the point indicated. Secure the wires at the back and trim.

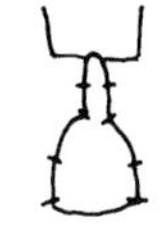

thorax/head

THORAX/HEAD (SNOUT)
The thorax/head shape is cut from blue suede. Pad the snout with two straight stitches (using six strands of dark blue thread). Apply the suede with stab stitches using nylon thread, squeezing into shape with tweezers. Leave the tip of the snout free for the antennae.

ANTENNAE
Wrap uncovered wire with bright blue thread. Bend into antennae shape (three sides of a square) and insert tails (wire and thread) through to the back. Secure the centre of the wrapped wire under the tip of the snout, then stitch the tip over the wire. Secure wire tails at the back and trim.

EYES
Using nylon thread, stitch black beads on either side of the snout for eyes.

LEGS
With two strands of blue/black metallic thread, work two straight stitches for the inner segments of each leg. Work the outer segment with one strand of green/black thread. Use the outline on the back as a guide.

Great Diving Beetle.

Family Dytiscidae

The large aquatic family Dytiscidae (predacious diving beetles), found in freshwater ponds and lakes, range from 1–40 mm (up to $1^1/_2$ in) in length. Diving beetles have very smooth, oval bodies, compressed from top to bottom to facilitate rapid underwater movement. The strong, grasping front legs and enlarged hind legs have a border of hairs on the tarsi ('toes'), acting as oars when the legs beat in unison. They occasionally fly from one pond to another.

The predacious diving beetle, though living permanently in water, still needs fresh air for its existence. Dytiscids breathe by coming to the surface backwards and exposing the tip of the abdomen, which draws in air to store under the elytra. These trips are repeated 4–7 times an hour. Both adults and larvae are fierce predators, feeding on aquatic insects, tadpoles and small fish.

While members of this family are generally black or brown, the Great Diving Beetle, *Dytiscus marginalis*, is a shiny bronze olive in colour, with a dark gold border around its thorax and elytra.

Dried specimens of the genus Cybister *in the same family are used by the Chinese as food and for medicinal purposes. They 'collect large adult dytiscids and hydrophilids under streetlights and prepare them in a number of ways. Basic preparation includes the removal of the elytra, wings, legs and head. Water beetles may be fried in oil, seasoned and eaten like nuts, or simply dropped in hot brine'.*

Evans and Bellamy, *An Inordinate Fondness for Beetles*, p. 157.

Great Diving Beetle

Dytiscus marginalis

ORDER: COLEOPTERA

SUBORDER: POLYPHAGA

FAMILY: DYTISCIDAE

Requirements

- 10 cm (4 in) embroidery hoop
- quilter's muslin, 15 cm (6 in) square
- olive green taffeta ribbon
- brown felt and Vliesofix
- stuffing and fine satay stick
- olive green stranded thread (Soie d'Alger 2215 or DMC 730)
- light old gold stranded thread (Cifonda 48 or DMC 729)
- old gold stranded thread (Cifonda 49 or DMC 3829)
- dark old gold stranded thread (Cifonda 50 or DMC 829)
- nylon thread (Madeira Monofil No.60, clear)
- Mill Hill antique beads (3038 ginger)
- 30-gauge green-covered wire

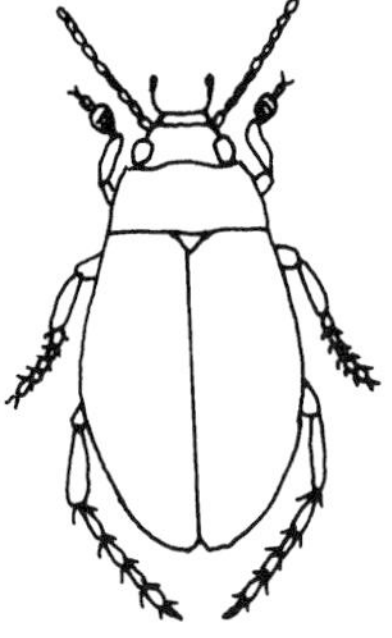

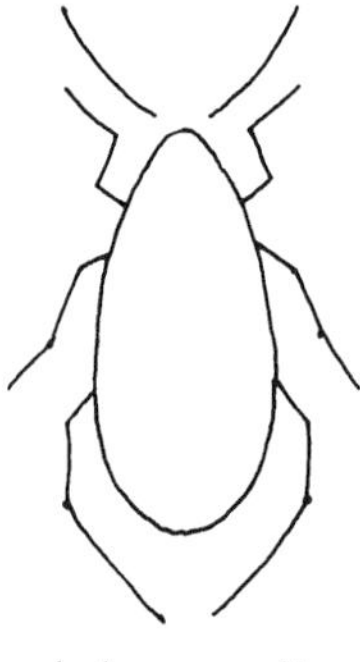

skeleton outline

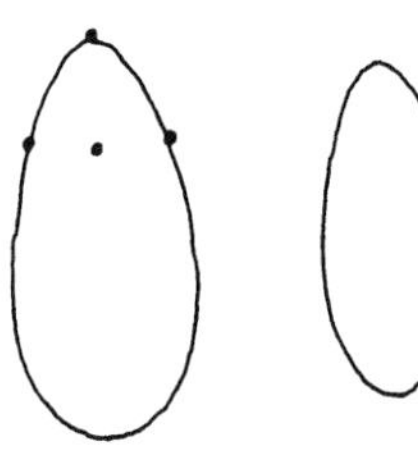

abdomen padding

Order of work

Trace a skeleton outline of the diving beetle onto the backing fabric. The abdomen and thorax are worked on the background fabric of the specimen box (silk or the fabric of your choice, backed with muslin or calico).

Abdomen

Apply two layers of felt to pad the abdomen then cover with satin stitch, worked horizontally, with olive green thread.

Elytra

elytra

1. Stitch the taffeta ribbon to the centre of the muslin, mount into the hoop and trace the elytra and thorax outlines (or use a paper template). Couch wire around the outline, leaving two wire tails, then buttonhole stitch the wire to the fabric, using old gold thread on the curved edge, and olive green on the straight edge. Work a row of chain stitches on the inside curved edge, using light old gold thread. Using a satay stick, insert a minute amount of stuffing to pad the elytra, between the ribbon and the muslin, through the space left between the wires (work from the edge of the ribbon).

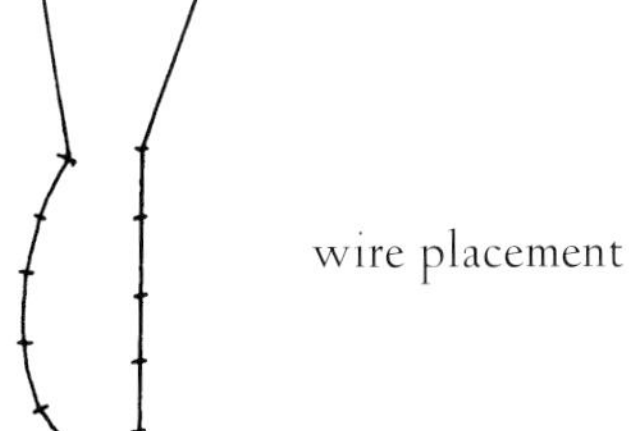

wire placement

2. Using old gold thread, couch the wire around the thorax outline, inserting both wire tails through to the back at A. Buttonhole stitch the wire to the fabric, avoiding the wire tails (stitch over the wire insertion point to make the buttonholing look continuous). Work a row of chain stitches close to the inside edge with light old gold thread. Cut a small slit in the muslin backing, insert a tiny amount of stuffing, then stitch slit closed.

3. Cut out the elytra and apply over the abdomen, inserting the wire tails at the points indicated. Secure the wires at the back and trim.

Thorax

Cut out the thorax and apply at the top of abdomen, inserting the wire tails at the point indicated. Secure the wires at the back and trim. Work an invisible stitch in each corner with nylon thread.

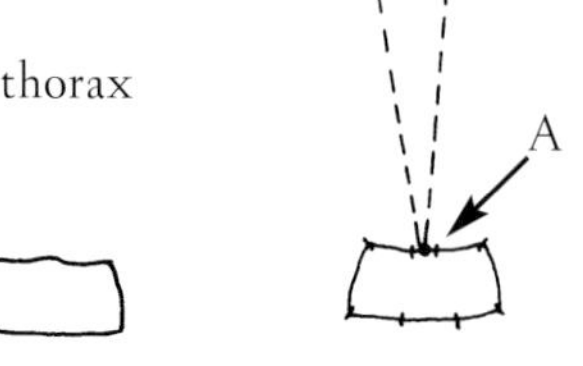

Head and eyes

Using olive green thread, work the head in satin stitch (covering the wire insertion point), then apply a bead on either side of the head for eyes. Work satin stitch at the top of the head with old gold thread.

Antennae

With one strand of dark old gold thread, work nine chain stitches for each antenna. Work three chain stitches with old gold thread for the mouthparts.

Legs

Using three strands of dark old gold thread, work two chain stitches for the inner segments of each leg. Make a straight stitch in the centre of each chain stitch with three strands of old gold thread. Work the outer segment with three or four chain stitches, using two strands of light old gold thread, and one strand for the hairs on the back legs.

Click Beetles.

Family Elateridae

The members of the large family Elateridae (the click beetles and skipjack beetles), with their long, slightly flattened bodies and saw-like antennae, vary widely in size, from 4–50 mm ($^{5}/_{32}$–2 in) in body length, colouration, patterning and distribution. Elaterids are well known (and named) for the unique clicking mechanism of the adults. Many species can be seen around lights at night, while others frequent flowers or surface litter, feeding upon seeds, plants, roots and decaying wood. Elaterid larvae, known as wireworms, are long and cylindrical, with a hardened, shiny rust-coloured body.

Also known as skipjacks, snapping beetles and spring beetles, the click beetle 'plays dead' when threatened by a predator, then springs high into the air with an audible click, propelled by a unique tension mechanism on its underside. Although the result of this action is slightly haphazard, the beetle will eventually alight on its feet, allowing it to escape. Click beetles can jump about 30 cm (12 in) into the air at a speed measured at 2.5 m per second, accelerating to 700 times the force of gravity!

Most species of click beetle are brown or black in colour with little or no ornamentation. However, a number of tropical and subtropical species are beautifully coloured, such as *Campsosternus gemma*, with its smooth, metallic green elytra and thorax of brilliant blue and coppery red. The more commonly known Skipjack Beetle, *Agrypnus murinas*, has ribbed, gleaming grey wing cases.

Campsosternus gemma

ORDER: COLEOPTERA

SUBORDER: POLYPHAGA

FAMILY: ELATERIDAE

Requirements

- 10 cm (4 in) embroidery hoop
- quilter's muslin, 15 cm (6 in) square
- green felt and Vliesofix
- green bupestrid beetle elytra or green metallic leather
- green stranded thread (Cifonda 525 or DMC 3345)
- dark green stranded thread (Cifonda 495 or DMC 890)
- red-copper stranded thread (Cifonda 105A or DMC 919)
- blue stranded thread (Cifonda 184 or DMC 796)
- indigo metallic thread (Kreinik Cord 202c)
- blue/black metallic thread (Kreinik Very Fine (#4) Braid 060)

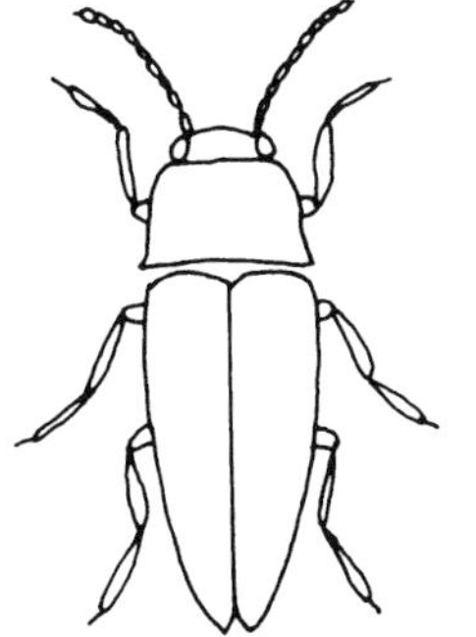

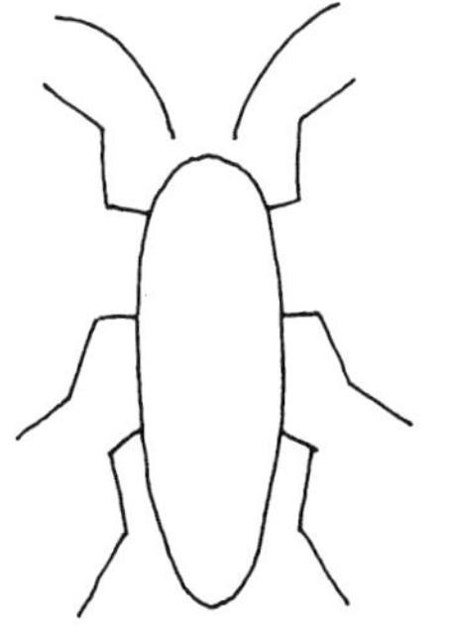

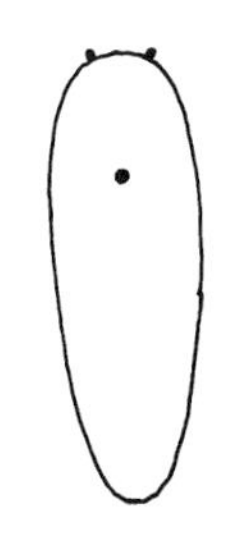

abdomen padding

skeleton outline

- nylon thread (Madeira Monofil No.60, clear)
- Mill Hill petite beads (42014 black)
- 30-gauge green-covered wire

Order of work

Trace a skeleton outline of the click beetle onto the backing fabric. The abdomen and thorax are worked on the background fabric of the specimen box (silk or the fabric of your choice, backed with muslin or calico).

Abdomen

Apply one layer of felt to pad the abdomen then cover with satin stitch, worked horizontally, with green thread.

Elytra

1. Mount the muslin into the hoop and trace the elytra and thorax outlines (work in the same hoop). Using green thread, couch the wire around the outline, inserting both wire tails through to the back at A. Buttonhole stitch the wire to the fabric, avoiding the wire tails (stitch over the wire insertion point to make the buttonholing look continuous). Work a row of split back stitch close to the inside wire. Cut elytra padding out of felt and apply with small stab stitches.

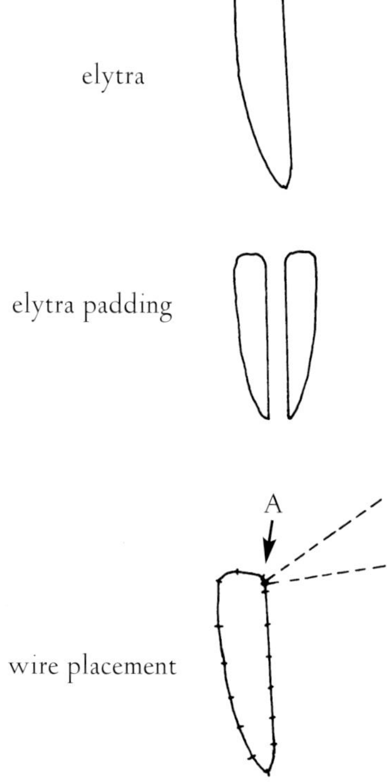

2. Cut the bupestrid elytra to fit inside the wire, make seven holes 1 mm in from the edge with a fine needle (refer to instructions on how to sew with beetle wings, page 64–66), then stab stitch the elytra inside the wire, using the green thread. Work a tiny French knot over the holes if desired.

3. Couch the wire around the thorax outline, leaving two wire tails at the front, then buttonhole stitch the wire to the fabric using red-copper thread, except for the small centre section, which is worked in blue. Embroider the thorax in long and short stitch, working the centre panel in blue shading to green, and the outer panels in red-copper. Work a tiny spot of blue at each corner.

4. Cut out the elytra and apply over the abdomen, inserting the wire tails at the point indicated. Secure the wires at the back and trim.

THORAX, HEAD AND EYES

1. Cut out the thorax, leaving a 1.5 mm (1/16 in) tab between the wires, and apply at the top of abdomen, inserting the wire tails at the points indicated. Secure the wires at the back and trim. Work an invisible stitch in each corner with nylon thread, if required.

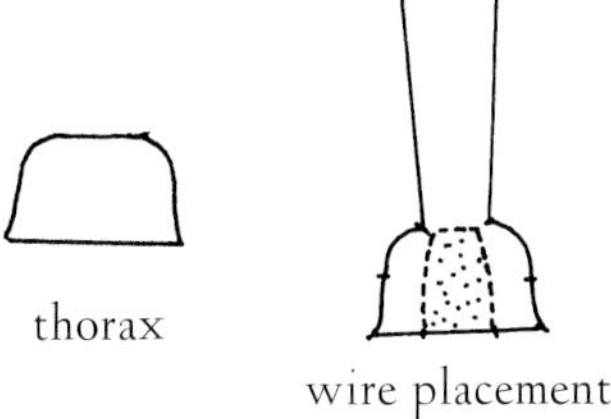

2. Using dark green thread, work the head in satin stitch (covering the tab of the thorax and the wire insertion points), then apply a bead on either side of the head for eyes.

ANTENNAE

With one strand of indigo metallic thread, work nine chain stitches for each antenna. Work two straight stitches, with two strands of thread, for the mouthparts.

LEGS

Using two strands of blue/black metallic thread, work two straight stitches for the inner segments of each leg. Work the outer segment with one strand of thread.

Skipjack Beetle

Agrypnus murinas

ORDER: COLEOPTERA

SUBORDER: POLYPHAGA

FAMILY: ELATERIDAE

Requirements

- 10 cm (4 in) embroidery hoop
- quilter's muslin, 15 cm (6 in) square
- black cotton (homespun), 15 cm (6 in) square
- black felt and Vliesofix
- black kid or snakeskin
- peacock feather or fine brown metallic thread (Kreinik Cord 201c)
- pad for working detached buttonhole stitch or a piece of felt
- small piece of clear self-adhesive plastic
- black stranded thread (Cifonda Black or DMC 310)
- steel metallic thread (Kreinik Very Fine #4 Braid 010HL)

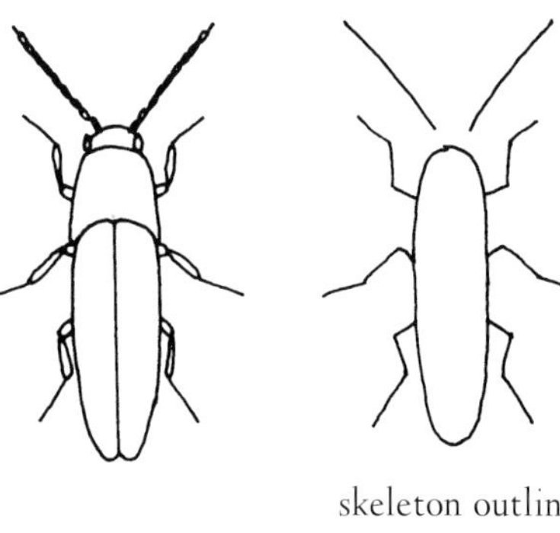

skeleton outline

abdomen padding

- brown-black metallic thread (Kreinik Very Fine (#4) Braid 022)
- Nylon thread (Madeira Monofil No.60, dark)
- Mill Hill petite beads (40374 blue-black)
- 30-gauge green-covered wire

Order of work

Trace a skeleton outline of the skipjack beetle onto the backing fabric. The abdomen and thorax are worked on the background fabric of the specimen box (silk or the fabric of your choice, backed with muslin or calico).

Abdomen

Apply one layer of felt to pad the abdomen then cover with satin stitch, worked horizontally, with black thread.

elytra outline

Elytra

The elytra are worked, over wire, in corded detached buttonhole stitch. For ease of working, support the wire on a pad or felt until the stitching is complete.

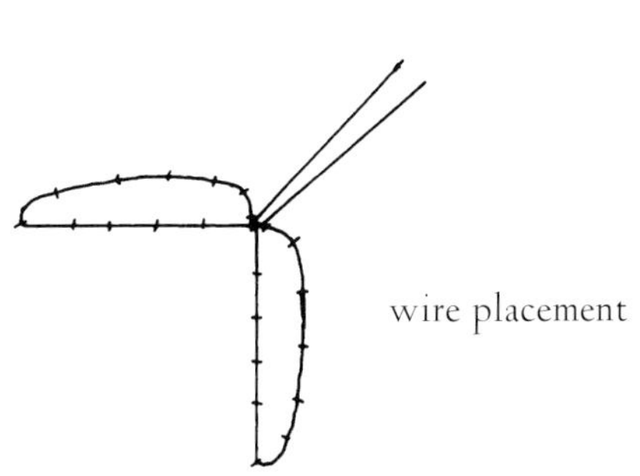

wire placement

1. Trace the elytra outline onto a square of tracing paper and secure to pad (or felt) with a larger square of self-adhesive plastic. Using tacking thread, couch the wire around the wing outline (through the plastic and pad), leaving two tails of wire (as the couching stitches are only temporary, do not work too many).

2. With one strand of steel metallic thread in a tapestry needle, work a row of spaced buttonhole stitch over the wire on the inside of one elytra (see diagram). Work two rows of corded detached buttonhole stitch to fill the shape, catching the second row to the remaining buttonholed edge (retain thread tails to insert through to the back when applying the elytra). Whip around the outside edge of the wire, between each buttonhole stitch, to cover the spaces. Repeat for the other elytra. Remove the couching stitches to release.

wire, showing spaced buttonhole stitch

3. Apply elytra over the abdomen, inserting the wire tails at the point indicated. Secure the wires at the back and trim.

Thorax, head and eyes

1. Mount the black homespun into the hoop. Using a paper template for the thorax outline and black thread, couch wire around the outline (leaving two tails of wire), then buttonhole stitch the wire to the fabric. Cut a thorax shape from black kid and apply inside the wire with stab stitches worked with nylon thread.

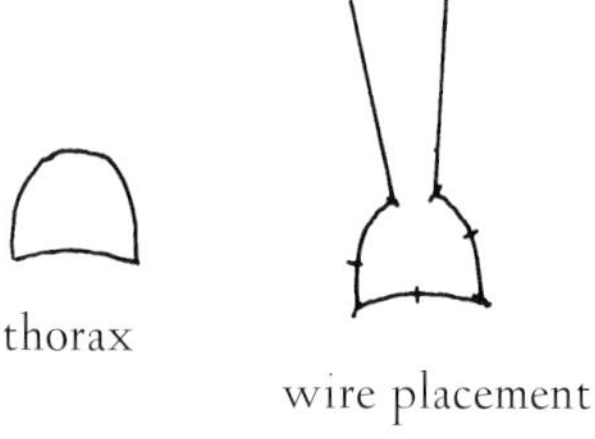

2. Cut out the thorax, leaving a 1.5 mm (1/16 in) tab of fabric between the wires, and apply at the top of abdomen, inserting the wire tails at the points indicated. Secure the wires at the back and trim.

3. Using black thread, work the head in satin stitch (covering the tab of the thorax and the wire insertion points), then apply bead on either side of the head for eyes.

Antennae

Having read that 'real peacock feathers, tightly rolled, were used for the knots of tree trunks and marking of butterfly wings' on eighteenth century Chinese silk bed-hangings, I thought that a plumule from a feather would give just the right effect for this beetle's antennae! Use the alternate method if preferred.

- Separate a plumule from a peacock feather and use for the antennae; insert each end through to the back at the appropriate points and secure with nylon thread.

Or

- With one strand of fine brown metallic thread, work nine chain stitches for each antenna.

Work two straight stitches, with two strands of thread, for the mouthparts.

Legs

Using two strands of brown/black metallic thread, work two straight stitches for the inner segments of each leg. Work the outer segment with one strand of thread.

Family Erotylidae

One of the clearest reasons for the success of the order Coleoptera is their ability to use a wide variety of resources as food, such as fungus. Many species of the family Erotylidae, the pleasing fungus beetles, have brightly decorated elytra—red, orange or yellow spots, purple with black spots, and zigzagging coloured lines.

Adults and larvae live and feed on fungi on the ground or growing up on the bark of trees. Although the fungus beetles' bright colours are a vivid warning to predators, they may also exude a foul-tasting fluid and/or feign death to avoid being attacked. *Cypherotylus guatemalae*, a native of Guatemala, is bright yellow and purple, 25 mm (1 in) in body length, and feeds on nectar and some fungi.

Fungus Beetle.

Fungus Beetle

Cypherotylus guatemalae

ORDER: COLEOPTERA

SUBORDER: POLYPHAGA

FAMILY: EROTYLIDAE

Requirements

- 10 cm (4 in) embroidery hoop
- quilter's muslin, 15 cm (6 in) square
- yellow cotton (homespun), 15 cm (6 in) square
- black felt and Vliesofix
- black snakeskin
- yellow stranded thread (Soie d'Alger 545 or DMC 972)
- dark purple stranded thread (Soie d'Alger 3326 or DMC 939)
- steel metallic thread (Kreinik Cord 011c)
- nylon thread (Madeira Monofil No.60, clear)
- Mill Hill petite beads (42014 black)
- fine flower wire (colour yellow if desired)

skeleton outline

abdomen padding

Order of work

Trace a skeleton outline of the fungus beetle onto the backing fabric. The abdomen and thorax are worked on the background fabric of the specimen box (silk or the fabric of your choice, backed with muslin or calico).

Abdomen

Apply two layers of felt to pad the abdomen then cover with satin stitch, worked horizontally, with dark purple thread.

Elytra

elytra

1. Mount the yellow fabric into the hoop and trace the elytra outlines. Using yellow thread, couch the wire around the outline, leaving two tails. Overcast the wire to the fabric.

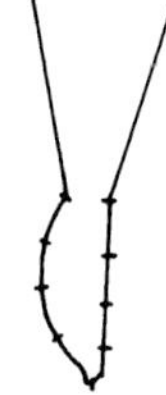

wire placement

2. Fill the elytra with French knots (two strands, one wrap), worked in irregular 'stripes', using yellow and dark purple thread.

3. Cut out the elytra and apply over the abdomen, inserting the wire tails at the points indicated. Secure the wires at the back and trim.

Thorax, head and eyes

thorax

Cut the thorax from black snakeskin and apply with nylon thread: work two stitches at each lower corner of the thorax, a stitch on either side of the head (in each corner), then stitch a bead on either side of the head for eyes (use tweezers to shape the thorax and the head as you work). To define the head, work a stitch across the leather (behind the eyes) with one strand of steel metallic thread.

Legs and antennae

Work the legs in straight stitches with two strands of steel metallic thread. Use one strand for the antennae.

Family Lycidae

Metriorrhynchus rhipidius belongs to the Lycidae family, the net-winged beetles, a medium sized group of soft, flat-bodied beetles, 5–20 mm (1/4–3/4 in) in length. The distinctive features are the flattened body, red or orange-red ribbed wing cases and a (usually) black thorax. The long antennae are serrate (saw-like), flattened and wide. Net-winged beetles can be found on vegetation and blossoms and on rotting, mossy stumps in clearings at the edge of forests.

The brilliant colouring of the family Lycidae serves as a warning to would-be predators that the insect is highly distasteful or even poisonous, a characteristic which makes them a model for mimicry. There are many examples of other families of beetles and even wasps, flies and moths, which mimic the colour and form of *Metriorrhynchus rhipidius* in order to avoid predation.

Net-winged Beetle.

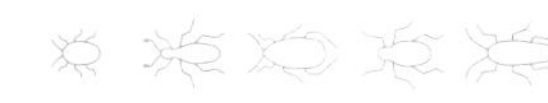

Net-winged Beetle

Metriorrhynchus rhipidius

ORDER: COLEOPTERA

SUBORDER: POLYPHAGA

FAMILY: LYCIDAE

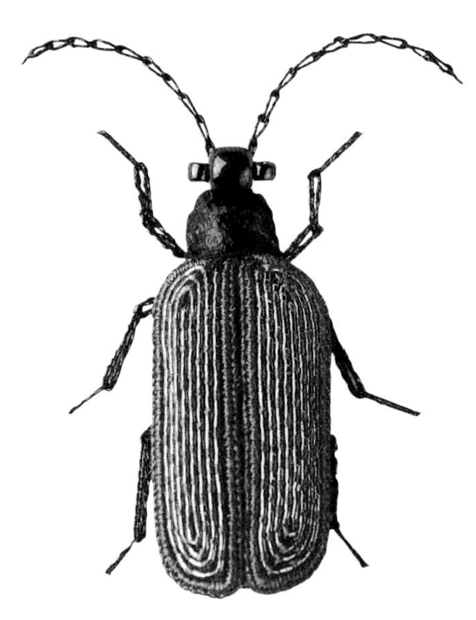

Requirements

- 10 cm (4 in) embroidery hoop
- quilter's muslin/calico, 15 cm (6 in) square
- brown felt and Vliesofix
- black snakeskin
- orange stranded thread (Cifonda 103 or DMC 921)
- brown stranded thread (Cifonda 225a or DMC 3371)
- Copper Metallic Couching Thread (or Copper No.6 Smooth Passing)
- fine brown/black metallic thread (Kreinik Cord 201c)
- nylon thread (Madeira Monofil No.60, clear)
- Hot Spotz 3 mm blue-black beads (SBXL-449)
- Mill Hill petite beads (40374 blue-black)
- fine flower wire (colour orange if desired)

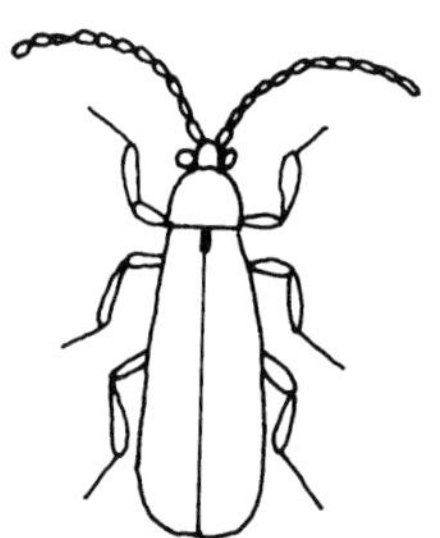

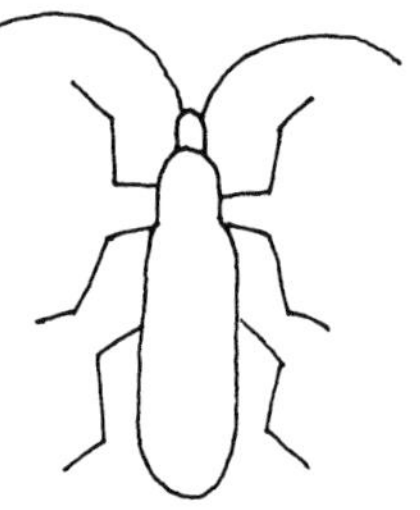

skeleton outline

abdomen padding

In its most fundamental aspect, mimicry is any behavior that enables an animal to avoid predation by adopting the characteristics or appearance of another animal. The resemblance may be in terms of shape, color, pattern or behavior.

Evans and Bellamy, *An Inordinate Fondness for Beetles*, p. 118.

Order of work

Trace a skeleton outline of the net-winged beetle onto the backing fabric. The abdomen and thorax are worked on the background fabric of the specimen box (silk or the fabric of your choice, backed with muslin or calico).

Abdomen

Apply one layer of felt to pad the abdomen then cover with satin stitch, worked horizontally, with brown thread.

Elytra

1. Mount the muslin into the hoop and trace the elytra outline. Using orange thread, couch the wire around the outline, leaving two tails, then buttonhole stitch the wire to the fabric.

2. The elytra are filled with rows of copper metallic thread, couched down in a brick pattern (whenever possible) with one strand of orange thread. To work one side of the elytra, sink an end of copper metallic thread at the top corner, then couch a row close to the inside edge of the wire outline. Continue couching the thread, close to the previous row, until the elytra is filled. Sink the remaining end, secure at the back and trim. Repeat for the other side.

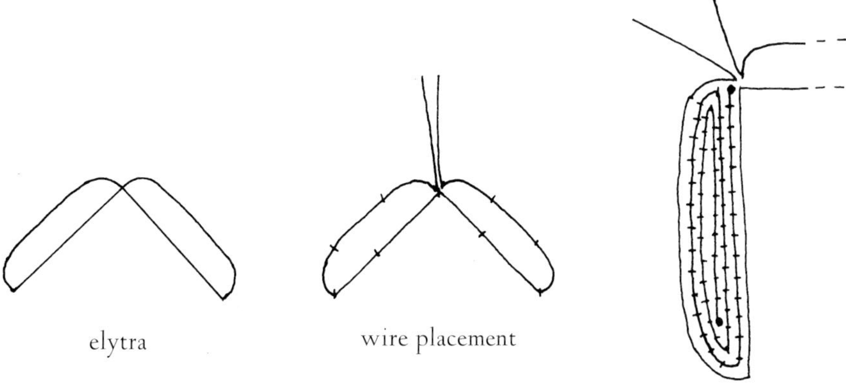

elytra

wire placement

couched metallic thread

3. Cut out the elytra and apply over the abdomen, inserting the wire tails at the point indicated. Secure the wires at the back and trim. Work a few stitches with brown thread over the bend in the wire for the elytra marking, then work a few satin stitches above the marking as extra padding for the thorax.

Thorax

The thorax is cut from black snakeskin and applied with nylon thread. Cut the snakeskin a little larger than the thorax shape, then trim to size when applying. Attach the snakeskin with five stitches—the first two at each corner next to the elytra, one stitch at centre front, then a stitch at each side.

thorax

Head and eyes

Using the nylon thread, stitch a 3 mm bead close to the thorax for the head, then, stitching through this larger bead in a figure of eight movement, apply a petite bead to each side for the eyes.

Antennae

With one strand of brown/black metallic thread, work 11 chain stitches for each antenna, using the outline on the back of the fabric as a guide.

Legs

Using two strands of brown/black metallic thread, work two chain stitches and a long tie-down stitch for each leg, following the outline on the back of the fabric.

Family Scarabaeidae

The second largest family of beetles, the scarabs are also the most versatile family in size, ranging from 2–70 mm (1/16–2 3/4 in) long, and sport a variety of sculptured body shapes. The usually stocky body is covered by a thick and durable exoskeleton, affording protection from predators. Essential to the ecosystem, scarab beetles recycle plant matter and faeces.

The family Scarabaeidae, which also includes the chafer beetles, dung beetles and Christmas beetles, is divided into many distinct subfamilies, each displaying quite different characteristics. Though many are brightly coloured, it was a black dung beetle, the 'sacred scarab', that the ancient Egyptians revered as a symbol of rebirth. Dung-rolling scarabs carefully cut and shape animal excrement into balls which serve not only as a protective chamber for a single larva, but also as a food source. Using their scoop-like head and flat, shovel-like forelegs, the beetles remove a small portion of dung and roll it into a ball. Then, using the hind legs, they roll the ball of dung over the surface of the ground, encasing it in a thin layer of dust. The females deposit an egg in the ball of dung and then bury it.

Members of the Cetoniinae (flower chafer) and Rutelinae subfamilies are brilliantly coloured scarabs, usually with a metallic sheen. Most adult chafers feed on flower pollen, tree foliage and fruit; in their search for energy-rich pollen and nectar, they have become important pollinators of some groups of plants. The Garden Chafer, *Phyllopertha horticola*, with its rusty-orange elytra and lustrous green thorax, may be found on the petals of large flowers, particularly roses. Their larvae feed primarily on plant roots or the organic material of decaying trees.

Sacred Scarab rolling a ball of dung.

The jewel-like members of the large subfamily Rutelinae, justifiably called 'gold chafers', are most sought after by collectors. Many gorgeously coloured beetles, like *Plusiotis chrysargyrea*, are found in the tropics, the gleaming, armour-like elytra being often worn as ornament.

Scarab Beetles.

Scarab Beetle

Plusiotis chrysargyrea

ORDER: COLEOPTERA

SUBORDER: ADEPHAGA

FAMILY: SCARABAEIDAE

Requirements

- 10 cm (4 in) embroidery hoop
- quilter's muslin or brown cotton (homespun), 15 cm (6 in) square
- black felt and Vliesofix
- bronze metallic leather
- bronze stranded thread (Soie d'Alger 526 or DMC 829)
- dark purple stranded thread (Soie d'Alger 3326 or DMC 310)
- brown metallic thread (Kreinik Very Fine (#4) Braid 154V)
- nylon thread (Madeira Monofil No.60, dark)
- Mill Hill seed beads (blue-black 374)
- 30-gauge green-covered wire, cut into three 18 cm (7 in) lengths

The iridescent cryptic patterns on the scarab beetle's back often glow with a green, velvety softness, a hard red metallic sheen, or an unmatched blue luminescence. These living gems have become literal jewels to the people of the Waugi Valley in the interior highlands of New Guinea. Stringing the insects side by side between two strands of plant fibre, they wear them as headbands or as headdress decorations.

Koch, *Dragonfly Beetle Butterfly Bee.*

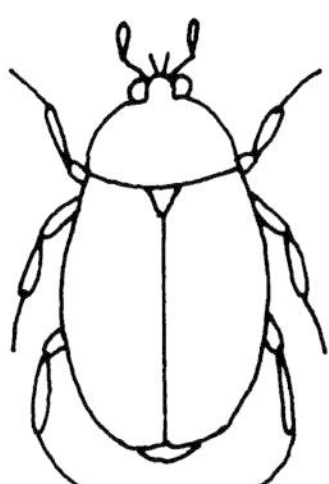

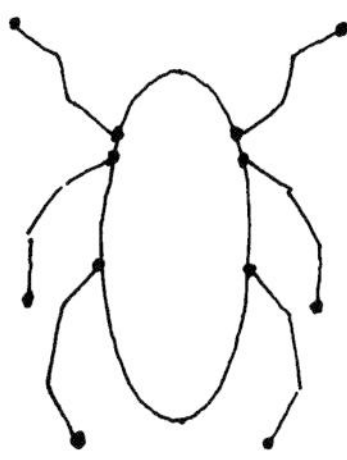

skeleton outline

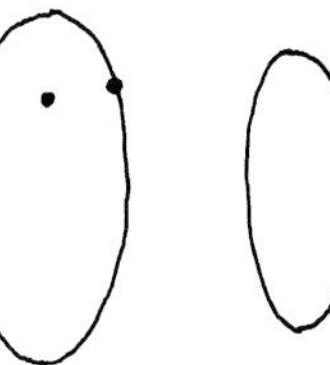

abdomen padding

Order of work

Trace a skeleton outline of the scarab beetle onto the backing fabric. The abdomen and thorax are worked on the background fabric of the specimen box (silk or the fabric of your choice, backed with muslin or calico).

Abdomen

Apply two layers of felt to pad the abdomen then cover with satin stitch, worked horizontally, with dark purple thread.

Elytra

1. Mount the muslin into the hoop and trace the elytra outlines. Using bronze thread, couch wire around the outline, leaving two long tails (these will be used for legs), then overcast the wire to the fabric. Cut an elytra padding shape from felt and apply inside the wire with stab stitches.

2. Cut a *slightly* enlarged elytra shape from bronze leather. (It is important that the leather shape is not too small—it needs to be slightly larger than the space inside the wire to allow for the padding and the curve of the finished elytra. Bevel the edges if the leather is thick.) Using nylon thread in a fine needle, stab stitch the leather inside the wire, pulling the leather down at the edges. Do not stitch across the gap between the wire tails. Stroke around the ditch between the wire and the leather with a blunt needle.

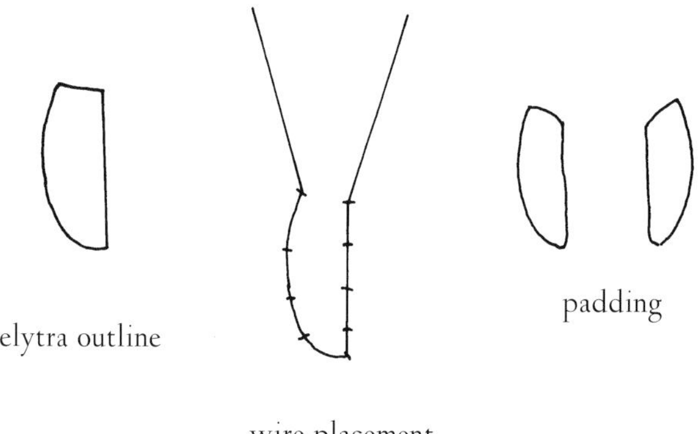

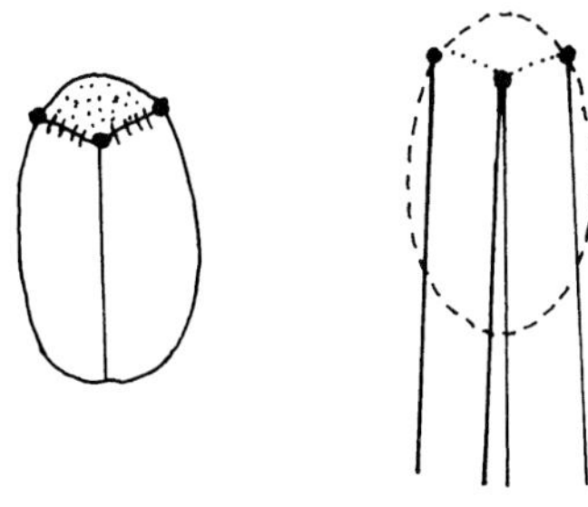

3. Cut out the elytra and apply over the abdomen, inserting the wire tails at the points indicated. Bend the wires towards the tail of the abdomen and secure, temporarily, to the muslin backing with masking tape. Using nylon thread, stab stitch the unwired leather edges of the elytra through the abdomen.

Thorax, head and eyes

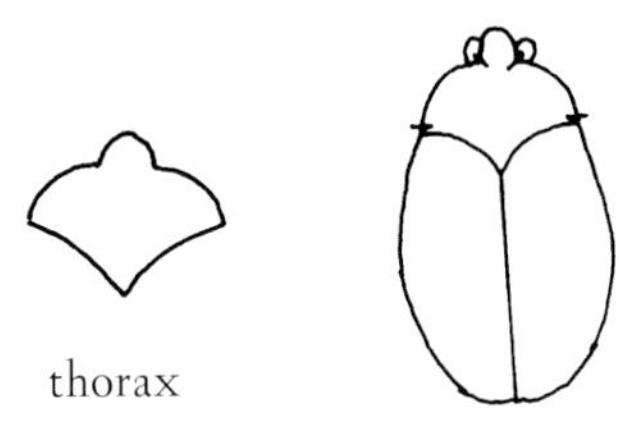

1. Cut a thorax shape out of bronze leather (bevel the edges if necessary). Using nylon thread, apply the thorax (to just overlap the elytra) with small stab stitches. Work two stitches at the lower corners of the thorax (just below the insertion points of the side elytra wires), then two stitches on either side of the head. Stitch a bead on either side of the head for eyes (use tweezers to shape the thorax and head as you work).

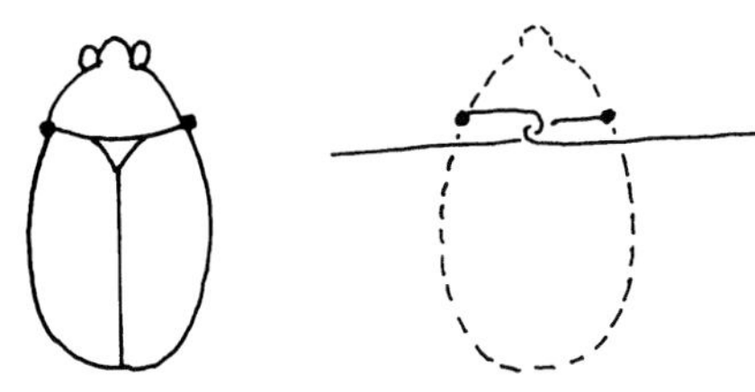

2. The lower edge of the thorax is held in place with a piece of wrapped wire (this also forms the scutellum, the small triangular shape at the top of the elytra). Using one strand of bronze thread, wrap the middle 2 cm (3/4 in) of a piece of green wire. Insert the wire tails on either side of the thorax, the wrapped wire overlapping the small triangle at the bottom of the thorax. Secure the wires by twisting around each other once at the back.

Legs

The legs are made by wrapping wire with brown metallic thread.

Bring the six tails of wire through to the front at the appropriate points using a large yarn darner (follow the leg outlines on the back of the fabric as a guide):

- the tails from the wire securing the thorax form the front legs
- the 'crossed' tails of wire from the sides of the elytra form the middle legs
- the tails from the centre wires of the elytra become the back legs

Wrap each leg with brown metallic thread, wrapping for at least 2 cm (3/4 in), which is longer than needed for each leg, then insert the ends through to the back. Shape the legs with tweezers. Bend the wire tails back under the leg, secure to the muslin, then trim.

ANTENNAE AND MOUTHPARTS

Using brown metallic thread, work each clubbed antenna with a straight stitch and a chain stitch. Separate a single strand of this thread to work two straight stitches for the mouthparts.

Garden Chafer

Phyllopertha horticola

ORDER: COLEOPTERA

SUBORDER: ADEPHAGA

FAMILY: SCARABAEIDAE

Requirements

- 10 cm (4 in) embroidery hoop
- quilter's muslin or orange cotton (homespun), 15 cm (6 in) square
- black felt and Vliesofix
- dark orange suede
- green leather
- copper stranded thread (DMC 920)
- dark green stranded thread (DMC 934)
- nylon thread (Madeira Monofil No.60, clear)
- brown/black metallic thread (Kreinik Very Fine (#4) Braid 022)

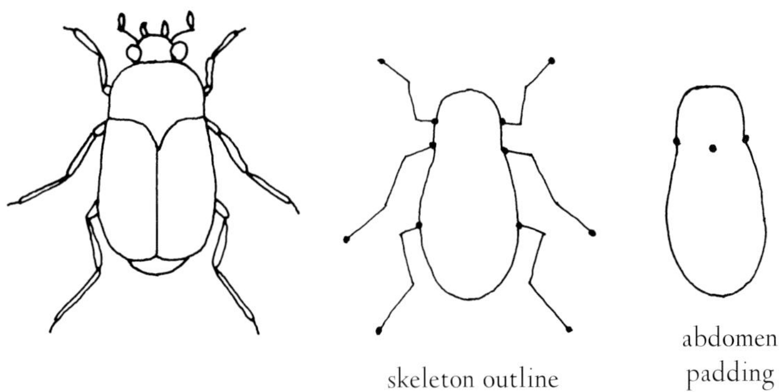

- copper/black metallic thread (Kreinik Very Fine (#4) Braid 2122)
- Mill Hill seed beads (374 blue-black)
- 30-gauge green-covered wire, cut in three 18 cm (7 in) lengths

Order of work

Trace a skeleton outline of the garden chafer onto the backing fabric. The abdomen and thorax are worked on the background fabric of the specimen box (silk or the fabric of your choice, backed with muslin or calico).

Abdomen

Apply two layers of felt to pad the abdomen then cover with satin stitch, worked horizontally, with dark green thread.

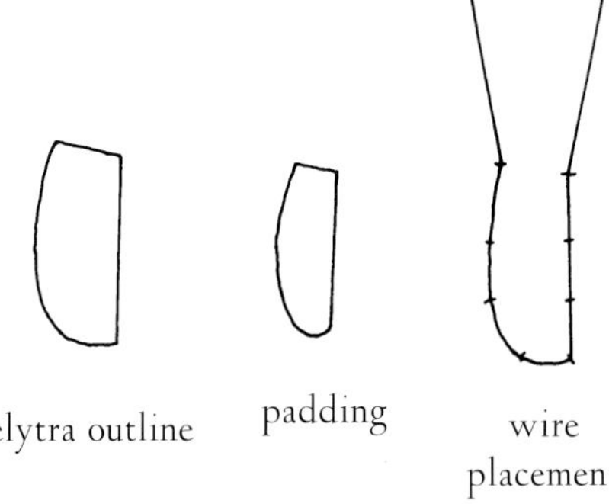

Elytra

1. Mount the muslin into the hoop and trace the elytra outlines. Using copper thread, couch wire around the outline, leaving two long tails (these will be used for legs), then overcast the wire to the fabric. Cut an elytra padding shape from felt and apply inside the wire with stab stitches.

2. Cut a *slightly* enlarged elytra shape from dark orange suede. (It is important that the suede shape is not too small—it needs

to be slightly larger than the space inside the wire to allow for the padding and the curve of the finished elytra.) Using nylon thread in a fine needle, stab stitch the suede inside the wire, pulling the suede down at the edges. *Do not stitch across the gap between the wire tails.* Stroke around the ditch between the wire and the suede with a blunt needle.

3. Cut out the elytra and apply over the abdomen, inserting the wire tails at the points indicated. Bend the wires towards the tail of the abdomen and secure, temporarily, to the muslin backing with masking tape. Using nylon thread, stab stitch the unwired suede edges of the elytra through the abdomen.

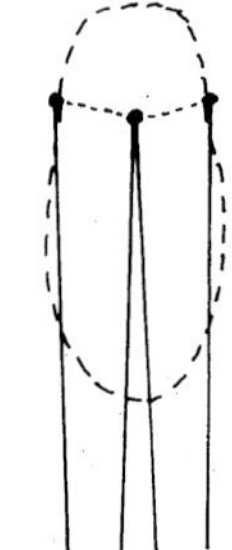

THORAX, HEAD AND EYES

1. Cut a thorax shape out of green leather (bevel the edges if necessary). Using nylon thread, apply the thorax (to just overlap the elytra) with small stab stitches. Work two stitches at the lower corners of the thorax (just below the insertion points of the side elytra wires), then two stitches on either side of the head. Stitch a bead on either side of the head for eyes (use tweezers to shape the thorax and head as you work).

thorax

LEGS

The legs are made by wrapping wire with brown/black metallic thread.

Bring six wire tails through to the front at the appropriate points at the edge of the abdomen, using a large yarn darner (use the leg outlines on the back of the fabric as a guide):

- insert a piece of wire on either side of the thorax to form the front legs (secure the centre of the wire at the back, under the thorax)
- the 'crossed' tails of wire from the sides of the elytra form the middle legs
- the tails from the centre wires of the elytra become the back legs

Wrap each leg with brown/black metallic thread, wrapping for at least 2 cm (3/4 in), which is longer than needed for each leg, then insert the ends through to the back. Shape the legs with tweezers. Bend the wire tails back under the leg, secure to the muslin, then trim.

Antennae and mouthparts

Using copper/black metallic thread, work each clubbed antenna with a straight stitch and a chain stitch. Separate a single strand of this thread to work two straight stitches for the mouthparts.

Family Staphylinidae

The Staphylinidae, the rove beetles, form one of the major beetle families with species ranging from 1 to 22 mm ($^{1}/_{32}$–$^{7}/_{8}$ in) in length, but by far the greatest number are very small (less than 3 mm). These beetles are recognised by having greatly reduced elytra, with most of the abdominal segments being visible. They have membranous wings folded below these small wing cases and most of them are good flyers.

The majority of rove beetles are predacious and play an important role as scavengers, disposing of the remains of plants and animals. They occur in the most diverse habitats; some are to be found near animal dung or in ant hills; others in fungi, decaying organic matter and beneath loose tree bark. Most staphylinids are black or brown, however, with their partly metallic colouring, the rove beetles of the genus *Paederus* are some of the prettiest of the entire family. Their metallic blue elytra contrast sharply with their yellowish red thorax and bicoloured abdomen. *Paederus riparius* is one of the most common species, inhabiting marshes, damp forest outskirts and the edges of small lakes and pools.

Rove Beetle.

Rove Beetle

Paederus riparius

ORDER: COLEOPTERA

SUBORDER: POLYPHAGA

FAMILY: STAPHYLINIDAE

Requirements

- 10 cm (4 in) embroidery hoop
- dark aqua metallic organdie and organza, each 15 cm (6 in) square
- red felt and Vliesofix
- ochre coloured suede
- rust-red metallic purl (Rusty Red No.6 Rough Purl)
- dark purple metallic purl (Purple No.6 Rough Purl)
- beeswax
- dark aqua stranded thread (Cifonda 685 or DMC 3765)
- rust-red stranded thread (DMC 900)
- dark purple stranded thread (Soie d'Alger 3326 or DMC 939)
- brown/black metallic thread (Kreinik Cord 201c)
- copper/black metallic thread (Kreinik Cord 215c)
- nylon thread (Madeira Monofil No.60, clear)
- Mill Hill petite beads (40374 blue-black)
- 28-gauge uncovered wire

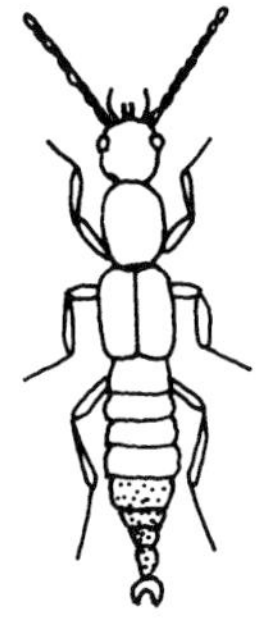

skeleton outline

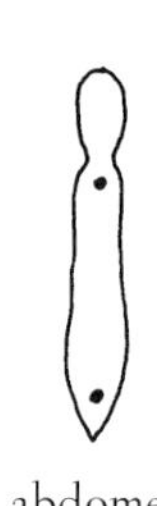

abdomen padding

Order of work

Trace a skeleton outline of the rove beetle onto the backing fabric. The abdomen and thorax are worked on the background fabric of the specimen box (silk or the fabric of your choice, backed with muslin or calico).

Abdomen

1. Work two stitches with six strands of rust-red thread (between the two dots) as the first layer of padding. Apply a layer of felt over these stitches for the second layer of padding.

2. The abdomen is covered with lengths of metallic purl cut to size, and applied with well-waxed, matching thread in a fine needle. Starting at the 'head' end, cut a piece of rust-red purl the width of the abdomen, bring the needle out on one side of the abdomen, thread on the purl then insert the needle on the other side of the abdomen. Repeat until the abdomen is covered, changing to purple metallic purl (and thread) for the final five rows (make sure that the purl is cut to the accurate length—it should just touch the background on either side of the padding).

3. To form the tail, work a fly stitch through the last piece of purl, with two strands of dark purple thread.

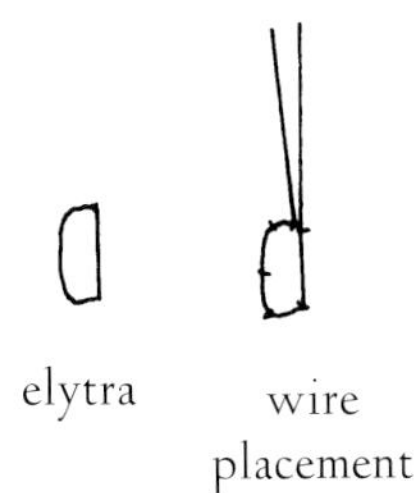
elytra wire placement

Elytra

1. Fuse a layer of organza to the back of the metallic organdie (for support), then mount the 'sandwich' into the hoop. Trace the elytra outline (or use a paper template) onto the fabric sandwich. Using dark aqua thread, couch wire around the outline, leaving two tails, then buttonhole stitch the wire to the fabric.

2. Cut out the elytra and catch both inner wires together. Apply over the abdomen, inserting the wire tails close to the first row of rust-red purl (the elytra overlaps some of the purl). Secure the wires at the back and trim.

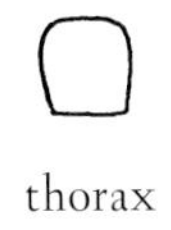
thorax

Thorax

The thorax shape is cut from ochre suede and applied with stab stitches, using nylon thread.

Head and eyes

Work the head in padded satin stitch with dark purple thread. Apply a bead on either side of the head for eyes.

Antennae

With one strand of copper/black metallic thread, work nine chain stitches for each antenna. Using two strands of brown/black metallic thread, work two chain stitches for the mouthparts, then a straight stitch either side.

Legs

With four strands of brown/black metallic thread, work two straight stitches for the inner segments of each leg. Work the outer segment with two strands of thread.

The Entomologist

This charming engraving exemplifies the nineteenth century's sometimes morbid fascination with insects and natural curiosities. The Entomologist *is completely composed of insects; his body comprises three large moths; caterpillars form his arms; moth wings and dragonflies his legs, above beetle shoes. His neck is also a beetle and he wears a grasshopper hat trimmed with a damselfly. He carries two butterfly nets—one about to capture a tiny blue butterfly.*

The Entomologist *is from a scrapbook believed to have belonged to the Langdon family of* Montacute, Bothwell, Tasmania*. The leather-bound book, with* Scrapbook *engraved on the binding, contains significant pictures, hand drawings and paintings, and memorabilia collected between 1790 and 1870. Inside is an original ticket to the Palace of Glass, constructed for the Industrial Exhibition in London's Hyde Park, in 1850. In the same scrapbook is a hand-coloured print, a companion to* The Entomologist, *featuring a lady composed of flowers and flower petals—rose petals surround her face and her shoes are fuchsias. Although the picture's title is missing, it was printed by* G.E. Madeley, Wellington Street, Strand.

The Entomologist, c.1800–1850.
Hand-coloured engraving, 15 x 20 cm (6 x 8 in)

Stumpwork Projects

The projects described in this section, worked with surface embroidery and stumpwork techniques, contain a variety of wild flowers, fruits and a peacock. Featured in each design is a stumpwork beetle, which could be almost any specimen, of a similar size, from the Specimen Box.

Note:

- The diagrams at the beginning of each project are actual size. The explanatory drawings accompanying the instructions may not be true to scale.
- If you wish to substitute another beetle into a design, enlarge or reduce the appropriate skeleton outline (with the aid of a photocopier) to a similar size, if necessary.
- For general information regarding techniques and equipment, please refer to Part 9, page 377.

As there is not the space to provide detailed instructions on stumpwork techniques, please refer to one of the stumpwork embroidery books available, some of which are listed in the bibliography.

Peacock, Grapevine and Beetle

This small stumpwork panel was inspired by illuminated mediaeval manuscripts. Worked on an exotic background of ivory/gold silk lame, this design features a vine of beaded grapes with wired tendrils and a peacock, embroidered in silk and metallic threads, with a beaded tail raised over a real peacock feather. At the base of the vine is a copper-coloured beetle, *Metriorrhynchus rhipidius*, which has its detached elytra worked in couched metallic thread.

Background requirements

- ivory silk or ivory/gold silk, 28 cm (11 in) square
- quilter's muslin (or fine calico) for backing, 28 cm (11 in) square
- 23 cm (9 in) embroidery hoop or a slate/square frame

Grapevine (see page 182)

Peacock (see page 187)

Net-winged Beetle (see page 160)

Order of work

1. Mount the background fabric and the backing fabric into the embroidery hoop or frame.
2. Trace the skeleton outline onto the backing fabric, then thread trace the vine outlines.
3. Vine and branches.
4. Beetle abdomen (then trace the beetle legs and antennae onto the backing fabric).
5. Grapes.
6. Peacock.
7. Complete the beetle.
8. Detached vine leaves.
9. Vine tendrils.

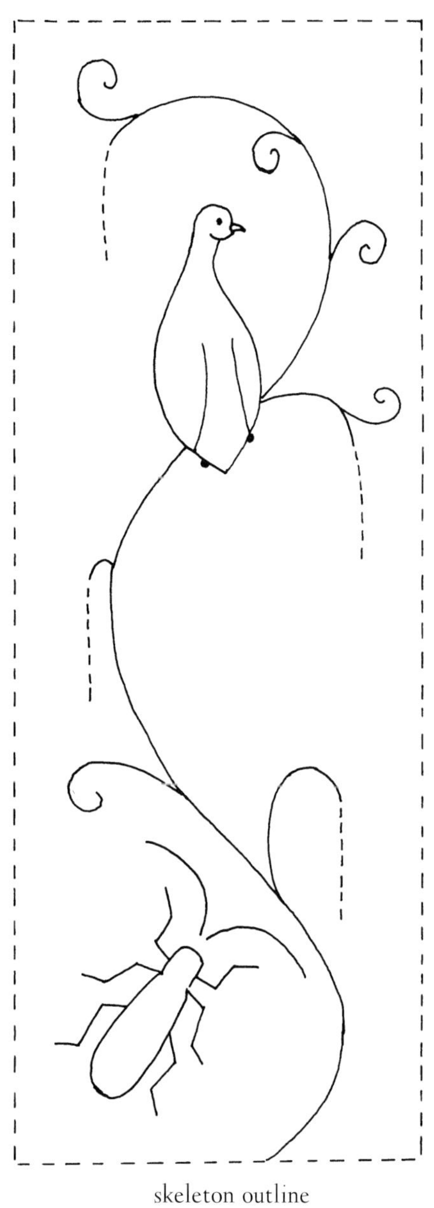

skeleton outline

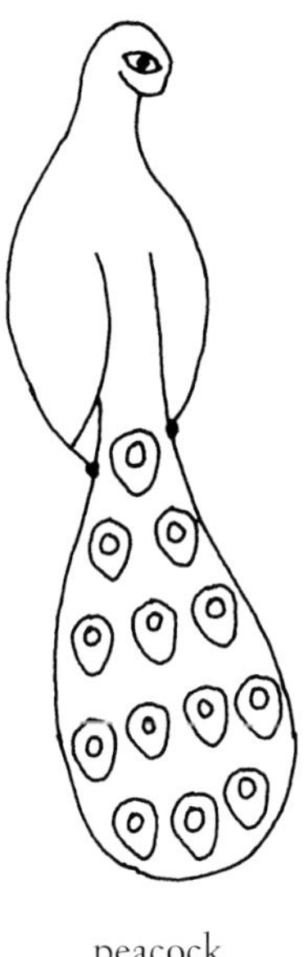

peacock

leaf

All diagrams actual size

Below: Two side panels from an eleventh century carved stone Romanesque doorway.
Right: an image of a vine twining around a tree.

A vineyard from its planting will last fifty, eighty, or an hundred years. The older the vineyard the fewer the grapes, but the better the wine. I have been told that a sheep's horn buried at the root of a vine will make it bear well even in barren ground. I have no great faith in it, but mention it because it may so easily be tried.

John Locke, *Observations Upon the Growth and Culture of Vines and Olives*, 1766.

GRAPEVINE

With its curving scroll-like lines, curling tendrils, serrated leaves and rounded fruits, the grapevine has long been a source of inspiration for designers, sculptors, carvers and embroiderers.

An ornamental grapevine border

Materials required

- quilter's muslin, 20 cm (8 in) square
- 10 cm (4 in) embroidery hoop
- fine flower wire (coloured green if desired)
- 28 gauge uncovered wire
- Mill Hill frosted beads (62056 boysenberry)
- Mill Hill frosted beads (60367 garnet)
- Mill Hill seed beads (367 garnet)
- dark green stranded thread (DMC 3345)
- green soft cotton thread (DMC Tapestry Cotton 2937)
- dark grape stranded thread (DMC 154)
- brown stranded thread (DMC 869)

VINE AND BRANCHES

1. Thread 50 cm (20 in) of green soft cotton into a large needle and make a tiny stitch (1 mm) at the base of the vine outline, leaving two lengths of thread on the front of the work (these will be used as padding).

2. Using one strand of dark green thread, couch the double length of soft cotton along the lower vine outline, separating into single lengths at the first branch. Couch a single length of soft cotton along all remaining vine outlines, working the major vine first, then the branches (remove the thread tracing as you go).

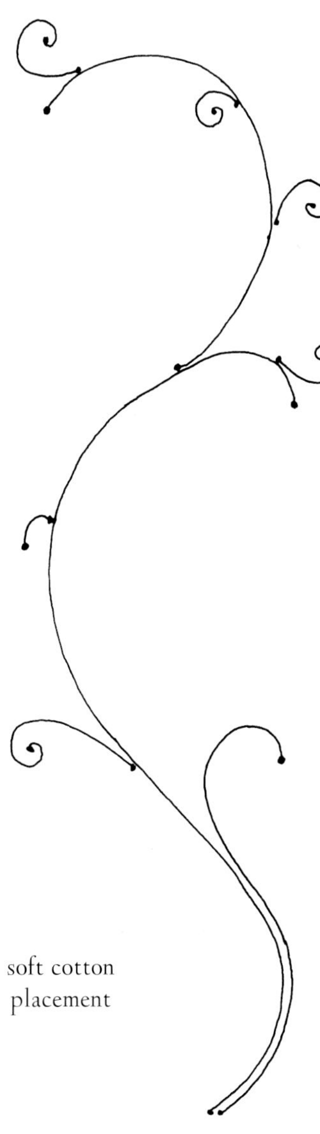

3. The soft cotton core is then wrapped (with detached overcast stitch) with one strand of dark green thread in a fine tapestry needle, inserting through to the back whenever necessary to change threads.

Hints: Work the couching stitches 3 mm (1/8 in) apart, entering and exiting on the vine outline. Keep the soft cotton under tension whilst couching, making the couching stitches the same tension as the eventual wrapping. Insert the soft cotton through to the back whenever required. Secure the ends of soft cotton to the back of the vine when all wrapping is finished.

Grapes

Apply beads 62056 (most), 60367 and 367 (a few for highlights) to form bunches of grapes. Stitch the beads one at a time, with one strand of grape coloured thread (use the dotted lines on the tracing pattern as a guide to the length and direction of each bunch).

Detached vine leaves

1. Mount muslin into the hoop and trace five leaf shapes—three curving to the right and two to the left. The leaves are worked with one strand of dark green thread and flower wire, cut into 10 cm lengths.

2. Insert one wire tail at the base of the leaf (at •) and secure to the muslin under the central vein (this wire will not be seen—it is used to help shape the leaf). Shape and couch the remaining wire around the outside edge of leaf, leaving the other wire tail on the front. Buttonhole stitch the wire to the muslin.

3. Work a row of split back stitch around inside edge of the wire before embroidering each lobe of the leaf with fishbone stitch (this is easier to do if you reverse the direction of the fishbone stitches). Work the lower two lobes first, the side lobes and finally the top lobe.

4. Carefully cut out the leaves, inserting the wire tails through to the back (using the photograph as a guide to placement). Secure the wire tails at the back of the vine, then shape the leaves with tweezers

VINE TENDRILS

Vine tendrils are made by wrapping uncovered wire with one strand of brown thread.

Peacock feathers were often worked into embroidery in early church decorations.

1. Tie the thread 1 cm (3/8 in) from the end of the uncovered wire. Wrap the wire (back over the thread end) to the required length. Secure, leaving a tail of thread and wire.

2. To shape the tendril, wind the wrapped wire around a daring needle to form a small coil, then cut off the unwrapped 1 cm (3/8 in) of wire.

3. Insert the tail of wire and thread through to the back, next to the grapes, and secure.

The male peacock has a fabulous fan which he opens when trying to charm a peahen. The peacock's fan, or train, contains about 200 iridescent ocelli (eye feathers), up to 2 metres (7 feet) long, and is supported by the tail. When courting, the peacock backs up to the peahen, then spins suddenly to face and dazzle her with his beautiful, quivering fan.

Italian peacock feathers.

Marble relief, Ravenna, mid sixth century.

As a Christian symbol, peacocks became a characteristic Byzantine motif, used in conjunction with the cross, circle, dove and vine, usually in pairs, placed one on each side of a chalice, pedestal or column.

Ware and Stafford, *An Illustrated Dictionary of Ornament*, p. 164.

In China, the feathers were valued highly during the T'ang dynasty over a thousand years ago. Districts paid their taxes with peacocks because the feathers were needed as decorations during imperial processions, and they were also presented to officials as rewards for loyal and faithful service.

Peacock tail feather, showing 'eye', as used in the project.

According to Greek legend, the peacock was sacred to the goddess Hera. She directed Argus, the creature with one hundred eyes, to spy on a rival. When Argus was slain, Hera placed his eyes on the tail of her favourite bird.

PEACOCK

Materials required

- quilter's muslin, 20 cm (8 in) square
- 10 or 12 cm (4 or 5 in) embroidery hoop
- small peacock feather (optional)
- stuffing and satay stick
- fine flower wire (coloured teal blue if desired)
- Mill Hill petite beads (40374 blue-black)
- Mill Hill petite beads (42014 black)
- dark teal stranded thread (Soie d'Alger 135)
- electric blue stranded thread (DMC 995)
- blue stranded thread (Cifonda 685)
- aquamarine stranded thread (Cifonda 7)
- copper stranded thread (Cifonda 103)
- light brown stranded thread (Cifonda 496)
- medium brown stranded thread (Cifonda 497)
- dark brown stranded thread (Cifonda 498)
- white stranded thread (Cifonda white)
- black stranded thread (Cifonda black)
  (Note: I chose Cifonda for its fineness and sheen)
- electric blue metallic thread (Madeira Metallic No.40 col.37)
- peacock metallic thread (Kreinik Blending Filament 085)
- nylon thread (Madeira Monofil No.60, clear)
- small peacock feather (optional)

Peacock tail

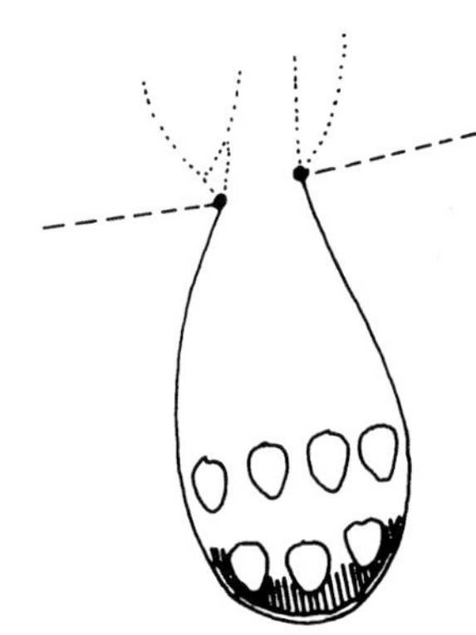

1. Mount muslin into the hoop and trace the peacock body, tail and feather 'eyes'. Insert each end of flower wire through to the back at the points (•) where the tail joins the body. Using dark teal thread, couch then buttonhole stitch the wire to the muslin around the tail outline (bend the wire tails out of the way and secure to the back with masking tape).

2. Work a row of long and short buttonhole stitch at the lower edge of the tail (inside the wire), following the outline of the feather 'eyes', then embroider the background of the tail in long and short stitch (around the feather 'eyes').

3. Work the feather 'eyes' as follows (they are basically an eyelet with a bead stitched in the hole):

a. Using one strand of copper thread:

- outline the 'eye' with back stitch (next to the dark teal background);
- to work the eyelet, make a hole at o with a large (14) yarn darner, then embroider around the 'eye' in buttonhole stitch (starting at the top), inserting the needle through the hole at o, the ridge of the buttonhole covering the backstitch outline;
- insert the darner through the centre of the eyelet again to define the hole.

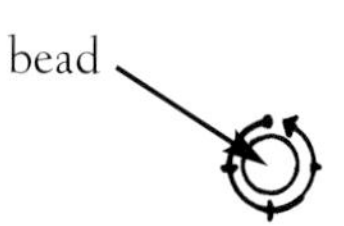

b. Using the same thread, stitch a blue-black bead into each eyelet hole (work from the back, making several stitches through the bead into the edges of the hole).

c. Thread a needle with one strand each of electric blue stranded and metallic thread. To make an electric blue 'circle' around each bead, work a chain stitch around the bead and secure in three places (instead of the usual one).

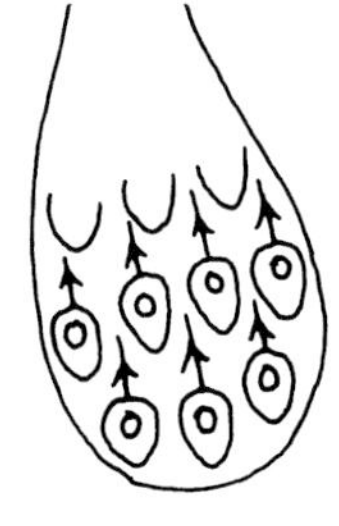

d. Use nylon thread to couch one or two strands of peacock metallic thread around outside edge of each 'eye', to add a little sparkle.

e. Using one strand of blue thread, work fly and straight stitches at the top of each feather (over the teal background), to add some 'blue' to the tail.

Peacock body

The peacock body is embroidered with encroaching satin stitch, using different coloured threads in two or three needles (worked at the same time), to achieve a feathered effect. Vary the length of the satin stitches a little for a more natural look.

1. Using dark teal thread, outline the wings, neck and head with split stitch.

2. Embroider the back, between the wings, with encroaching satin stitch, working with dark teal thread in one needle, and (blue 685 + aquamarine 7) threads in another, blending the two colour combinations. Where the tail meets the body, work a few straight stitches in peacock metallic thread.

3. The area starting from the top of the wings up to the head is embroidered with rows of encroaching satin stitch, blending three different colour combinations (repeating the rows as required, working with three needles at once):

- work two rows with (blue 685 + aquamarine 7) threads;
- then work one row of (electric blue 995 + electric blue metallic) threads;
- work a few stitches in each row with dark teal thread.

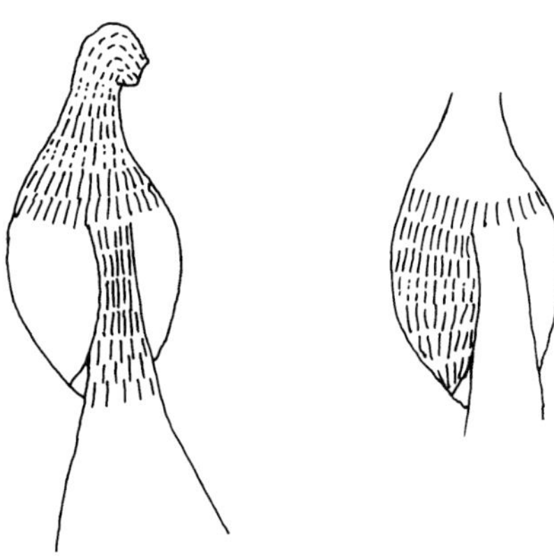

4. Embroider the head in (blue 685 + aquamarine 7) threads in tiny stitches (following the 'feather' direction). Do not leave a space for the eye as this will be worked later.

5. The wings are embroidered with rows of encroaching satin stitch, starting at the top of the wings and working to the tip, blending three different colour combinations (repeating the rows as required, working with three needles at once):

- work one row of (blue 685 + aquamarine 7) threads;
- then work one row of (light brown 496 + medium brown 497) threads;
- then work one row of (medium brown 497 + dark brown 498) threads.

In each row work a few stitches with one of the other colour combinations to avoid 'rainbow' bands of colour.

Apply peacock body to main fabric

1. Snip the muslin to the wire insertion points (where the tail joins the body) and at the neck edges, then work a row of small running stitches around body 1.5 mm (1/16 in) from embroidered edge (these will be used as gathering stitches) leaving two thread tails.

2. Cut out the tail close to the wired edge, then cut out the body leaving a 3–4 mm (approx. 1/8 in) turning allowance (take care not cut the gathering threads or the tails of wire). Gently pull up the gathering threads and finger press the turning allowance under the body.

3. Using a yarn darner, insert the wire tails through two holes at • and •, twist tails around each other once at the back and hold temporarily with masking tape (check the placement of the peacock). With blue thread, stab stitch the body and head in place (from • to •), using the outline on the back as a guide. Stitch the twisted wire behind the body then trim the tails.

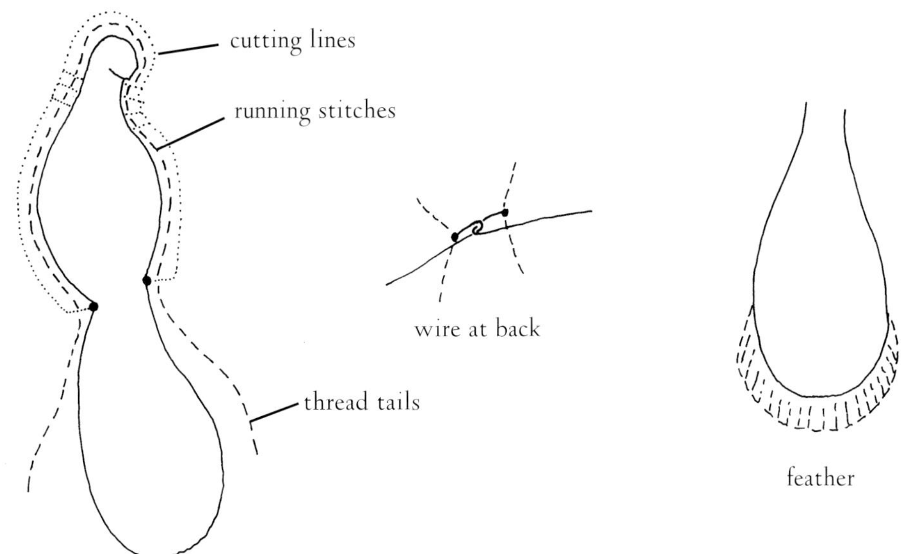

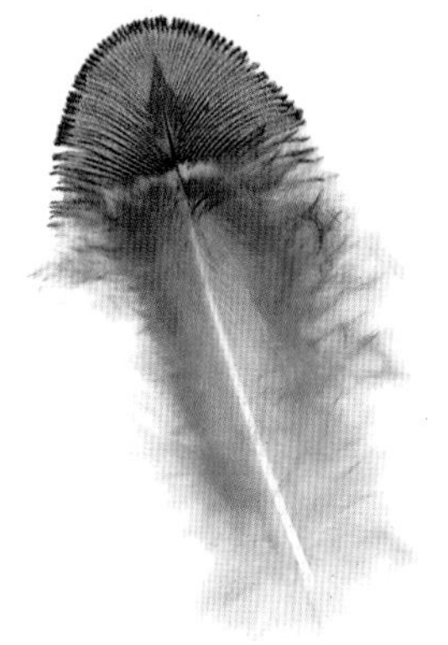

4. Lightly stuff the peacock body, inserting the stuffing through the gap under the tail with the satay stick. With blue thread, work stab stitches along the internal wing outlines to accentuate the wings. If necessary, work straight stitches around the edge of the body (in blending colours), to hide the stab stitches.

To complete the peacock

1. Make a hole for the eye with the yarn darner, then insert a black bead with black thread and work a few stitches in black. Work stitches around the eyes in white thread.

2. Work five straight stitches with medium brown 497 for the beak, then whip to form a curved shape. For the crest on the head, make five straight stitches with blue thread, then work a French knot at the end of each with (aquamarine7 + blue 685) threads.

3. Shape the peacock feather with sharp scissors (if necessary), then apply under the tail with small stitches. (The feather used is one of the small feathers found on the lower back, just above the long tail feathers. This feather is optional.)

NET-WINGED BEETLE

Follow the instructions for the Net-winged Beetle on pages 160–162, working the abdomen on the background fabric (step 4, order of work) after completing the embroidery for the peacock, and completing the beetle as step 7 in the order of work.

Crocus, Clover and Jewel Beetle

This small stumpwork panel was inspired by mediaeval flowers and insects. Embroidered on ivory satin, the design features the bright purple Saffron Crocus, *Crocus sativus,* with detached petals, leaves and stems, and Red Clover, *Trifolium pratense,* with padded flower heads and detached sepals. At the base of the flowers is a glittering Jewel Beetle, with its detached elytra worked in metallic thread.

Crocus sativus, the Saffron Crocus, whose name comes indirectly from Arabic za-faran, meaning 'yellow', was much prized in the Middle Ages for its culinary, medicinal, disinfectant and dyeing properties. Originally from Asia Minor, it was spread throughout the Mediterranean by the Arabs, and the rest of southern Europe by the Crusaders.

Inside each bright lilac bloom are three vivid, orange-red stigmas, the source of the world's costliest spice, saffron. This is obtained from the dried stigmas, 500 flowers being required to produce three or four grams of the spice. The laborious, time-consuming process of harvesting and growing was considered labour well spent. The industry was highly important, for saffron was used in medicine for its sedative properties and as a disinfectant, as well as making a splendid hair and clothing dye and paint for illuminating manuscripts. The spice was greatly prized by mediaeval cooks for colouring and flavouring food, especially sauces and puddings.

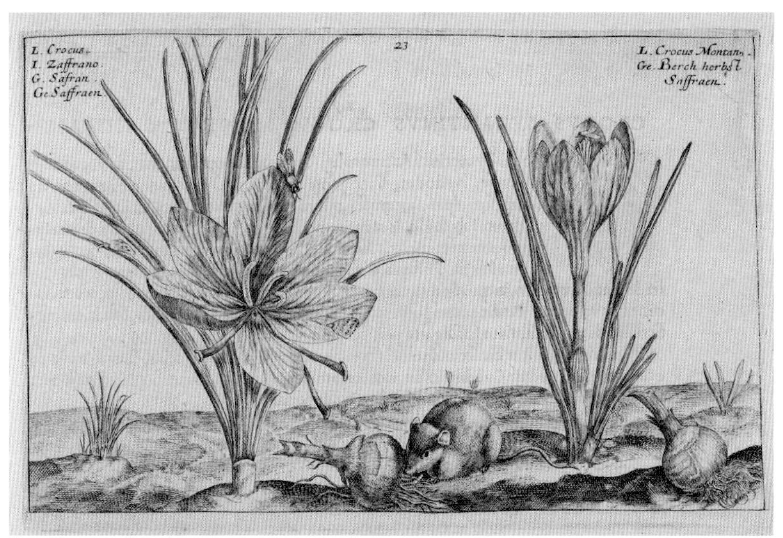

Saffron Crocus (Crocus sativus) *with Long-tailed Field Mouse* (Apodermus sylvaticus). *Engraving by Crispin de Passe from his* Hortus Floridus, 1614.

Crocus, Clover and Jewel Beetle

Background requirements

- ivory satin, 28 cm (11 in) square
- quilter's muslin (or fine calico) for backing, 28 cm (11 in) square
- 23 cm (9 in) embroidery hoop or a slate/square frame

Crocus (see below)

Clover (see page 204)

Jewel Beetle (see pages 90–91)

Order of work

1. Mount the background fabric and the backing fabric into the embroidery hoop or frame.
2. Trace the skeleton outline onto the background fabric.
3. Crocus surface leaves and bud stem.
4. Beetle abdomen (then trace the beetle legs onto the backing fabric).
5. Clover stems, flowers and detached leaflets.
6. Crocus flowers and detached stems.
7. Complete the beetle.
8. Detached crocus leaves.

Saffron can be used in savoury as well as sweet dishes; to colour food a beautiful buttercup yellow, to scent it with a warm, subtly woody smell, and to flavour it with an elegant bittersweet taste. Italian risottos, Indian birianis, Persian pilafs and Spanish paellas attest to its widespread affinity with rice; and paella, Provençal bouillabaisse and most Mediterranean fish soups, to how well it combines with fish.

CROCUS

Materials required

- quilter's muslin, three 20 cm (8 in) squares
- 10 and 15 cm (4 and 6 in) embroidery hoops

All diagrams actual size

skeleton outline

upper crocus flower petal

bud petal

clover leaflet

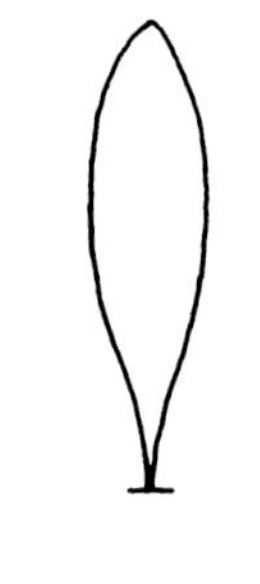

lower crocus flower petal

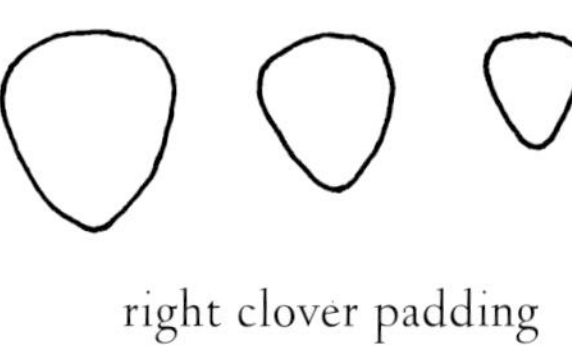

right clover padding

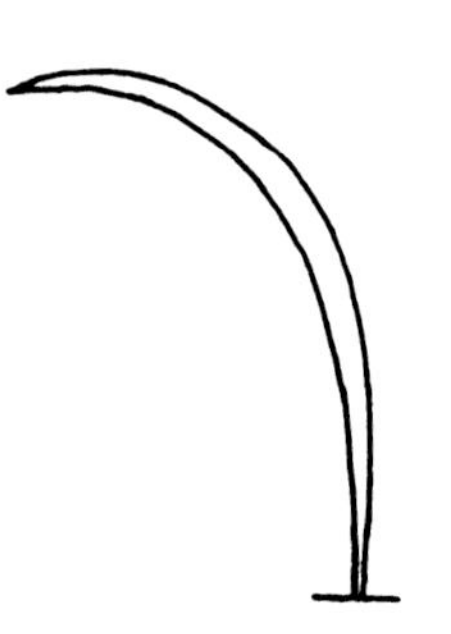

left detached leaf

right detached leaf

left clover padding

- fine flower wire (coloured purple, green and red if desired)
- medium green stranded thread (DMC 3345)
- dark green stranded thread (DMC 895)
- light purple stranded thread (Soie d'Alger 3314 or DMC 553)
- medium purple stranded thread (Soie d'Alger 3315 or DMC 552)
- dark purple stranded thread (Soie d'Alger 3316 or DMC 550)
- red stranded thread (DMC 349)

Surface stems and leaves

The crocus leaves are worked with close rows of stem or outline stitch, using one strand of thread.

1. Work the left crocus leaf with five rows of stem stitch, working the centre row in dark green thread (for the vein) and the other four rows in medium green thread. Starting at the base of the leaf, work the first row of stem stitch on the left

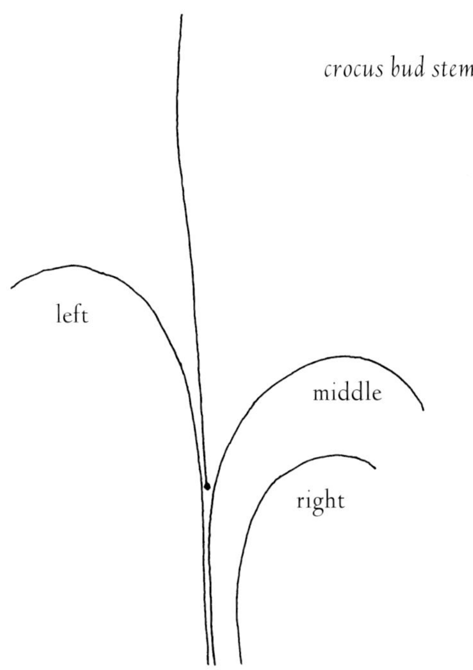

leaf outline. Starting at the base, work each of the next four rows to the left of this line, stopping each row slightly short of the previous row to ensure a tapering leaf point.

2. Work the middle crocus leaf with five rows of outline stitch, working the centre row in dark green thread (for the vein) and the other four rows in medium green thread. Starting at the base of the leaf, work the first row of outline stitch on the middle leaf outline. Starting at the base, work each of the next four rows to the right of this line, stopping each row slightly short of the previous row to ensure a tapering leaf point (this leaf is embroidered over the clover stem line).

3. Work the right crocus leaf in the same way as the middle crocus leaf.

4. Work the stem of the crocus bud in whipped chain stitch, using three strands of thread (two of dark green 895 and one of medium green 3345) for both the chain stitch and the whipping. Start at the upper edge of the left leaf (•) and stop just below the bud leaves (these leaves will be worked after the detached bud petal is applied).

Surface bud petal

Crocus petals are bright lilac, with purple veins (the centre vein being prominent) and a deep purple throat. Embroider the petals with rows of split stitch, using several shades of purple to suggest their delicately veined surface.

direction of veins in petal

1. Outline the crocus bud petal in split stitch in medium purple thread. Work the central vein in split stitch with dark purple thread.

2. Embroider the petal with rows of split stitch, alternating two rows in medium thread with one row in dark. Work all rows from the base to the tip, with the stitches covering the outline.

Surface flower petals

1. Outline the crocus flower petals in split stitch in light purple thread. Work the central vein in split stitch with medium purple thread.

2. Embroider the petals with rows of split stitch, alternating two rows in light purple thread with one row in medium purple. Work all rows from the base to the tip, with the stitches covering the outline (adjust as required for the side petals).

3. Work a dark purple blush with a few stitches at the base of the petals.

Stigmas

The crocus stigmas, the source of saffron, are 'long, drooping and scarlet'.

Make eight stigmas, each requiring 10 cm (4 in) of flower wire (coloured red if desired), and one strand of red thread.

1. Tie the thread to the wire (near one end), then wrap 4 mm (a bit more than 1/8 in) over the tail of thread.

2. Bend the wrapped wire and squeeze with tweezers, cut the short tail of wire.

3. Starting near the bend, wrap the doubled wire (stigma tip), then continue wrapping the single wire for 25 mm (1 in). Secure the thread (leaving wire and thread tails).

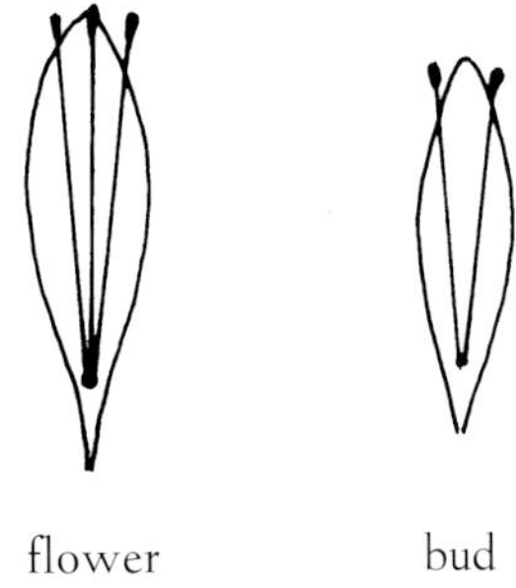

4. Using a large yarn darner, insert the stigmas 5 mm (approx. 1/4 in) above the base of the surface petals (they need to be slightly shorter than the petals). Apply three stigmas for each flower and two for the bud. Bend the wires back behind the petals, secure and trim.

Detached bud petal

1. Mount muslin into the 10 cm (4 in) hoop and trace the bud petal outline (and the length line). Cut 15 cm (6 in) of flower wire (coloured purple if desired).

2. Using medium purple thread, couch wire around the bud outline, leaving two wire tails (the wires touch but do not cross at the base of the petal—the line indicates the petal length). Overcast the wire to the muslin (do not stitch over both wires).

3. Work a row of split stitch inside the wire with medium purple thread, then the central vein with dark purple thread. Embroider the petal with rows of split stitch, alternating two rows in medium purple with one row in dark purple. Work all rows from the base to the tip (insert the needle close to the wire, *into* the split stitch).

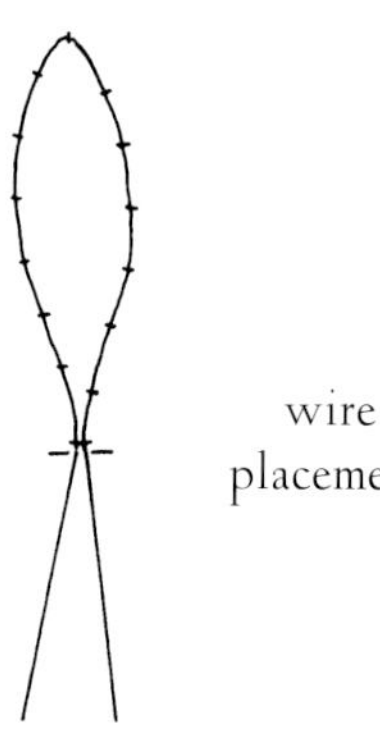

wire placement

4. Cut out the bud petal, secure one strand of dark purple thread at the back then wrap the wire tails for 1.5 cm (5/8 inch) to form the flower 'tube'. Insert the wrapped wire at the top of the stitched bud stem, covering the surface petal and stigmas. Secure the wire to the back of the stem and trim. Secure the detached petal (where the wrapping begins) at the base of the surface petal with an invisible stitch. Shape the petal with tweezers.

wrapping

5. Embroider the leaves on either side of the bud in stem or outline stitch (as for the surface leaves) with medium green thread; work the first row of stitching on the leaf outline, work two more rows inside this line, stopping each row slightly short of the previous row to ensure a tapering point.

Detached flower petals

Crocus flower petals are fused at the base to form a long thin tube, which continues as the stem. The detached flower petals are embroidered with long wire tails which will be wrapped to form the flower tubes and stems.

1. Trace six flower petals onto the muslin in the 15 cm (6 in) hoop (three petals for the upper flower and three for the lower flower). Indicate the petal length with a line. Cut three 30 cm (12 in) lengths of flower wire for the upper flower petals, and three 20 cm (8 in) lengths, for the lower flower petals. Check that the correct wires are being used for

each petal! Colour the middle 9 cm ($3^1/_2$ in) of each wire purple, if desired.

2. Work the upper flower petals first. Using light purple thread, couch wire around the petal outline, leaving two wire tails (the wires touch but do not cross at the base of the petal). Overcast the wire to the muslin (do not stitch over both wires—hold wire tails out of the way with masking tape).

3. Work a row of split stitch inside the wire with light purple thread, then the central vein with medium purple thread. Embroider the petal with rows of split stitch, alternating two rows in light purple with one row in medium purple. Work all rows from the base to the tip (insert the needle close to the wire, *into* the split stitch).

4. Work a dark purple blush with a few stitches at the base of the petals.

5. Cut out the three detached upper flower petals (colour the long tails of wire green, if desired). Sort the petals into left, right and middle petals. Stack the petals—middle on top, the left and right underneath. Thread one strand of dark purple thread into a fine needle, secure to the back of the lower petal. Bend the *inner* wire of the left and the right petals at right angles to the petals (keep them free as they will be inserted into the main fabric when applying the petals). To form the flower tube, wrap the remaining four wires with the dark purple thread for 10–12 mm (approx. $^1/_2$ in), secure the thread with a buttonhole loop around the wires and retain the tail. Slide a strand of dark green thread between the wires, leaving a tail of thread, and continue wrapping the wires to form the stem. When the thread runs out, secure with a buttonhole loop (retaining the tail) and join in a new thread as before. Wrap about 9 cm ($3^1/_2$ in) with green thread.

6. To apply the upper crocus flower, insert the two reserved wires at the base of the upper flower surface petals—bend back under the petals and hold with tape. Using a large yarn darner, insert the wrapped stem wires at the base of the

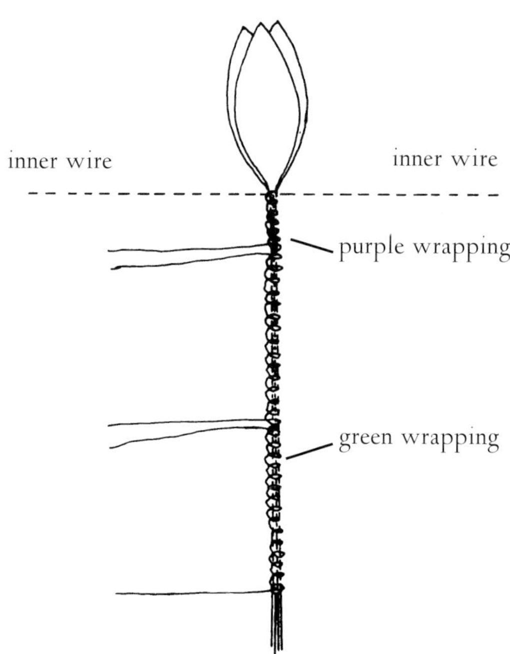

leaves, next to the lower right leaf (curving over the surface stems and leaves), bend back behind the leaves and hold with masking tape. Take the purple and green wrapping-thread tails through to the back (under the wrapped stem) and stitch to the backing, thus securing the stem. Grade (cut to different lengths) and secure all wires and trim. Shape the petals with tweezers. Hold the detached petals in place with invisible stitches (using nylon thread), if necessary.

7. Embroider the leaves on either side of the stem in stem or outline stitch, as for the surface leaves: with medium green thread, work the first row of stitching on the leaf outline; work three more rows inside this outline, stopping each row slightly short of the previous row to ensure a tapering point.

8. Apply the lower crocus flower in the same way (omitting step 7), inserting the wrapped wires at the base of the left leaf, curving the stem over all the other stems and leaves.

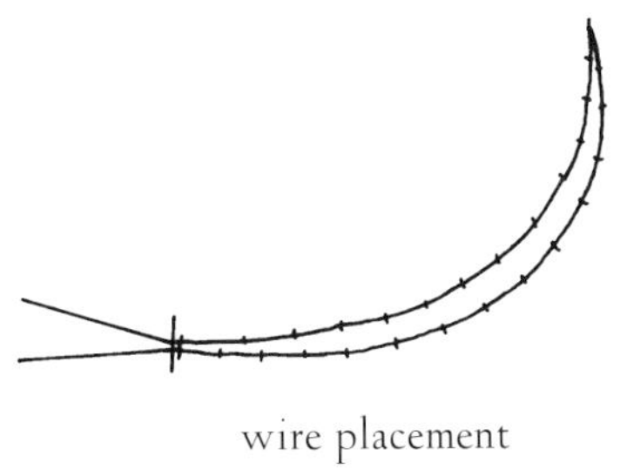
wire placement

Detached crocus leaves

The dark green leaves of the crocus are long, narrow and channelled.

1. Mount muslin into the 15 cm (6 in) hoop and trace both the leaf outlines, and their length lines.

2. Using medium green thread, couch wire around the leaf outline, leaving two wire tails (the wires touch but do not cross at the base of the leaf—the line indicates the leaf length). Buttonhole stitch the wire to the muslin.

3. Embroider the leaves, inside the wire, with rows of stem or outline stitch (as for the surface leaves), working all rows in medium green thread.

4. Carefully cut out the leaves and insert at the points marked as (•). Secure the wires at the back and trim.

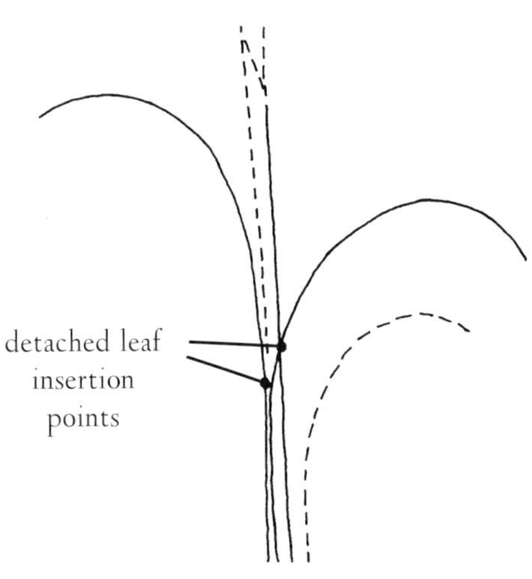

Clover ornament from Henri Gillet's LA VIE NORMAL, 1905.

CLOVER

Requirements

- quilter's muslin, 20 cm (8 in) square
- pink felt and Vliesofix
- flower wire (coloured green if desired)
- dark pink stranded thread (Soie d'Alger 2934 or DMC 309)
- medium pink stranded thread (Soie d'Alger 2933 or DMC 3832)
- green stranded thread (DMC 3346)
- light green stranded thread (DMC 3347)

Stems

Embroider the clover stems in chain stitch using three strands of green thread, stitching over the crocus surface leaves and bud stem.

Flowers

1. To pad the flower, trace the clover outline (and two successively smaller shapes) onto Vliesofix and fuse to the felt. Cut out the shapes (remove the paper). Using one strand of medium pink thread, apply the padding to the main fabric with small stab stitches, applying the smallest layer first (inside the clover outline).

Red Clover, Trifolium pratense, *a small, pink-purple wildflower, takes its name from the Latin* trifolium, *meaning 'three-leaved'. Clovers which produce leaves with four instead of three leaflets have long been considered to be lucky. Besides being a good bee and butterfly attracting plant, clover (meaning 'industry') plays an important role in agriculture, the nodules in the plants' roots putting nitrogen into the soil.*

Once regarded as an antidote for all poisons, clover has been used medicinally for centuries; a syrup made from the flowers was given to children to ease whooping cough, while old herbals claim that it will cleanse the blood.

2. Starting at the tip of the clover, cover the shape with 'rows' of bullion knots (about five wraps in a size 5 or 6 straw/milliners needle), worked with two strands of dark pink thread, shading to medium pink at the base of the clover (work the bullions over the edge of the felt and not too close together).

3. After each row of bullion knots, work a fly stitch with a long tie-down at the base of each bullion, with one strand of light green thread (to represent the tiny leaves around each flower segment and to cover the pink felt—the next row of bullions will cover most of the long tie-down).

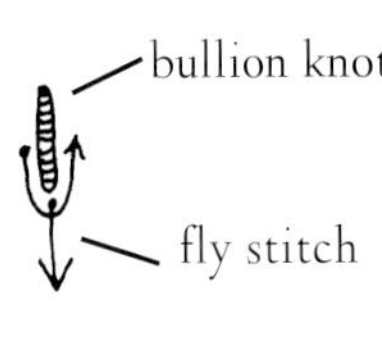

wire placement

4. Mount the muslin into the 10 cm (4 in) hoop and trace four clover leaflets. Using one strand of green thread, couch wire around the outline leaving two tails of wire (the wires touch but do not cross at the base of the leaf). Buttonhole stitch the wire to the muslin. Embroider the leaf, inside the wire, with padded satin stitch in one strand of green 3346.

JEWEL BEETLE

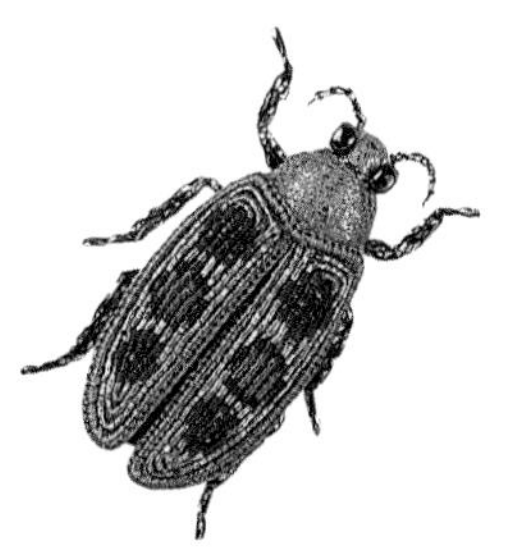

Follow the instructions for the Jewel Beetle on page 90, working the abdomen on the background fabric (step 4, order of work) after completing the surface embroidery for the crocus, and completing the beetle as step 7 in the order of work.

Fritillary, Fennel and Scarab Beetle

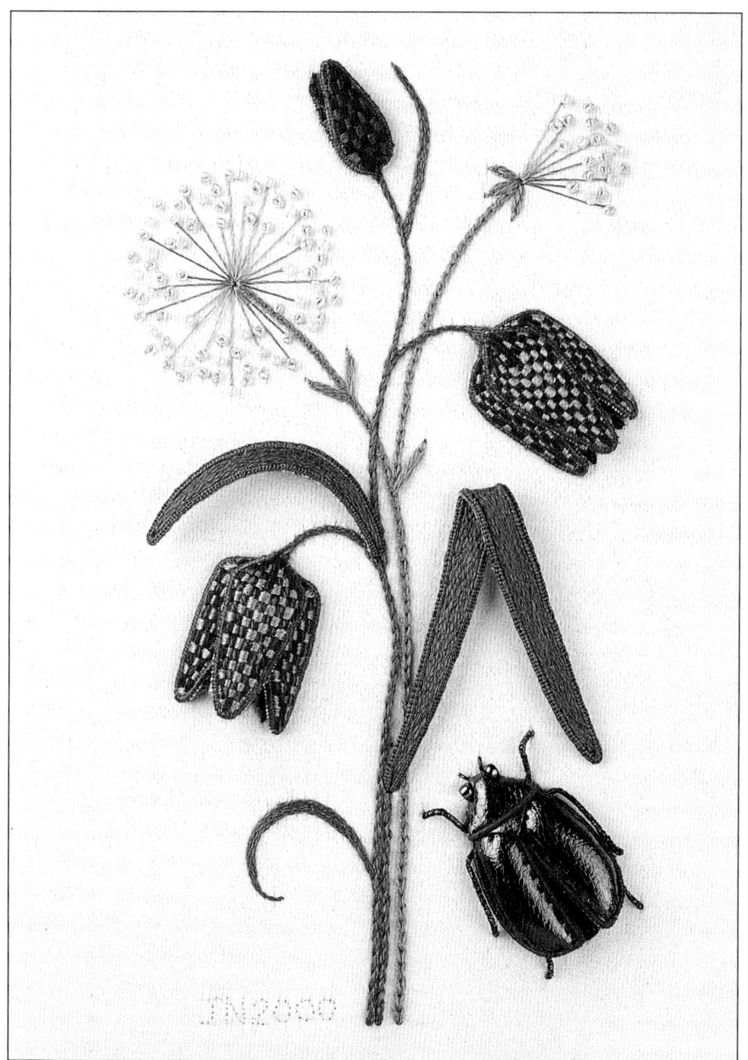

This small stumpwork panel was inspired by wildflowers and insects. Embroidered on ivory satin, the design features the Snake's-head Fritillary, *Fritillaria meleagris*, with its extraordinary chequer-patterned flowers and long, narrow detached leaves, and Fennel with stitched and beaded flowerheads. At the base of the wildflowers is a shiny metallic Scarab Beetle, with its detached elytra worked in bronze leather.

All diagrams actual size

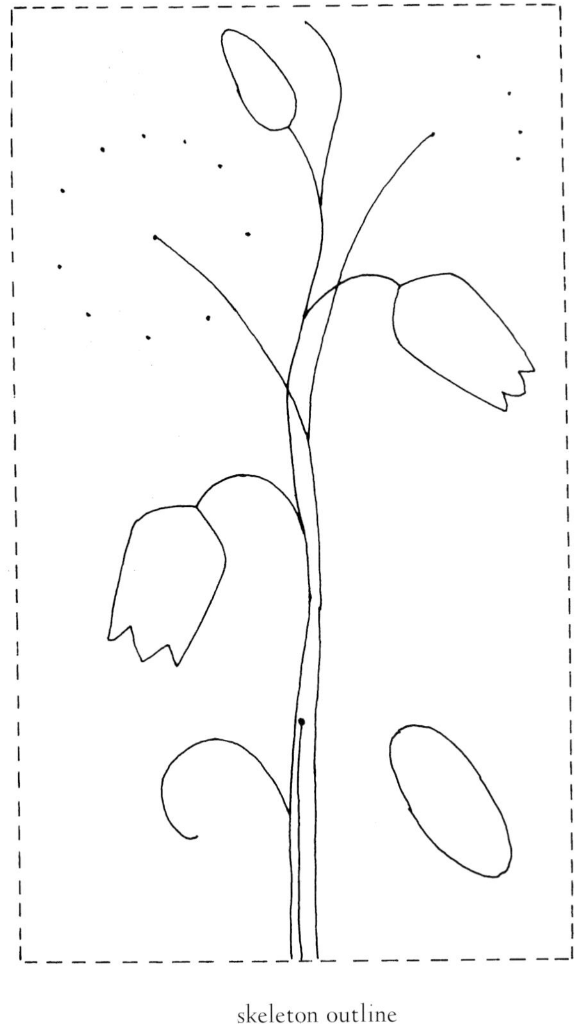

skeleton outline

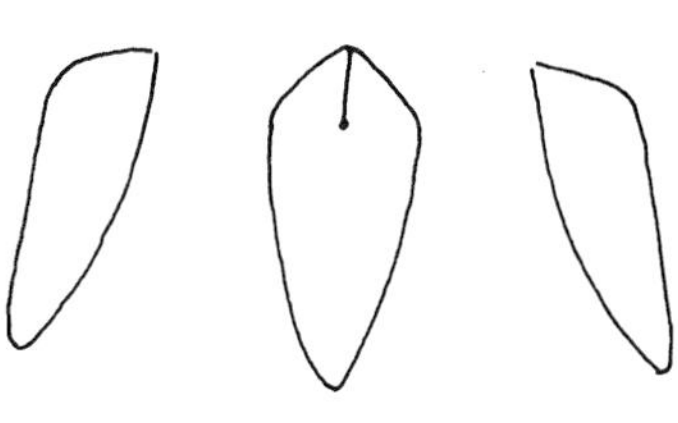

left fritillary petals

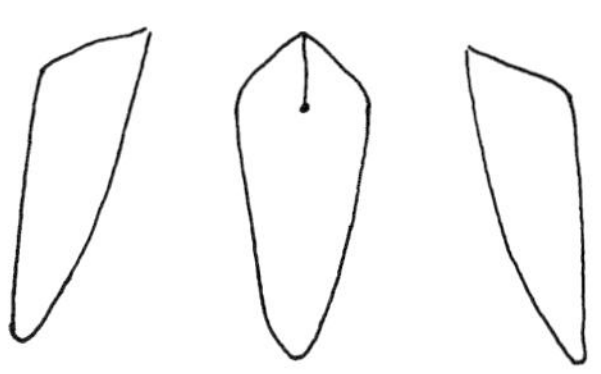

right fritillary petals

bud

left leaf

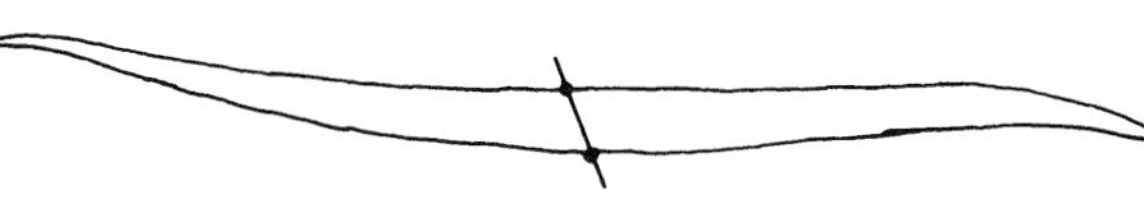

right leaf

Requirements

- ivory satin, 28 cm (11 in) square
- quilter's muslin (or fine calico) for backing, 28 cm (11 in) square
- 23 cm (9 in) embroidery hoop or a slate/square frame

Fennel (see opposite page)

Fritillary (see page 210)

Scarab Beetle (see page 165)

Order of work

1. Mount the background fabric and the backing fabric into the embroidery hoop or frame.
2. Trace the skeleton outline onto the background fabric.
3. Fennel stems.
4. Fritillary stems and leaves.
5. Beetle abdomen (then trace the beetle legs onto the backing fabric).
6. Fennel flowers.
7. Fritillary flowers.
8. Complete the beetle.
9. Detached fritillary leaves.

Fennel has been used in the kitchen since Roman times; the seeds as a spice, the stems and bulbs as a vegetable, and the young leaves as a medicinal herb. Credited with powers against all kinds of pain, the delicate, feathery fennel leaves were used to cure rheumatism and digestive ailments, improve eyesight and memory, and generally promote good health and longevity.

In mediaeval times, fennel was regarded as having mystical properties, being one of the 'nine sacred and all-powerful herbs—atterlothe, chervil, crabapple, fennel, maythen (chamomile), stime (watercress), waybroad (plantain), wergulu (nettle) and mugwort—lauded in the tenth century Anglo-Saxon Lacnunga *as having the power to protect against just about every evil known, including worm blast, thistle blast, dusky venom, flying things and loathed things'.*

Innes and Perry, *Medieval Flowers*, pp. 70, 89.

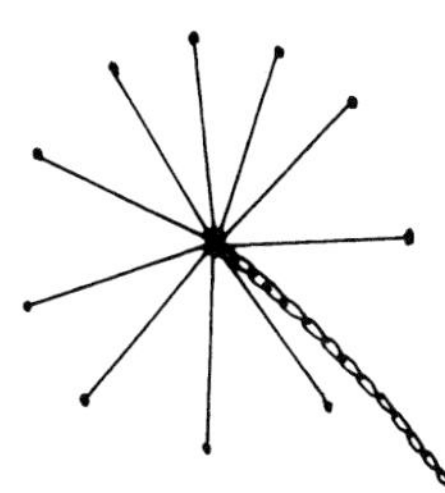

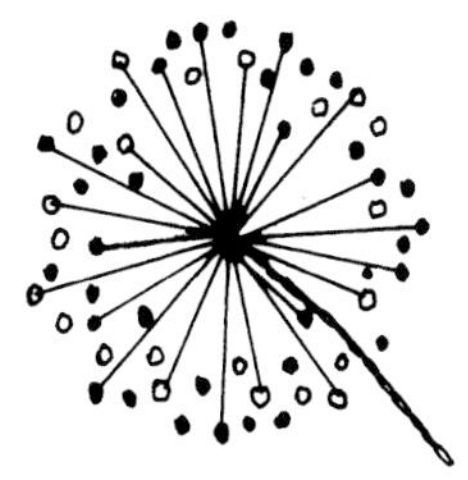

FENNEL

Materials required

- Mill Hill petite beads (40123 cream)
- light green stranded thread (DMC 470)
- light green fine silk thread (Cifonda 522 or DMC 470)
- pale yellow-green stranded thread (Soie d'Alger 2131 or DMC 3047)
- pale yellow rayon thread (Madeira Decora 1426 or DMC Rayon 30745)

Fennel stems

Work the stem of the fennel in chain stitch, starting at the base with three strands of light green thread, changing to two strands, where the stem divides, to work the branches to the fennel flower and fennel bud.

Fennel flower and bud

1. The flower stalks are straight stitches, worked into one central point at the top of the stem, using one strand of light green fine silk (or cotton). Work the longer stalks first, one from each dot, then a number of stitches at random, varying lengths inside the 'circle' outline.

2. The flowerhead is formed by stitching beads or French knots at the end of each stalk, then at random in the spaces in between. Apply the beads with one strand of pale yellow-green thread. Work some French knots with pale yellow-green thread (two strands/two wraps) and some with the pale yellow rayon thread (two strands/one wrap).

3. Work the fennel bud in the same way, at the end of the other stem.

4. The fennel leaflets are worked in detached chain stitches with two strands of light green thread, using the photograph as a guide to placement.

FRITILLARY

Materials required

- quilter's muslin, three 20 cm (8 in) squares
- 10 and 15 cm (4 and 6 in) embroidery hoops
- fine flower wire (coloured antique mauve, green and yellow if desired)
- medium green stranded thread (Soie d'Alger 514 or DMC 469)
- dark green stranded thread (Soie d'Alger 516 or DMC 937)
- light antique mauve stranded thread (Soie d'Alger 4643 or DMC 778)
- medium antique mauve stranded thread (Soie d'Alger 4635 or DMC 3726)
- dark antique mauve stranded thread (Soie d'Alger 4636 or DMC 3802)
- yellow stranded thread (DMC 743)

Stems

The fritillary stems are embroidered in stem stitch, working over the fennel stems. Stitch the stems to the left and right fritillary flowers with three strands of thread (two of dark green plus one of medium green), the bud stem with two strands (one of each green), and the middle stem with three strands (stopping at • the insertion point shown on the skeleton outline, for the right detached leaf).

Surface leaves

Fritillary leaves are very long and narrow.

Work both leaves with close rows of stem stitch, using one strand of medium green thread. Starting at the stem, work a row of stem stitch along the leaf outline. Work a second row, on the inside curve of the line, stopping slightly short of

Cultivated since ancient times, the exotic fritillary has delicate bell-shaped flowers, very narrow grey-green leaves and grows up to 30 cm (12 in) high. These cold climate flowers, closely related to liliums, can be found in a variety of beautiful colours, often with distinctive chequering or stripes, and flourish in damp meadows or open woodland.

One of the most beautiful is the Snake's-head Fritillary, Fritillaria meleagris, *whose creamy white, bell-shaped blooms are distinctly chequered with green, deep chocolate, pinkish lilac or reddish purple.*

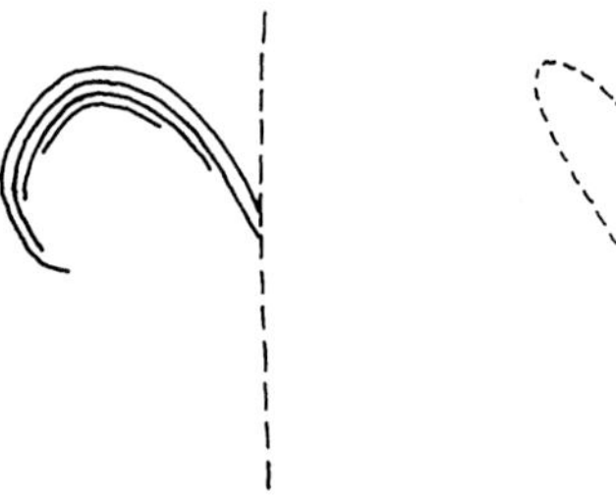

the previous row to ensure a tapering leaf point. Work another one or two rows, inside the curve, to shape the leaf, using the diagram as a guide.

Fritillary flowers

The flower petals are embroidered in plaited stitch, imitating the extraordinary chequering of the Snake's-head Fritillary. Plaited stitch, weaving over three or four threads in a basket-work pattern, is a variation of surface darning (weaving over one thread). Traditionally, a foundation was worked in surface satin stitch, but here regular satin stitch, worked horizontally, is used as the base for these petals. Use a fine tapestry needle

Charles Rennie Mackintosh, *Fritillaria*, 1915

(or the eye of a crewel needle) to weave four rows with a darker colour, under and over approximately four threads, to form the chequered pattern.

Hints:

- I found that weaving three rows with dark antique mauve and one row with medium antique mauve (selected randomly) gave a pleasing result.
- The thread is taken through to the back of the petal at the end of each row, inside the wire.
- The rows can be woven in either direction.
- The third and/or fourth rows of weaving can be stopped (or started) short of the end of the column to facilitate shaping, if desired.

SURFACE FLOWER PETALS

1. With one strand of pale antique mauve thread, embroider the flower shape with satin stitch, starting at the top and working horizontally (keeping the edges as even as possible).

2. Starting in the middle, weave a row vertically, over and under approximately four threads, with one strand of dark antique mauve thread; work three more rows (three dark and one medium, in any order) to complete the first column of weaving. The second and third columns of weaving are worked concurrently, on either side of the first column (this helps to give a slightly curved shape to the weaving). Continue weaving columns of dark and medium threads, on either side of the previous weaving, until the shape is filled. Work short columns at the side edges if necessary to give a good shape.

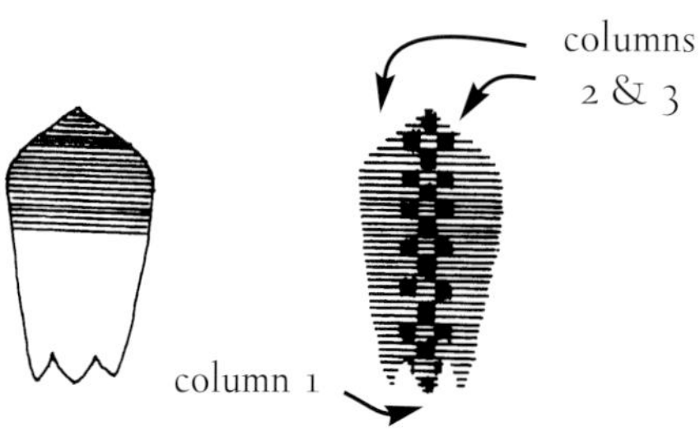

John Gerard, herbalist and author of the famous Herball or Generall Historie of Plants *in 1597, was fascinated with* Fritillaria meleagris, *and carefully described its squares of colour, adding that 'every leafe seems to be the feather of a Ginnie hen, whereof it took its name'—the guinea-hen flower. Also known by less favourable common names such as death bell, sullen lady or leper's bell, the genus name is from* fritillus, *Latin for 'dice-box', and its species name, meleagris, means 'speckled'.*

Surface bud petal

1. With one strand of medium antique mauve thread, embroider the bud shape with satin stitch, starting at the top and working horizontally (keeping the edges as even as possible).

2. Starting in the middle, weave a row vertically, over and under approximately four threads, with one strand of dark antique mauve thread; work three more rows to complete the first column of weaving. The second and third columns of weaving are worked concurrently, on either side of the first column (this helps to give a slightly curved shape to the weaving). Continue weaving in this way until the shape is filled.

Stamens

Make six stamens, each requiring 10 cm (4 in) of flower wire (coloured yellow if desired), and one strand of yellow thread.

1. Tie the thread to the wire (near one end), then wrap 4 mm (approx. 1/8 in) over the tail of thread.

2. Bend the wrapped wire and squeeze with tweezers, cut the short tail of wire.

3. Starting near the bend, wrap the doubled wire (stamen tip), then continue wrapping the single wire for 25 mm (1 in). Secure the thread (leaving wire and thread tails).

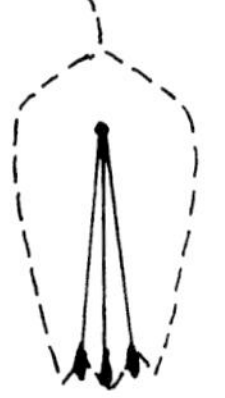

4. Using a large yarn darner, insert the stamens through the surface flower petals, 5 mm (a bit less than 1/4 in) below the stem (they need to be slightly shorter than the petals). Apply three stamens for each flower. Bend the wires back behind the petals, secure and trim.

Detached flower petals

Mount the muslin into the 15 cm (6 in) embroidery hoop and trace six petals—one middle petal and two side petals for each fritillary flower. Cut 12 cm (5 in) lengths of flower wire for the petals and an extra 3 cm (1 1/4 in) piece for each middle petal (coloured antique mauve, if desired).

DETACHED SIDE PETALS

1. Using one strand of medium antique mauve thread, couch wire around the outline, leaving two wire tails (the wires touch but do not cross at the base of the petal). Buttonhole stitch the wire to the muslin—with the buttonhole edge *on the inside of the wire* (work the buttonhole stitches close together—not too tight). The satin stitch base will be worked over this buttonhole edge (for support), inside the wire.

2. Using one strand of pale antique mauve thread, cover the petal with horizontal satin stitch, worked *into* the buttonhole stitch—between the wire and the buttonholed edge (start in the middle and work the stitches very close together).

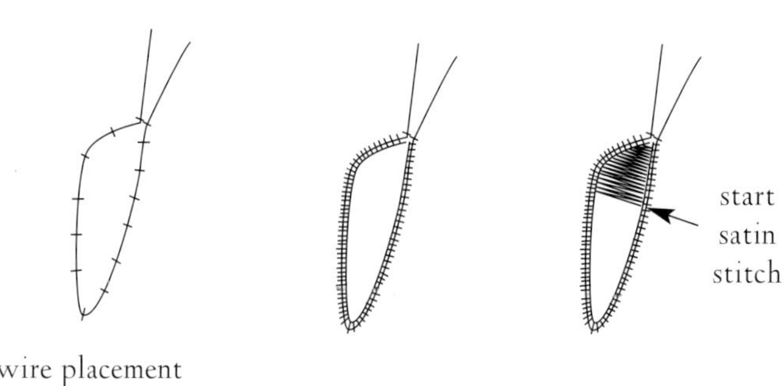

3. Starting close to the outside edge of the petal, weave a row vertically (slightly curved), over and under approximately four threads, with one strand of dark antique mauve thread; work three more rows (three dark mauve and one medium mauve, in any order) to complete the first column of weaving. The second and third columns of weaving are worked concurrently, on either side of the first column. Continue weaving columns only on the inside edge of the petal until the shape is filled (forcing the first three columns close to the outside edge of the petal).

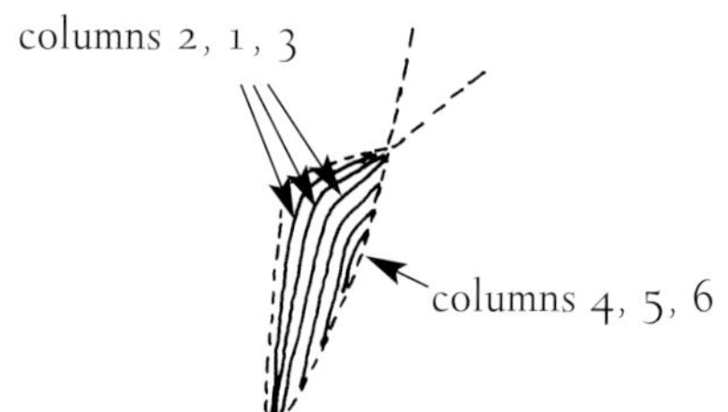

DETACHED MIDDLE PETAL

1. Using one strand of medium antique mauve thread, couch wire around the outline, leaving two wire tails (the wires touch but do not cross at the base of the petal). Buttonhole stitch the wire to the muslin—with the buttonhole edge on the inside of the wire (do not pull the buttonhole stitches too tight).

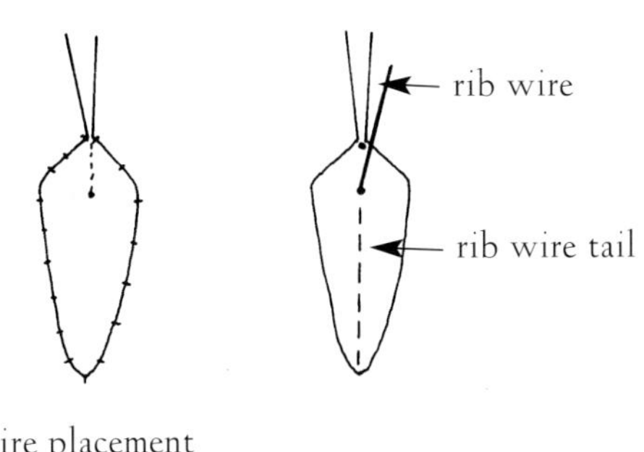

wire placement

2. To form the rib of the fritillary petal, insert one tail of a short length of flower wire at the end of the rib line (•) and secure to the back of the petal (keep the remaining wire tail free until the petal surface has been covered in satin stitch).

3. Using one strand of pale antique mauve thread, cover the petal with horizontal satin stitch, worked *into* the buttonhole stitch (between the wire and the buttonholed edge). Starting at the wire insertion point, satin stitch to the base of the petal, then to the top of the petal, working the stitches very close together. Insert the remaining wire tail at the base of the petal, inside the wires (hold tail out of the way with masking tape).

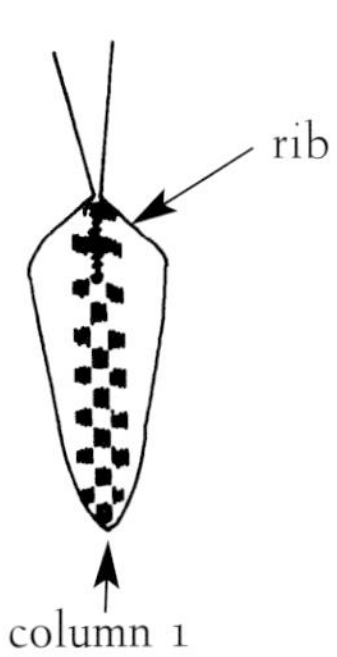

4. With one strand of dark antique mauve thread, overcast the rib wire to the fabric, through the satin stitch. Trim the wire tail.

5. Starting in the middle, below the wire insertion point • , weave a row vertically, over and under approximately four threads, with one strand of dark antique mauve thread; work three more rows (three dark mauve and one medium mauve, in

any order) to complete the first column of weaving. The second and third columns of weaving are worked concurrently, on either side of the first column, and on either side of the rib. Continue weaving columns of dark mauve and medium mauve threads, on either side of the previous weaving, until the shape is filled. Work short columns at the side edges if necessary to give a good shape.

To complete the fritillary flowers

Carefully cut out the petals. Apply the two side petals over the surface petals and stamen, inserting the wires at the end of the stem. Bend the wires under the flower and secure to the back. Apply the middle petal through the same hole, and secure. Cover the wire insertion points with stitches in green thread if necessary. Shape the petals into a lantern shape with tweezers. The petals can be held in place with invisible stitches in nylon thread, if desired.

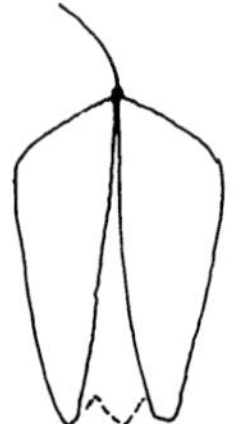

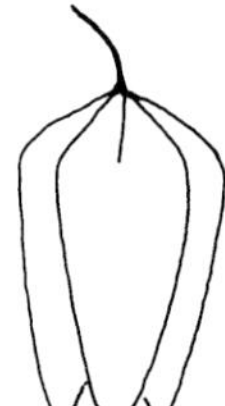

Detached bud petal

1. Mount muslin into the 10 cm (4 in) embroidery hoop and trace the bud petal. Cut a 10 cm (4 in) length of flower wire (colour antique mauve, if desired). Using one strand of medium antique mauve thread, couch wire around the outline, leaving two wire tails (the wires touch but do not cross at the base of the petal). Buttonhole stitch the wire to the muslin—with the buttonhole edge *on the inside of the wire.*

2. Using one strand of medium antique mauve thread, cover the petal with horizontal satin stitch, worked *into* the buttonhole stitch.

3. Starting in the middle, weave a row vertically, over and under approximately four threads, with one strand of dark antique mauve thread; work three more rows to complete the first column of weaving. The second and third columns of weaving are worked concurrently, on either side of the first column (this helps to give a slightly curved shape to the weaving). Continue weaving in this way until the shape is filled.

4. Cut out and apply the petal to cover the surface petal, inserting the wires at the end of the stem. Bend the wires back under the petal, secure and trim.

DETACHED FRITILLARY LEAVES

Mount muslin into the 15 cm (6 in) hoop and trace the larger leaf outline (and the 'fold' line) in the centre of the hoop (this is to facilitate the working, as half of the leaf will be stitched on the back to allow it to fold over when applied). Trace the smaller leaf at the side. Cut two lengths of flower wire, 15 and 25 cm (6 and 10 in) (coloured green if desired).

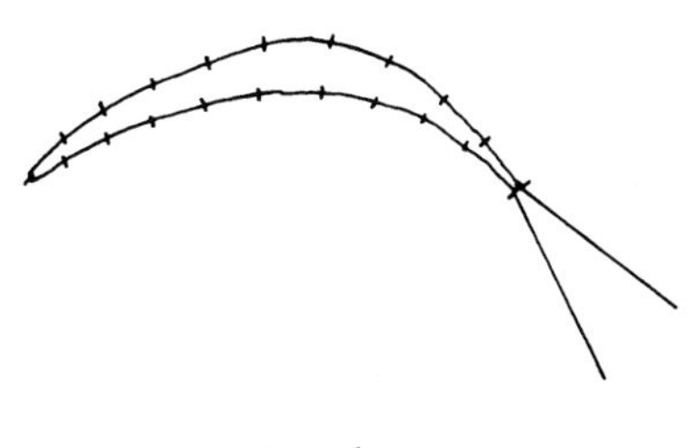

wire placement

LEFT LEAF

Using one strand of dark green thread, couch the shorter length of wire around the outline. Buttonhole stitch the wire to the muslin (leaving two tails of wire—do not cross the wires). Embroider the leaf, inside the wire, with rows of stem stitch (stem stitch filling), working the rows alternately in one strand of dark and medium green thread.

RIGHT LEAF

One half of the leaf is embroidered on the front of the muslin; the other half (the tip) is embroidered on the back—this enables the leaf to fold over when applied.

1. Using one strand of dark green thread, couch the longer length of wire around the leaf outline, inserting the wire through to the back at the points marked (fold line), leaving the wire tails on the front. The tip end of the leaf is couched on the back, using the tracing on the front as a guide.

2. Buttonhole stitch the wire to the muslin using one strand of dark green thread, around the outside edge of the leaf, working sections 1 and 3 on the front of the muslin (leaving two tails of wire on the front—do not cross the wires) and section 2 on the back.

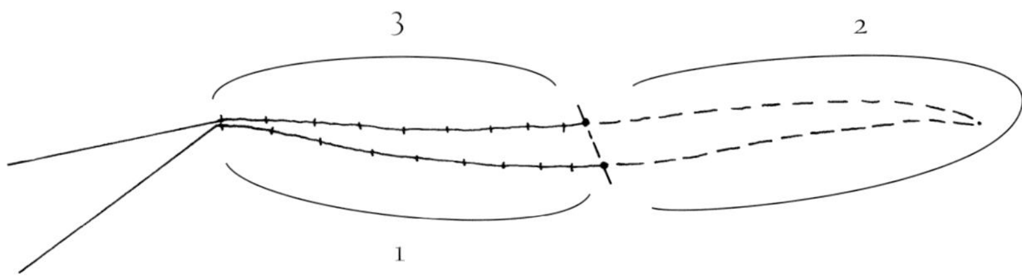

3. Embroider the leaf in stem stitch filling, working the rows alternately in one strand of dark and medium green thread. Work one half of the leaf on the front and the other half (the tip) on the back. Take care when working the section on either side of the wire insertion points, as this will be the fold when the leaf is applied.

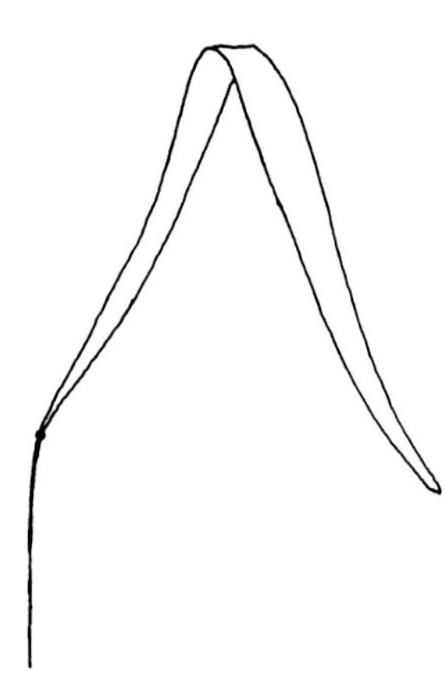

4. Carefully cut out the leaves and insert the wires through to the back; the left leaf at the junction of the left fritillary stem, and the right leaf at the end of the middle stem. Secure the wires at the back of the stems, then trim. Bend the right leaf at the fold line, bringing the tip of the leaf to the front in a smooth curve.

SCARAB BEETLE

Follow the instructions for the Scarab Beetle on page 165, working the abdomen on the background fabric (step 5, order of work) after completing the fritillary flowers, and completing the beetle as step 8 in the order of work.

Beetle and Boysenberries

Work a bronze Scarab Beetle, or other similarly sized beetle, inside a garland of beaded boysenberries, then frame, or mount into a paperweight, gilt bowl or music box.

Requirements

- ivory silk or satin, 20 cm (8 in) square
- quilter's muslin (or fine calico) for backing, 20 cm (8 in) square
- 10 cm (4 in) embroidery hoop

Boysenberries (see opposite page)

Scarab Beetle (see page 165)

Paperweight, gilt bowl or music box

Order of work

1. Mount the background fabric and the backing fabric into the embroidery hoop.
2. Trace the skeleton outline onto the background fabric.
3. Boysenberry stems and leaves.
4. Beetle abdomen (then trace the beetle legs onto the backing fabric).
5. Boysenberries.

actual size
skeleton outline

6. Complete the beetle.
7. Mount the finished piece into a small paperweight (see pages 386–387).

BOYSENBERRIES

Materials required

- Mill Hill frosted glass beads (62056 boysenberry)
- Mill Hill frosted glass beads (60367 garnet)
- Mill Hill glass seed beads (367 garnet)
- dark green stranded thread (Soie d'Alger 2126 or DMC 3345)
- medium green stranded thread (Soie d'Alger 2125 or DMC 3346)
- dark purple stranded thread (Soie d'Alger 3326 or DMC 154)

STEMS

Embroider the stems in chain stitch with one strand of dark green thread.

LEAVES

Embroider the leaves in fishbone stitch with one strand of dark green thread.

BOYSENBERRIES

The centres of the boysenberries are indicated by the short lines on the design outline. The berries are formed by stitching beads on to the satin, in two layers, using one strand of dark purple thread. Apply the beads one at a time, selecting the colours at random.

LOWER LAYER

a. Stitch two beads on the centre line.

b. Back stitch nine beads around the two centre beads, then run three rounds of thread through these beads (like a necklace) to draw them into a tight oval

UPPER LAYER

c. Stitch one bead in the centre, over the lower layer (take the needle between the beads in the lower layer and through to the back)

d. Back stitch seven beads around the centre bead (take the needle between the in the lower layer and through to the back), then run three rounds of thread through these beads to draw them into a tight oval and secure the thread at the back

SEPALS

Work three or four detached chain stitches at the base of each boysenberry with one strand of medium green thread.

SCARAB BEETLE

Follow the instructions for the Scarab Beetle on page 165 (or any beetle you prefer), working the abdomen on the background fabric (step 4, order of work) after completing the surface embroidery for the boysenberries, and completing the beetle as step 6 in the order of work.

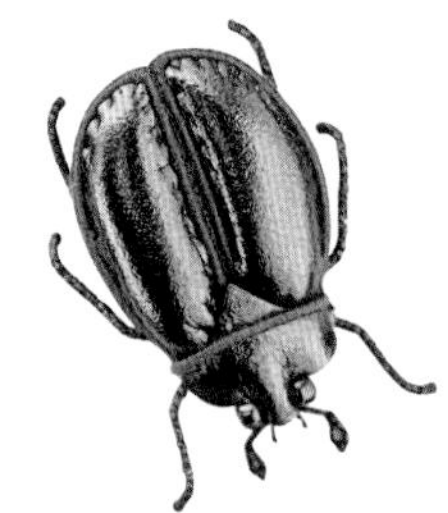

MOUNTING

Mount the finished work in a paperweight following the suggestions given on pages 386–387, or perhaps into a gilt bowl or music box.

Scarab Beetle Brooch

A single Scarab Beetle looks gorgeous mounted as a brooch, or into the lid of an oval black porcelain bowl. My beetle was worked with green emu-leg skin, embroidered on a background of burnt orange-gold kimono silk. A scarab can be worked in a variety of leathers—green, bronze, grey-violet metallic or dark mahogany—on a rich burnt orange or ivory silk background.

Requirements

- burnt orange dupion, 15 cm (6 in) square (or colour of your choice).
- quilter's muslin (or fine calico) for backing, 15 cm (6 in) square
- 10 cm (4 in) embroidery hoop
- brooch back, 40 x 30 mm oval (1 1/2 x 1 1/8 in)
- double-sided adhesive tape or Jac paper
- template plastic or thin card

Follow the instructions for the Scarab Beetle on pages 165–168, substituting as required for the different colours.

DARK GREEN SCARAB BEETLE

- quilter's muslin or dark green cotton (homespun), 15 cm (6 in) square
- black felt and Vliesofix
- dark green kid
- dark green stranded thread (Soie d'Alger 1846)

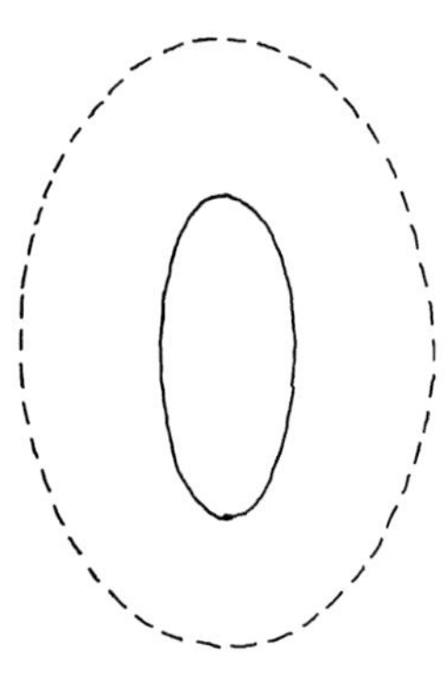

actual size
skeleton outline

- dark purple stranded thread (Soie d'Alger 3326 or DMC 310)
- brown metallic thread (Kreinik Very Fine (#4) Braid 154V)
- nylon thread (Madeira Monofil No.60, clear)
- Mill Hill seed beads (374 blue-black)
- 30-gauge green-covered wire, cut in 18 cm (7 in) lengths

DARK MAHOGANY SCARAB BEETLE

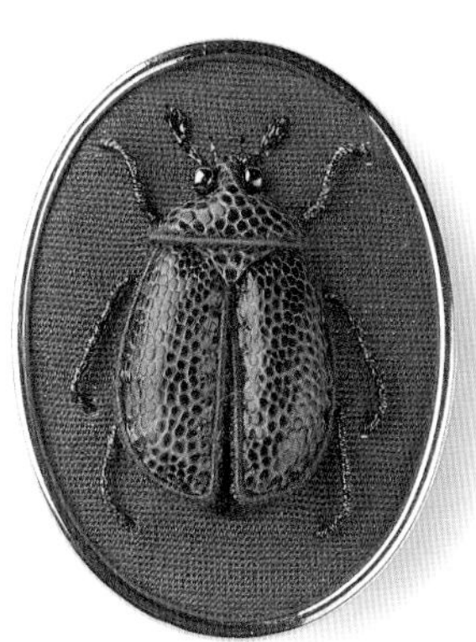

- quilter's muslin or dark brown cotton (homespun), 15 cm (6 in) square
- black felt and Vliesofix
- dark mahogany metallic leather
- dark mahogany stranded thread (Soie d'Alger 4144)
- dark purple stranded thread (Soie d'Alger 3326 or DMC 310)
- brown metallic thread (Kreinik Very Fine (#4) Braid 154V
- nylon thread (Madeira Monofil No. 60, clear)
- Mill Hill seed beads (374 blue black)
- 30-gauge green-covered wire, cut in 18 cm (7 in) lengths

GREY/VIOLET SCARAB BEETLE

- quilter's muslin or grey/violet cotton (homespun), 15 cm (6 in) square
- black felt and Vliesofix
- grey/violet metallic leather
- grey/violet stranded thread (Soie d'Alger 3415)

- dark purple stranded thread (Soie d'Alger 3326 or DMC 310)
- grey metallic thread (Kreinik Very Fine (#4) Braid 010HL)
- nylon thread (Madeira Monofil No. 60, clear)
- Mill Hill seed beads (374 blue black)
- 30-gauge green-covered wire, cut in 18 cm (7 in) lengths

Order of work

1. Mount the silk and muslin backing into the embroidery hoop. Trace the skeleton outline onto the backing fabric.

2. Work the scarab beetle.

3. Mount the project into an oval gilt frame as follows: Cut an oval out of template plastic to fit inside the brooch back, and trim the muslin backing to an oval slightly smaller than the template plastic. With a small seam allowance, gather the background fabric over the template plastic oval. (Insert a layer of thin padding between the fabric and the template plastic if desired.) Insert the embroidery into the brooch, using double-sided adhesive to secure. If using a Framecraft brooch, mount the embroidery into the frame and secure with the backing plate as instructed.

Part 5: Goldwork Beetles

Gold, one of the first metals to be discovered by early man and valued for its beauty and malleability, was originally associated with myth and magic, and with the worship of the sun, later also becoming a symbol of status and wealth. Gold and precious jewels have long been used to embellish hangings, furnishings, tents, trappings and garments. The Egyptians, Assyrians and Babylonians have left descriptions of their gilded textiles, and in the Bible the Old Testament describes how 'gold leaf was hammered out and cut into threads to work into the blue and purple and the scarlet stuff, and into the fine twined linen in skilled design' (Exodus 39: 3).

The first gold threads were strands of beaten pure gold, cut into narrow strips from the flattened metal. However, once the technique of bonding gold to silver was discovered, the original pure gold flat strip developed into a gilded silver strip, which could be drawn into a wire of any thickness and still retain its gold coating. The gilded wire could then be hammered flat, wrapped around a silk core and used for couching; or coiled into bullions and purls to be used as gold beads.

Gold thread originally came from the East, travelling slowly across Central Asia via the silk caravans to the West, where its use became widespread. Goldwork reached a peak in the mediaeval period, when the highly regarded 'English work' or opus anglicanum was in demand all over Europe. Gold and metal threads were used extensively on the domestic embroideries of the Elizabethan era, particularly in combination with blackwork and silk embroidery, and continued to embellish dress and court attire until almost the end of the eighteenth century.

Metal thread embroidery, still employed for ecclesiastical and ceremonial items, is perhaps the most challenging and exciting technique available to the embroiderer. The attraction of goldwork is not just the colour—the different textures the various threads produce, and the interesting play of light obtained from a myriad padding and couching techniques, are a continual source of delight, whether used in traditional or more experimental ways.

Note: 'Goldwork' refers to the technique rather than to the choice of metal, as silver, copper and a whole range of colours can be included in this form of embroidery. I have used the term 'gold' in reference to thread colour only, as very few threads containing real gold are available today.

How to Embroider a Goldwork Beetle

The beetle, with its perfect symmetry, variety of shapes and often metallic colouration, makes a wonderful subject for interpretation in goldwork. Some of the scarabs (from the genus *Chrysina*) have colours that appear to be made of polished metal—some gold, some silver, some with a golden thorax and silver elytra.

This chapter contains diagrams and instructions for embroidering an assortment of beetles, drawn from the Specimen Box, in a variety of goldwork techniques, and concludes with a section on 'goldwork stumpwork'. As there is not the space in this book to provide detailed instructions on goldwork techniques and threads, please refer to one of the goldwork books available, some of which are listed in the Bibliography.

Silver and gold scarab beetles.

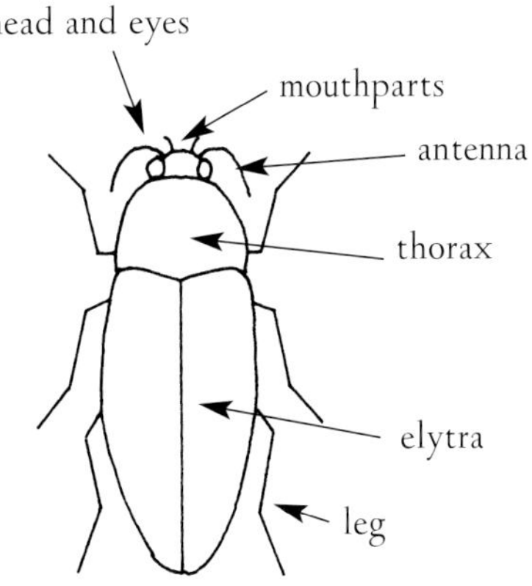

Beetle parts to embroider.

Order of work

A goldwork beetle is usually embroidered in the following order: elytra, thorax, head and eyes, antennae and finally the legs.

Tools

In addition to your regular embroidery equipment, the following tools will be useful.

Frames and hoops

An embroidery frame or hoop, larger than the design being worked, is essential for goldwork, as the fabrics must be kept taut at all times. If working a small piece, a hoop is suitable—bind the inner ring with tape to prevent slipping. For larger work, use a slate or square frame. Refer to a goldwork manual for instructions on dressing a slate frame.

NEEDLES

- *Sharps* size 8 or 9: use with metallic sewing thread for couching metal threads.
- *Sharps* size 11 or 12: use with silk and nylon sewing threads for couching metal threads and applying beads.
- *Crewel/embroidery* sizes 8–10: use with embroidery threads, and with polyester thread for couching metal threads, tacking and general stitching.
- *Straw/milliners* sizes 3–9: use for stitching with metallic threads.
- *Chenille* sizes 18–22 or *sharp yarn darners* sizes 14–18: use to sink thread ends and to stitch with thicker metallic threads. The largest darner can be used as a stiletto.

BEESWAX

The silk, metallic, cotton or polyester sewing thread used for applying metallics should be pulled over a block of beeswax to give it a protective coating, which strengthens the thread and helps prevent fraying. Run the thread between your fingers (away from your work) before you stitch to remove any loose flakes of wax.

SCISSORS

Small, strong scissors with sharp points (such as nail scissors) are required to cut the metal threads. Do not use your embroidery scissors.

CUTTING BOARD

A small square of cardboard covered with velveteen makes a good surface for cutting metal purl into accurate lengths, as it helps stop the pieces from jumping about.

TWEEZERS

Fine tweezers are useful for picking up small pieces of purl, and for manipulating it around points and corners.

Mellor

A mellor is a traditional goldwork tool, with one sharp pointed end which can be used as a stiletto, and a rounded end which is used for manipulating metal threads into position. An old metal nailfile makes a good substitute.

Materials

Background fabric

Almost any closely woven fabric can be used as a background for goldwork, such as silk, satin, linen, velvet and wool flannel. Silk, with its rich lustre, is a popular choice.

Backing fabric

A backing fabric of calico or linen is essential for most goldwork. The weight of the backing fabric is determined by the amount of support required for the metal threads being used.

Padding

Goldwork depends on reflected light for many of its effects and this is often achieved by the use of a variety of padding materials. Yellow felt and dyed, smooth cotton string have been used to pad the beetles: the felt, often applied in several layers, as padding under gold thread and metallic leather; the string, couched into rows, as a padding for basket stitch with metal threads.

Leather

Metallic coated leather or kid is used to provide a smooth, gleaming contrast in goldwork. Apply leather with fine silk or nylon thread, over padding, for best results.

Spangles and beads

Spangles, small circular shapes made from flattened gold wire, and beads can be used to embellish goldwork. Apply with fine gold or nylon thread.

Threads

Goldwork is an embroidery technique where the majority of gold threads are applied to the background with another sewing thread, either by means of couching, or cut into appropriate lengths and sewn down like beads. As gold thread is quite fragile, very few are actually sewn through fabric. There is a bewildering array of gold and metallic threads available to the embroiderer, varying greatly in quality, price and construction. The following information relates only to the goldwork threads used for the beetles, listed in groups for easy reference.

Sewing threads

The following threads, coated with beeswax, are used to couch or apply metal threads:

- fine metallic thread (YLI Metallic Yarn col. Gold)
- fine silk thread (YLI Silk Thread #100 col. 215 or #50 col. 79)
- polyester thread (Gütermann col. 488)
- clear nylon thread (Madeira Monofil No.60 col. 1001)
- one strand of stranded cotton, either gold or a colour

Couched gold threads

This group of threads is couched down with a beeswaxed sewing thread. Some of them can also be sewn through fabric.

Jap gold (Japanese gold)

Japanese gold, known as Jap gold, was originally made from a flattened strip of real gold or gilded silver, wrapped around a silk core. These days it has been replaced with substitute Jap gold, or the much easier to work imitation Jap gold, which is available in four sizes—T69, T70, T71 and T72 (T72 being the finest). The goldwork beetles use imitation Jap gold which, for convenience, is referred to as Jap gold.

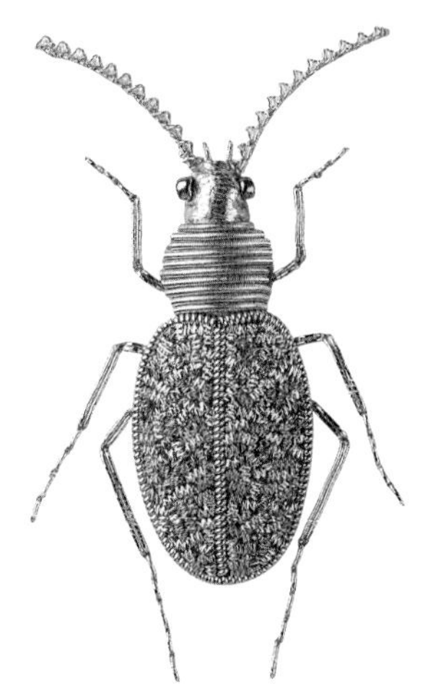

Passing thread

Smooth passing thread, similar to Jap gold in appearance although less shiny, is made by wrapping a very fine wire around a soft thread core. Usually couched on the surface, smooth passing thread can also be sewn through fabric.

Couching thread

A synthetic version of passing thread, referred to as couching thread, can be obtained in a variety of colours as well as gold (often called Jacobean gold). An English version of this thread, Standard Couching Thread 371, is used in these projects. Couching thread, usually couched on the surface, can be also sewn through fabric.

Rococo (Check) thread

Rococo is a gold thread with a crinkled, wavy finish, available in several sizes.

Twists

Twists are made from two or more strands of metal thread twisted together and are available in many different sizes and combinations.

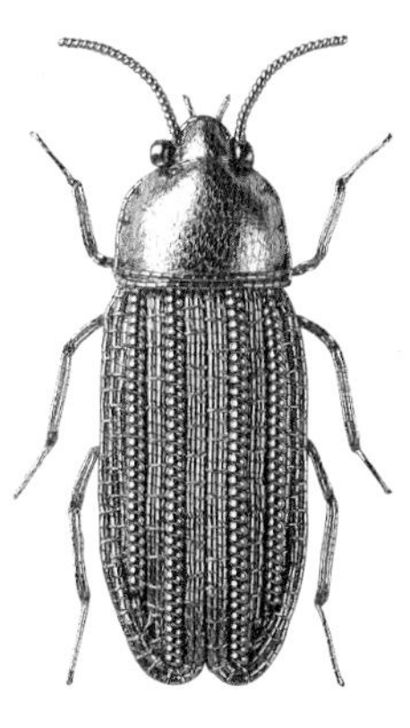

Milliary

Milliary is a fancy goldwork thread consisting of a stretched coil of metal wire whipped onto a fine smooth metal thread. It is available in gold, silver and copper.

Broad plate

Broad plate is a thin flat strip of metal that can be couched down. It is available in several widths.

Pearl Purl

(See Cut Gold Threads.) Pearl Purl, often used for the outline of a design, is couched onto the surface with stitches that are pulled firmly between the coils of the metal thread (thus

being invisible). It is available in several sizes, size 3 being larger than size 1, and super pearl purl the smallest. It can also be cut into lengths and sewn on like a bead.

Cut gold threads

The metal threads called purls are cut into appropriate lengths and sewn down like beads, mostly over padding, using a beeswaxed sewing thread. Purls, made from a very fine wire, tightly coiled around a long needle to make a hollow spring, are available in many qualities, textures, colours and sizes, with size 8 being smaller than size 6.

Note: When working with cut purls, the pieces must be cut to an accurate length and applied with a stitch of the same length. If the purl is too long, it will bulge above the surface; if too short, there will be a gap at the edge.

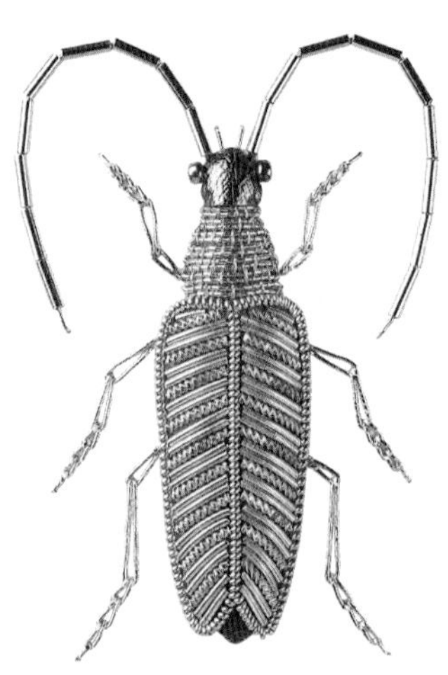

Smooth Purl

Smooth Purl is a smooth coil with a very shiny smooth surface.

Rough Purl

Rough Purl, a smooth coil with a dull surface, is also available in a range of colours.

Bright Check Purl

Bright Check Purl, made by coiling wire around a square or triangular needle, is a faceted coil which reflects light in a glittering fashion.

Pearl Purl

Pearl Purl is made with a thicker wire than purl wires, producing a stiff but pliable coil of wire. It is usually couched on to the surface with a waxed sewing thread, but it can also be cut into lengths and sewn on like a bead. It is available in several sizes, size 3 being larger than size 1, and super pearl purl being the smallest.

SYNTHETIC METALLIC EMBROIDERY THREADS

Synthetic metallic embroidery threads, usually a mixture of rayon and polyester, are made for all types of needlework, both hand and machine. These threads are available in a wide range of colours, textures and thicknesses, and can be couched on to the surface or sewn through the fabric.

Goldwork Beetle Sampler

This collection of five gold beetles is worked with a variety of gold threads using traditional goldwork techniques. They may also be worked individually, or perhaps three beetles could be displayed in a specimen box.

Requirements

- cream silk, at least 20 x 35 cm (8 x 14 in)
- calico backing fabric
- 45 cm (18 in) slate or square frame
- yellow felt
- yellow or cream silk organza

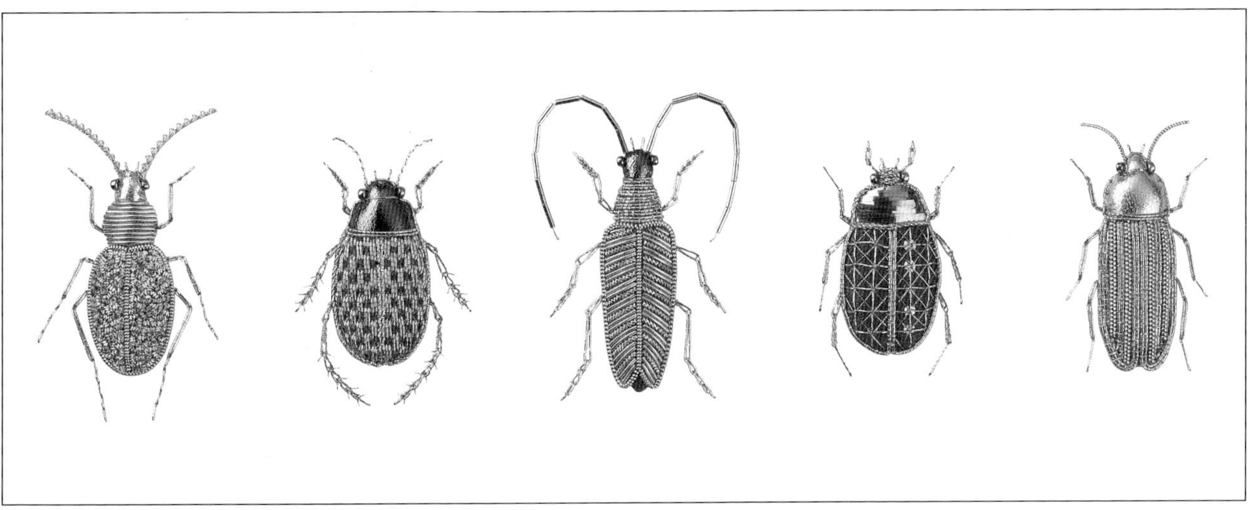

Goldwork Beetle Sampler

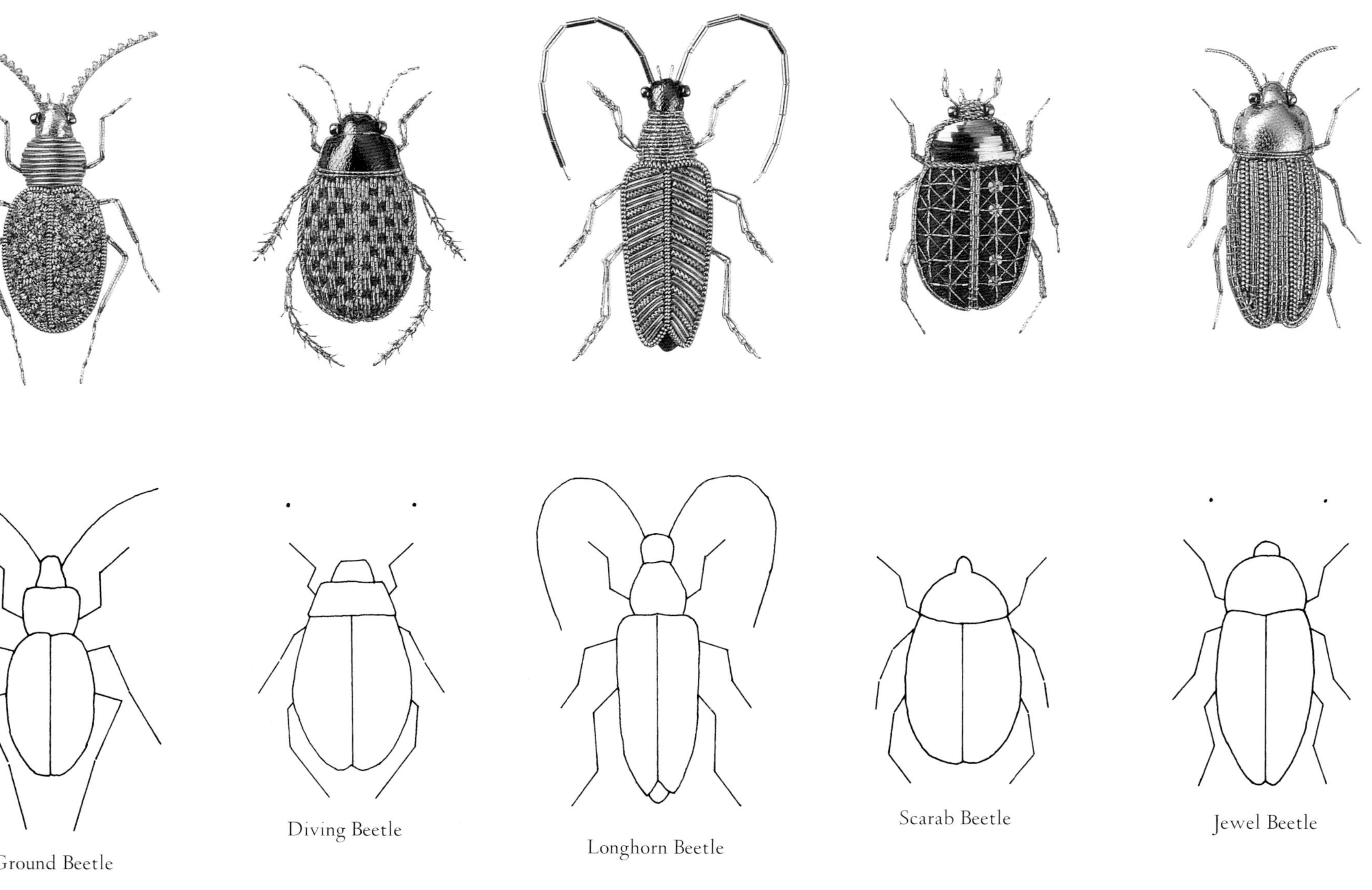
Ground Beetle
Diving Beetle
Longhorn Beetle
Scarab Beetle
Jewel Beetle
actual size
skeleton outlines

- Vliesofix
- silk sewing thread (YLI Silk Thread #100 col. 215)
- metallic sewing thread (YLI Metallic Yarn col. Gold)
- polyester sewing thread (Gütermann col. 488)
- clear nylon thread (Madeira Monofil No.60 col. 1001)

Gold Ground Beetle (see page 240)

Gold Diving Beetle (see page 242)

Gold Longhorn Beetle (see page 244)

Gold Scarab Beetle (see page 245)

Gold Jewel Beetle (see page 247)

Preparation

1. Mount the cream silk and calico backing into a square frame, making sure that both fabrics are drum tight.

2. Trace the skeleton outlines of the beetles onto the calico backing. The beetles will be embroidered using these outlines as a guide.

3. Each beetle is padded with four layers of felt—one the actual size of the skeleton outline and three successively smaller. To obtain an accurate outline, and to provide guidelines on the top layer, use the following method to cut the four layers. For each step, use baking parchment (GLAD Bake) to protect the iron and the ironing board:

- iron/fuse Vliesofix to silk organza;
- place the fused organza, silk side up, over the padding outlines; using a fine lead pencil, trace all outlines (including the internal lines of the top layer);
- remove the paper backing and iron/fuse the organza to the felt, then carefully cut out the four shapes.

With polyester thread, stitch each layer of felt to the background fabric (silk side up), with small stab stitches around the outside edge, applying the smallest layer first. Use the skeleton outline on the backing as a guide. Stitching through all layers of felt, work a row of back stitches along all the traced internal lines (centre line of elytra, thorax and head lines). These will be used as a guide when embroidering the beetles (and also help to mould the felt into the body parts).

Gold Ground Beetle

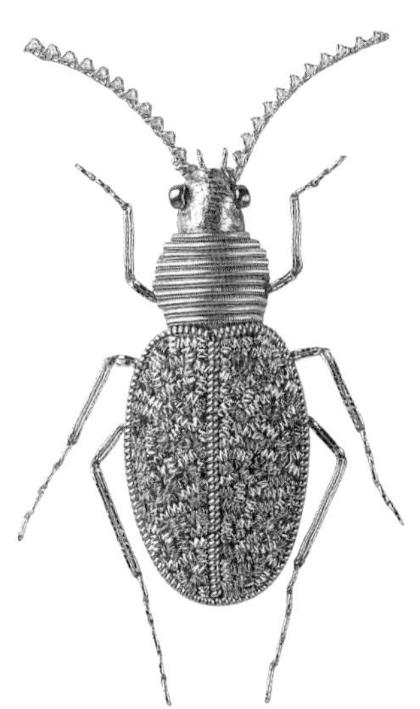

Materials required

- silk, metallic and nylon sewing threads (beeswaxed)
- gold No.1 Pearl Purl
- gold No.8 Smooth Purl
- gold No.8 Bright Check Purl
- gold Milliary
- gold Couching Thread 371
- gold leather
- Mill Hill antique beads (3037 abalone)

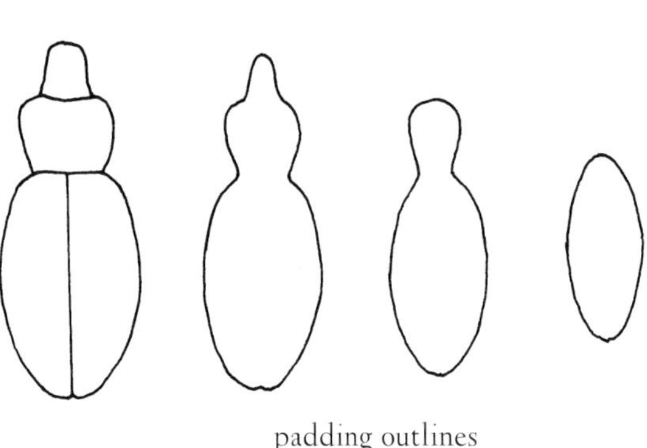

padding outlines

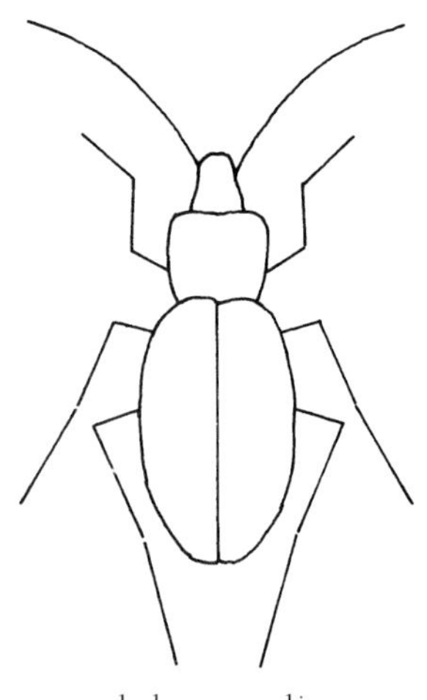

skeleton outline

Elytra

Using silk sewing thread, couch gold Pearl Purl around the edge and down the centre line of the elytra. Fill the elytra with Bright Check Purl chips, sewn on individually in as many different directions as possible.

Thorax

Cover the thorax with lengths of gold Smooth Purl, cut to appropriate lengths, stitched in place with silk sewing thread.

Head and eyes

head shape

Cut a head shape from gold leather and stitch in place with nylon thread. Apply two beads for the eyes.

Antennae

Cut a length of Milliary for each antenna. Using the outline on the back of the fabric as a guide, couch in place with nylon thread.

Legs and mouthparts

Using two strands of gold Couching Thread, work the inner leg segments with straight stitches. With one strand of thread, embroider each outer leg segment in back stitch. Work two straight stitches between the antennae for the mouthparts.

Gold Diving Beetle

Materials required

- silk, metallic, polyester and nylon sewing threads (beeswaxed)
- bronze stranded thread (Soie d'Alger 526 or DMC 829)
- smooth string for padding
- gold No.3 Twist
- fine gold Rococo Thread
- Jap gold T71
- fine gold twisted metallic thread (Au Papillon Fil d'Or)
- bronze leather
- Mill Hill antique beads (3037 abalone)

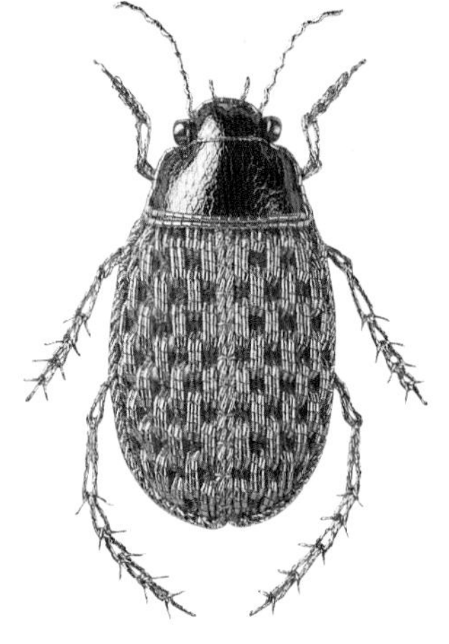

Elytra

The elytra is covered in Jap gold couched in a basket pattern over string padding.

1. Using polyester thread, sew down a foundation of nine bars of string, a string width apart, across the elytra.

2. Couch a row of double gold Twist down the centre line of the elytra with metallic sewing thread, retaining the tails of gold Twist to outline the elytra at the end.

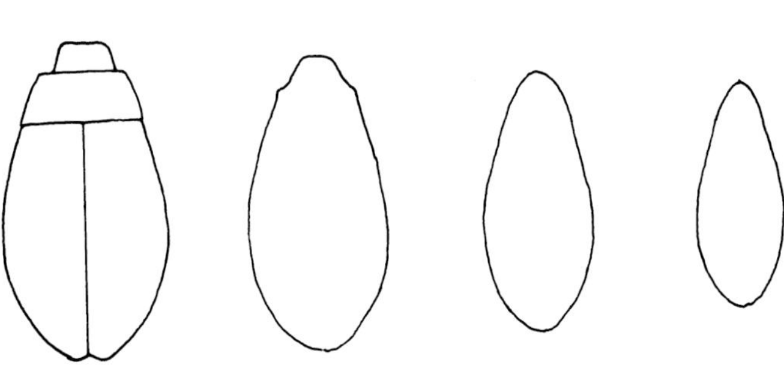

padding outlines

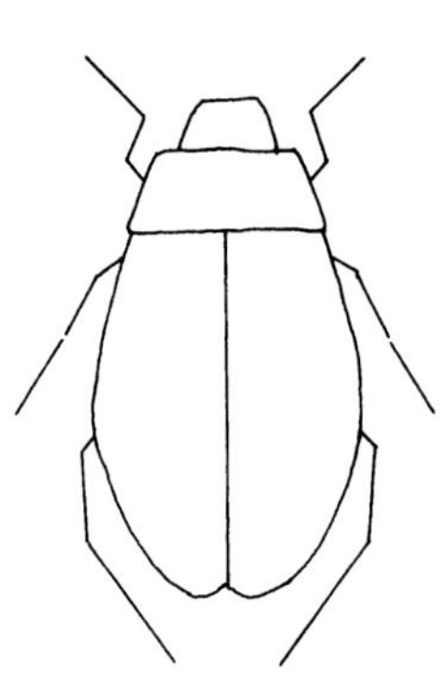

skeleton outline

3. Couch rows of double Jap gold over the string padding, on either side of the centre line, to cover the elytra (sink the tails at the end of each row). To form a basket pattern, couch the gold thread over every second string, with a firm double stitch using bronze thread. Couch the next row of gold in the alternate spaces to form a basket pattern.

4. Using the retained tails, couch a line of gold Twist around the edge of the elytra.

THORAX, HEAD AND EYES

thorax–head shape

Cut a thorax–head shape from bronze leather and stitch in place with nylon thread. Outline the shape with couched Jap gold; single around the outside edge; double between the thorax and elytra (secure at the corners only). With a double strand of metallic sewing thread, work a stitch across the leather to define the head. Apply two beads for the eyes.

ANTENNAE

Each antenna is a straight stitch worked with a single strand of gold Rococo thread, couched into a curve with nylon thread.

LEGS AND MOUTHPARTS

Using gold Fil d'Or, work two chain stitches for the inner segments of each leg. Work each outer leg segment with three of four chain stitches. Work two straight stitches between the antennae for the mouthparts. The hairs on the back legs are straight stitches using gold sewing thread.

Gold Longhorn Beetle

Materials required

- silk, metallic and nylon sewing threads (beeswaxed)
- bronze stranded thread (Soie d'Alger 526 or DMC 829)
- gold No.1 Pearl Purl
- gold No.8 Smooth Purl
- gold No.8 Bright Check Purl
- Jap gold T71
- gold Couching Thread 371
- bronze leather
- gold metal bugle beads (or Jap Gold T69)
- Mill Hill antique beads (3037 abalone)

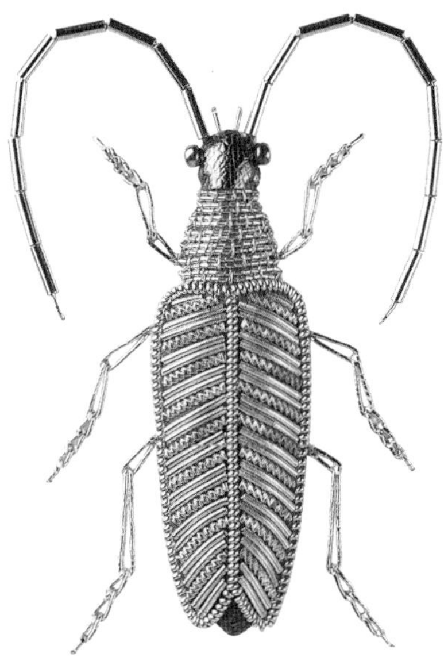

Elytra

Satin stitch the tail of the abdomen with one strand of bronze thread. Using silk sewing thread, couch gold Pearl Purl around the edge and down the centre line of the elytra. Starting at the tail end, cover the elytra, inside the Pearl Purl outline, with lengths of cut purl, stitching down two lengths of Smooth Purl, then one length of Bright Check Purl, alternately.

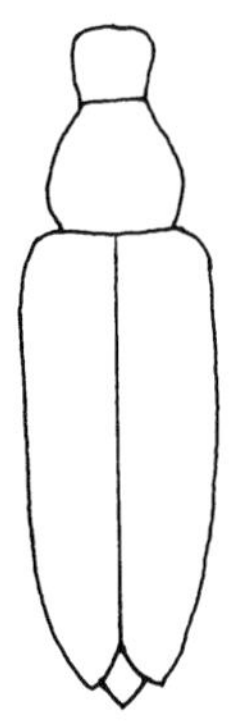

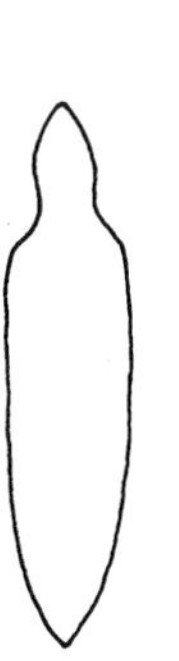

padding outlines

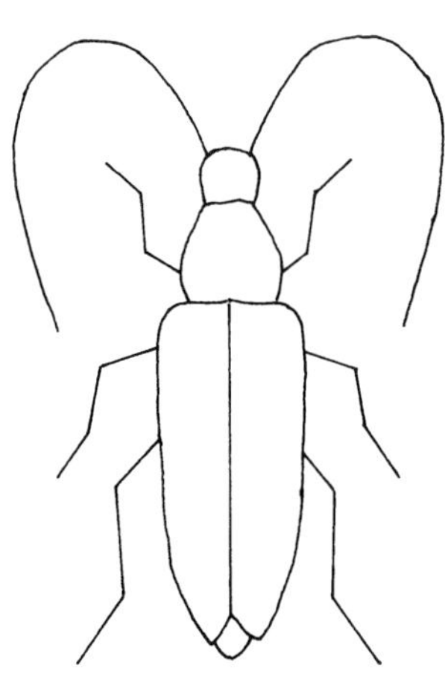

skeleton outline

THORAX

Cover the thorax with couched Jap gold, using metallic sewing thread.

head shape

HEAD AND EYES

Cut a head shape from bronze leather and stitch in place with nylon thread. Apply two beads for the eyes.

ANTENNAE

Thread nine bugle beads on to a length of gold Couching Thread for each antenna. Using the outline on the back as a guide, couch in place with nylon thread, working a stitch between each bead, sinking the gold thread tails through to the back at each end. Alternatively, couch the antennae in Jap gold T69, using the outline on the back of the fabric as a guide.

LEGS AND MOUTHPARTS

Using gold Couching Thread, work two chain stitches for the inner segments of each leg. Work each outer leg segment with three chain stitches. Work two straight stitches between the antennae for the mouthparts.

Gold Scarab Beetle

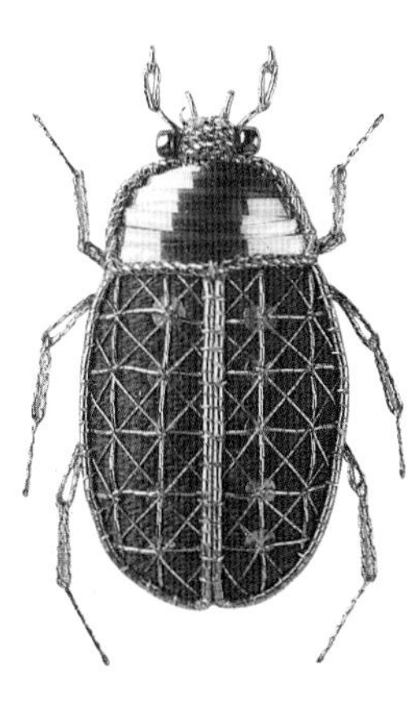

Materials required

- silk and metallic sewing threads (beeswaxed)
- bronze stranded thread (Soie d'Alger 526 or DMC 829)
- Jap Gold T72
- Jap Gold T70
- gold Broad Plate (width 2 mm)
- gold No.3 Twist
- gold Couching Thread 371

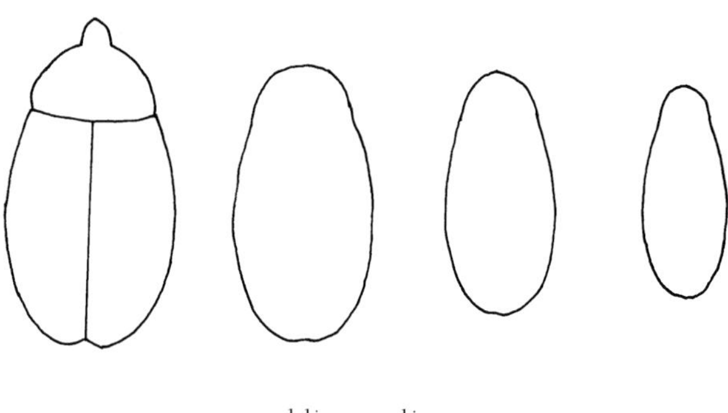
padding outlines

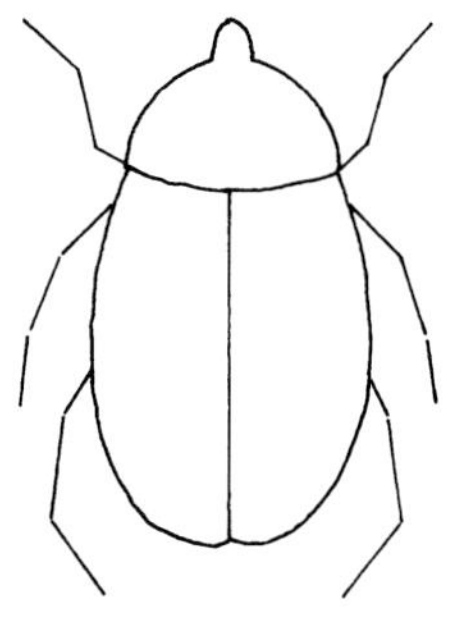
skeleton outline

- fine gold twisted metallic thread (Au Papillon Fil d'Or)
- gold spangles (2 mm)
- Mill Hill antique beads (3037 abalone)

Elytra

Work satin stitch across the elytra with one strand of bronze thread. Cover the elytra with an open laid work filling, worked with two weights of metallic thread. Stitch a square grid first with the Jap gold T72 (thicker thread), then work a diagonal grid with the metallic sewing thread (finer thread). Using metallic sewing thread, work a securing stitch where both grids intersect, catching in a tiny gold spangle if desired (optional). Couch a row of double Jap gold T70 down the centre line of the elytra, and a single row around the outside edge.

Thorax

Cover the thorax with couched Broad Plate, using silk sewing thread. Start couching at the top edge and work in a zigzag down to the elytra. Outline the thorax with a line of gold Twist, couched with metallic sewing thread.

Head and eyes

Work the head in satin stitches with gold Twist. Apply two beads for the eyes.

ANTENNAE AND MOUTHPARTS

Using gold Couching Thread, work each antenna with a straight stitch and a chain stitch. Work two straight stitches between the antennae for the mouthparts.

LEGS

Each leg is worked with two chain stitches and a straight stitch, using gold Fil d'Or (it is easier to work reverse chain stitch, starting with the straight stitch).

GOLD JEWEL BEETLE

Materials required

- silk, metallic and nylon sewing threads (beeswaxed)
- gold No.2 Pearl Purl
- gold Super Pearl Purl
- Jap Gold T69
- Jap Gold T70
- gold Couching Thread 371
- gold leather
- Mill Hill antique beads (3037 abalone)

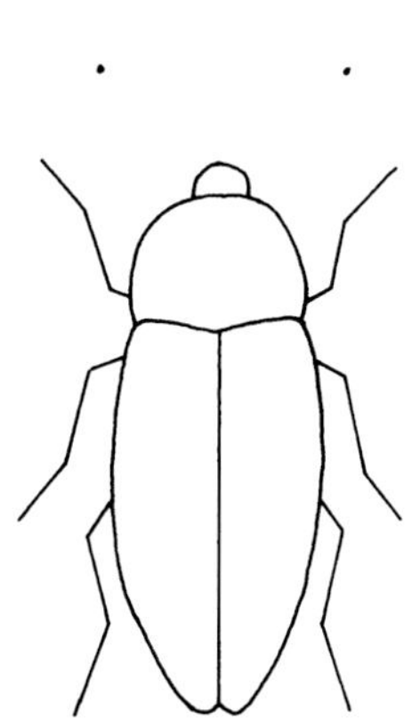

skeleton outline

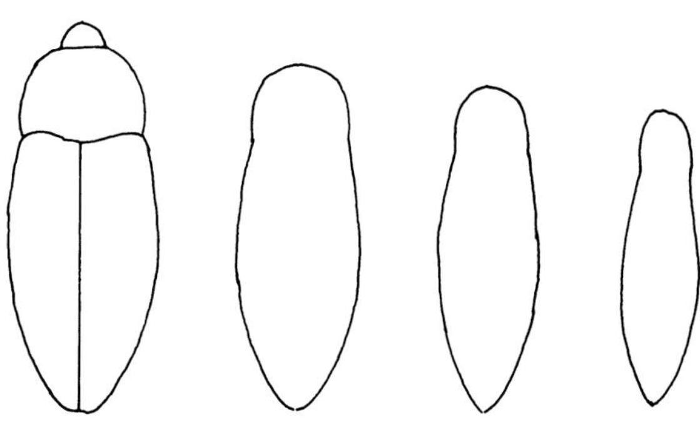

padding outlines

Elytra

The elytra is covered with alternate rows of couched double Jap gold T69 (using metallic sewing thread), and couched gold No.2 Pearl Purl (using silk sewing thread).

- Couch rows of double Jap gold on either side of the centre line of the elytra, retaining the tails to outline the elytra when the filling is complete.
- Couch a row of Pearl Purl (on either side of the Jap gold); a row of double Jap gold; a row of Pearl Purl; finishing with a row of single or double Jap gold (depending on the space). Sink the ends of Jap gold at the lower edge of the elytra.

Using the retained tails, couch a line of double Jap gold around the outer edge of the elytra.

Thorax, head and eyes

Cut a head-thorax shape from gold leather and stitch in place with nylon thread. Outline the shape with couched Jap gold T70—single around the outside edge, double between the thorax and elytra (secure at the corners only). With a double strand of metallic sewing thread, work a stitch across the leather to define the head. Apply two beads for the eyes.

head-thorax shape

Antennae

Cut a length of gold Super Pearl Purl for each antenna. Couch in place with nylon thread, using the outline on the back as a guide.

Legs and mouthparts

Using gold Couching Thread, work each leg in straight stitches, using two strands of thread for the two inner segments, and one strand for the outer segment. Work two straight stitches between the antennae for the mouthparts.

Pomegranates, Snail and Gold Beetle

The pomegranate, Punica granatum, native to Persia, was associated with religious ceremonies and rites amongst the Phoenicians, and later amongst the Greeks and the Romans, because of the rather mysterious qualities of both the flowers and the fruit. In the Mediterranean region, the plant was thought to give protection against evil spirits, and the fallen blossoms were often threaded on necklaces and hung round the necks of children to alleviate stomach ailments.

The fruits have a pleasantly acid taste and can be eaten fresh, or used in the preparation of syrups such as Grenadine, and jellies. The first sherbet is believed to have consisted of a preparation of pomegranate juice mixed with snow.

This design from The Embroidress, 1930, was inspired by Elizabethan blackwork.

skeleton outline

All diagrams actual size

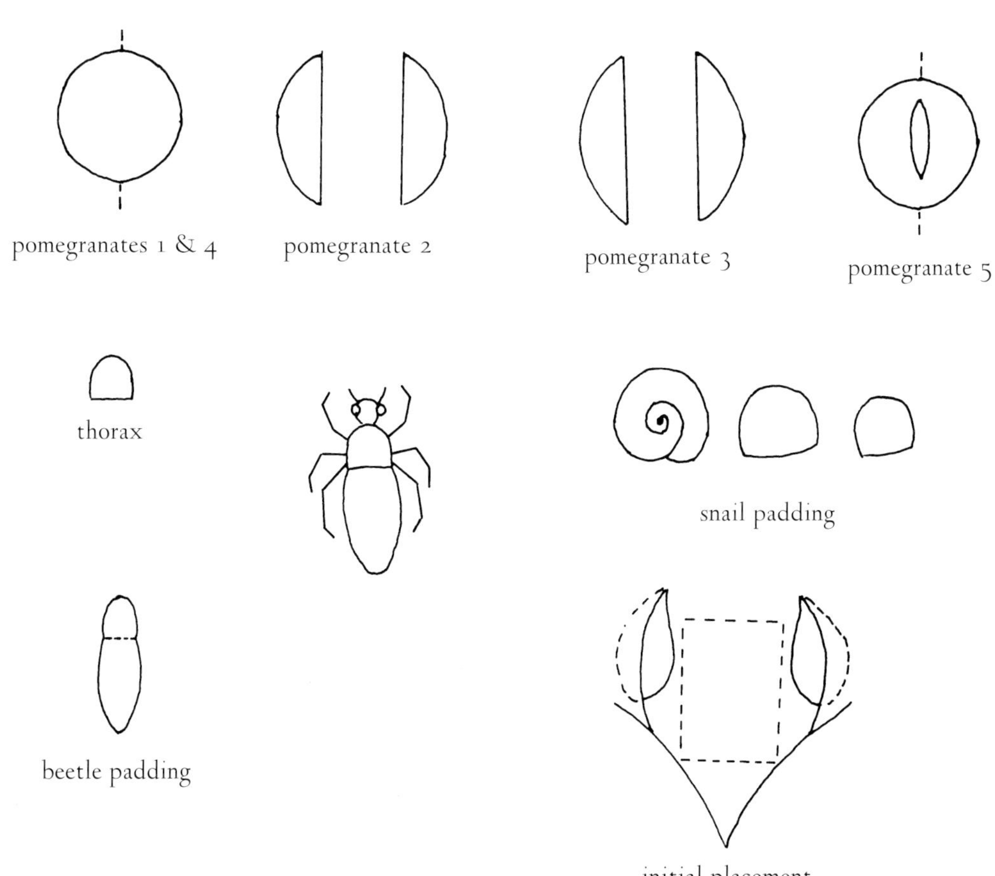

Requirements

- ivory satin, 20 cm (8 in) square
- quilter's muslin (or fine calico) for backing, 20 cm (8 in) square
- 15 cm (6 in) embroidery hoop

Pomegranates (see below)

Snail (see page 257)

Initial (see page 259)

Gold Checkered Beetle (see page 259)

Order of work

1. Mount the main fabric and the backing fabric into the embroidery hoop.
2. Trace the skeleton outline onto the main fabric.
3. Branches, leaves and pomegranate flowers.
4. Snail.
5. Pomegranates.
6. Initial.
7. Gold Checkered Beetle.

Pomegranates

Materials required

- quilter's muslin, 20 cm (8 in) square
- 15 cm (6 in) embroidery hoop
- small amount of stuffing and satay stick
- Mill Hill glass seed beads (165 Christmas red)

- gilt No.6 Smooth Passing Thread
- fine gold couching thread (Kreinik Japan 002J)
- dark olive green stranded thread (Soie d'Alger 2215 or DMC 936)
- olive green stranded thread (Soie d'Alger 2134 or DMC 469)
- dark red stranded thread (Soie d'Alger 915 or DMC 817)
- medium red stranded thread (Soie d'Alger 914 or DMC 349)
- dark coral stranded thread (Soie d'Alger 913 or DMC 350)
- medium coral stranded thread (Soie d'Alger 912 or DMC 351)
- light coral stranded thread (Soie d'Alger 911 or DMC 3341)
- dark orange stranded thread (Cifonda 64 or DMC 301)

The Pomegranates, Snail and Gold Beetle project was inspired by the Chesterfield coat-of-arms.

Branches

The branches are worked with close rows of stem or outline stitch, worked on both sides of the skeleton outlines, using two strands of dark olive green thread.

1. Stitching on the outlines, work one row of stem stitch from the base to *pomegranate* 2, and one row of stem stitch from the base to *pomegranate* 4.

2. Stitching close to these rows, work one row of stem stitch from the base to *pomegranate* 1, and one row of stem stitch from the base to *pomegranate* 5 (start each row slightly ahead of the previous row to ensure tapering points at the base).

3. Stitching next to the previous rows, work another row of stem stitch from the base to *pomegranate* 1, and another row of stem stitch from the base to the *lower pomegranate flower*.

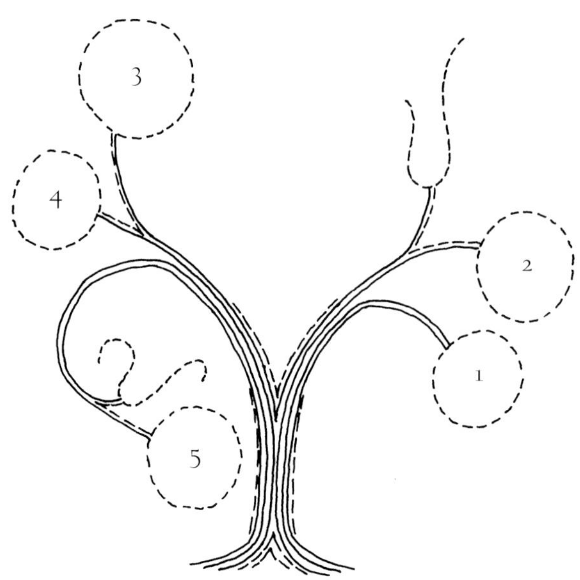

4. Stitching inside the first rows, work one row of stem stitch to the *upper pomegranate flower*, and one row of stem stitch to *pomegranate* 3.

5. Work extra rows of stem stitch inside the Vs of the lower and upper trunk, and the branches, to achieve a pleasing shape.

6. Outline the trunk and the branches with couched Gilt Passing Thread, using one strand of fine metallic thread to work the couching stitches. Starting at the point inside the lower V of the trunk, couch the passing thread around the edges of the trunk and all the branches, working back to the starting point. Sink the tails of the passing thread through to the back, secure and trim.

Hints: To help prevent tangling, run the metallic couching thread twice through beeswax. Using a size 8 or 9 sharps or straw/milliners needle, work the couching stitches 2–3 mm (approx. 1/16 in) apart, with the stitch direction towards the tree.

Leaves

The leaves are worked in padded buttonhole stitch with one strand of olive green thread. Smooth Passing, couched with fine metallic thread, forms the central veins and leaf stems.

1. Pad the leaf with straight stitches—leave a 1 mm space for the central vein. Starting at the base of the leaf, embroider each side with close buttonhole stitches, leaving a small space for the central vein.

2. Couch the Passing thread along the stem and central vein of the leaf, sinking the tails through to the back at each end.

3. To give a neat point to the leaf, work a small fly stitch at the tip with one strand of olive green thread.

FLOWERS

1. Outline the petals in split stitch with one strand of medium red thread. Starting at the top edge, embroider the petals in long and short stitch, blending in the dark red thread towards the base of the flower.

2. Work the sepals, over the base of the flower, with rows of chain stitch using one strand of dark olive green thread.

3. Embroider the stamen with straight stitches and French knots, using one strand of dark orange thread.

POMEGRANATES

Mount the muslin into the hoop and trace all the pomegranate shapes; two whole shapes (*pomegranates 1 and 4*); one whole shape with a small split (*pomegranate 5*); and two half shapes for each split pomegranate (*pomegranates 2 and 3*), their straight edges on the straight grain of the fabric. The pomegranates are embroidered in long and short stitch, with one strand of thread, blending the three shades of coral.

Whole Pomegranate

1. Outline the shape in split stitch, with medium coral thread. Embroider the shape (covering the outline) following

the curve of the fruit, blending the three shades to give a rounded effect (lighter in the centre).

2. Make a row of small gathering stitches around the shape, 1.5 mm from the edge, retaining two tails of thread. Cut out the shape with a small turning allowance (outside the stitches). Pull up the gathering stitches and finger press the seam allowance under. Apply the pomegranate (over the end of the branch) with small stab stitches, easing the edge to fit the outline, and leaving a small opening at the top. Insert a small amount of stuffing with the satay stick, then stitch the opening. Cover the stab stitches with straight stitches, worked around the edge of the pomegranate in blending shades, if required.

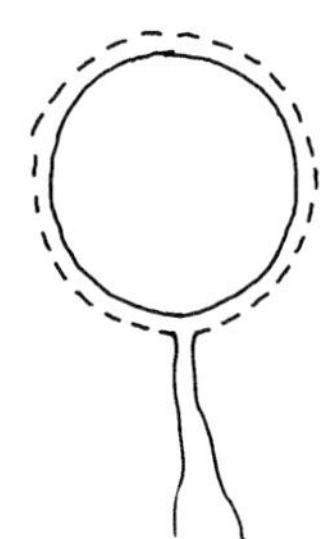

Pomegranate with a Small Split

1. Outline the shape in split stitch, with medium coral thread. Work a row of small chain stitches on each side of the split then cover these stitches with close buttonhole stitch, the ridge edging the split (just like a small buttonhole on a garment). Embroider the shape on either side of the split, following the curve of the fruit.

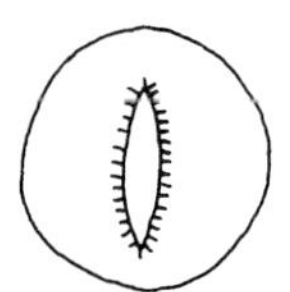

2. Carefully cut out the split inside the buttonhole edges. Cut out and apply the shape as for the whole pomegranate—do not leave an opening at the top. Pad the pomegranate through the split with a little stuffing, using a satay stick. Stitch beads into the split, one at a time, with medium coral thread.

Split Pomegranate

1. With one strand of medium coral thread, work a row of small chain stitches along the straight edge then cover with close buttonhole stitch, the ridge on the outside edge.

2. Outline the curved edge in split stitch, then embroider the shape (inside the buttonhole edge), following the curve of the fruit. Work the other half of the pomegranate.

3. Make a row of small gathering stitches around curved edge (1.5 mm away), retaining two tails of thread. Cut out the shape with a small turning allowance (outside the stitches). Pull up the gathering stitches and finger press the seam allowance under. Apply one half of pomegranate (over the end of the branch) with small stab stitches, easing the edge to fit half the outline (the straight edge should bulge slightly). Apply the other half.

4. Stitch beads into the pomegranate, one at a time, using medium coral thread. Apply a bottom layer of beads first, then gradually fill the shape.

Sepals

Complete all pomegranates by working three sepals in needleweaving at the top of the fruit, using one strand of medium coral thread.

Snail

Materials required

- beige felt, organza and Vliesofix (small pieces)
- Mill Hill petite beads (42028 ginger)
- grey stranded thread (DMC 3023)
- variegated bronze-grey stranded thread (Needle Necessities Overdyed 128)
- grey soft cotton thread (DMC Tapestry Cotton 2647)
- brown soft cotton thread (DMC Tapestry Cotton 2829)

Body

The snail's body is worked in raised stem stitch over a padding of soft cotton thread.

1. Outline the body in backstitch with one strand of grey thread. Pad with three rows of grey soft cotton, held in place with couching stitches worked over the outline stitches with grey stranded thread.

2. Starting at the tail, work raised stem stitch band over the couching stitches using grey stranded thread in a fine tapestry needle (start each row at the tail and insert the needle at various points to form a rounded head).

3. Work four tentacles in bullion knots (7 wraps for long and 5 wraps for short) with grey thread. Stitch a petite bead to the ends of the long tentacles for eyes.

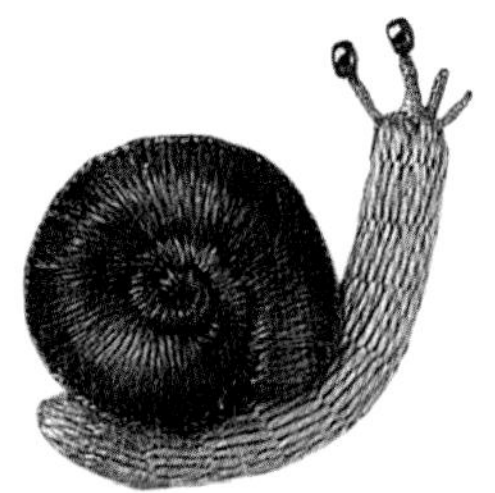

SHELL

1. Fuse the Vliesofix to the organza. Trace the shell (and the internal scroll line) and the two smaller padding shapes on to the organza. Remove the paper, fuse the organza to the felt then cut out the shapes.

2. To pad the snail shell, stab stitch the first and second layers of felt in place (organza side up) with variegated thread. Apply the top layer with small buttonhole stitches, leaving the opening of the shell. Make sure all layers are sitting level with the top of the snail body.

3. The snail shell is embroidered in buttonhole stitch with variegated thread, using the scroll line as a guide. The inner coil of the snail shell is wrapped soft cotton thread.

Bring the brown soft cotton through at • , wrap closely with variegated thread for about 4 mm (approx. 1/8 in), twist into a coil to start the shell then secure with a stitch. Continue embroidering the shell with buttonhole stitch, working through the felt (over the soft cotton padding), following the scroll outline on the organza and stitching over the edge of the buttonhole stitches of the previous coil (one or two lengths of soft cotton can be added for extra padding as the shell widens, if desired). Insert the tails of soft cotton under the felt at the shell opening and through to the back. Secure.

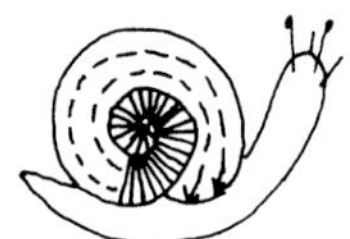

INITIAL

The initial may be omitted, or replaced with leaves (repositioned) or a spiderweb and spider, if desired. I drew the J freehand, using the initial rectangle as a guide, but you may choose to use a letter from the ornamental alphabet on the next page.

Materials required

- gilt No.6 Smooth Passing Thread
- fine gold couching thread (Kreinik Japan 002J)
- dark purple or navy stranded thread (Soie d'Alger 3326 or DMC 939)

1. Using the rectangle as a guide, draw the initial then trace onto the satin.

2. Outline the initial in backstitch with one strand of purple thread and pad with chain stitch. Embroider the initial in satin stitch, covering the outline.

3. Couch a line of gilt Passing Thread around the edge of the initial, couching with fine metallic thread. Sink the tails of thread through to the back and secure. Embellish the initial with extra lines of gilt and purple thread if desired.

GOLD CHECKERED BEETLE

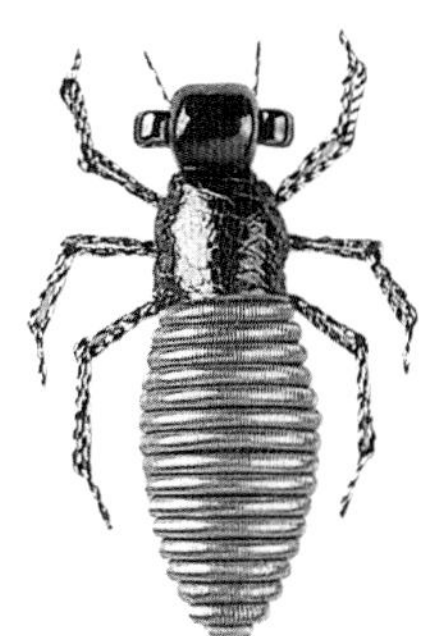

Materials required

- gold felt and Vliesofix (small pieces)
- bronze snakeskin (or kid)
- gold Smooth Purl no. 8
- 4 mm blue/bronze bead (SBX6-449)
- Mill Hill seed beads (374 blue-black)

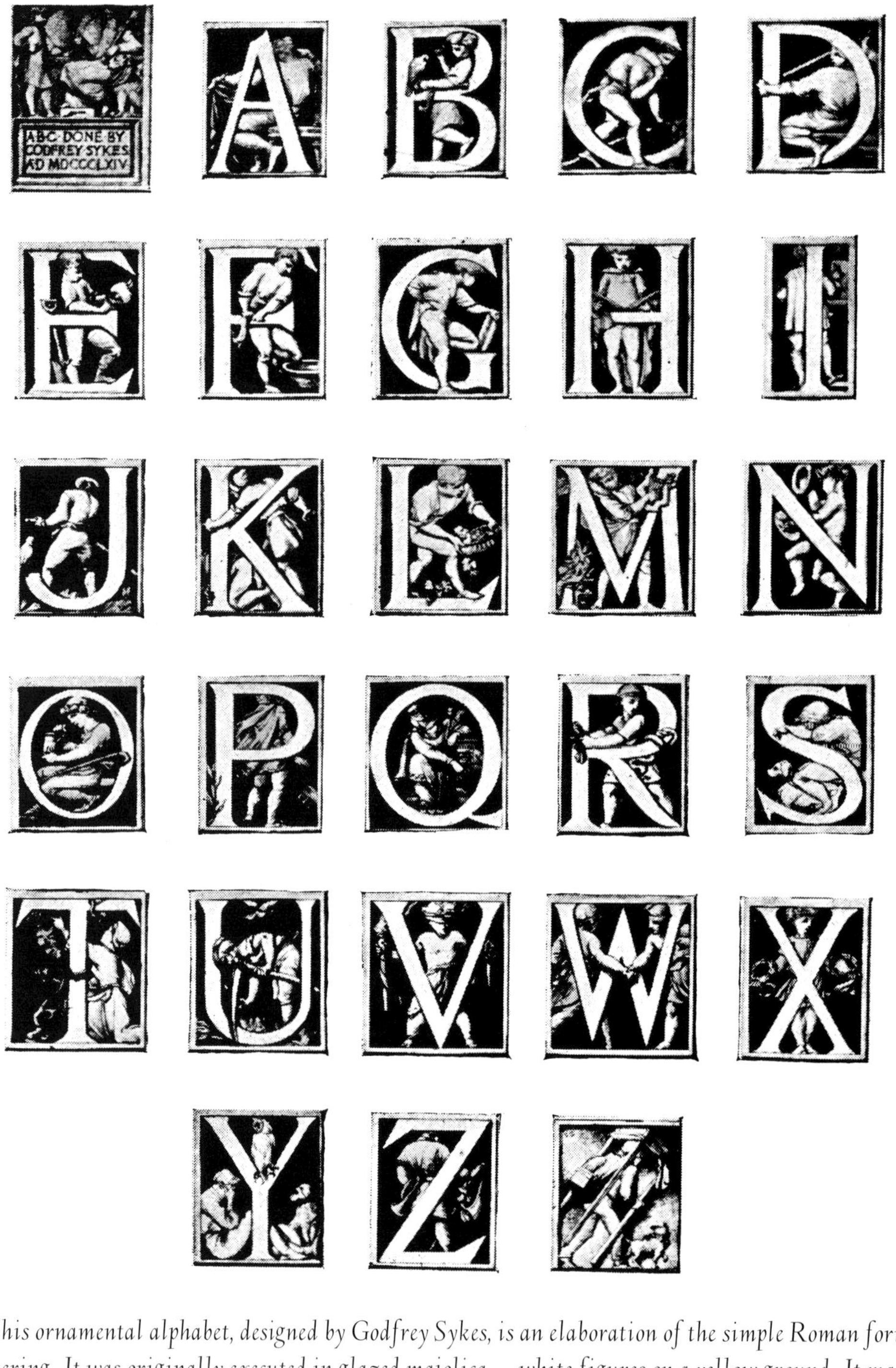

This ornamental alphabet, designed by Godfrey Sykes, is an elaboration of the simple Roman form of lettering. It was originally executed in glazed majolica—white figures on a yellow ground. It may help when drawing your own initial.

- fine gold/black metallic thread (Kreinik Cord 205c)
- old gold stranded thread (DMC 729)
- nylon thread (Madeira Monofil No.60, clear)

Preparation

Cut a beetle padding shape from yellow felt; apply with stab stitches using one strand of old gold thread. Backstitch the line dividing the thorax and the elytra.

Elytra

Using well-waxed old gold thread in a size 12 sharps needle, stitch cut lengths of smooth purl, over the padding, to form the elytra (the purl need to be cut into lengths just long enough cover the felt—if it is too long it will bulge and split). Start at the top of the elytra and work down to the tail.

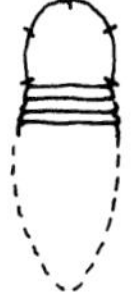

Thorax

The thorax is cut from bronze snakeskin and applied with nylon thread. Attach the snakeskin with five stitches—the first two at each corner next to the elytra, one stitch at centre front, then a stitch at each side.

Head, eyes and antennae

Using the nylon thread, stitch the 4 mm bead close to the thorax for the head, then, stitching through this bead in a figure of eight movement, apply a seed bead to each side of the bead for eyes. With one strand of gold/black metallic thread, make two straight stitches for the antennae, taking the needle through the big bead to make the stitch on either side.

Legs

Using two strands of gold/black metallic thread, work two chain stitches and a long tie-down stitch for each leg, using the diagram as a guide to placement.

Gold Violin Beetle

The elytra of this Violin Beetle have been worked in Burden stitch, a goldwork technique dating back to the Middle Ages, when it was used to decorate Italian and German ecclesiastical embroideries. Burden stitch is a type of couching, where horizontal, evenly spaced long stitches (or laid gold threads) are couched with rows of vertical stitches, in a brick-like fashion, often in varying shades of silk. This exotic beetle could also be worked in other colours, such as dark purple, burnt orange or deep magenta.

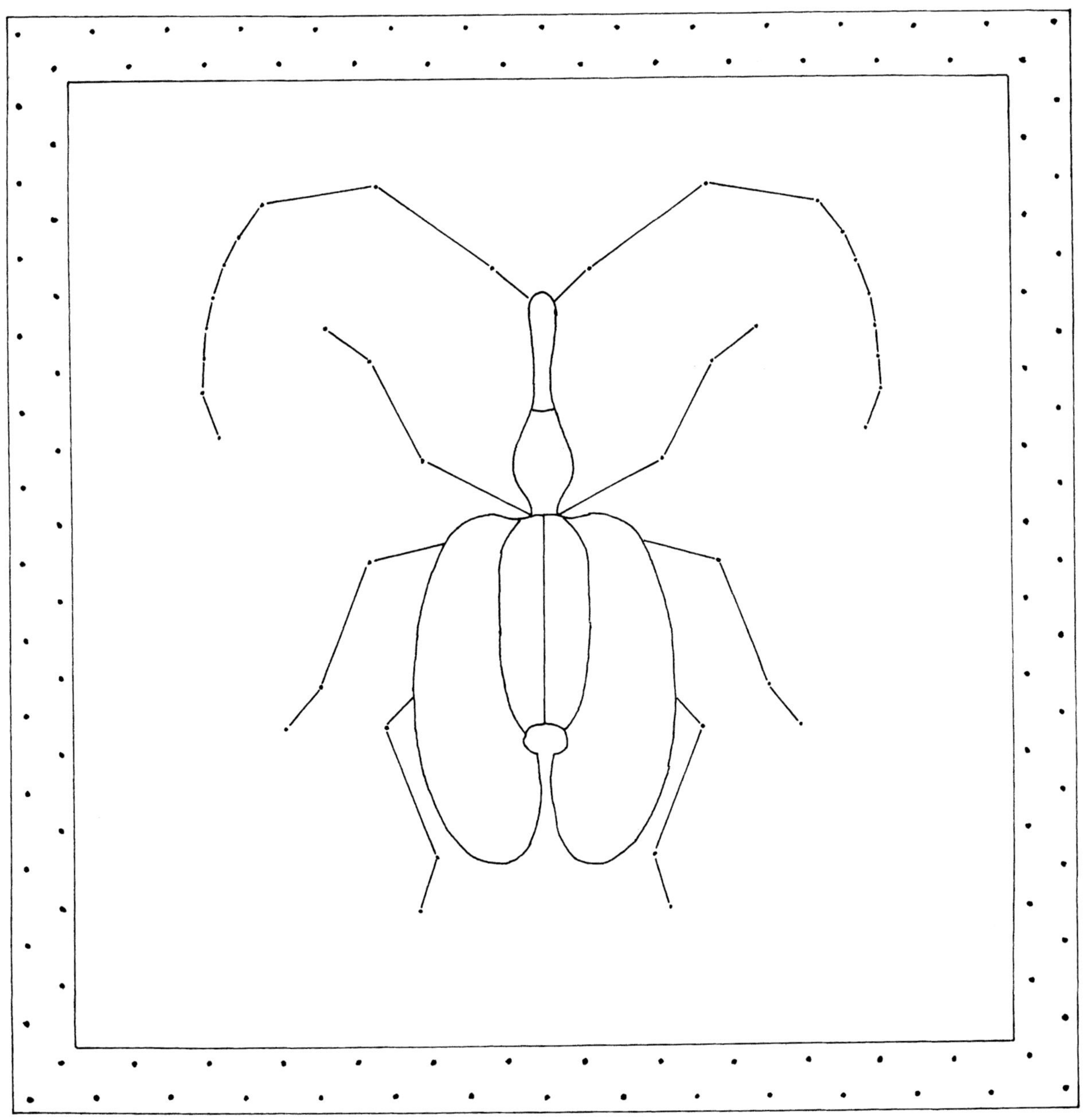

skeleton outline
actual size

Requirements

- cream silk (or ivory/gold silk), 30 cm (12 in) square
- calico backing fabric
- 45 cm (18 in) slate or square frame
- sea green silk ribbon or fabric, 10 cm (4 in) square (optional)
- yellow felt
- yellow or cream silk organza
- Vliesofix
- silk sewing thread (YLI Silk Thread #100 col. 215)
- metallic sewing thread (YLI Metallic Yarn col. Gold)
- polyester sewing thread (Gütermann col. 488)
- clear nylon thread (Madeira Monofil No.60, col. 1001)
- dark teal stranded thread (Soie d'Alger 135 or DMC 3808)
- sea green stranded thread (Soie d'Alger 1826 or DMC 3847)
- dark green thick pearl thread (DMC Coton Perlé No.3, col. 500)
- emerald green metallic braid (Kreinik Fine (#8) Metallic Braid col. 009HL)
- gold No.1 Pearl Purl
- gold No.2 Pearl Purl
- gold No.6 Smooth Passing
- Jap Gold T69
- Jap Gold T70
- dark gold Couching Thread 371

- gold No.3 Twist
- Mill Hill antique beads (3033 claret)
- Mill Hill petite beads (45270 bottle green)
- gilt metal 4 mm bugle beads or substitute

Note: I have had the gilt bugle beads for many years and just had to use them! They can be replaced with glass bugle beads; couched Jap gold T69; or gold Super Pearl Purl—gently pulled out into a spiral and couched, in the grooves, with coloured silk.

Preparation

1. Mount the cream silk and calico backing into a square frame, making sure that both fabrics are drum tight.

2. Trace the skeleton outline, including the border, onto the calico backing (I drew over the lines, marking the antennae and legs with a series of dots, with a fine Pigma marking pen as the pencil outline tends to disappear). Tack around the border lines with silk sewing thread. The project will be worked using these outlines as a guide.

Elytra

The 'wings' of the elytra are worked in Burden stitch. I have padded the elytra (before working the Burden stitch) with a layer of felt and sea green silk ribbon. This is optional—the area could be painted with fabric paint, or just embroidered.

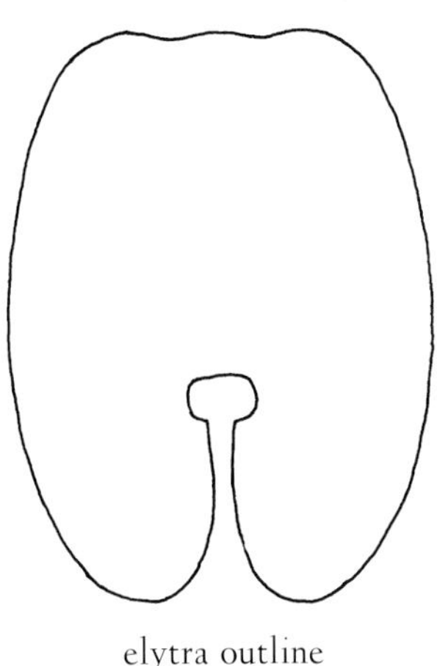
elytra outline

1. Fuse the ribbon to the felt with Vliesofix. Trace the elytra outline onto the paper side of a piece of Vliesofix and fuse to the other side of the felt. Cut out the elytra shape and apply to the background fabric (silk side up), with small, close stab stitches around the outside edge, using one strand of sea green thread. Use the outline on the back as a guide to placement.

2. Prepare the gold foundation for Burden stitch: using double gold Passing thread and a large needle, work evenly

spaced, horizontal satin stitches over the padded shape, the spaces being the same width as the Passing thread (work the satin stitches with as much thread on the back as the front for best results). Couch the Passing threads in place with nylon sewing thread, securing each row before proceeding to the next.

3. Cut three layers of felt to pad the centre panel of the elytra; one the actual size, and two successively smaller (use organza, Vliesofix and felt; see page 381). Using polyester thread, stitch each layer of felt to the centre of the elytra (over the laid threads) with stab stitches around the outside edge, applying the smallest layer first. Work a row of back stitch along the centre line of the elytra (stitching through to the back).

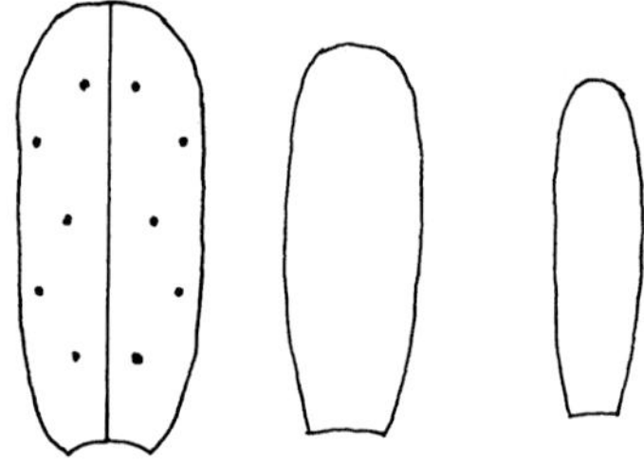

central elytra padding

4. Using one strand of either dark teal or sea green thread, work vertical stitches, in a brick-like pattern, over the laid gold thread, blending the shades from the lighter sea green at the edges, to the darker teal near the centre. Work a row of stem stitch around the outside to neaten the edge. Starting and ending at the top of the elytra, couch a row of gold No.1 Pearl Purl around the outside edge (over the stem stitch), using nylon thread.

5. The padded centre panel of the elytra is covered with alternate rows of couched Jap gold T70, and gold No.1 Pearl Purl and green petite beads, using nylon thread.

- Couch a row of double Jap gold along centre line of the elytra (insert the tails through to the back).
- Thread pieces of Pearl Purl (cut to size) and green beads onto nylon thread and couch on either side of the centre Jap gold (use the photograph as a guide to the bead and Pearl Purl pattern, or make up your own).
- Couch a row of single Jap gold on either side of the couched Pearl Purl and beads.

Detail of central elytra.

- Repeat the last two rows until the third row of Pearl Purl and beads has been applied.
- To help achieve the rounded ends of the panel, insert the tails of Jap gold through to the back, slightly short of the ends of each row, before working the row of Pearl Purl and beads. Ease the end of each row of Pearl Purl towards the centre when securing.
- Couch a row of double Jap gold around the outer edge of the panel, using dark teal thread.

THORAX, NECK AND HEAD

1. Outline the thorax, neck and head in backstitch with one strand of sea-green thread. Pad the thorax with three layers of felt, cutting the top layer from the scraps of the silk-covered felt if desired. Stab stitch in place, applying the smallest layer first.

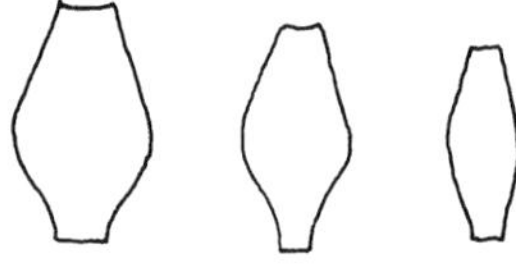

thorax padding

2. The head and neck are embroidered in raised stem stitch with sea green thread. Pad the head and neck with a bundle of sea green threads (inserting the ends through to the back) held in place with couching stitches, 2–3 mm (approx. 1/8 in) apart, worked over the backstitched outline. Cover the head and neck in raised stem stitch, worked over the couching stitches with one strand of thread. Outline the thorax, neck and head with couched Jap gold T69, using nylon sewing thread.

3. Cover the padded thorax with French knots, worked with two strands of thread (one each of green and teal).

4. To form the band between the thorax and the elytra, expand a piece of gold No.2 Pearl Purl cut to the appropriate length and wrap with seven strands of dark teal thread, leaving a tail of thread at each end. Apply the wrapped wire by inserting the thread tails at each lower corner of the thorax, tying the threads in a knot at the back to secure. Form the band between the thorax and the neck in the same manner, using gold No.1 Pearl Purl and two strands of thread.

5. Work couching stitches over the embroidered neck with gold Couching Thread. Apply two claret seed beads for eyes with nylon thread.

Antennae

A 5 mm (1/4 in) piece of gold No.1 Pearl Purl and several gilt bugle beads (I needed 14) are threaded onto gold Couching Thread and couched in place for each antenna. Insert the tails of gold thread at each end of the antenna then work couching stitches between every bead with nylon thread, using the outline on the back of the fabric as a guide.

Legs and mouthparts

Using emerald green metallic braid, work two chain stitches and a straight stitch for each leg. It is easier to work the outer leg segment first, with a straight stitch, then the two threaded chain stitches for the inner segments (use the dots on the back as a guide). Embroider two straight stitches, between the antennae for mouthparts.

Border

This border, inspired by an embroidered band on a nineteenth century ecclesiastical vestment, is great fun to work; however, it requires precision, both in the placement of the border threads and the beads (see detail photograph). The border threads are gold No.3 Twist, dark green Coton Perlé, and Jap gold T69. They are couched in place with gold metallic sewing thread, or nylon thread if preferred. The inner part of the border is worked with claret-coloured antique beads and dark gold Couching Thread 371.

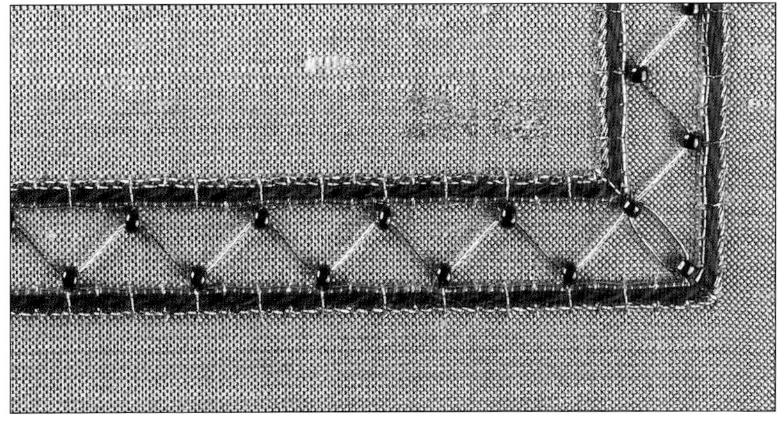

Detail of border, showing a corner.

1. Couch the three border threads (with the green in the middle) over the silk tacking lines; work a couching stitch over all three (taking care not to 'pinch' the threads), then a stitch over each gold thread only (opposite each other). Work both lines of couched threads with the gold Twist on the outside edge. Hold the border threads under tension as you couch, to maintain a straight line, and make sure that the three threads are long enough to work the entire border—sinking the tails of thread at one corner only. The border threads may be couched individually if preferred.

2. Using nylon thread, stitch an antique bead over each dot inside the border, with the hole of the bead parallel to the couched threads. Apply the beads with a firm back stitch motion (this looks like herringbone on the back), close to the Jap gold border threads.

3. Now the fun part! Thread the gold Couching Thread through the beads in a zigzag fashion (forming a loop in the corners), to complete the border. Again, work with a long length of thread to avoid too many joins.

Or Nué Beetle

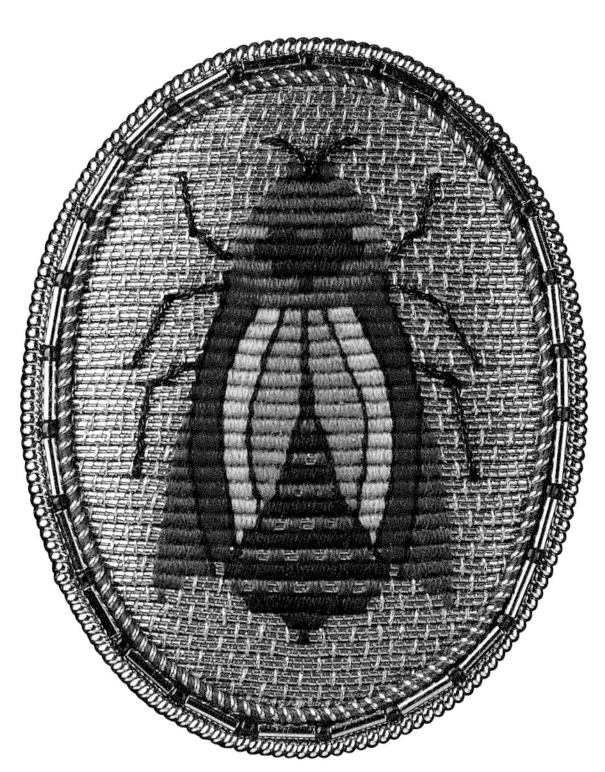

Right: Or Nué Beetle

Above: Early twentieth century Italian mosaic button.

Inspired by an early twentieth century Italian mosaic button, this beetle has been embroidered in the goldwork technique of Or Nué. Regarded as the supreme example of the embroiderer's art in the thirteenth and fourteenth centuries, Or Nué had its origins in Europe, where it was used to work ecclesiastical vestments and hangings.

A very time-consuming technique, Or Nué is a method of couching gold thread to cover an area completely. The gold thread is couched, usually in pairs, across a design drawn or painted on the background fabric; the design lines are picked out in coloured silk couching stitches. The shading of the design depends on the closeness and/or the colour of the silk couching stitches; areas not requiring any colouring are couched in fine gold thread. The aim is to cover the surface with perfectly straight, couched gold threads with no background fabric showing through.

Requirements

- unwashed calico, 20 cm (8 in) square
- slate frame, or 15 cm (6 in) hoop bound with tape
- fine marking pen and paints, felt-tip pens or coloured pencils
- Jap Gold T71
- metallic sewing thread (YLI Metallic Yarn col. Gold), beeswaxed
- red stranded thread (DMC 349)
- orange stranded thread (DMC 900)
- yellow stranded thread (DMC 741)
- green stranded thread (DMC 505)
- teal stranded thread (DMC 924)
- dark purple stranded thread (Soie d'Alger 3326)

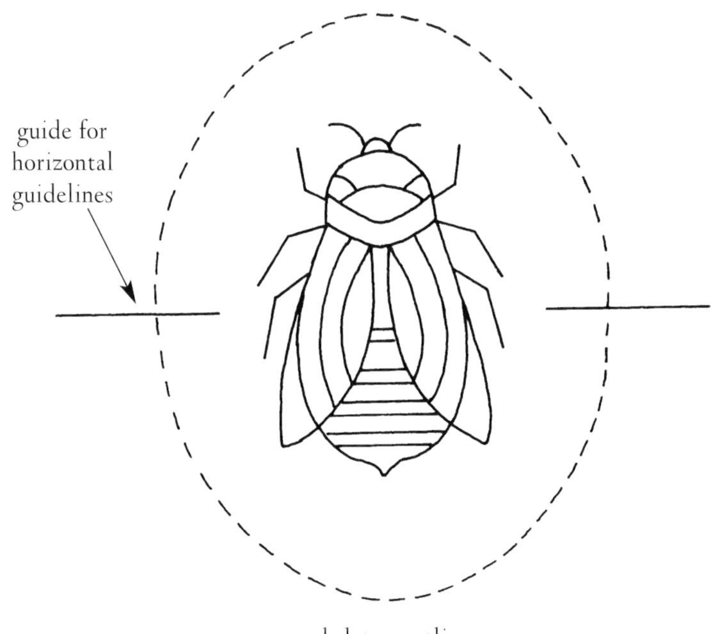

skeleton outline

Preparation

1. Mount the calico in a square frame (or embroidery hoop) making sure that the fabric is drum tight.

2. Trace the design onto the calico and draw over the outlines with a fine marking pen. Colour the interior shapes of the beetle as desired, using the photograph as a guide. With a sharp lead pencil, rule horizontal lines across the calico, approximately 5 mm ($^1/_4$ in) apart, to help keep the couched Jap gold in straight rows.

To Work the Or Nué Beetle

Following the instructions below, couch rows of double Jap gold to completely cover the surface, couching with either stranded thread or gold metallic thread as dictated by the design painted on the calico.

- Starting at the bottom, couch rows of double Jap gold to the calico, over the painted beetle design, to completely cover the surface.
- Couch the background of the design, using gold metallic sewing thread, with spaced couching stitches 2–3 mm (approx. $^1/_8$ in) apart, worked in a brick pattern.
- Couch the beetle, using one strand of thread, with close, vertical couching stitches in the colours painted on the calico. Use separate threads and needles for each block of colour. It may be necessary to work some of the coloured stitches at an angle to follow the design.
- Lastly, work the legs, antennae and fine dark outlines, with straight stitches in dark purple thread (take care not to pierce the couched Jap gold).
- As the edge of the design will not be seen, it is only necessary to couch the Jap gold background within the oval outline. Leave the ends of Jap gold on the surface (holding them out of the way with masking tape).

- The finished embroidery has been mounted over cardboard and the edges embellished with a border of Pearl Purl and beads. As it is a companion piece to the two Beaded Beetles, completed in the same way, refer to these beetles for the finishing instructions (see pages 43–45).

You may like to refer to a goldwork manual for more detailed information on the technique of working Or Nué (see Bibliography).

Gold Stumpwork Beetles

Gold stumpwork beetles—perhaps the ultimate challenge! A collection of beetles embroidered in gold, combining the techniques of stumpwork and goldwork (both disciplines requiring practice and patience), would look wonderful and be very rewarding to work. The unique characteristic of stumpwork—embroidered detached shapes with wired edges—is ideal for working the hardened wing cases of the beetle, which are lifted away from the body for flight. The curved, raised surfaces of stumpwork elytra, embellished with the different textures of the metallic threads, reflect light in a spectacular way, a distinguishing feature of goldwork. The felt padding employed to give a mounded shape to the body of the beetle is an element shared by both techniques.

How to Embroider a Gold Stumpwork Beetle

Most of the beetles in the Specimen Box could be interpreted in gold; indeed, six of them have been worked in coloured metallic materials using goldwork techniques. These beetles form the basis of a Gold Stumpwork Beetle Collection. (I have to confess that my Collection is still in a box, together with the selected threads and materials, 'virtual beetles' awaiting completion ...)

If you wish to take up the challenge, this section contains information and ideas for embroidering goldwork stumpwork beetles. A list of the substitute threads required to work the six stumpwork beetles in gold is included for each one. Many gold threads, such as the purls and couching threads, are also available in silver and copper—combining gold and silver, or gold and copper, can look very effective. You may wish to enlarge the stumpwork beetle outlines slightly to facilitate their execution in goldwork.

A gold stumpwork beetle is embroidered in the same way as a traditional stumpwork beetle, except for the working of the elytra. Embroider the elytra on light gold cotton homespun or muslin, stitching the wire around the outside edge with light gold stranded thread (Soie d'Alger 2533 or DMC 833). Embellish the surface of the elytra with the goldwork thread and technique of your choice, then cut out the elytra and complete the beetle as for traditional stumpwork.

Suggestions for Goldwork Elytra

Work the elytra with one of the following:

- Bright Check Purl chips, sewn on individually in as many different directions as possible; see the Gold Ground Beetle (pages 240–241).
- Jap gold, couched in a basket pattern over string padding; see the Gold Diving Beetle (pages 242–243).
- Diagonal lengths of cut Smooth Purl and Bright Check Purl; see the Gold Longhorn Beetle (pages 244–245).
- A laid-work filling, using different weights of metallic thread and embellished with tiny spangles or beads; see the Gold Scarab Beetle (pages 245–247).
- Alternate rows of couched Jap gold and couched gold Pearl Purl; see the Gold Jewel Beetle (pages 247–249).
- Couched gold thread, working a pattern (a variation of Or Nué) with a contrasting stranded thread; see the stumpwork Jewel Beetle (pages 90–92).
- Padded gold kid or snakeskin; see the stumpwork Scarab Beetle (pages 165–168).
- Vertical lengths of Rough Purl, cut to size; see the stumpwork Leaf Beetle (pages 124–127).
- Work the elytra on a coloured metallic background in Burden stitch; see the Gold Violin Beetle (pages 262–269).
- Fill a wire elytra shape with metallic needlelace; see the stumpwork Skipjack Beetle (pages 152–155).

Gold Stumpwork Scarab Beetle

To embroider a gold version of the stumpwork Scarab Beetle, use the diagrams, requirements and instructions on pages 165–168, making the following substitutions.

Requirements

- light gold cotton homespun (*elytra*)
- dark gold felt (*abdomen*)
- gold leather or snakeskin (*elytra, thorax–head*)
- light gold stranded thread (Soie d'Alger 2533 or DMC 833) (*elytra*)
- dark gold stranded thread (Soie d'Alger 526 or DMC 892) (*abdomen*)
- gold metallic braid (Kreinik Very Fine (#4) Japan Braid 002J) (*legs, antennae*)
- Mill Hill antique beads (3037 abalone) (*eyes*)

Gold Stumpwork Rove Beetle

To embroider a gold version of the stumpwork Rove Beetle, use the diagrams, requirements and instructions on pages 173–175, making the following substitutions.

Requirements

- gold metal organdie and organza (*elytra*)
- dark gold felt (*abdomen*)
- gold leather or snakeskin (*thorax*)
- gold No.8 Smooth Purl (*abdomen*)
- gold No.8 Bright Check Purl (*abdomen*)
- light gold stranded thread (Soie d'Alger 2533 or DMC 833) (*elytra, abdomen*)
- dark gold stranded thread (Soie d'Alger 526 or DMC 892) (*head*)
- antique gold metallic thread (Kreinik Cord 205c) (*legs, antennae*)
- Mill Hill petite beads (42028 ginger) (*eyes*)

Gold Stumpwork Skipjack Beetle

To embroider a gold version of the stumpwork Skipjack Beetle, use the diagrams, requirements and instructions on pages 152–155, making the following substitutions.

Requirements

- light gold cotton homespun (*thorax*)
- dark gold felt (*abdomen*)
- gold kid or snakeskin (*thorax*)
- fine antique gold metallic thread (Kreinik Cord 205c) (*antennae*)
- dark gold stranded thread (Soie d'Alger 526 or DMC 892) (*abdomen, head*)
- light gold stranded thread (Soie d'Alger 2533 or DMC 833) (*thorax*)
- gold metallic braid (Kreinik Very Fine (#4) Japan Braid 002J) (*elytra*)
- gold Couching Thread 371 (*legs*)
- Mill Hill petite beads (42028 ginger) (*eyes*)

Gold Stumpwork Net-winged Beetle

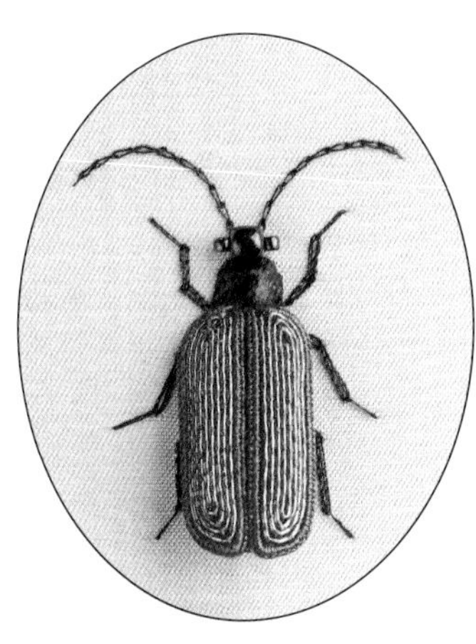

To embroider a gold version of the stumpwork Net-winged Beetle, use the diagrams, requirements and instructions on pages 160–162, making the following substitutions.

Requirements

- light gold cotton homespun (*elytra*)
- dark gold felt (*abdomen*)
- gold snakeskin (*thorax*)
- light gold stranded thread (Soie d'Alger 2533 or DMC 833) (*elytra*)
- dark gold stranded thread (Soie d'Alger 526 or DMC 892) (*abdomen*)
- gold Metallic Couching Thread (or gold No.6 Smooth Passing) (*elytra*)
- gold metallic sewing thread (YLI Metallic Yarn col. Gold) (*elytra*)
- fine antique gold metallic thread (Kreinik Cord 205c) (*legs, antennae*)
- 3 mm gold/bronze bead (*head*)
- Mill Hill petite beads (42028 ginger) (*eyes*)

Note: Cover the elytra with couched gold Passing thread, using gold metallic sewing thread.

Gold Stumpwork Jewel Beetle

To embroider a gold version of the stumpwork Jewel Beetle, use the diagrams, requirements and instructions on pages 90–92, making the following substitutions.

Requirements

- light gold cotton homespun (*elytra*)
- dark gold felt (*abdomen*)
- gold kid (*thorax*)
- light gold stranded thread (Soie d'Alger 2533 or DMC 833) (*elytra*)
- gold metallic sewing thread (YLI Metallic Yarn col. Gold) (*elytra*)
- dark gold stranded thread (Soie d'Alger 526 or DMC 892) (*abdomen*)
- dark gold Metallic Couching Thread 371 (*elytra*)
- gold metallic braid (Kreinik Fine (#8) Japan Braid 002J) (*legs*)
- Mill Hill antique beads (3037 abalone) (*eyes*)

Note: Cover the elytra with couched dark gold Couching Thread, couching the background with gold metallic sewing thread, and working the blotches with dark gold stranded thread.

Gold Stumpwork Leaf Beetle

To embroider a gold version of the stumpwork Leaf Beetle, use the diagrams, requirements and instructions on pages 124–127, making the following substitutions.

Requirements

- light gold cotton homespun (*elytra*)
- dark gold felt (*abdomen*)
- gold leather (*thorax*)
- gold No.8 Smooth Purl (*elytra*)
- gold No.8 Bright Check Purl (*elytra*)
- light gold stranded thread (Soie d'Alger 2533 or DMC 833) (*elytra, head*)
- dark gold stranded thread (Soie d'Alger 526 or DMC 892) (*abdomen*)
- antique gold metallic thread (Kreinik Cord 205c) (*legs, antennae*)
- Mill Hill petite beads (42028 ginger) (*eyes*)

Embroidered Initial and Beetle

An embroidered initial embellished with a goldwork or stumpwork beetle, mounted into a frame or small glass paperweight, is a very personal gift. Almost any beetle could be combined with these fairly plain letters—either surrounded by the initial, or crawling over it! The initial can be embroidered in many ways. Instructions are provided for a simple and effective method of working an initial, and for mounting the finished piece into a paperweight; the beetle, background fabric and thread colour is your choice. I have used the stumpwork Scarab Beetle, one worked in bronze leather and the other in green emu-leg skin, for the D and G paperweights; and a gold version of the stumpwork Leaf Beetle for the J, which has been mounted into a frame.

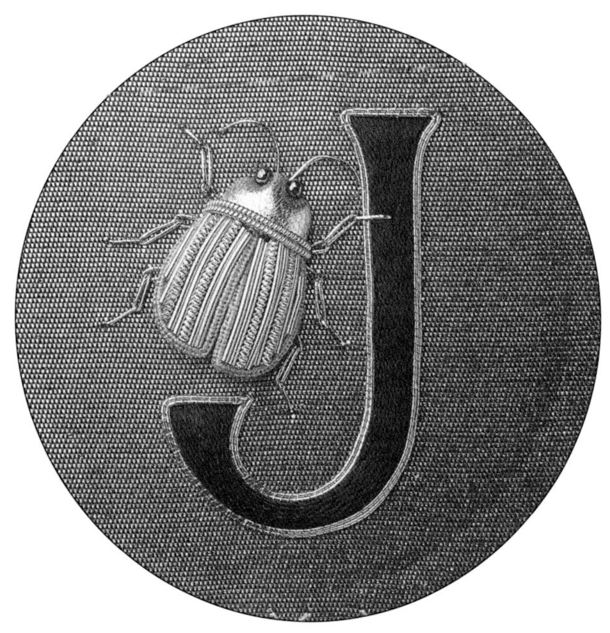

Initials (adapted from woodcut initials by G. Tory) Enlarge at 125% on a photocopier

M
N
O
P
Q
R
S
T
U
V
W
Y

Requirements

- silk background fabric, 20 cm (8 in) square
- quilter's muslin (or fine calico) for backing, 20 cm (8 in) square
- 10 or 12 cm (4 or 5 in) embroidery hoop
- threads and materials for the beetle of your choice
- threads to work the initial:

  – to pad the initial, use DMC Soft Tapestry Cotton, in a colour that blends, or lengths of the silk that will be used to embroider the initial.

  – to embroider the initial, use stranded silk in the colour of your choice. I chose Soie d'Alger 4615 (russet), and 3326 (dark purple).

  – to outline the initial, use gold thread, Gold Super Pearl Purl, Milliary, DMC Perlé 3 in a contrasting colour, or the thread of your choice. I used Jap Gold T71 for the J and copper metallic thread (Madeira art No 9803 Col 3027) for the D and G.

  – clear nylon thread (Madeira Monofil No.60 col.1001) for couching.

The initials in the alphabet on pages 285–286 are suitable for a Framecraft small glass paperweight and recessed wooden base with a 6 cm (2 1/4 in) inside diameter.

Order of work

1. Mount the silk and calico backing into a hoop, making sure that both fabrics are drum tight.

2. Trace the initial and circle outline onto a piece of white paper. Trace the skeleton outline of the beetle onto tracing paper; experiment with the position of the beetle until a pleasing arrangement is found, then tape the skeleton outline in place over the initial. Trace a skeleton outline of the beetle, initial and circle, onto the calico backing. Tack around the circle with sewing thread. The project will be worked using these outlines as a guide.

3. Outline the initial in back stitch with one strand of silk.

4. Pad inside the initial with three lengths of soft cotton, reducing to two lengths in the narrow sections. Couch the padding in place inside the initial outlines, leaving a small space (1 mm) between the padding and the back stitch. Stitch the ends of the padding to the surface and trim.

5. Apply a layer of silk padding over the soft cotton padding—three lengths of silk (separated into strands), couched in place with one strand of silk. As these couching stitches are also the foundation stitches for the raised stem stitch, they need to enclose the back stitch outline and be worked fairly close together, about 3 mm (a bit less than 1/8 in); closer around curves, at 2 mm (1/16 in). Take the ends of the silk padding threads through to the back.

6. Using one strand of silk, cover the initial in raised stem stitch band, starting and ending each row as for satin stitch. Add short rows to the wider sections of the initial as required (sometimes every alternate row) to fill the shape.

7. Couch double Jap gold (or the outline thread of your choice) around the outside edge of the initial, working the couching stitches in nylon thread. Sink the tails at an inconspicuous point on the initial.

8. Embroider the beetle.

9. Mount the finished piece into a small paperweight (see pages 386–387).

This delightful hand-coloured print of a frock-coated, top-hatted beetle has no identifying marks; however, his head and fan-like antennae, and the shape of his red elytra-coat, indicate that he belongs to the scarab family.

Unattributed hand-coloured print c.1850s, 10 x 15 cm (4 x 6 in)

PART 6:

Beetles in Surface Embroidery

Traditional surface embroidery, with its extensive repertoire of flat, durable stitches, is the most suitable method to work decorative beetles on clothing and accessories. The passion for embellishing both dress and furnishings with 'creatures' was at its zenith in sixteenth and seventeenth century England, with the embroiderer filling every available space with the most extraordinary assortment of insects. Bees, beetles, flies, ladybirds, dragonflies, moths, snails, worms, grasshoppers and crickets, craneflies, caterpillars and centipedes, spider webs and spiders, butterflies and unidentifiable insects can all be found amidst the foliage and flowers of Elizabethan and Stuart embroideries. A fascinating example is a seventeenth century pillow cover, 'worked in pale shades of coloured silk in chain, satin and back stitch with couched work and French knots on linen ... 10 flowers, 3 birds, 4 fishes, 1 shell, 4 beasts, 1 reptile, 4 large and 23 small insects, and 41 little beetles scattered as if sequins'

(Snook, English Embroidery, p. 72).

The enthusiasm for the natural world (and all its inhabitants) as subjects for embroidery is evident in the coats and waistcoats of the eighteenth-century gentleman. Made from silk, often woven with delicate stripes and sprig designs, these garments, and their numerous embroidered buttons and buttonholes, were worked in coloured silks and metal threads. A particularly interesting example is the ivory satin waistcoat, c.1780, with a variety of beetles (some in flight with outspread elytra), dragonflies, wasps, snails, spiders and grasshoppers, embroidered in a border on either side of the front opening and around the hem. The front of the vest is scattered with flying insects of all kinds including ladybirds, bees, flies, spiders and centipedes. An enchanting ladybird design embellishes the pocket flaps.

Insects continue to be a popular theme with contemporary embroiderers. One of the most innovative, Chilean artist Miguel Cisterna, working on traditional backgrounds of silk, taffeta or organdie, uses raffia, wooden beads, metallic

Embroidered ivory satin waistcoat, c. 1780.

thread, mussel shells, horsehair and splinters of jet to embroider exotic boxes, lampshades, stools and chairs. Cisterna's scarab beetles—smooth mussel shells applied to a silk and linen ground with black shiny raffia, silk-strung beads and silver and bronze metallic threads—and his dragonflies—raffia and diamantés on ivory silk ottoman—are just stunning.

How to Work a Beetle in Surface Embroidery

This chapter contains the diagrams and instructions for working more than 20 different beetles, using a variety of traditional surface embroidery stitches. Based on the beetles in the Specimen Box, the drawings have been simplified and enlarged a little, and were used to work the endpapers of the book.

There are many items that would benefit from the addition of a beetle:

- Embroider one beetle on a pocket or collar; on children's clothing; in the corner of table napkins; on shoe or gift bags; or in the centre of a plump pincushion.
- Work a row of beetles on a hat band; on the placket of a shirt; around a mirror or picture frame; at the edge of sheets; or on the border of a woollen scarf.
- Scatter a handful of beetles over a carry bag; a cushion; a linen shirt; a woollen wrap; a baby's blanket; or embellish a crazy quilt.

Before you start embroidering these beetles, the following information may be helpful:

- An embroidered beetle can be worked on almost any background fabric—silk, satin, linen twill, cottons, velvet, wool or felt. Unless the background fabric needs support, there is no need for a backing fabric. Mount the fabric into a hoop or frame, although surface embroidery can be worked in the hand if preferred.

- The embroidery can be worked with a wide variety of threads—silks, rayons, cottons, crewel wools, and metallic threads, using the appropriate needles. Check that the laundering requirements of the threads are suitable for the future use of the embroidered item.
- There is not enough space in this book to give detailed instructions on how to work these surface embroidery stitches. Please refer to one of the stitch manuals listed in the Bibliography.
- Trace a skeleton outline of the beetle onto the background using the method most appropriate for the fabric selected.
- The size of the beetle outline may be altered with aid of a photocopier. The Ladybird Notebook Cover, for example, uses three different sizes of ladybird.
- Embroider the beetle in the following order: elytra (wing cases), thorax, head and eyes, antennae and finally the legs.

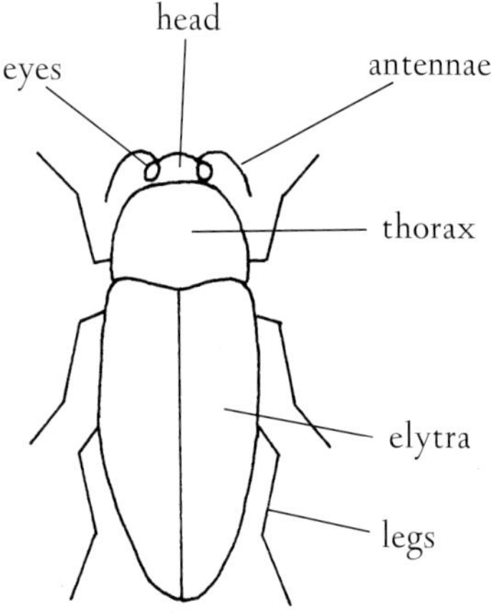

Beetle parts to embroider

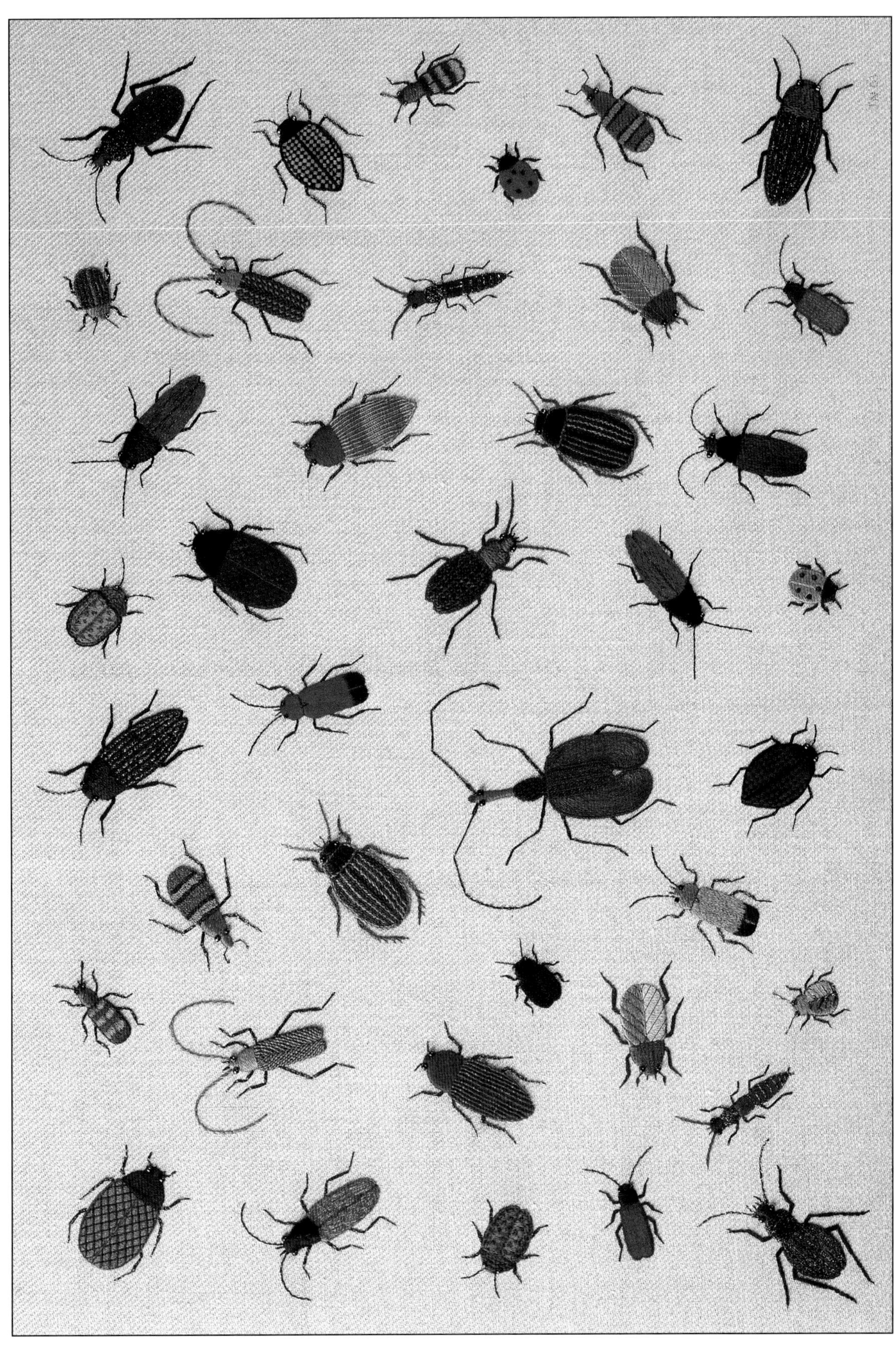

Violet Jewel Beetle
Orange Jewel Beetle

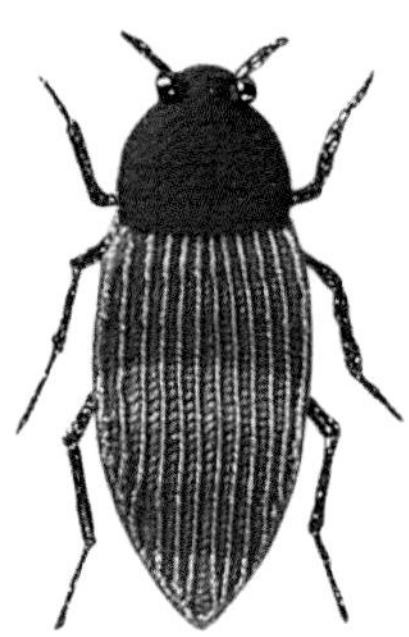

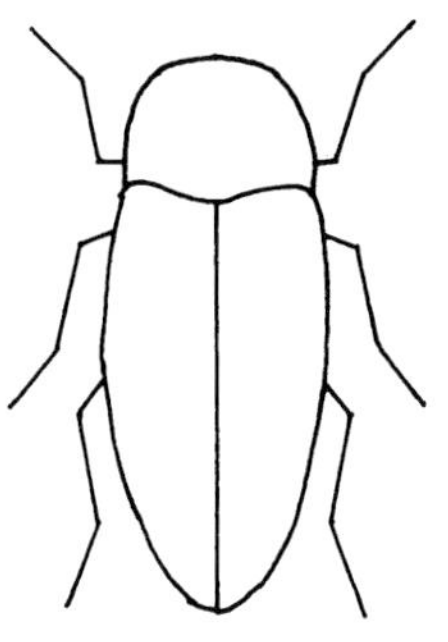

skeleton outline

Requirements

Violet Jewel Beetle

- violet stranded thread (DMC 791)
- teal stranded thread (DMC 3808)
- Madeira Metallic No.40 (aqua 37)
- Kreinik Very Fine (#4) Metallic Braid (bronze 154V)
- Mill Hill Seed Beads 374 (blue-black)

Orange Jewel Beetle

- dark orange stranded thread (Soie d'Alger 615)
- medium orange stranded thread (Soie d'Alger 614)
- light orange stranded thread (Soie d'Alger 612)
- copper stranded thread (Soie d'Alger 616)
- Mill Hill seed beads (374 blue-black)

Trace the skeleton outline of the beetle onto the background fabric. All embroidery is worked with two strands of thread unless otherwise indicated. The instructions relate to the violet beetle. Substitute the alternate colours for the orange beetle.

Elytra

The elytra are worked in whipped spider web stitch. Using violet thread, outline the elytra in stem stitch, then work a grid of 10 vertical straight stitches within the outline. Using three strands of thread (one each of violet, teal and aqua), fill the elytra with whipped spider web stitch, whipping each of the laid threads *and* the outline on each side of the elytra to form a ribbed surface.

(For the Orange beetle, whip with two strands of thread in bands of each shade of orange.)

Thorax

With violet thread, outline the thorax in split stitch then cover with padded satin stitch.

Head and eyes

Embroider the head in padded satin stitch with violet thread. Stitch a bead on either side of the head for eyes.

Antennae

Using one strand of bronze metallic thread, work the antennae with straight stitches.

Legs

Using one strand of bronze metallic thread, work two chain stitches for the two inner leg segments, with a long tie-down stitch forming the outer segment.

Aubergine Pill Beetle
Honey Pill Beetle

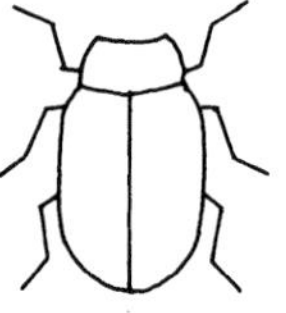

skeleton outline

Requirements

Aubergine Pill Beetle

- dark purple stranded thread (Soie d'Alger 3326)
- dark plum stranded thread (Soie d'Alger 4626)
- Kreinik Very Fine (#4) Braid (brown 022)
- Kreinik Metallic Cord (wine 208c)
- Mill Hill petite beads (40374 blue-black)

Honey Pill Beetle

- old gold stranded thread (Soie d'Alger 526)
- honey stranded thread (Soie d'Alger 524)
- Kreinik Very Fine (#4) Braid (bronze 154V)
- Kreinik Metallic Cord (brown 201c)
- Mill Hill petite beads (40374 blue-black)

Trace the skeleton outline of the beetle onto the background fabric. All embroidery is worked with two strands of thread unless otherwise indicated. The instructions relate to the aubergine beetle. Substitute the alternate colours for the honey beetle.

Elytra

Outline the elytra in stem stitch with dark plum thread. Fill the elytra with alternate rows of French knots in dark purple thread, and stem stitch in dark plum.

Thorax

With dark plum thread, outline the thorax in split stitch then cover with padded satin stitch.

Head and eyes

Embroider the head in padded satin stitch with dark plum thread. Stitch a bead on either side of the head for eyes.

Antennae

Using a double strand of wine metallic thread, work the antennae with straight stitches.

Legs

Work the leg in straight stitches, using two strands of brown metallic thread for the inner segments and one strand for the outer segment.

Amber Soldier Beetle
Rouge Soldier Beetle

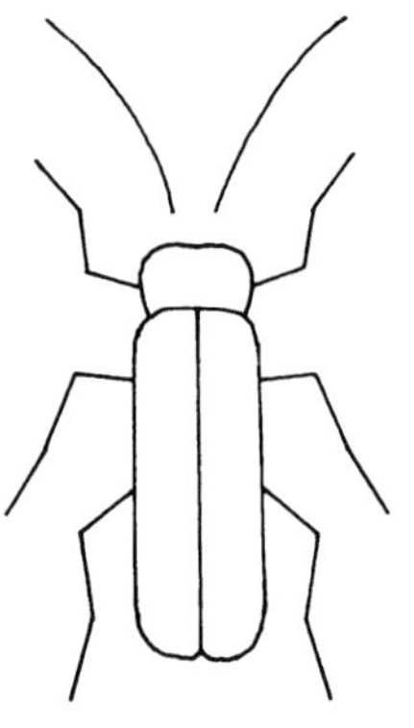

skeleton outline

Requirements

Amber Soldier Beetle

- orange stranded thread (Soie d'Alger 614)
- dark brown stranded thread (Soie d'Alger 4136)
- Kreinik Very Fine (#4) Braid (orange 152V)
- Kreinik Very Fine (#4) Metallic Braid (brown 022)
- Mill Hill petite beads (42014 black)

Rouge Soldier Beetle

- red stranded thread (Soie d'Alger 916)
- dark purple stranded thread (Soie d'Alger 3326)
- Kreinik Very Fine (#4) Braid (red 061)
- Mill Hill petite beads (42014 black)

Trace the skeleton outline of the beetle onto the background fabric. All embroidery is worked with one strand of thread unless otherwise indicated. The instructions relate to the amber beetle. Substitute the alternate colours for the rouge beetle.

Elytra

Outline the elytra in stem stitch with orange thread, changing to dark brown for the tips of the elytra. Work the centre line in chain stitch with orange thread. Embroider the elytra in long and short stitch, starting with dark brown thread at the tip then blending to orange for the remainder.

Thorax

With orange thread, outline the thorax in split stitch then cover with padded satin stitch. Work a straight stitch between the thorax and the elytra with orange metallic thread.

Head and eyes

Embroider the head in padded satin stitch with orange thread. Stitch a bead on either side of the head for eyes.

Antennae

Using one strand of brown metallic thread, work the antennae in back stitch and the mouthparts with straight stitches.

Legs

Work the leg in straight stitches, using two strands of orange metallic thread for the inner segments, and one strand of brown metallic thread for the outer segment.

Tan Violin Beetle

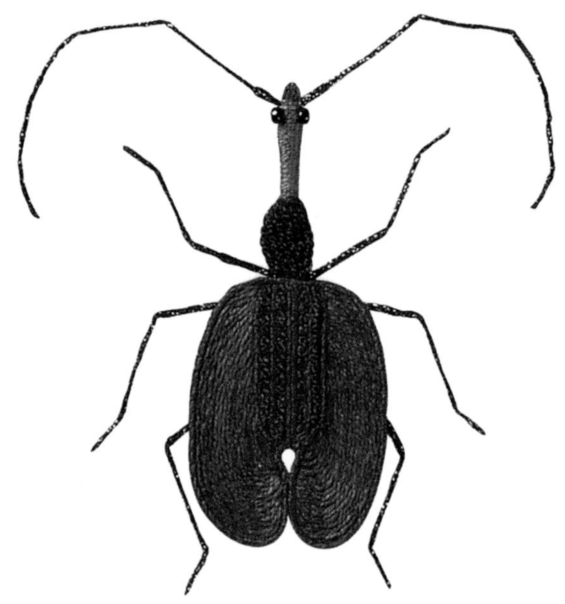

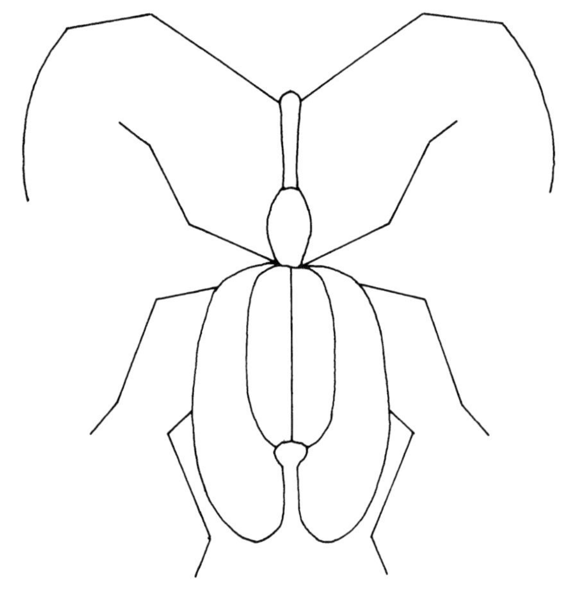

skeleton outline

Requirements

- dark tan stranded thread (DMC 300)
- medium tan stranded thread (DMC 400)
- light tan stranded thread (DMC 301)
- dark brown stranded thread (DMC 3371)
- medium brown stranded thread (DMC 938)
- Kreinik Fine (#8) Metallic Braid (brown 022)
- nylon thread (Madeira Monofil No.60, dark)
- Mill Hill seed beads (2014 black)

Trace the skeleton outline of the beetle onto the background fabric. All embroidery is worked with two strands of thread unless otherwise indicated.

Elytra

Outline the elytra in whipped chain stitch with dark tan thread. Work the centre panel with alternate rows of French knots (three strands—two dark tan and one medium brown) and whipped chain stitch (dark tan). Fill the remaining elytra with rows of stem stitch (dark and medium tan threads).

Thorax

Fill the thorax with French knots worked with three strands of mixed threads (dark tan, dark and medium brown).

Head and eyes

Embroider the head in padded satin stitch with light tan thread. Stitch a bead on either side of the head for eyes.

Antennae

Using brown metallic braid, work each antenna with a chain stitch (near the head) and back stitches, following the outline. Couch the longer stitches in place with nylon thread. Work two chain stitches for the mouthparts with dark tan thread.

Legs

Work each leg with straight stitches in brown metallic braid—two strands for the inner leg segment and one strand for the middle and outer leg. Couch the long straight stitches in place with nylon thread.

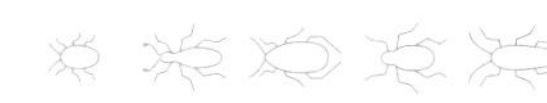

Green Ground Beetle

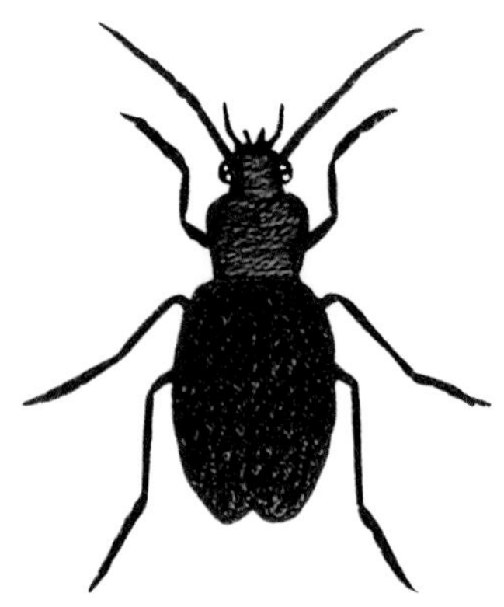

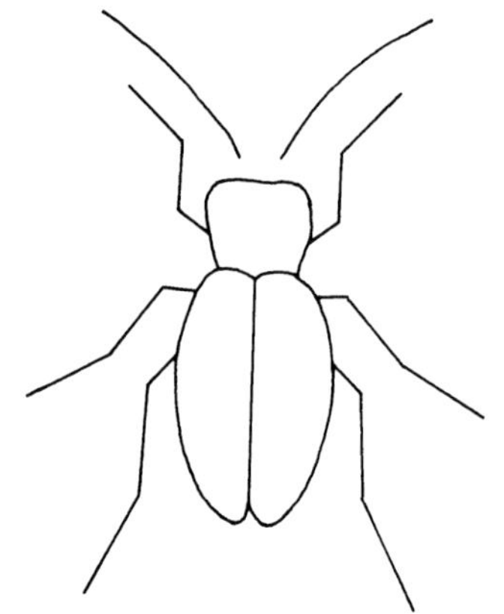

skeleton outline

Requirements

- dark green stranded thread (Soie d'Alger 216)
- medium green stranded thread (Soie d'Alger 215)
- navy blue stranded thread (Soie d'Alger 163)
- rust stranded thread (Soie d'Alger 2636)
- dark rust stranded thread (Soie d'Alger 4615)
- Mill Hill seed beads (374 blue-black)

Trace the skeleton outline of the beetle onto the background fabric. All embroidery is worked with two strands of thread unless otherwise indicated.

Elytra

Outline the elytra in stem stitch with rust thread. Starting in the centre, fill the elytra with rows of back stitched chain stitch, using mixed green threads for the chain stitch and navy for the back stitches.

Thorax

Outline the thorax in stem stitch with rust thread. Work the thorax in flat stitch with mixed green threads.

Head and eyes

Embroider the head in padded satin stitch with mixed green threads. Stitch a bead on either side of the head for eyes.

Antennae

Using one strand of thread, work the antennae in chain stitch with rust, and the mouthparts in back stitch with dark rust.

Legs

Using dark rust thread, work two straight stitches for each inner leg segment and one straight stitch for the middle segment. Work the outer leg segment with three or four chain stitches, using one strand of thread.

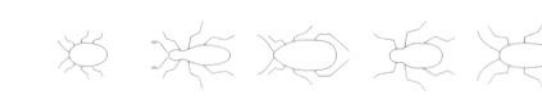

Steel Ground Beetle
Bronze Ground Beetle

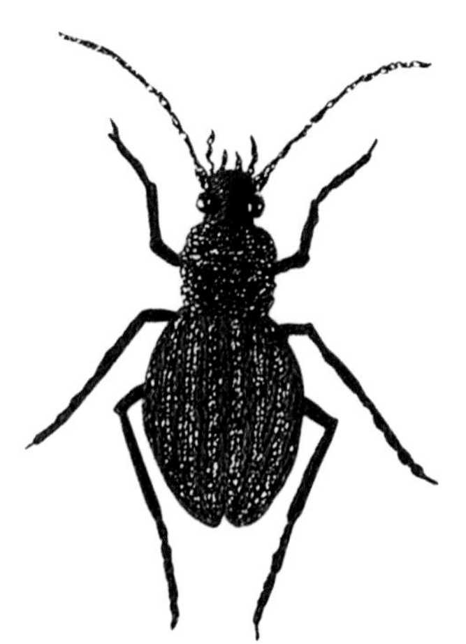

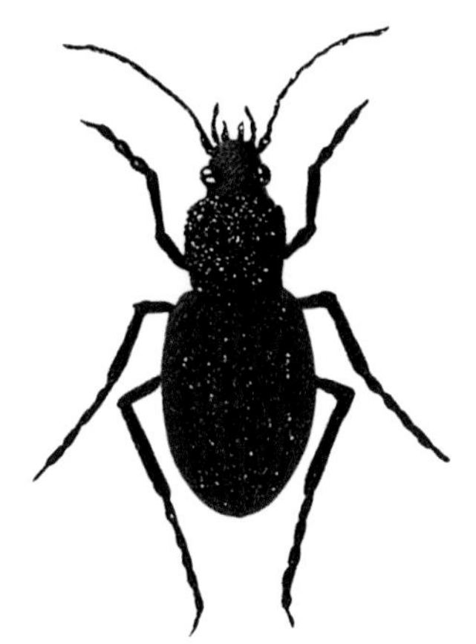

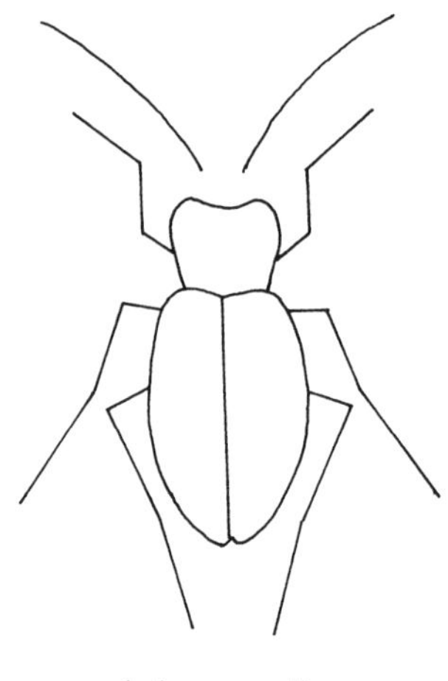

skeleton outline

Requirements

Steel Ground Beetle

- dark grey stranded thread (DMC 3799)
- dark purple stranded thread (Soie d'Alger 3326)
- Kreinik Fine (#8) Braid (steel grey 010HL)
- Kreinik Very Fine (#4) Braid (steel grey 010HL)
- Nylon thread (Madeira Monofil No.60, dark)
- Mill Hill seed beads (374 blue-black)

Bronze Ground Beetle

- Tan stranded thread (DMC 300)
- dark brown stranded thread (Soie d'Alger 4136)
- Kreinik Fine (#8) Braid (brown 022)
- Kreinik Very Fine (#4) Braid (brown 022)
- Nylon thread (Madeira Monofil No.60, dark)
- Mill Hill seed beads (374 blue-black)

Trace the skeleton outline of the beetle onto the background fabric. All embroidery is worked with two strands of thread unless otherwise indicated. The instructions relate to the steel beetle. Substitute the alternate colours for the bronze beetle.

Elytra

Work the elytra outline and centre lines in stem stitch with dark grey thread. Couch a double row of Fine #8 steel grey metallic thread inside the centre line (couch with nylon thread), then work two rows of stem stitch in dark grey thread. Fill the elytra with alternate rows of stranded and metallic threads to form stripes.

Thorax

Work the thorax in satin stitch using one strand of Fine #8 steel metallic thread.

Head and eyes

Embroider the head in padded satin stitch with dark grey thread. Stitch a bead on either side of the head for eyes.

Antennae

Using one strand of Very Fine #4 steel metallic thread, work the antennae and mouthparts in back stitch.

Legs

Using dark purple thread, work two chain stitches for the inner segments of each leg. Work each outer leg segment with three or four chain stitches, using one strand of thread.

Purple Longhorn Beetle
Mustard Longhorn Beetle

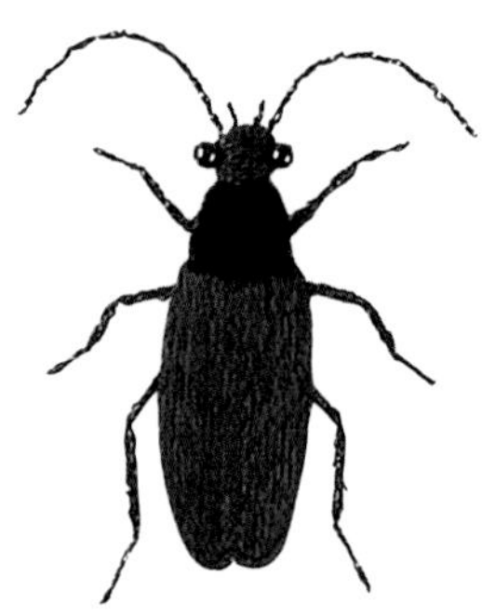

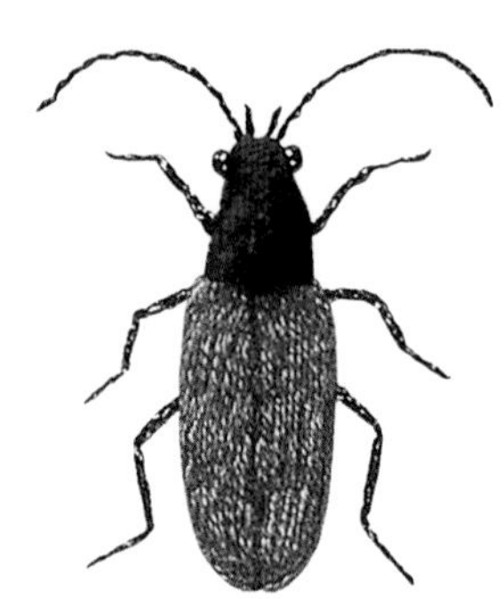

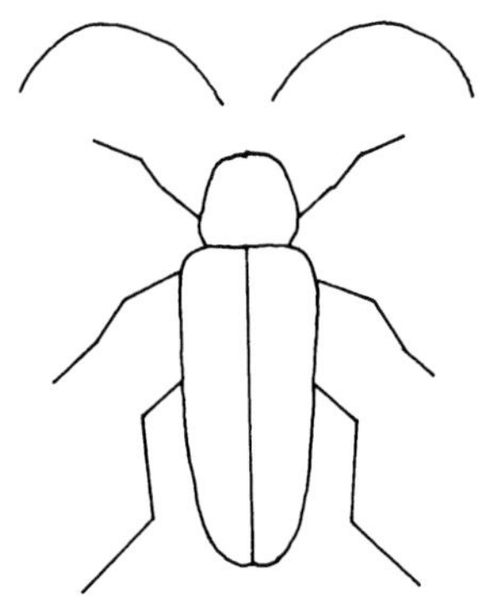

skeleton outline

Requirements

Purple Longhorn Beetle

- purple stranded thread (Soie d'Alger 3336)
- dark teal stranded thread (Soie d'Alger 135)
- Kreinik Very Fine (#4) Braid (purple 026V)
- Kreinik Very Fine (#4) Braid (emerald 009)
- Mill Hill seed beads (374 blue-black)

Mustard Longhorn Beetle

- old gold stranded thread (Soie d'Alger 524)
- purple stranded thread (Soie d'Alger 3336)
- Kreinik Very Fine (#4) Braid (bronze 154V)
- Kreinik Very Fine (#4) Braid (purple 026V)
- Mill Hill seed beads (374 blue-black)

Trace the skeleton outline of the beetle onto the background fabric. All embroidery is worked with two strands of thread unless otherwise indicated. The instructions relate to the purple beetle. Substitute the alternate colours for the mustard beetle.

ELYTRA

Using purple thread, outline the elytra in stem stitch, then embroider in Rumanian couching.

THORAX

With dark teal thread, outline the thorax in split stitch then fill with Turkey knots. Trim and comb the Turkey knots to form a short velvety mound.

HEAD AND EYES

Embroider the head in padded satin stitch with dark teal thread. Stitch a bead on either side of the head for eyes.

ANTENNAE

Using one strand of green metallic thread, work the antennae and mouthparts in back stitch.

LEGS

Work the leg in straight stitches, using two strands of purple metallic thread for the inner segments and one strand for the outer segment.

Chartreuse Longhorn Beetle
Peacock Longhorn Beetle

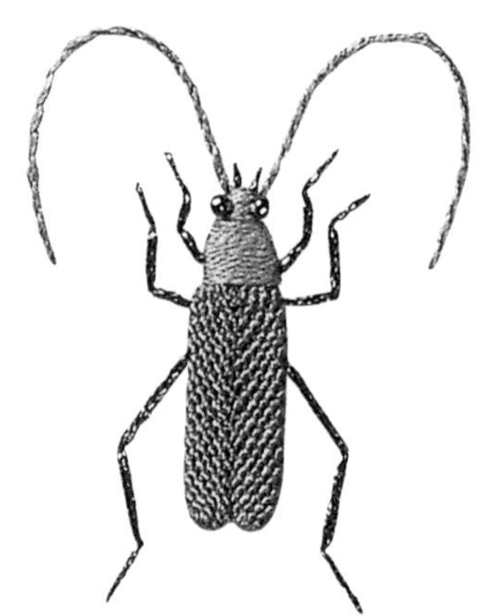

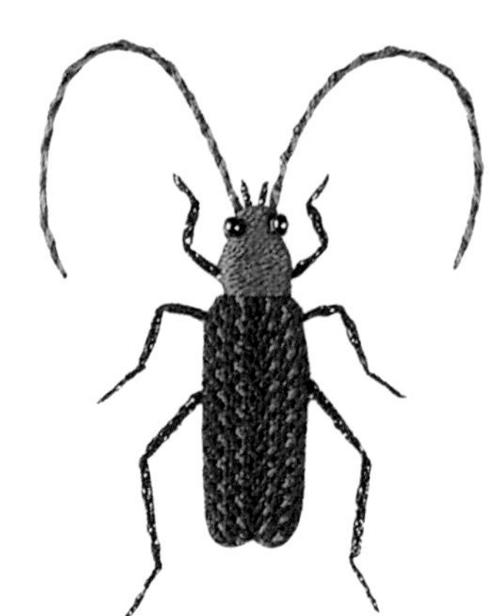

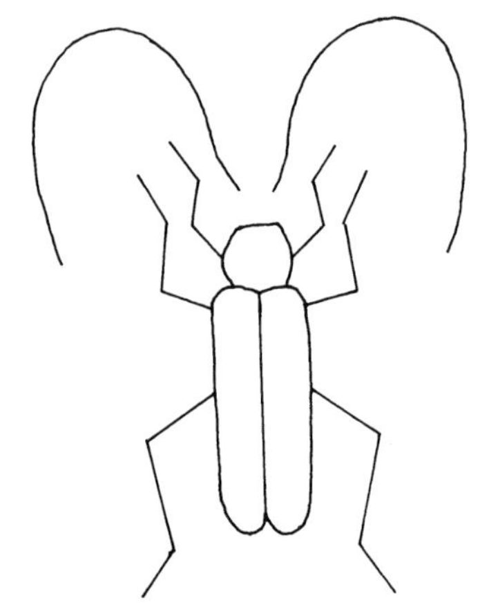

skeleton outline

Requirements

Chartreuse Longhorn Beetle

- grass green stranded thread (Soie d'Alger 514)
- lime green stranded thread (Soie d'Alger 2145)
- Kreinik Very Fine (#4) Metallic Braid (bronze 154V)
- Mill Hill antique beads (3036 cognac)

Peacock Longhorn Beetle

- teal stranded thread (Soie d'Alger 135)
- turquoise stranded thread (Soie d'Alger 134)
- Kreinik Very Fine (#4) Metallic Braid (bronze 154V)
- Mill Hill antique beads (3036 cognac)

Trace the skeleton outline of the beetle onto the background fabric. All embroidery is worked with two strands of thread unless otherwise indicated. The instructions relate to the chartreuse beetle. Substitute the alternate colours for the peacock beetle.

Elytra

Using grass green thread, outline the elytra in back stitch. The elytra are worked in trellis stitch, working two rows with grass green thread to one row with lime green. Starting at the outer edge, work the first row of trellis stitch into the back stitches of the elytra outline. Catch both inner edges along the centre line.

Thorax

With lime green thread, outline the thorax in split stitch then cover with padded satin stitch.

Head and eyes

Embroider the head in padded satin stitch with lime green thread. Stitch a bead on either side of the head for eyes.

Antennae

Using one strand of thread, work the antennae in whipped chain stitch, using lime green thread for the chain stitches and grass green to whip. Using one strand of bronze metallic thread, work the mouthparts with straight stitches.

Legs

Work the leg in straight stitches, using two strands of bronze metallic thread for the inner segments and one strand for the outer segment.

Kelly Green Leaf Beetle

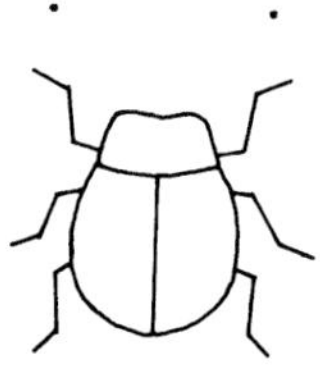

skeleton outline

Requirements

- pale green stranded thread (DMC 701)
- medium green stranded thread (DMC 700)
- dark green stranded thread (DMC 895)
- Kreinik Blending Filament (peacock 085)
- Mill Hill petite beads (40374 blue-black)

Trace the skeleton outline of the beetle onto the background fabric. All embroidery is worked with two strands of thread unless otherwise indicated.

Elytra

Embroider the elytra in fishbone stitch, using one strand of each of pale green thread and peacock blending filament in the needle. Using one strand of peacock filament, outline the elytra with stem stitch and work two straight stitches down the centre line.

Thorax

With medium green thread, outline the thorax in split stitch then cover with padded satin stitch.

Head and eyes

Embroider the head in satin stitch with medium green thread. Stitch a bead on either side of the head for eyes.

ANTENNAE
Using two strands of peacock filament, work a straight stitch with a French knot at the end for each antenna.

LEGS
Using one strand of dark green thread, work two chain stitches for the two inner leg segments; with a long tie-down stitch forming the outer segment (the first chain stitch is very short).

MARINE TORTOISE BEETLE AQUA TORTOISE BEETLE

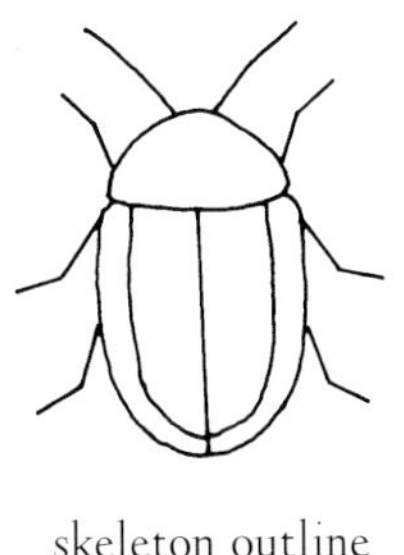

skeleton outline

Requirements

Marine Tortoise Beetle

- medium green stranded thread (Soie d'Alger 215)
- dark green stranded thread (Soie d'Alger 216)
- bright blue stranded thread (DMC 3842)
- Kreinik Very Fine (#4) Metallic Braid (blue 060)
- Mill Hill petite beads (40374 blue-black)

Marine Tortoise Beetle

- turquoise stranded thread (Soie d'Alger 134)
- bright blue stranded thread (DMC 3842)

- navy blue stranded thread (DMC 823)
- Kreinik Very Fine (#4) Metallic Braid (blue 060)
- Mill Hill petite beads (40374 blue-black)

Trace the skeleton outline of the beetle onto the background fabric. All embroidery is worked with two strands of thread unless otherwise indicated. The instructions relate to the marine beetle. Substitute the alternate colours for the aqua beetle.

Elytra

Using medium green thread, embroider the centre of the elytra in padded satin stitch, then work dark green spots with French knots. Work two rows of chain stitch to form the elytra rim—the inner row in medium green thread and the outer row in dark green. Outline the elytra in stem stitch using one strand of bright blue thread.

Thorax

Outline and fill the thorax with rows of chain stitch worked with dark green thread.

Head and eyes

Embroider the head in satin stitch with dark green thread. Stitch a bead on either side of the head for eyes.

Antennae

Work the antennae in back stitch with one strand of blue metallic thread.

Legs

Using one strand of blue metallic thread, work a chain stitch for the inner leg segment, with a long tie-down stitch forming the outer segment.

Teal Checkered Beetle
Wine Checkered Beetle

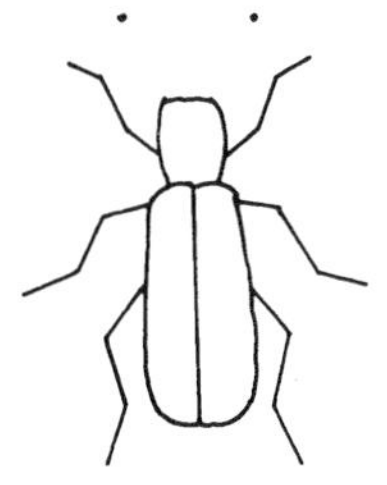

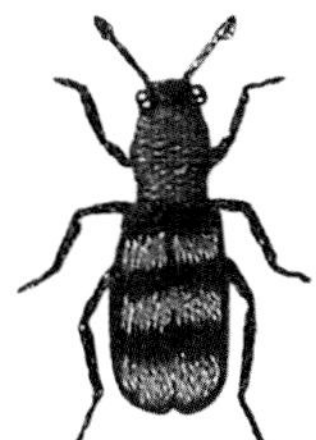

skeleton outline

Requirements

Teal Checkered Beetle

- teal stranded thread (Soie d'Alger 135)
- orange stranded thread (Soie d'Alger 614)
- blue green stranded thread (Soie d'Alger 1826)
- Kreinik Very Fine (#4) Braid (emerald 009)
- Kreinik Very Fine (#4) Braid (bronze 154V)
- Mill Hill petite beads (42028 ginger)

Wine Checkered Beetle

- lime stranded thread (Soie d'Alger 2144)
- wine stranded thread (Soie d'Alger 4636)
- light wine stranded thread (Soie d'Alger 4635)
- Kreinik Very Fine (#4) Braid (purple 026V)
- Kreinik Very Fine (#4) Braid (orange 152V)
- Mill Hill petite beads (42028 ginger)

Trace the skeleton outline of the beetle onto the background fabric. All embroidery is worked with two strands of thread unless otherwise indicated. The instructions relate to the teal beetle. Substitute the alternate colours for the wine beetle.

Elytra

The elytra are embroidered in striped woven bands. Using orange thread, outline the elytra in split stitch, pad with long stitches, then work a foundation grid of six horizontal stitches across the elytra. Work a row of split stitch along the centre line to secure the grid stitches. Starting the weaving near the thorax, fill the elytra with striped woven bands, using orange and teal threads.

Thorax

With blue green thread, outline the thorax in split stitch then cover with padded satin stitch.

Head and eyes

Embroider the head in satin stitch with teal thread. Stitch a bead on either side of the head for eyes.

Antennae

Using one strand of bronze metallic thread, work a tiny chain stitch with a long tie-down for each antenna.

Legs

Work the leg in straight stitches, using two strands of emerald metallic thread for the inner segments and one strand for the outer segment.

Red Ladybird
Yellow Ladybird

skeleton outline

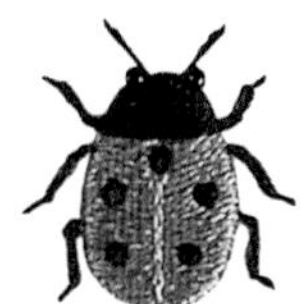

Requirements

Red Ladybird

- red stranded thread (DMC 321)
- black stranded thread (DMC 310)
- Mill Hill petite beads (42014 black)

Yellow Ladybird

- yellow stranded thread (Soie d'Alger 612)
- dark purple stranded thread (Soie d'Alger 3326)
- Mill Hill petite beads (42014 black)

Trace the skeleton outline of the ladybird onto the background fabric. All embroidery is worked with one strand of thread unless otherwise indicated. The instructions relate to the red ladybird. Substitute the alternate colours for the yellow ladybird.

Elytra

Using red thread, outline the elytra in split stitch, then pad with straight stitches. Embroider the elytra in flat stitch, starting at the thorax and covering the outline. Work a row of split stitch down the centre line. Embroider the black spots in satin stitch (across the flat stitches).

Thorax

With black thread, outline the thorax in split stitch then cover with padded satin stitch.

HEAD AND EYES
Embroider the head in satin stitch with black thread. Stitch a bead on either side of the head for eyes.

ANTENNAE
Work two straight stitches in black thread for the antennae.

LEGS
Using black thread, work two chain stitches for the two inner leg segments; with a long tie-down stitch forming the outer segment (the first chain stitch is very short).

Turquoise Weevil
Pumpkin Weevil

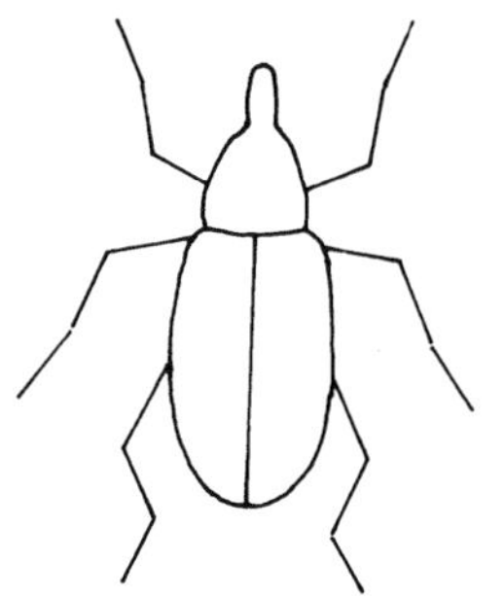

skeleton outline

Requirements

Turquoise Weevil

- turquoise stranded thread (Soie d'Alger 134)
- bright blue stranded thread (DMC 3842)
- navy blue stranded thread (DMC 823)
- Kreinik Very Fine (#4) Braid (blue 060)
- Kreinik Metallic Cord (blue/black 202c)
- Mill Hill seed beads (374 blue-black)

Pumpkin Weevil

- yellow stranded thread (Soie d'Alger 612)
- orange stranded thread (Soie d'Alger 614)
- grey stranded thread (DMC 3799)
- Kreinik Very Fine (#4) Braid (steel 010HL)
- Kreinik Metallic Cord (nickel 011c)
- Mill Hill seed beads (374 blue-black)

Trace the skeleton outline of the beetle onto the background fabric. All embroidery is worked with two strands of thread unless otherwise indicated. The instructions relate to the turquoise weevil. Substitute the alternate colours for the pumpkin weevil.

Elytra

Using bright blue thread, outline the elytra and work the centre line in split stitch. The elytra is filled with rows of French knots (one row of navy blue, two rows of turquoise, one row of navy blue, four rows of bright blue—repeat).

Thorax, head and eyes

Outline the thorax and the head in split stitch then cover with padded satin stitch using one strand of bright blue thread. Stitch a bead on either side of the head for eyes.

Antennae

Using two strands of blue/black metallic thread, work two straight stitches with a French knot at the end for each antenna.

Legs

With one strand of blue metallic thread, work two chain stitches for the two inner leg segments, with a long tie-down stitch forming the outer segment.

Khaki Diving Beetle
Chocolate Diving Beetle

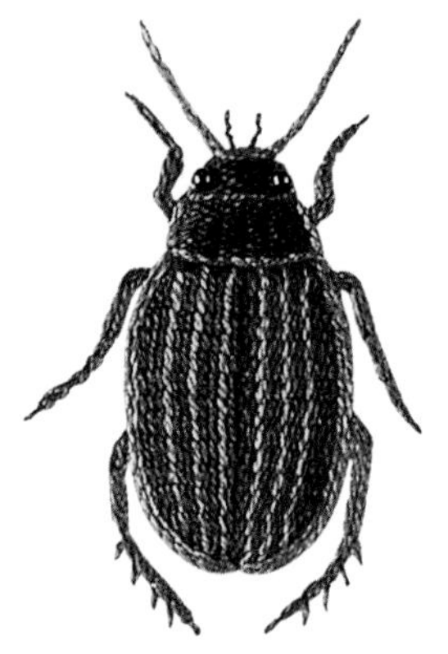

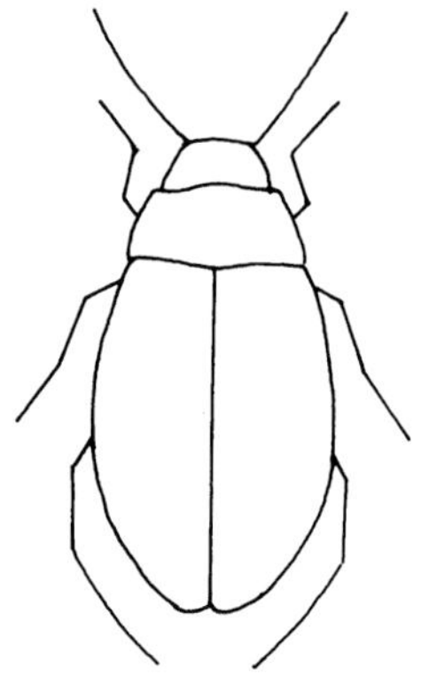

skeleton outline

Requirements

Khaki Diving Beetle

- khaki stranded thread (Soie d'Alger 2216)
- medium gold stranded thread (Soie d'Alger 525)
- dark gold stranded thread (Soie d'Alger 526)
- Mill Hill seed beads (374 blue-black)

Khaki Diving Beetle

- dark brown stranded thread (Soie d'Alger 4136)
- light tan stranded thread (Soie d'Alger 4214)
- medium tan stranded thread (Soie d'Alger 4215)
- Mill Hill seed beads (374 blue-black)

Trace the skeleton outline of the beetle onto the background fabric. All embroidery is worked with two strands of thread unless otherwise indicated. The instructions relate to the khaki beetle. Substitute the alternate colours for the chocolate beetle.

Elytra

The elytra are worked in raised stem stitch. Work a grid of straight stitches, 2 mm (1/16 in) apart, across the elytra with khaki thread (hold in place on the centre line with a row of stem stitch). Starting from the centre, fill the elytra with rows of raised stem stitch, two rows of khaki to one row of medium gold, to form stripes. Outline the elytra with two rows of stem stitch in medium gold thread.

Thorax

Fill the thorax with raised stem stitch in khaki thread (worked over a grid of four stitches), then outline in stem stitch with medium gold thread.

Head and eyes

Embroider the head in padded satin stitch with khaki thread. Stitch a bead on either side of the head for eyes. Work a few satin stitches in medium gold at the front edge.

Antennae

Using one strand of thread, work the antennae in split stitch with medium gold, and the mouthparts in back stitch with khaki.

Legs

Using dark gold thread, work two chain stitches for the inner segments of each leg. With one strand of thread, work each outer leg segment with three or four chain stitches, and the hairs on the back legs with straight stitches.

Amethyst Click Beetle
Emerald Click Beetle

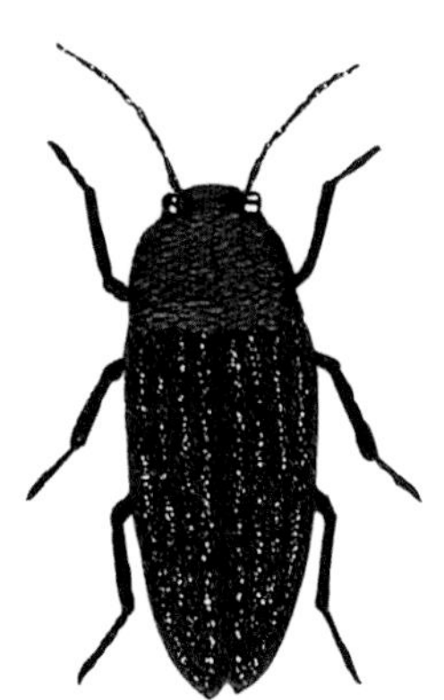

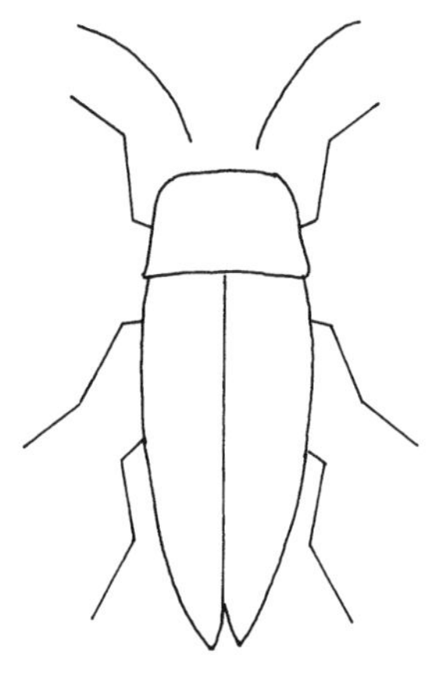

skeleton outline

Requirements

Amethyst Click Beetle

- medium purple stranded thread (Soie d'Alger 3316)
- dark purple stranded thread (Soie d'Alger 3326)
- Kreinik Medium (#16) Braid (peacock 850)
- Kreinik Blending Filament (peacock 085)
- nylon thread (Madeira Monofil No.60, clear)
- Mill Hill seed beads (374 blue-black)

Emerald Click Beetle

- emerald stranded thread (Soie d'Alger 216)
- black stranded thread (Soie d'Alger Noir)
- Kreinik Medium (#16) Braid (emerald 009)
- Kreinik Blending Filament (emerald 009)
- nylon thread (Madeira Monofil No.60, clear)
- Mill Hill seed beads (374 blue-black)

Trace the skeleton outline of the beetle onto the background fabric. All embroidery is worked with two strands of thread unless otherwise indicated. The instructions relate to the amethyst beetle. Substitute the alternate colours for the emerald beetle.

Elytra

Work the elytra outline and centre lines in stem stitch with three strands of medium purple thread. Couch a row of peacock metallic braid inside these stitched lines (couch with nylon thread). Fill the elytra with alternate rows of stranded and metallic threads to form stripes.

Thorax

Outline the thorax in split stitch then cover with raised stem stitch in medium purple thread (worked over a grid of five stitches).

Head and eyes

Embroider the head in padded satin stitch with medium purple thread. Stitch a bead on either side of the head for eyes.

Antennae

Work the antennae in chain stitch with two strands of peacock blending filament.

Legs

Using dark purple thread, work two chain stitches for the two inner leg segments, with a long tie-down stitch forming the outer segment.

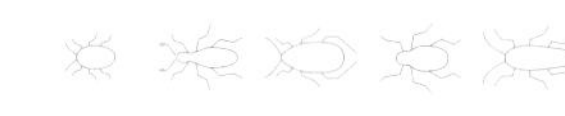

Crimson Skipjack Beetle
Tangerine Skipjack Beetle

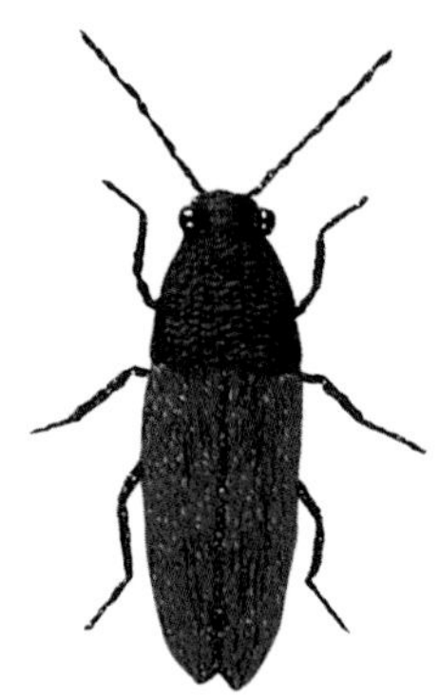

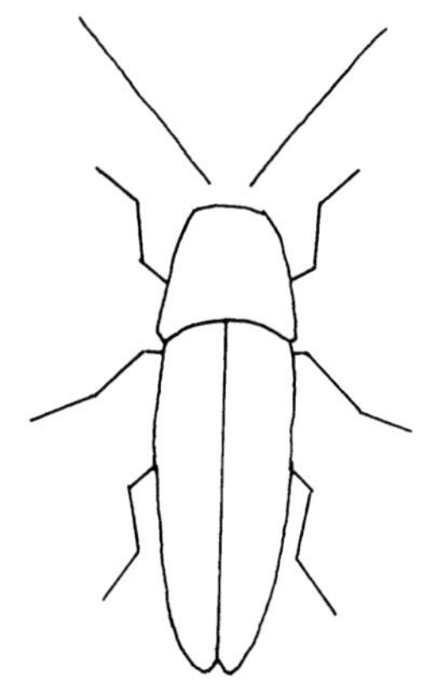

skeleton outline

Requirements

Crimson Skipjack Beetle

- red stranded thread (Soie d'Alger 916)
- dark purple stranded thread (Soie d'Alger 3326)
- black stranded thread (Soie d'Alger noir)
- Kreinik Blending Filament (ruby 061)
- Kreinik Very Fine (#4) Metallic Braid (ruby 061)
- Kreinik Very Fine (#4) Metallic Braid (black 005)
- nylon thread (Madeira Monofil No.60, clear)
- Mill Hill antique beads (3004 eggplant)

Tangerine Skipjack Beetle

- orange stranded thread (Soie d'Alger 646)
- purple stranded thread (Soie d'Alger 3336)
- dark purple stranded thread (Soie d'Alger 3326)
- Kreinik Blending Filament (ruby 061)
- Kreinik Very Fine (#4) Metallic Braid (ruby 061)

- Kreinik Very Fine #4 Metallic Braid (black 005)
- nylon thread (Madeira Monofil No.60, clear)
- Mill Hill antique beads (3004 eggplant)

Trace the skeleton outline of the beetle onto the background fabric. All embroidery is worked with two strands of thread unless otherwise indicated. The instructions relate to the crimson beetle. Substitute the alternate colours for the tangerine beetle.

Elytra

Starting at the outer edge, fill the elytra with rows of stem stitch (working towards the tip), using two strands of red thread and one strand of ruby blending filament. Couch a double row of ruby metallic braid down the centre line (couch with nylon thread).

Thorax

Using one strand each of black and dark purple thread, outline the thorax in split stitch then cover with raised stem stitch (worked over a grid of four stitches).

Head and eyes

Embroider the head in padded satin stitch with the combined black and dark purple threads. Stitch a bead on either side of the head for eyes.

Antennae

Work the antennae in back stitch with one strand of black metallic braid.

Legs

Work the leg in straight stitches, using two strands of black metallic thread for the inner segments and one strand for the outer segment.

Rust-purple Fungus Beetle
Navy-green Fungus Beetle

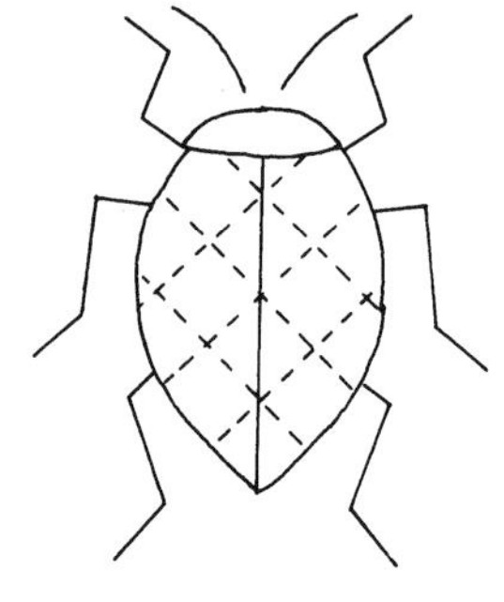

skeleton outline

Requirements

Rust-purple Fungus Beetle

- rust stranded thread (Soie d'Alger 616)
- dark purple stranded thread (Soie d'Alger 3326)
- Kreinik Very Fine (#4) Braid (brown 022)
- Mill Hill seed beads (374 blue-black)

Navy-green Fungus Beetle

- green stranded thread (DMC 701)
- navy stranded thread (DMC 939)
- Kreinik Very Fine (#4) Braid (emerald 009)
- Mill Hill seed beads (374 blue-black)

Trace the skeleton outline of the beetle onto the background fabric. All embroidery is worked with one strand of thread unless otherwise indicated. The instructions relate to the rust-purple beetle. Substitute the alternate colours for the navy-green beetle.

ELYTRA

The elytra are worked in plaited stitch (woven over four threads), a variation of surface darning. Using rust thread, cover the elytra with a foundation of diagonal satin stitch. Weave in and out of the foundation (under and over four threads) with dark purple thread, forming a basket-work pattern. Using two strands of dark purple thread, outline the elytra in stem stitch and work a row of split stitch along the centre line.

THORAX

With dark purple thread, outline the thorax in split stitch then cover with padded satin stitch.

HEAD AND EYES

Embroider the head in padded satin stitch with dark purple thread. Stitch a bead on either side of the head for eyes.

ANTENNAE

Work the antennae in back stitch with brown metallic thread.

LEGS

Using brown metallic thread, work two chain stitches for the two inner leg segments, with a long tie-down stitch forming the outer segment.

Garnet Net-winged Beetle
Coral Net-winged Beetle

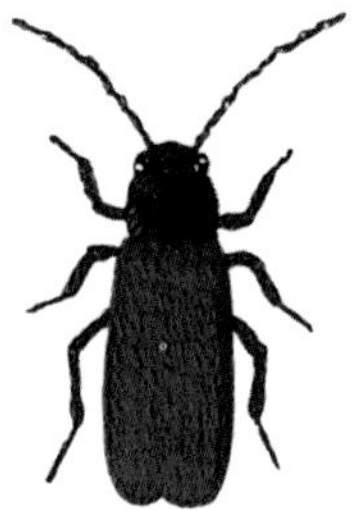

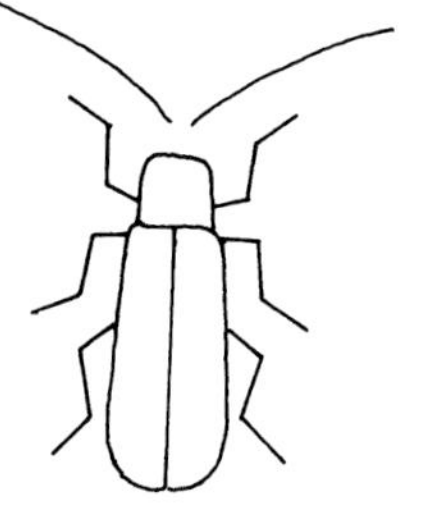

skeleton outline

Requirements

Garnet Net-winged Beetle

- wine stranded thread (Soie d'Alger 945)
- dark wine stranded thread (Soie d'Alger 946)
- garnet stranded thread (Soie d'Alger 4626)
- Kreinik Very Fine (#4) Braid (red 003V)
- Mill Hill petite beads (42014 black)

Coral Net-winged Beetle

- burnt orange stranded thread (Soie d'Alger 646)
- copper stranded thread (Soie d'Alger 616)
- russet stranded thread (Soie d'Alger 4615)
- Kreinik Very Fine (#4) Braid (orange 152V)
- Mill Hill petite beads (42014 black)

Trace the skeleton outline of the beetle onto the background fabric. All embroidery is worked with one strand of thread unless otherwise indicated. The instructions relate to the garnet beetle. Substitute the alternate colours for the coral beetle.

Elytra

The elytra are worked in raised stem stitch. Work a grid of straight stitches, 2 mm ($^1/_{16}$ in) apart, across the elytra with two strands of wine thread (hold in place on the centre line with a row of split stitch). Starting from the centre, fill the elytra with rows of raised stem stitch, two rows of wine to one row of dark wine, to form stripes. Outline the elytra with a row of stem stitch in dark wine thread.

Thorax

With two strands of garnet thread, outline the thorax in split stitch then cover with padded satin stitch.

Head and eyes

Embroider the head in padded satin stitch with two strands of garnet thread. Stitch a bead on either side of the head for eyes.

Antennae

Embroider the antennae in back stitch with red metallic thread.

Legs

Using garnet thread, work two chain stitches for the two inner leg segments, with a long tie-down stitch forming the outer segment.

Burnt-Orange Scarab Beetle
Mahogany Scarab Beetle

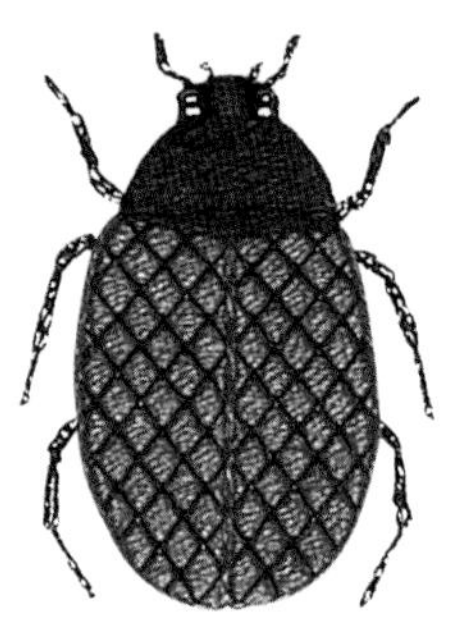

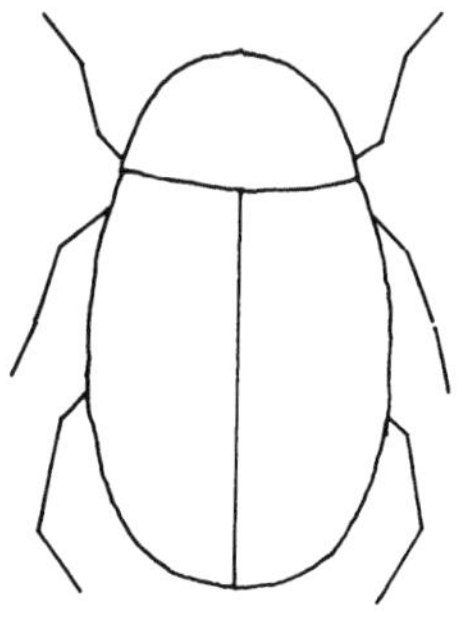

skeleton outline

Requirements

Burnt-orange Scarab Beetle

- burnt orange stranded thread (Soie d'Alger 646)
- dark purple stranded thread (Soie d'Alger 3326)
- Kreinik Metallic Cord (black 005c)
- Kreinik Very Fine (#4) Braid (steel 010HL)
- Mill Hill seed beads (374 blue-black)

Mahogany Scarab Beetle

- mahogany stranded thread (Soie d'Alger 2926)
- garnet stranded thread (Soie d'Alger 4626)
- Kreinik Metallic Cord (chocolate 201c)
- Kreinik Very Fine (#4) Braid (brown 022)
- Mill Hill seed beads (374 blue-black)

Trace the skeleton outline of the beetle onto the background fabric. All embroidery is worked with one strand of thread unless otherwise indicated. The instructions relate to the burnt orange beetle. Substitute the alternate colours for the mahogany beetle.

Elytra

Using burnt orange thread, embroider the elytra with padded horizontal satin stitch, inserting the needle at the centre line. Cover the satin stitch with lattice couching worked with fine black metallic thread. Work a row of stem stitch around the edge of the elytra, and a row of split stitch down the centre, with burnt orange thread.

Thorax

With dark purple thread, outline the thorax in split stitch then cover with flat stitch.

Head and eyes

Embroider the head in satin stitch with dark purple thread. Stitch a bead on either side of the head for eyes.

Antennae

Using steel metallic thread, work the antennae and mouthparts with straight stitches

Legs

With steel metallic thread, work two chain stitches for the two inner leg segments, with a long tie-down stitch forming the outer segment.

Lime Green Garden Chafer
Old Gold Garden Chafer

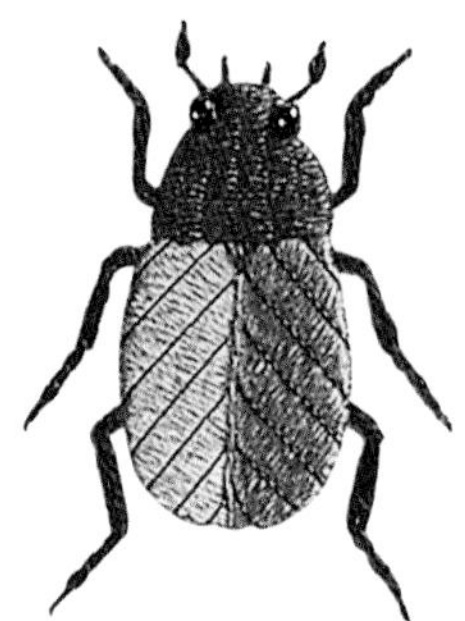

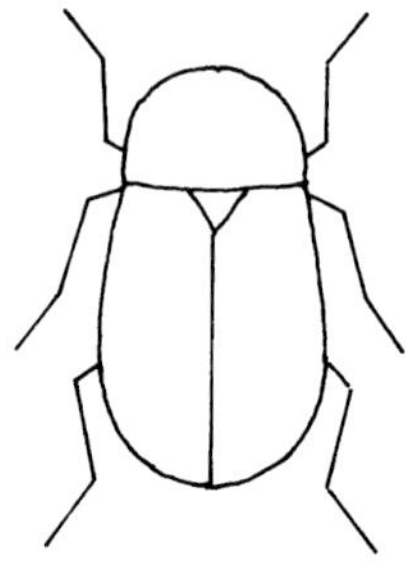

skeleton outline

Requirements

Lime Green Garden Chafer

- lime green stranded thread (Soie d'Alger 2144)
- mauve stranded thread (Soie d'Alger 4635)
- dark mauve stranded thread (Soie d'Alger 4636)
- Kreinik Metallic Cord (wine 208c)
- Mill Hill seed beads (374 blue-black)

Old Gold Garden Chafer

- old gold stranded thread (Soie d'Alger 524)
- dark old gold stranded thread (Soie d'Alger 526)
- khaki stranded thread (Soie d'Alger 2216)
- Kreinik Metallic Cord (gold/black 205c)
- Mill Hill seed beads (374 blue-black)

Trace the skeleton outline of the beetle onto the background fabric. All embroidery is worked with one strand of thread unless otherwise indicated. The instructions relate to the lime green beetle. Substitute the alternate colours for the old gold beetle.

Elytra

Using lime green thread, outline the elytra in split stitch, then cover with padded diagonal satin stitch, inserting the needle at the centre line. Work a row of split stitch down the centre of the elytra. Using fine black metallic thread, work a grid of parallel lines 2 mm ($^1/_{16}$ in) apart across the satin stitch, inserting the needle under the split stitches at the centre.

Thorax

With mauve thread, outline the thorax in split stitch then cover with raised stem stitch (worked over a grid of five double stitches).

Head and eyes

Embroider the head in satin stitch with mauve thread. Stitch a bead on either side of the head for eyes.

Antennae

Using dark mauve thread, work the antennae and mouthparts with straight stitches and chain stitches.

Legs

Using two strands of dark mauve thread, work two chain stitches for the inner segments of each leg. With one strand of thread, work each outer leg segment with three or four chain stitches.

Copper Rove Beetle
Pewter Rove Beetle

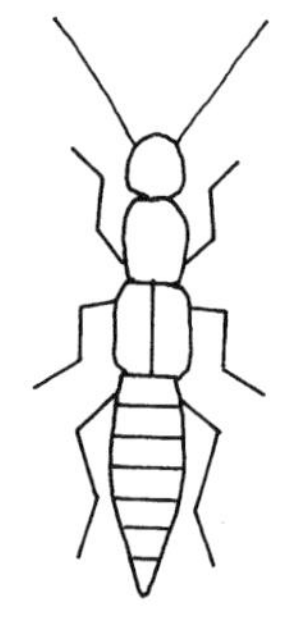

skeleton outline

Requirements

Copper Rove Beetle

- copper stranded thread (DMC 919)
- brown stranded thread (DMC 938)
- dark copper stranded thread (DMC 918)
- Kreinik Very Fine (#4) Braid (orange 152V)
- Kreinik Fine (#8) Braid (brown/black 022)
- Mill Hill petite beads (42014 black)

Pewter Rove Beetle

- dark grey stranded thread (DMC 3799)
- garnet stranded thread (DMC 814)
- ruby stranded thread (DMC 498)
- Kreinik Very Fine (#4) Braid (steel 010HL)
- Kreinik Fine (#8) Braid (burgundy 153V)
- Mill Hill petite beads (42014 black)

Trace the skeleton outline of the beetle onto the background fabric. All embroidery is worked with two strands of thread unless otherwise indicated. The instructions relate to the copper beetle. Substitute the alternate colours for the pewter beetle.

Elytra and abdomen

Using copper thread, work long satin stitches to fill the elytra and abdomen, tapering to a point at the tail. With one strand of orange metallic thread, work open chain stitch over the satin stitch, using the elytra and segment lines as a guide to stitch placement. Work a straight stitch for the centre of the elytra, and a fly stitch at the tail.

Thorax

Fill the thorax with French knots worked with one strand of orange metallic thread.

Head and eyes

Embroider the head in satin stitch with brown thread. Stitch a bead on either side of the head for eyes.

Antennae

Work the antennae in chain stitch with one strand of dark copper thread.

Legs

Work the legs in straight stitches with one strand of brown/black metallic thread.

The Ladybird Notebook Cover

Ladybirds, in three different sizes, were embroidered on this notebook cover, using the threads and instructions on pages 319–320. The removable cover, which could be adjusted to fit a notebook of any size, was made from a vintage linen tea-towel. Other beetles could replace the ladybirds and any fabric could be used for the background.

The ladybird is a symbol of fire and the sun. If a ladybird alights on your clothing, you will soon wear your wedding dress. If it settles upon your flesh or hair, good fortune is prophesied: you will have as many good months as there are spots. A ladybird with seven spots on its back is a fairy's pet, and you may make three wishes before it flies away.

Nahmad, *Garden Spells*, p. 70.

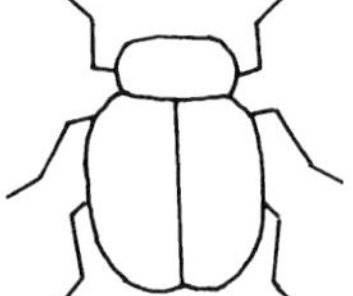
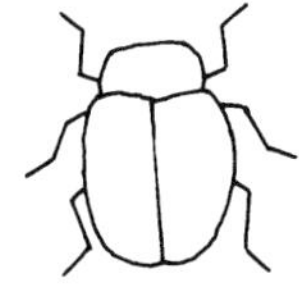
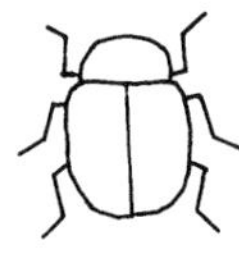

skeleton outlines

Hint: Instead of tracing the outline onto the uneven weave of the tea-towel linen, I traced the elytra and thorax onto red homespun (backed with Vliesofix), cut out the shape and fused it onto the linen to use as a template. This technique gave a lovely raised effect to the embroidery and could be used on any unusual background material.

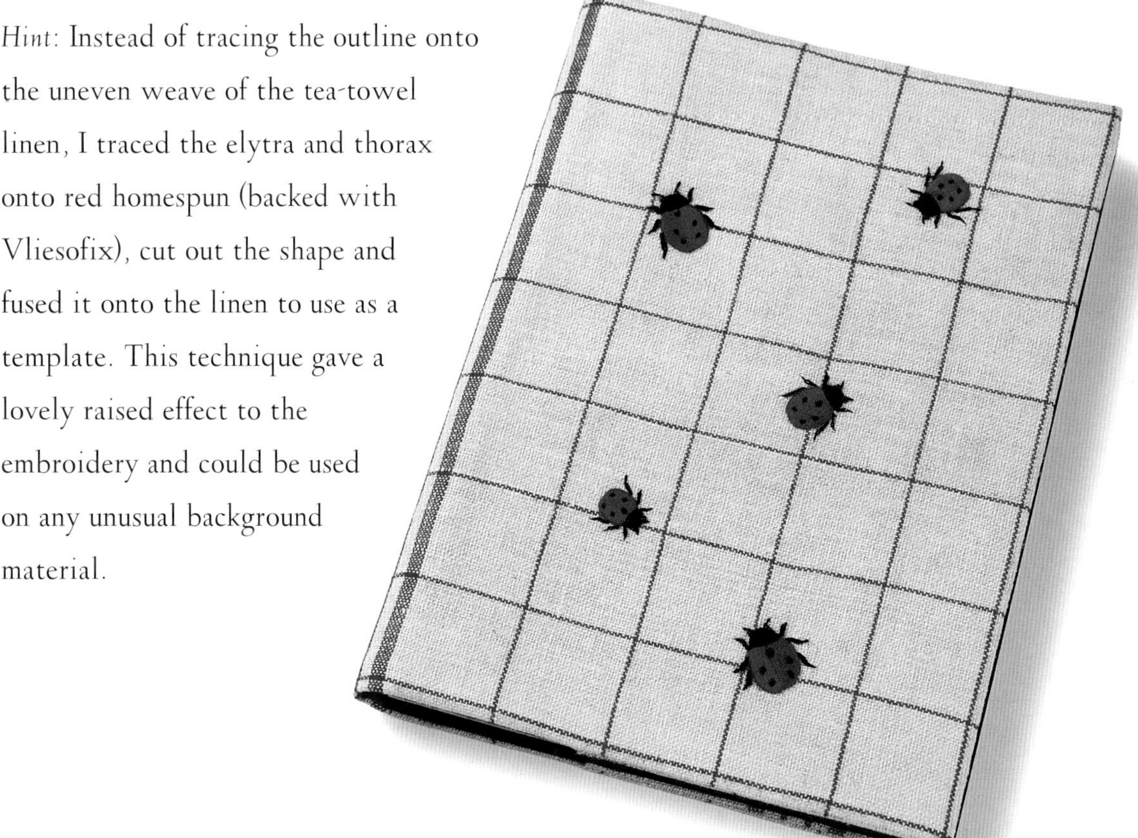

The Ladybird Notebook Cover.

Redwork Beetles

While attending a lecture about early American crazy quilts, I was amused to see that beetles had even crept into the world of patchwork. There they were; three scarab beetles, occupying an elongated hexagon in the middle of an antique redwork quilt!

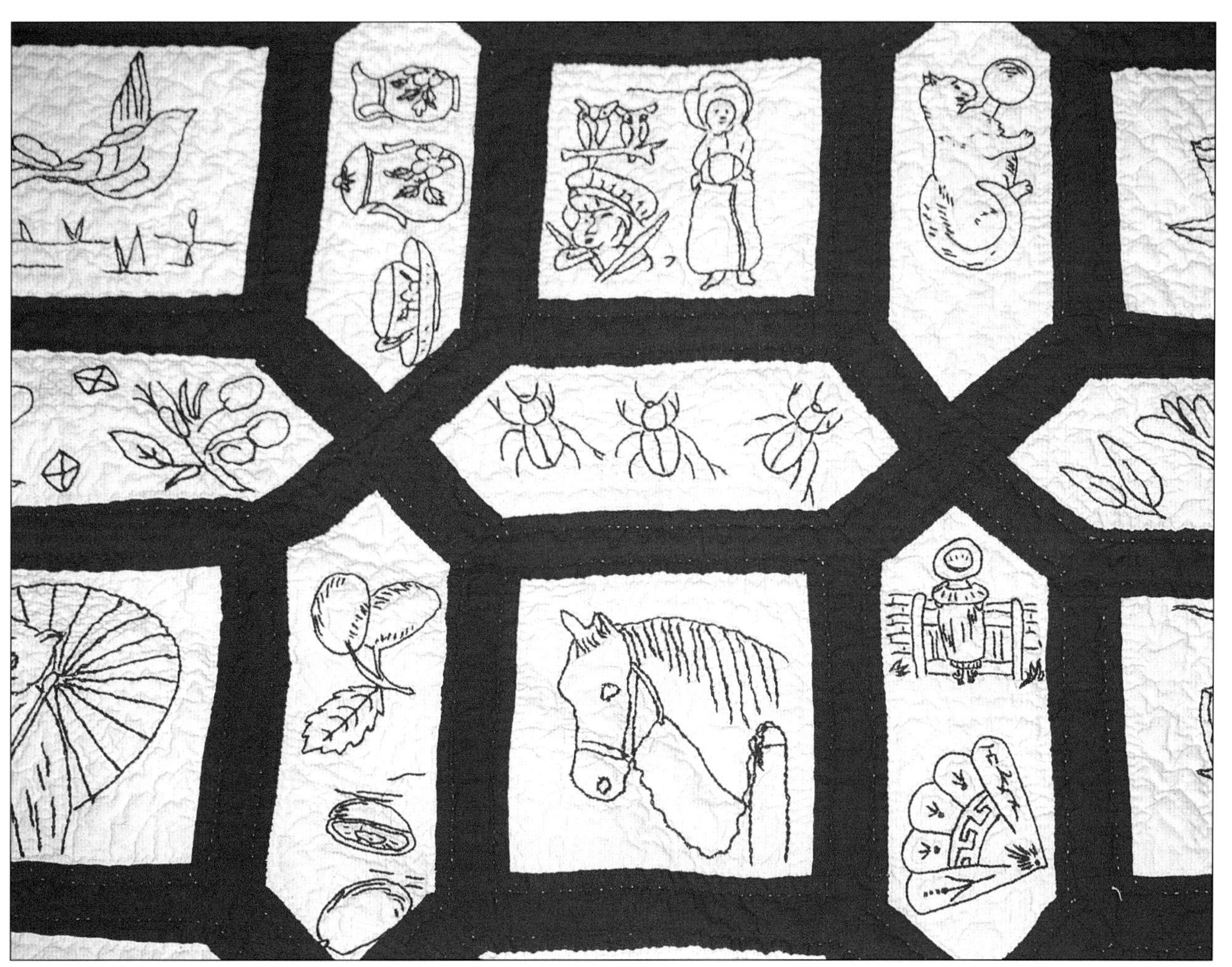

Detail from the quilt Redwork Garden Maze, c. 1880.

Redwork is the term used to describe a colourful and simplistic genre of embroidery popular in America between 1885 and the 1930s. Taking its name from the Turkey red cloth and embroidery threads used, redwork involved embroidering simple designs with basic stem or outline stitches, with the occasional French knot, onto a linen or muslin background, using Turkey red or, to a lesser extent, indigo blue embroidery thread. Believed to have been inspired by the Polish, French and German immigrants who embroidered words and pictures onto fabrics creating pieces that were pretty as well as functional, redwork was used to embellish household linens, such as pillow shams, dresser scarves and decorative towels. Embroidered muslin squares were combined with the colourfast Turkey red fabric to produce the charming patchwork quilts so sought after today. At the turn of the nineteenth century, redwork had become very popular with children, both as a pastime and as a way of developing their embroidery skills. The designs often included subjects that would appeal to children such as animals, birds, flowers, historical figures, everyday household objects and children at play (such as the Kate Greenaway figures).

The popularity of redwork was primarily due to the indelible nature of the dye used to produce Turkey red cloth and embroidery threads, 'the color being proof against any amount of washing'. The brilliant scarlet dye evolved in Turkey and was in widespread use in the nineteenth century, being particularly valued for 'marking' linens. This description of the dyeing process is fascinating:

'The method of dyeing this cloth is as follows: The bleached yarn is soaked in oil, then dipped in carbonate of soda, and exposed to the action of the air and of steam in a hot room. It is then passed through a solution of nut-galls and a red mordant successively, and is thus ready for dyeing. To effect this it is boiled for two or three hours in a vessel containing madder-root, or munjeet, and, lastly, it is boiled in a solution of soap.'

Caulfield and Saward, *Encyclopedia of Victorian Needlework*, Vol. 2, p. 503.

How to Embroider Redwork Beetles

I could not resist embroidering a few redwork beetles onto an old French linen tea-towel of a beautiful flax colour, but any linen or heavy calico background would look charming with the addition of a beetle or two. Worked in simple surface embroidery stitches with stranded thread, the beetles would look equally effective worked in green, dark blue or black, scattered on cushions (fastened with mother-of-pearl buttons), shoe bags or table linen.

Redwork Beetle Bag

This drawstring bag, made from an old linen tea-towel and lined with red cotton homespun, and measuring 25 x 30 cm (10 x 12 in) is the ideal size for a paperback, or perhaps a sketchbook and pencils. It has been embroidered in DMC stranded cotton, colour 321—very similar to Turkey red.

Order of work

Trace the skeleton outlines of the beetles onto the background fabric. All the beetles are embroidered in the same way, except for the fillings of their elytra.

Redwork Beetle Bag.

ELYTRA

Outline the elytra in stem stitch using two strands of thread. With one strand of thread, decorate the elytra with one of the following filling stitches:

- Checkered Beetle—bands of French knots
- Fungus Beetle—seed stitches in pairs
- Ground Beetle—rows of running stitch
- Jewel Beetle—cross-stitches in the shape of a star
- Pill Beetle—detached chain stitches

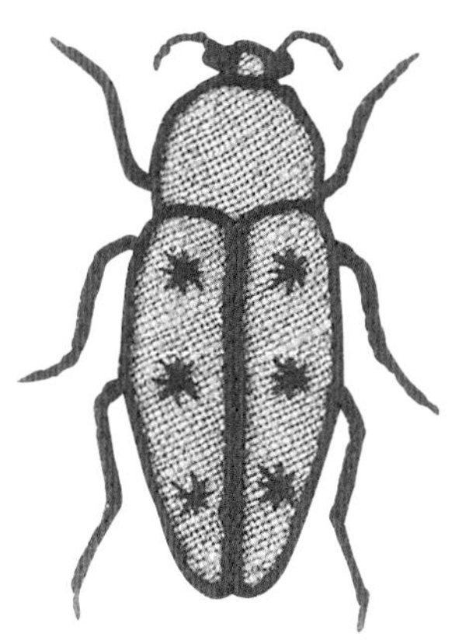

Jewel Beetle

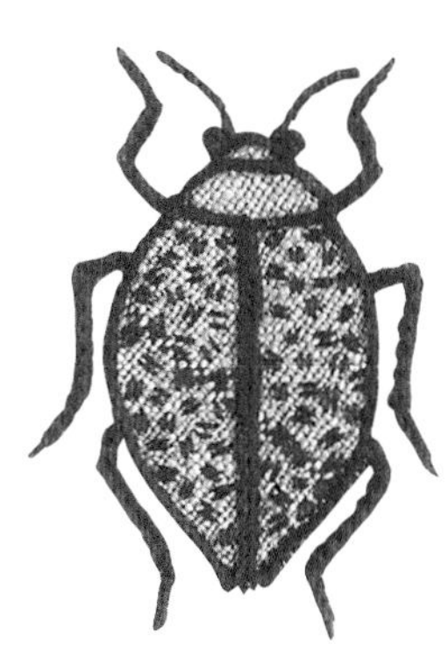

Fungus Beetle

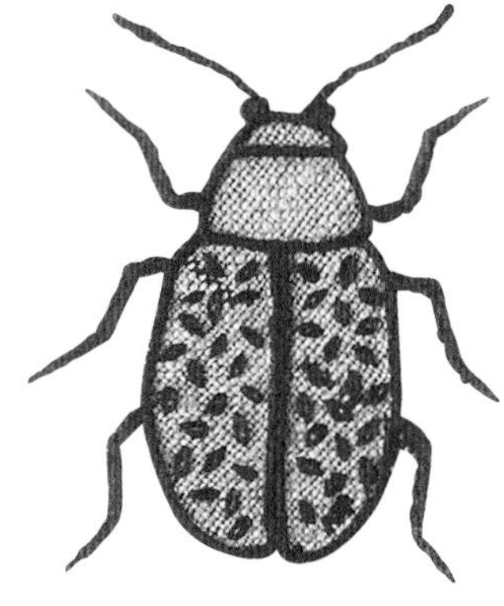

Pill Beetle

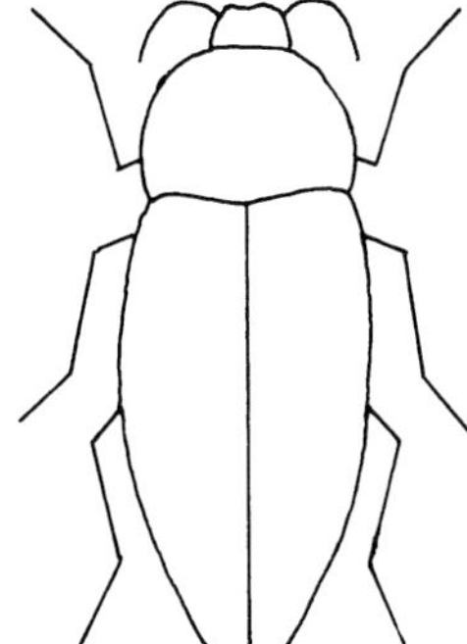

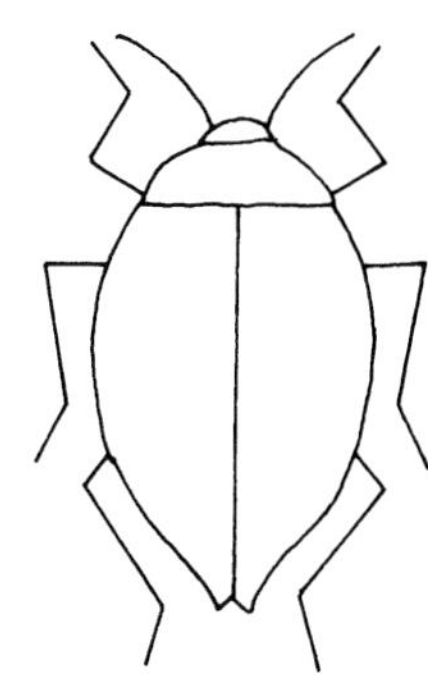

THORAX AND HEAD

Outline the thorax and the head in stem stitch worked with two strands of thread.

EYES

Work the eyes with French knots, using three strands of thread.

ANTENNAE

Embroider the antennae in back stitch with two strands of thread.

LEGS

Work the legs in chain stitch, using two strands of thread for the two inner segments, and one strand for the outer segment.

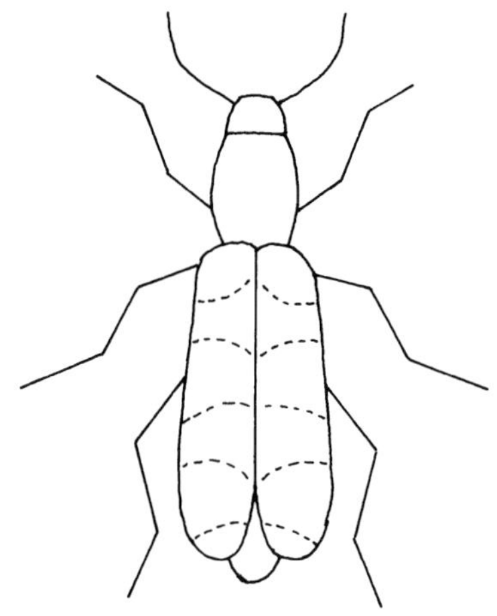

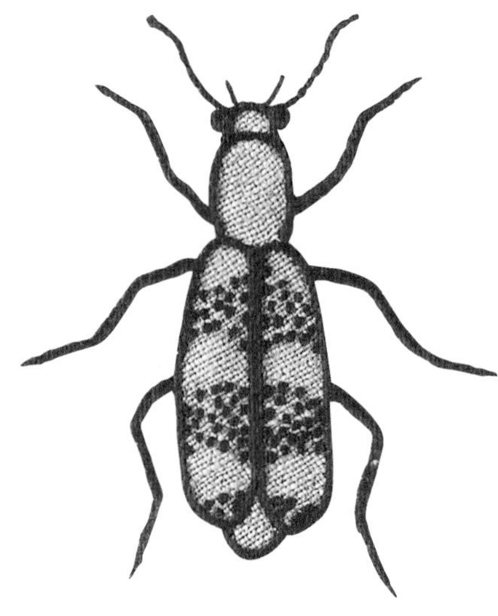

Checkered Beetle

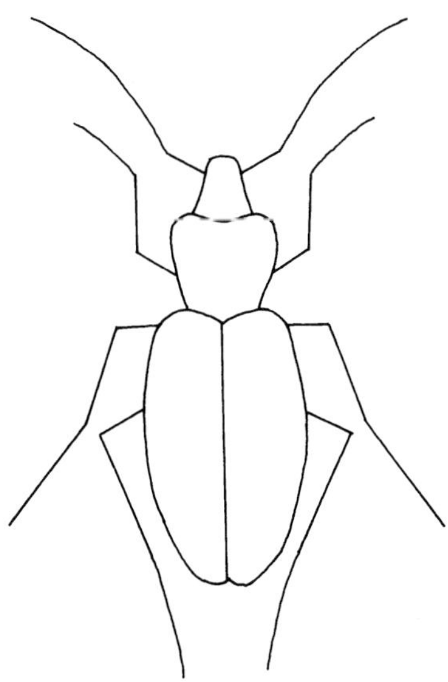

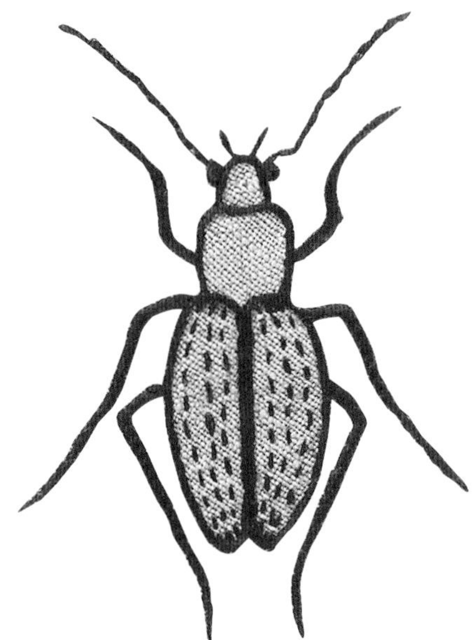

Ground Beetle

Part 7:

Appliqué Beetles

Applied embroidery, known as appliqué since the mid-nineteenth century, includes all work in which a shape or embroidered motif is cut from one material and applied to the surface of another, background material, often by means of decorative stitching, to form a design. It has a long history; the technique was used by the ancient Greeks and Egyptians. An early example, preserved in the Cairo Museum, is the funeral tent of Queen Isiemkheb, c.980 BC, decorated with hundreds of pieces of dyed gazelle hide. In Asia, nomadic cattle-herding tribes were decorating their tents, floor coverings and saddle covers with applied felt and leather as early as 200 BC. Throughout the ages, and in all parts of the world, appliqué has been used to decorate (and repair) a wide variety of textiles (from the surcoats of the Mediaeval crusaders to the finely appliquéd quilts of nineteenth century America), using a diverse array of techniques and materials. Applied work, in its many forms, continues to be a fascinating field for the contemporary embroiderer; as Mary Thomas claims, 'appliqué affords the widest scope for individual expression; admitting no limit to subject or material' (Mary Thomas's Embroidery Book, p. 1).

Beetles, with their simple, elegant shapes, are great fun to work in appliqué. They can be used to decorate a variety of articles such as bags, wraps, scarves, ties, hats, garments, quilts, cushions and book-covers. This chapter provides instructions for two methods of appliqué; however, other techniques could be substituted. Five beetles, their outlines enlarged and simplified, are drawn from the Specimen Box. The remaining beetles, treated the same way, could provide further inspiration.

Appliquéd ladybirds featured on a greeting card.

How to Appliqué a Beetle

- A beetle can be applied to almost any background fabric—silk, satin, linen, cotton, denim, velvet, wool and felt. If the background fabric needs support, use a backing fabric. Mount the fabrics into a hoop or frame.
- Many fabrics can be used for appliqué, including silks and satins, cottons, leather, wools and felt. If the item is to be laundered, take this into account when selecting your fabrics.
- These beetles have been padded with felt to give them a rounded shape. The internal lines of the body segments are stitched, giving a quilted effect.
- The edges of appliqué are often treated decoratively. A variety of threads and beads can be used to apply and embellish the applied shapes.
- Embroider the beetle in the following order—body padding, elytra (wing cases), thorax and head, antennae and mouthparts, and finally the legs.

Appliqué Beetles in Fabric

Japanese cotton fabrics, lined with felt, have been used for the elytra, thorax and head of each of these beetles. The fabric shapes have been appliquéd, over a layer of felt padding, to an indigo-dyed cotton background fabric. These appliquéd beetles can be made into a bag or a cushion cover.

Materials required

- assorted cotton fabrics for the beetle
- background fabric and backing fabric, mounted into a hoop or frame
- felt and Vliesofix
- machine sewing thread to match the cotton fabrics
- stranded threads to match and contrast with the cotton fabrics
- 3–4 mm beads for eyes

Preparation

Trace the skeleton outlines of the beetles onto the backing fabric. All the beetles are worked in the same way, except for the decorative stitches on some of the head and thorax shapes.

Body padding

Trace the body padding shape onto Vliesofix and fuse to the felt. Cut out the felt shape. With one strand of sewing thread, apply the felt shape to the background fabric (inside the elytra and thorax outlines) with small stab stitches, using the skeleton outline on the back of the fabric as a guide.

Elytra

1. Trace an elytra shape (or pair of shapes) onto Vliesofix and fuse to the felt. Cut out the felt shape (or shapes) and fuse to

the back of the elytra fabric (the felt shape is used as a template).

2. Cut out the fabric shape, leaving a 4 mm (approx. 1/8 in) turning allowance outside the felt. Fold the allowance to the back (over the edge of the felt) and tack around all edges. If using a pair of separate shapes to form the elytra (e.g. for diagonal stripes), stitch the centre seams together before folding the allowance around the outside edges.

3. With matching sewing thread, appliqué the elytra shape in place, over the body padding, with small stab stitches, using the outline on the back as a guide. Remove the tacking stitches.

4. The elytra is outlined with six strands of stranded thread (matching or contrasting in colour), couched in place with one strand. Work a double row of couched thread along the centre line of the elytra, and a single row around the outside edge.

Thorax and head

1. Trace a combined thorax and head shape (or separate shapes if desired) onto Vliesofix and fuse to the felt. Cut out the felt shape and fuse to the back of the thorax fabric (the felt shape is used as a template).

2. Cut out the fabric shape, leaving a 4 mm (approx. 1/8 in) turning allowance outside the felt. Fold the allowance to the back (over the edge of the felt) and tack around all edges. If using a pair of separate shapes to form the thorax and the head, stitch the seams together before folding the allowance around the outside edges.

3. With matching sewing thread, appliqué the shape in place with small stab stitches, using the outline on the back as a guide. Remove the tacking stitches.

4. The thorax and head are outlined with six strands of stranded thread (matching or contrasting in colour), couched in place with one strand. Define the line between the thorax and head, and work any decoration (if required) with one strand of thread.

5. Stitch a bead on either side of the head for eyes.

Antennae and mouthparts

Using two strands of thread, work the antennae in chain stitch, and the mouthparts (if required) in whipped backstitch.

Legs

The legs are worked in back stitch, using 12 strands of thread for the two long inner leg segments, and six strands for the outer segments. Couch the long back stitches in place with one strand of contrasting thread.

Appliqué Click Beetle

Work the Click Beetle following the general instructions. The head is embellished with French knots.

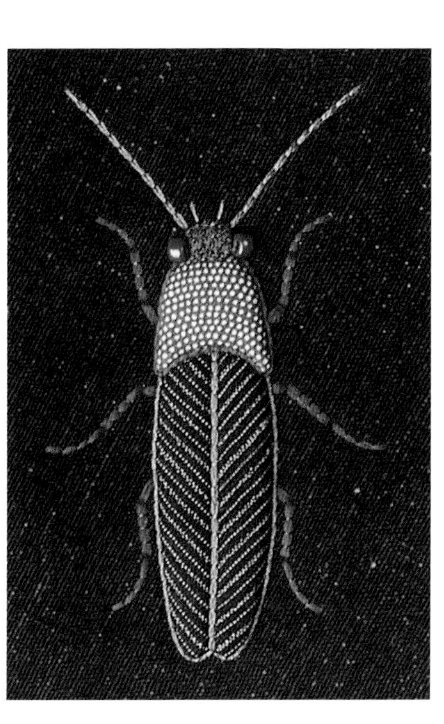

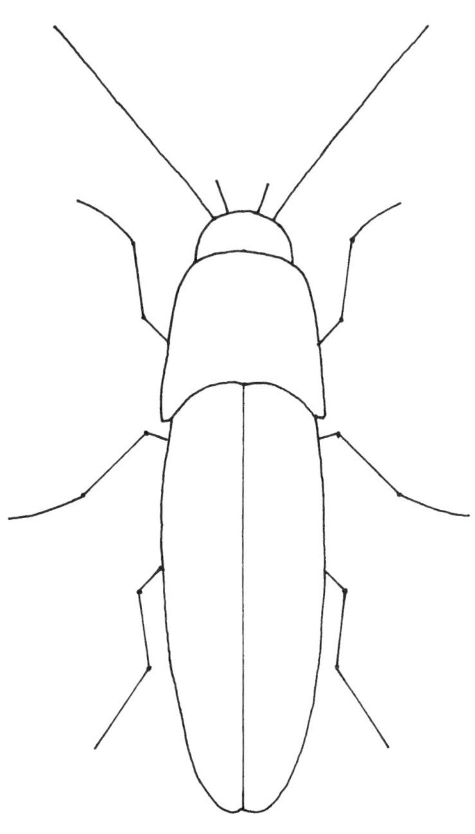

skeleton outline

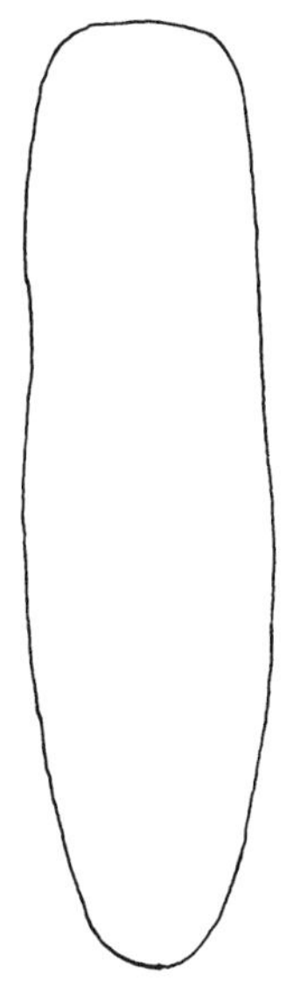

body padding

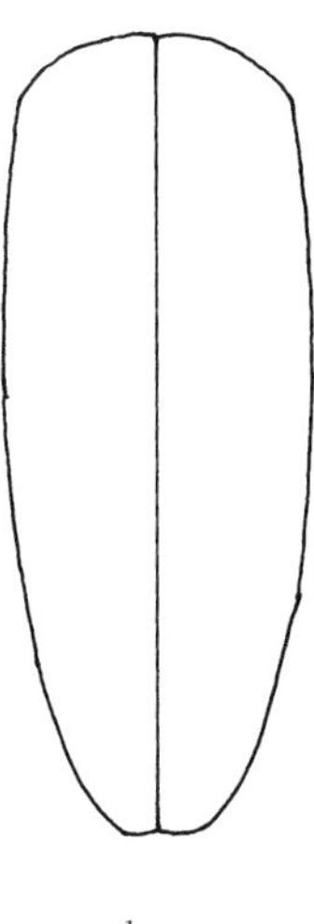

elytra

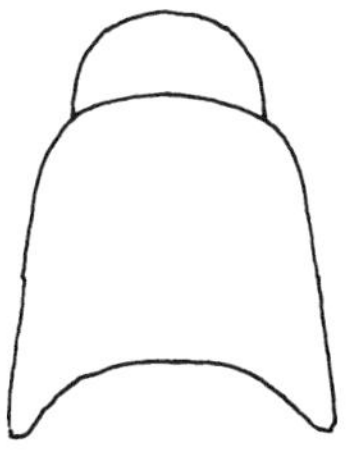

thorax and head

Appliqué Diving Beetle

Work the Diving Beetle following the general instructions. The thorax is embellished with lattice couching.

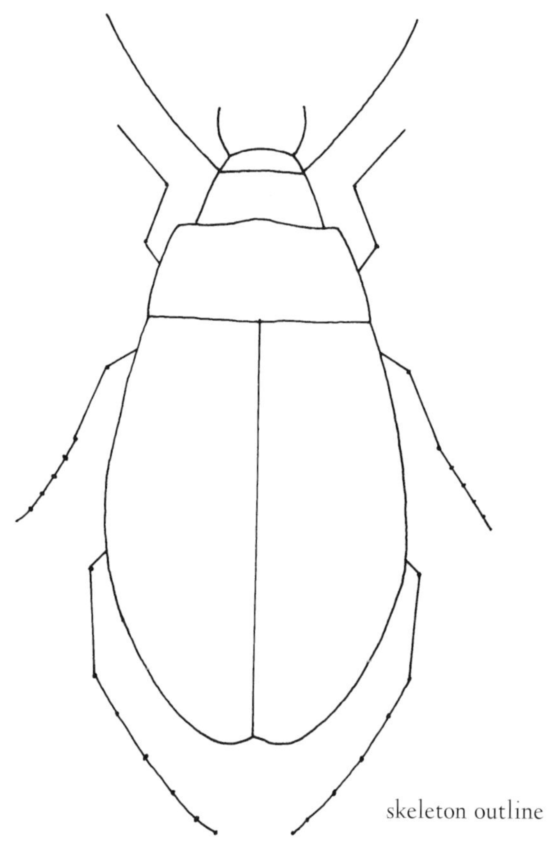

skeleton outline

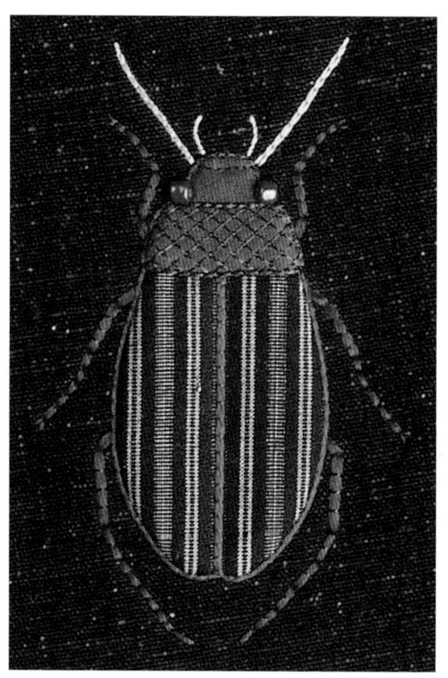

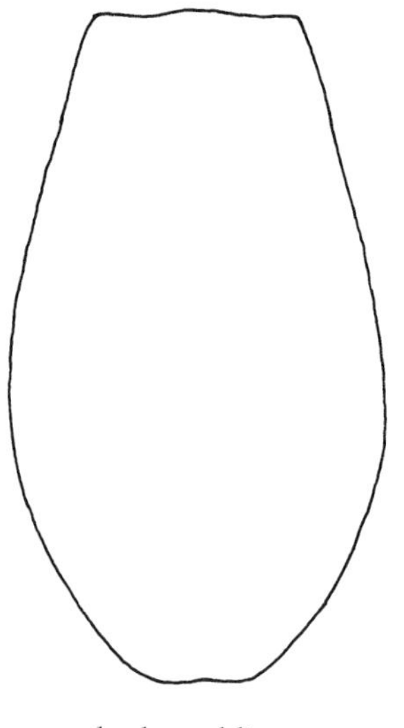

body padding

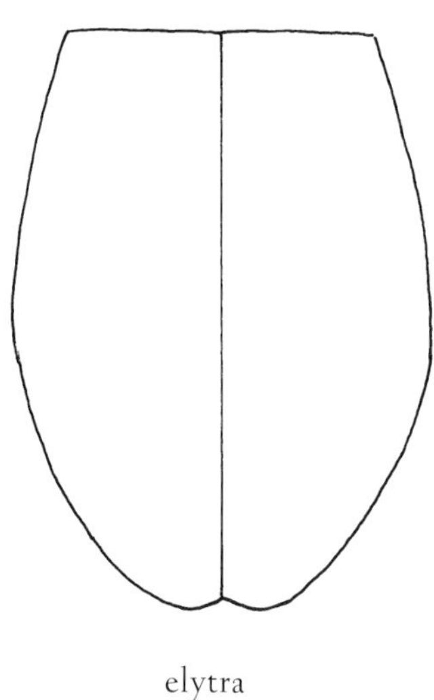

elytra

thorax and head

Appliqué Ground Beetle

Work the Ground Beetle following the general instructions. The head and thorax are separate pieces of fabric, stitched together at the join.

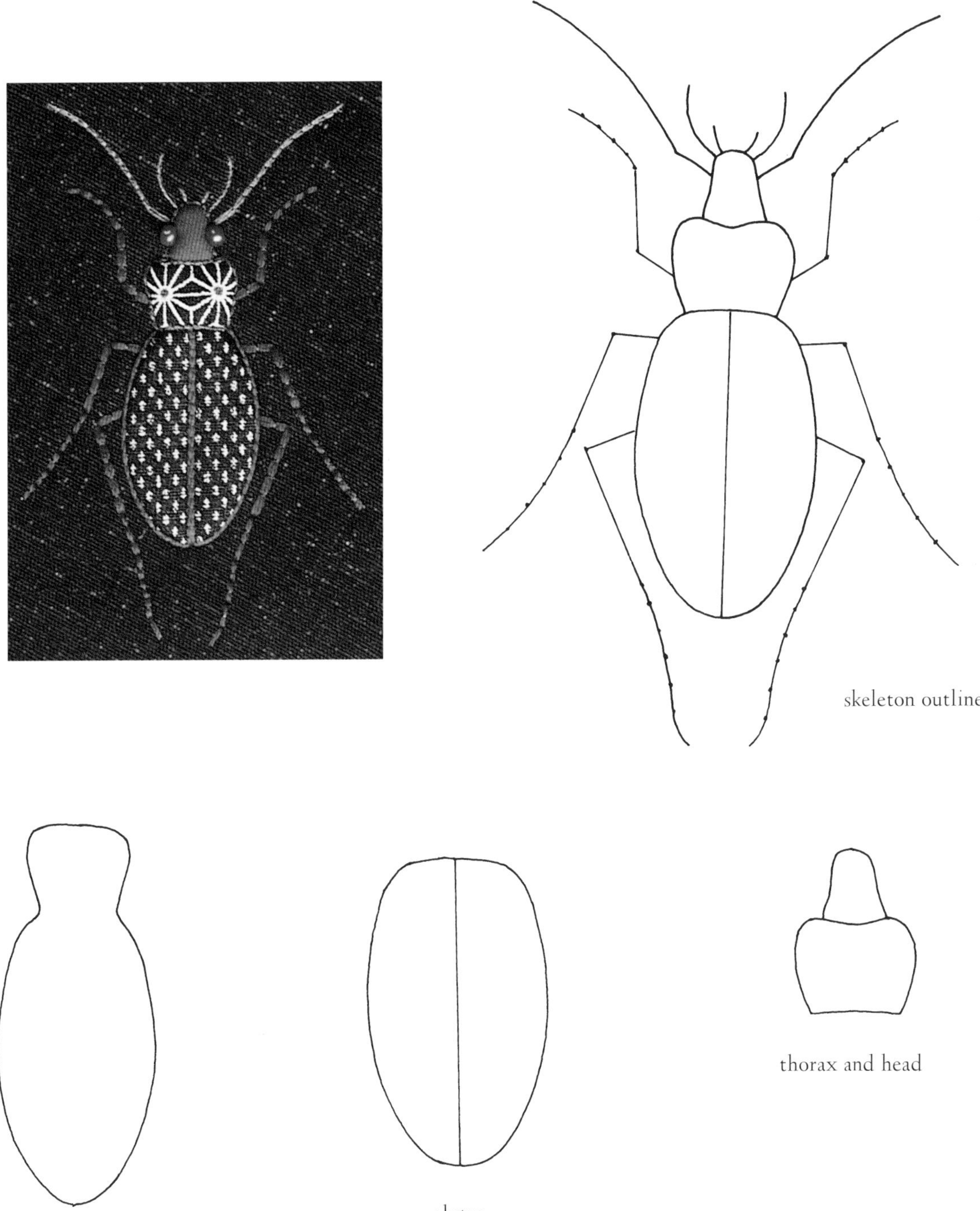

body padding

Appliqué Longhorn Beetle

Work the Longhorn Beetle following the general instructions. The thorax is embellished with parallel rows of couched thread.

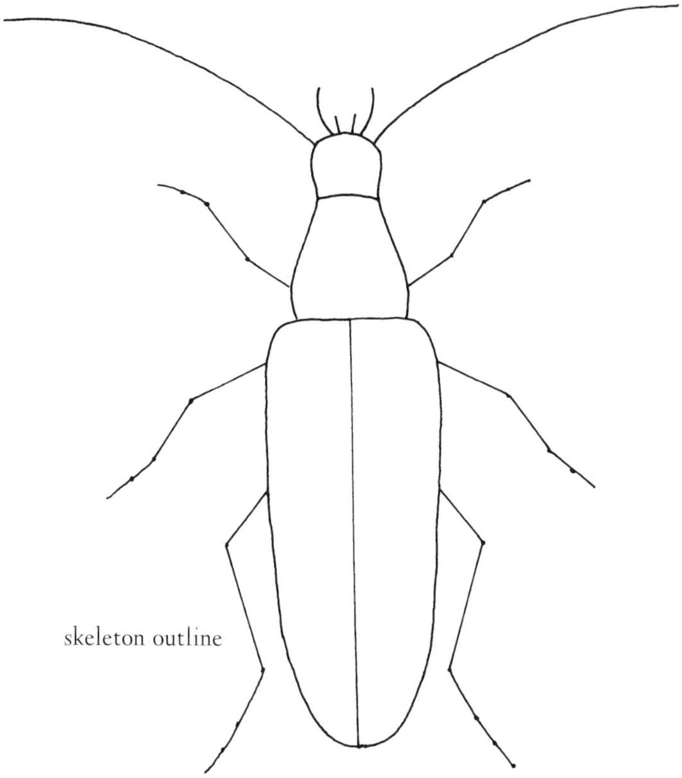

skeleton outline

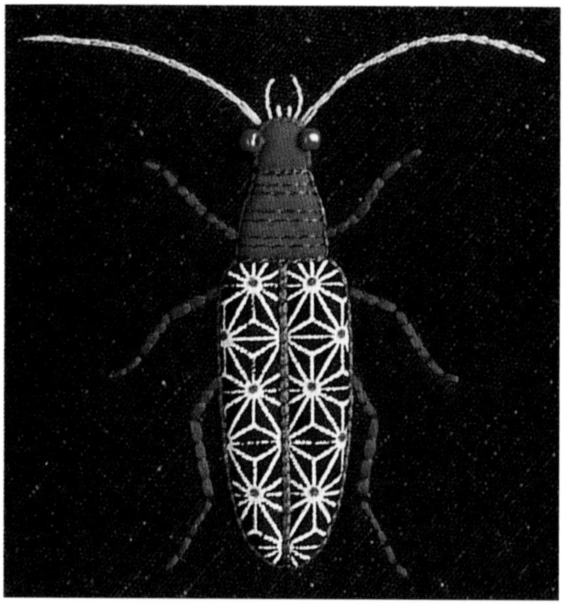

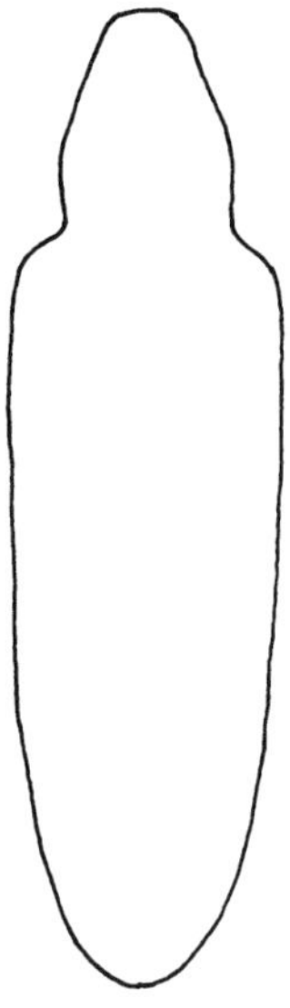

body padding

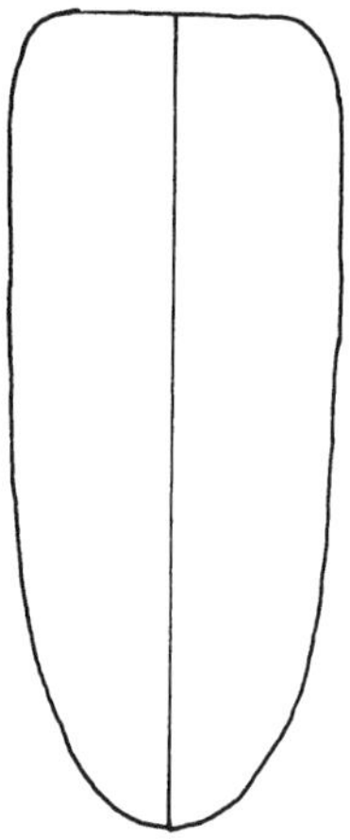

elytra

thorax and head

Appliqué Scarab Beetle

Work the Scarab Beetle following the general instructions.

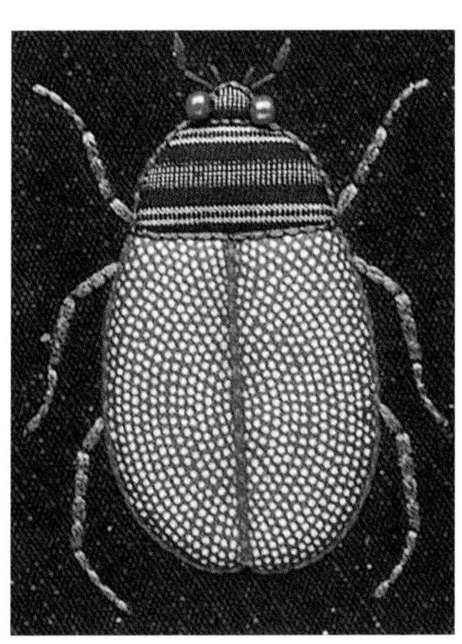

skeleton outline

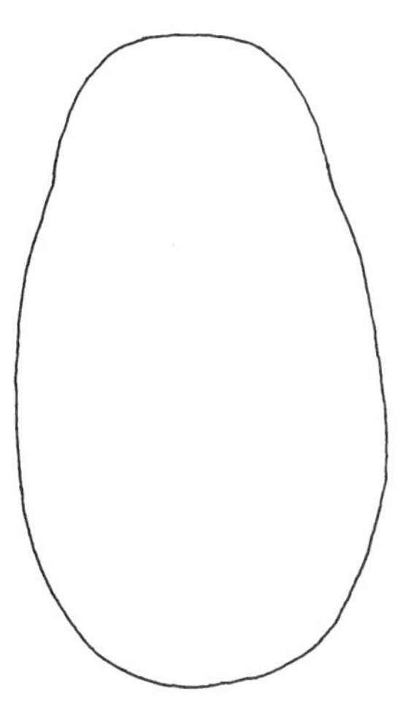

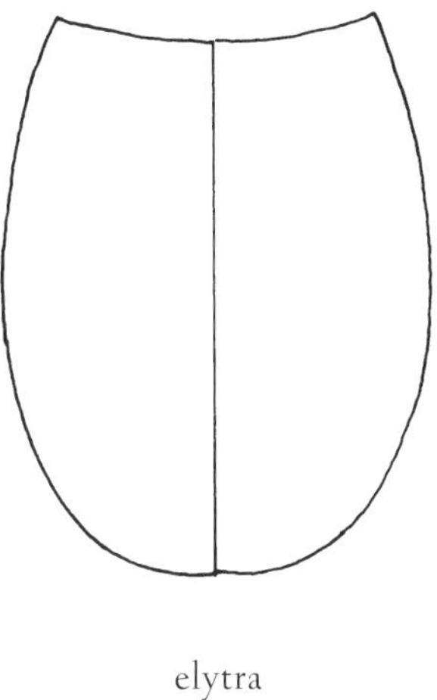

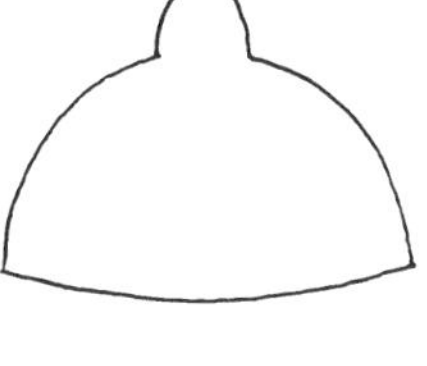

thorax and head

elytra

body padding

Appliqué Beetle in Felt

Brightly coloured felt has been appliquéd, over a layer of padding, to a woollen background fabric to make this cheerful Diving Beetle. A felt beetle can decorate rugs, cushions, clothing or a simple little bag.

Felt appliqué Diving Beetle on small woollen bag.

Materials required

- coloured felt for the beetle and Vliesofix
- background fabric and backing fabric, mounted into a hoop or frame
- machine sewing thread to match the felt
- stranded threads to match and contrast with the felt
- 3–4 mm beads for eyes

Trace the skeleton outline of the beetle onto the backing fabric.

Body padding

Trace the body padding shape onto Vliesofix and fuse to felt. Cut out the felt shape. With one strand of sewing thread, apply the felt body padding shape to the background fabric (inside the elytra and thorax outlines) with small stab stitches, using the skeleton outline on the back of the fabric as a guide.

Elytra

1. Trace an elytra shape onto Vliesofix and fuse to the felt. Cut out the felt shape.

2. With matching sewing thread, apply the felt elytra shape in place (fusible web side down), over the body padding, with small stab stitches. Work a row of back stitch along the centre line of the elytra to shape.

3. The elytra is outlined with 12 strands of stranded thread (matching or contrasting in colour), couched in place with one strand. Work a row of couched thread along the centre line of the elytra and around the outside edge.

4. Embellish the elytra with French knots (worked with seven strands of thread) or beads if desired.

skeleton outline

Felt Appliqué Diving Beetle.

body padding

elytra

head

thorax

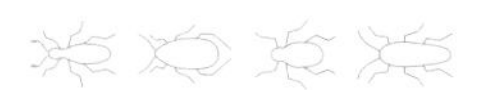

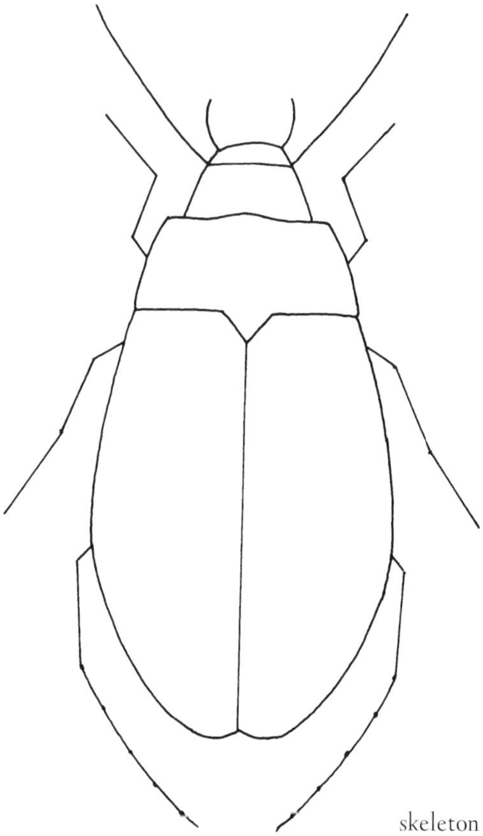

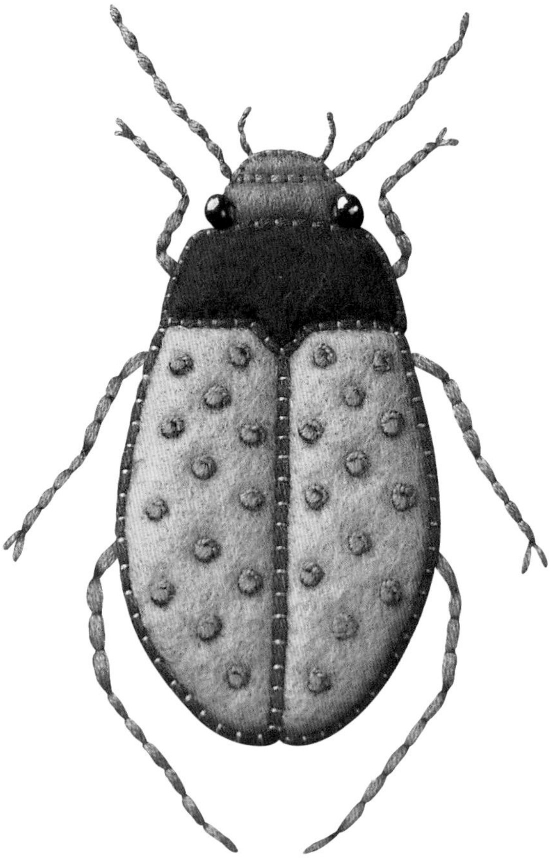

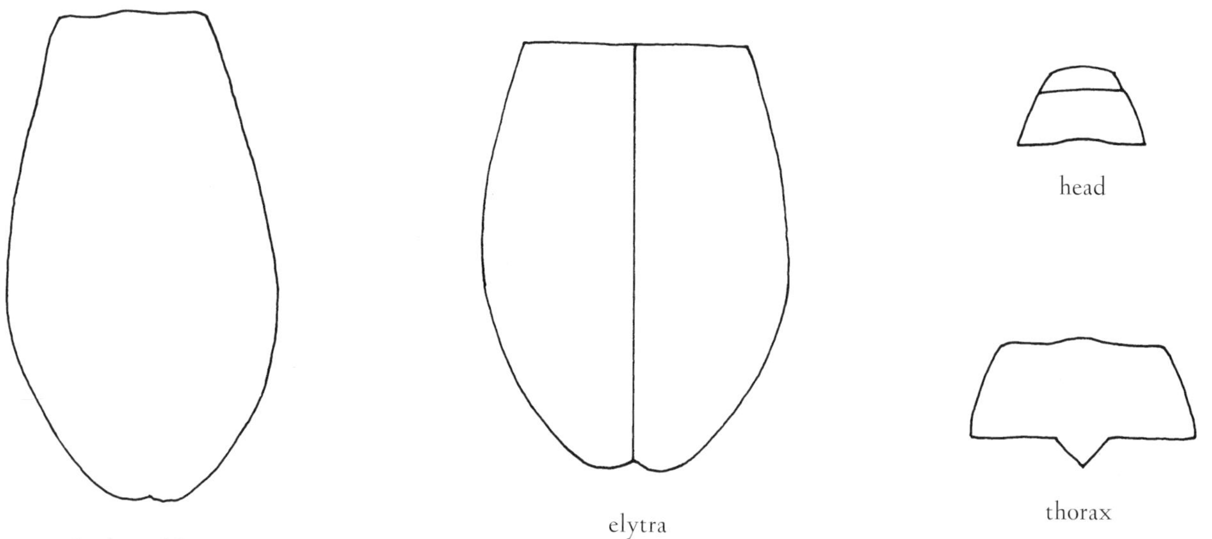

Thorax

1. Trace a thorax shape onto Vliesofix and fuse to the felt. Cut out the felt shape.

2. With matching sewing thread, apply the thorax shape with small stab stitches.

3. The thorax is outlined with six strands of stranded thread (matching or contrasting in colour), couched in place with one strand

Head

1. Trace a head shape onto Vliesofix and fuse to the felt. Cut out the felt shape.

2. With matching sewing thread, apply the head shape with small stab stitches.

3. The head and 'snout' is outlined with six strands of stranded thread (matching or contrasting in colour), couched in place with one strand.

4. Stitch a bead on either side of the head for eyes.

Antennae and mouthparts

Each antenna is worked with six strands of stranded thread couched in place with one strand. Using three strands, work the mouthparts in whipped backstitch.

Legs

The legs are worked in back stitch, using 12 strands of thread for the two long inner leg segments, and six strands for the outer segments. Couch the long back stitches in place with one strand of contrasting thread.

Never kill a beetle, but leave him to go about his important work in the garden. Folks say bad luck and seven days' soaking rain is the penalty for stamping on a beetle. This is because cruel behaviour angers the fairies, who can visit bad luck on us. If a black beetle crawls over your shoe, it is a warning against illness which bids you to take better care of your health. Many nocturnal flying beetles predict fine weather.

Nahmad, *Garden Spells*, p. 68.

Part 8:
Beetle Bags

The Beetle Shape as Inspiration

The shape of many beetles, such as the ladybird, scarab and jewel beetles, begs for interpretation into objects. Examples abound, small and large, where the beetle is the object: jewellery, ornaments, perfume containers, paperweights, bags, cushions, candles, chocolates, and the legendary Volkswagen 'beetle'—my first car.

The beetle shape provides endless inspiration for stitched items, such as bags, pouches, glasses cases and pincushions. Using a simplified beetle outline from the Specimen Box (enlarged at 200% or 300%), have fun designing your own handbags and pouches, using the following projects as a guide. The fabrics, from exotic silks to practical cottons, can be embellished with embroidery, beads or found objects. To close your bag, use buttons and loops (as 'eyes'), a zipper, drawstring, or a traditional, curved, metal handbag frame.

Scarab Beetle Pouch

The inspiration for this little scarab pouch came from a traditional Japanese chirimen bag, made in the shape of a cicada. In nineteenth century Japan, the daughters of privileged households were taught to sew tiny, hand-stitched bags from scraps of chirimen, the silk crepe used to make kimono. These amusing little bags, often used to hold the plectra for the girl's koto, were made in a wide variety of shapes, from cherry blossoms, pinecones and persimmons to cats, cicadas and kimono-clad dolls. It is believed that chirimen bags were first made about 1750 (after the newly-arrived silk crepe fabric became widespread), using the precious scraps of the fabric left over from making kimono.

Scarab Beetle Pouch.

A scarab beetle pouch makes a charming container for a lipstick and handkerchief, jewellery, buttons, potpourri, or a special gift. They can be made in a variety of fabrics; silks, cottons or thin leather, and decorated with beads or embroidery. I have used Japanese cottons, some of them quite old, to make these examples.

Materials required

- selection of fabrics for the body, elytra, thorax and scutellum, top band and linings
- thin pellon (wadding) and Vliesofix for interfacing (optional)
- stuffing (optional)
- 1 m (40 in) of thin cord or fine leather thonging
- 2 buttons or beads, 9–10 mm (3/8 in) for the eyes
- beads for cord ends (optional)
- sewing thread to match

Preparation

Transfer the pattern outlines onto tracing paper and cut out fabric shapes.

Note:

- All seam allowances are 6 mm (1/4 in), except for the short ends of the top band which are 12 mm (1/2 in).
- All stitching is done by hand, either with running stitch, or back stitch when a stronger seam is required.
- Press all seams after stitching—either finger press or use an iron.
- Trim seams and clip curves before turning, if required.
- The thorax is improved if a layer of pellon (cut to thorax shape, without seam allowance) is fused to the back with Vliesofix.

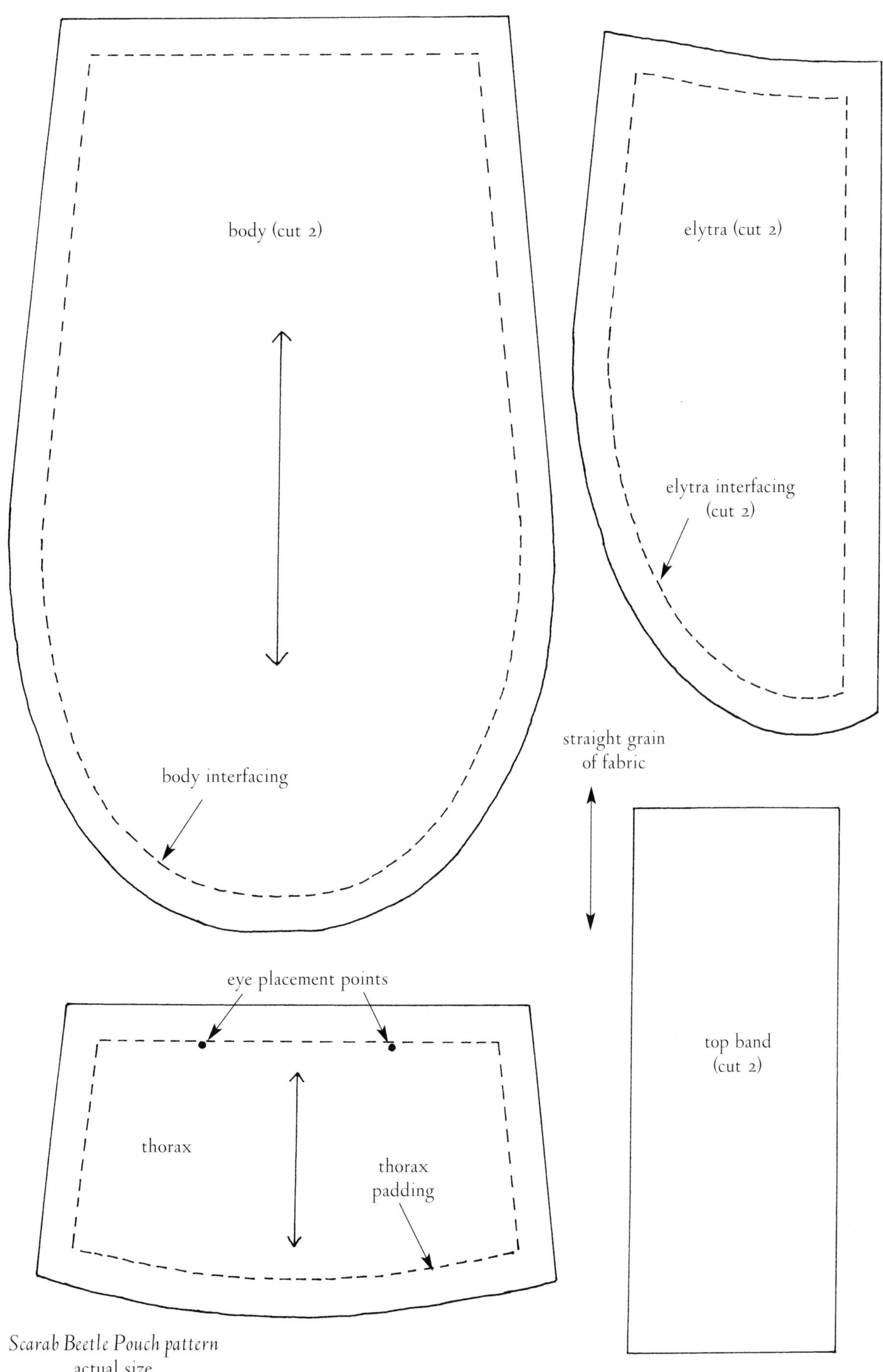

Scarab Beetle Pouch pattern
actual size

Scarab Beetle Pouch pattern
actual size

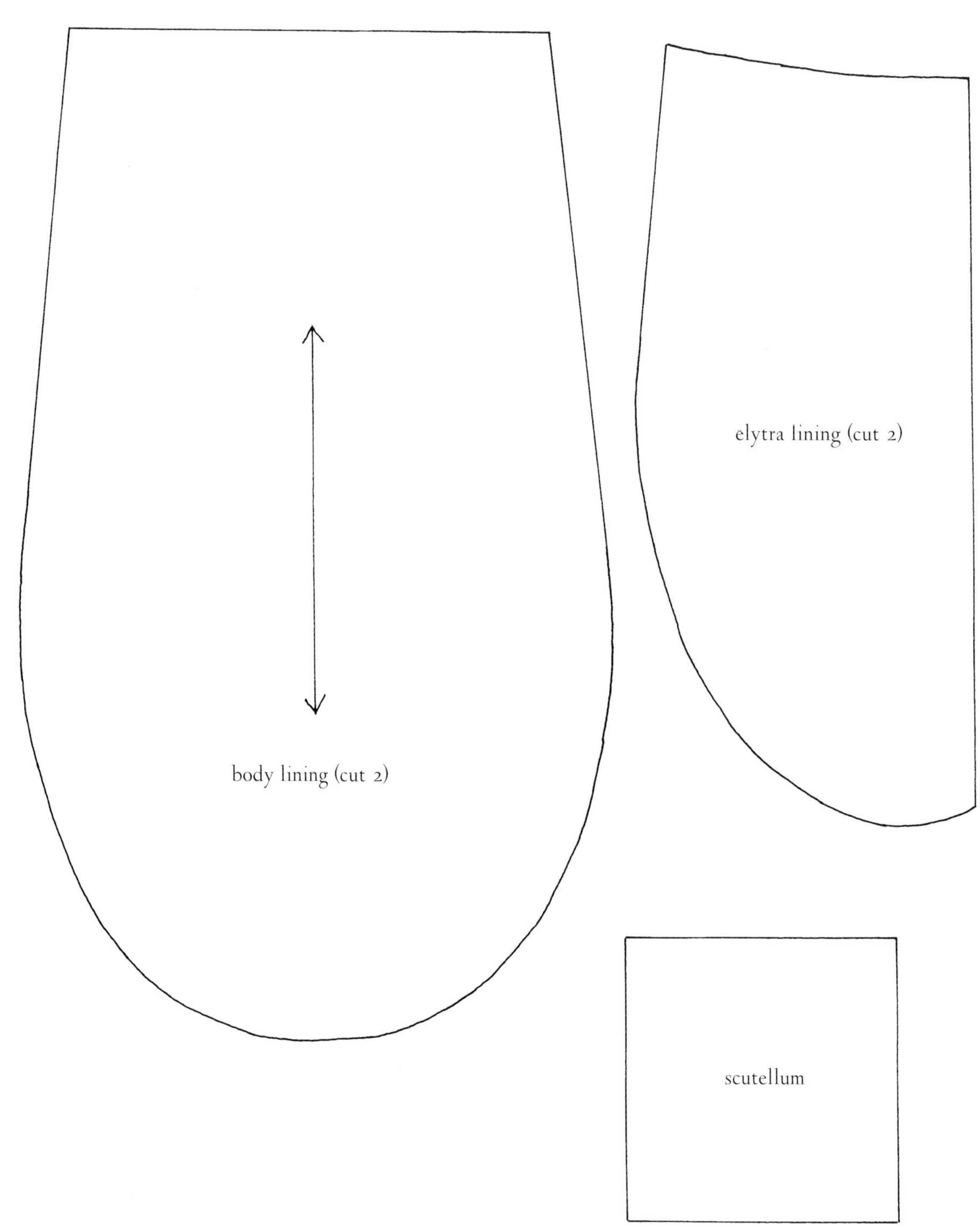

- The body and elytra pieces may be interfaced with a layer of pellon (cut without seam allowances) fused to the back of each shape with Vliesofix. This step is optional and is not needed for thicker fabrics.
- Join strips of fabric together, horizontally, to form a segmented body, if desired.

Elytra

1. With right sides facing, stitch the elytra to the elytra linings around the edges, leaving open at the top. Turn to the right side and press. With the straight edges touching, join the elytra together with a tacking stitch, 6 mm ($^1/_4$ in) down from the top.

2. To form the scutellum, the triangular shape at the top of the elytra, fold the square of fabric in half to make a rectangle. Press. Fold the corners of the folded edge to the centre of the opposite edge, making a triangle. Press.

3. Place the triangle (fold side down) on top of the elytra, raw edges level, and tack together.

Body and thorax

1. Fuse a layer of wadding to the back of the thorax. Turn the lower, curved seam allowance to the back and tack. Place the thorax on top of the front body piece, top and side edges level (there will be a slight bulge in the thorax as it is slightly wider). Tack the side edges together. Place the two body pieces together, right sides facing.

2. Place the two body lining pieces together, right sides facing. Place the two body pieces over the two body lining pieces, matching the edges. Back stitch all four layers together around the edges, leaving the top ('mouth') open. Turn to the right side.

3. Slide the elytra under the tacked thorax edge, scutellum side up. Slip stitch the folded edge of the thorax to the elytra and scutellum along the seam line, keeping the front of the bag free, at this stage.

4. Leaving the mouth open, tack the raw edges together around the top edge.

Top band (mouth)

1. Turn short edges of the top bands under 12 mm (1/2 in) and tack (or fuse). With the right sides facing, pin the top bands to the mouth edges of the bag, the short edges meeting at the sides, then back stitch.

2. Turn under the seam allowance on the remaining long edges of the band. Fold the band to the inside of the bag and slip stitch the folded edge over the seam.

3. Stitch buttons or beads to the points on the thorax, as marked, for eyes.

4. Lift up the elytra and insert a little stuffing between the thorax and the upper body (this helps to give a rounded shape to the thorax). To keep the stuffing in place, invisibly stitch the top of the elytra to the bag front, at the edge of the thorax (insert your fingers into the bag and stitch through all front layers).

5. Cut two pieces of cord, each 50 cm (20 in) long. Thread the cords through the openings in the top bands to form drawstrings. Knot the ends of each cord, first threading them through a bead if desired.

Beetle Evening Bag

The beetle evening bag, with its heavily beaded elytra and segmented satin body, uses an enlarged scarab beetle outline for its shape. This design lends itself to interpretation in a variety of materials (from silks and satins to leathers, velvets and corduroys) and embellishment techniques (such as beading, crazy patchwork, or trapunto quilting)—the possibilities are endless!

Beetle Evening Bag.

Materials required

- fabrics for body, elytra, thorax and scutellum, thorax and linings
- thin wadding or felt and Vliesofix for padding (optional)
- 20 cm (8 in) zipper
- twisted cord for handle
- 2 buttons or beads for the eyes (optional)
- embellishment materials of your choice
- sewing thread to match

Preparation

Transfer the pattern outlines onto tracing paper and cut out fabric shapes.

Note:

- All seam allowances are 6 mm (1/4 in).
- All stitching is done by hand, either with running stitch, or back stitch when a stronger seam is required.
- Press all seams after stitching—either finger press or use an iron.
- Trim seams and clip curves before turning, if required.
- The thorax is improved if a layer of felt (cut to thorax shape, without seam allowance) is fused to the back with Vliesofix.
- The body and elytra pieces may be padded with a layer of wadding or felt (cut without seam allowances). This step is optional and may not be needed for thicker fabrics.
- Join strips of fabric together, horizontally, to form a segmented body, if desired.

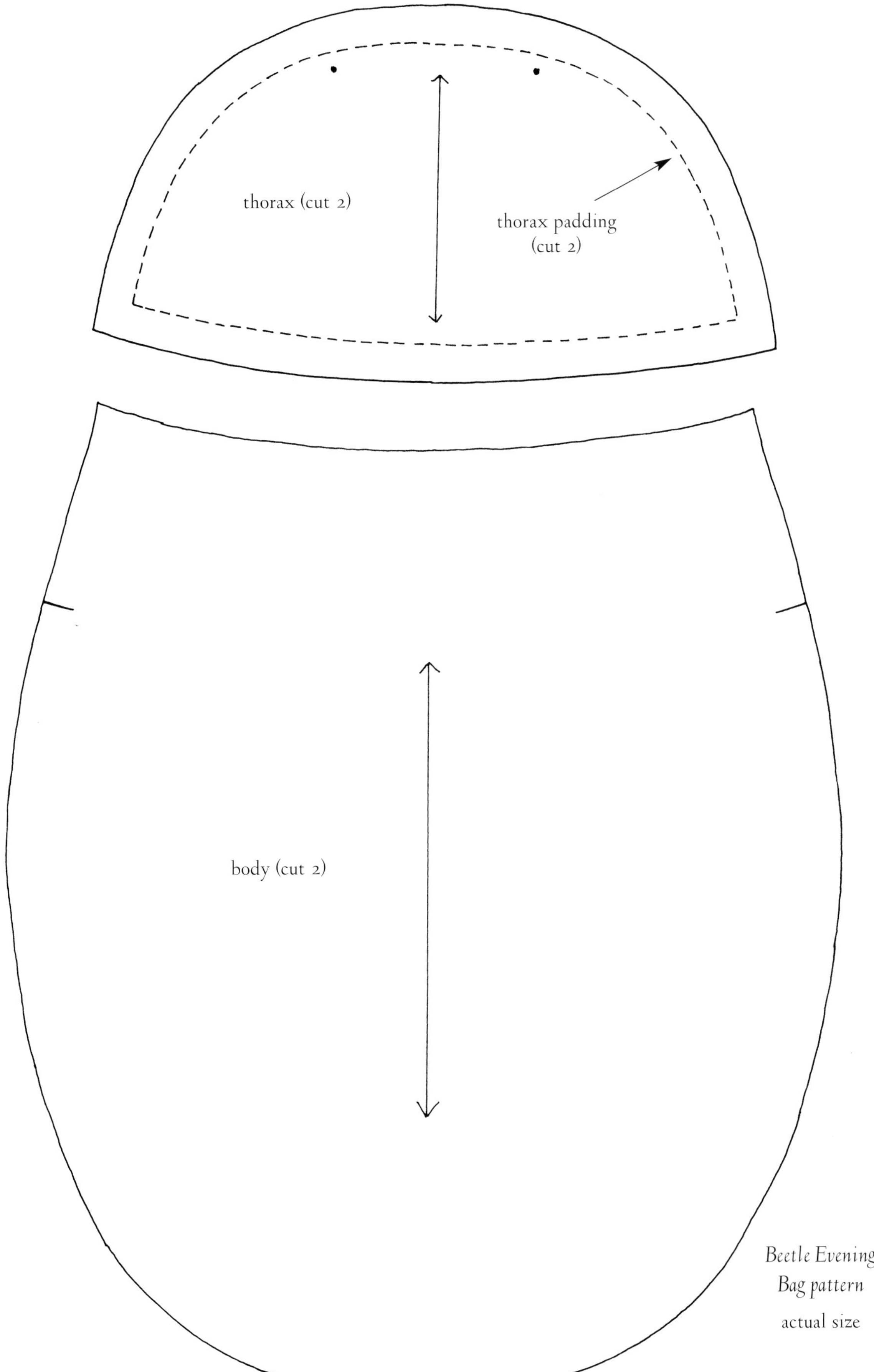

Beetle Evening Bag pattern

actual size

Beetle Evening Bag pattern

actual size

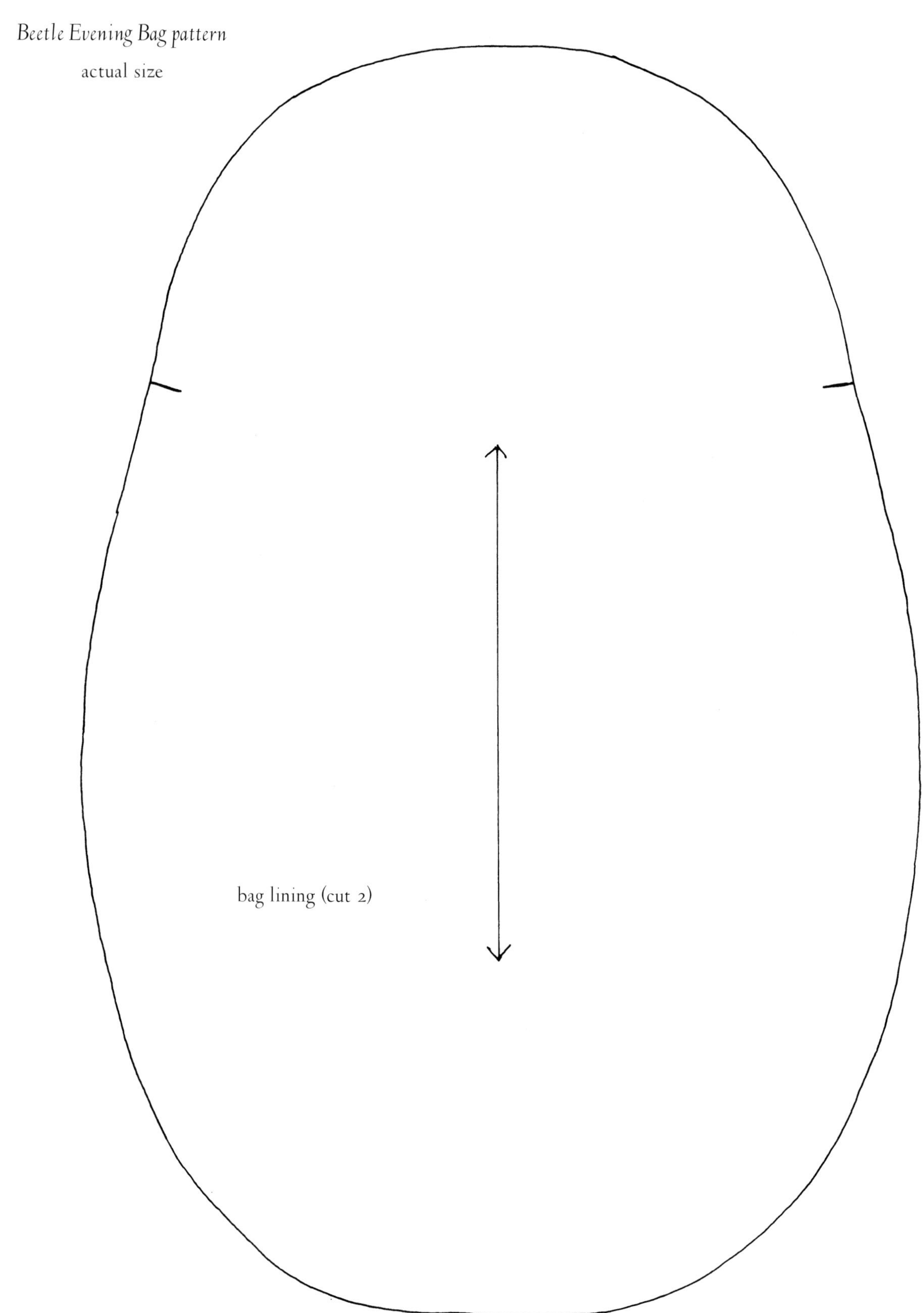

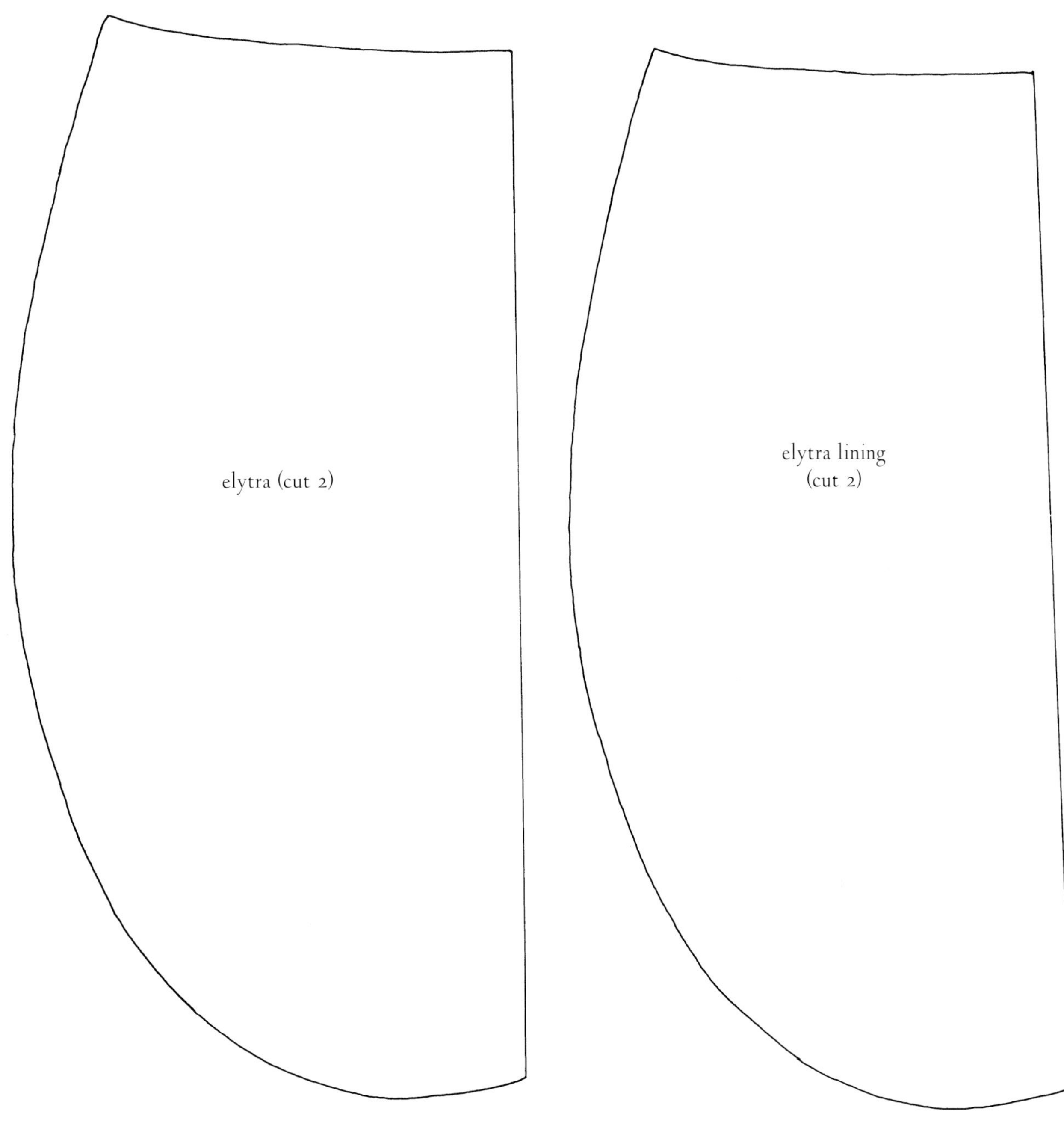

scutellum (cut 1)

Beetle Evening Bag pattern
actual size

Elytra

Decorate the elytra shape (before cutting out) if desired. I used a ribbed fabric (silk ottoman) for the elytra, and couched rows of bugle beads and seed beads, and narrow silver metallic braid, alternately, in the grooves.

1. With right sides facing, stitch the elytra to the elytra linings around the edges, leaving open at the top. Turn to the right side and press. With the straight edges touching, join the elytra together with a tacking stitch, 6 mm ($^1/_4$ in) down from the top.

2. To form the scutellum (the triangular shape at the top of the elytra), fold the square of fabric in half to make a rectangle. Press. Fold the corners of the folded edge to the centre of the opposite edge, making a triangle. Press.

3. Place the triangle (fold side down) on top of the elytra, raw edges level, and tack together.

Body

Cut two body padding shapes if required. The body fabric can be quilted to the padding, in a segment pattern; or join strips of fabric together, horizontally, to form a segmented body (optional).

1. With right sides facing, stitch the body shapes together around the curved outside edge, starting and ending 3 cm (1 $^1/_4$ in) below the top edge, as marked.

2. Tack the elytra, scutellum side up, to the top edge of one side of the body, matching the centre points.

Thorax

Fuse the layer of felt to the back of the thorax shapes if desired.

1. With right sides facing and raw edges even, stitch the lower edge of a thorax shape to the body front. Repeat for the body back. Press the seams towards the thorax.

2. Stitch the zipper tapes to the curved edges of the thorax (the zip is longer than the thorax; the ends will be tucked inside the bag). Slip stitch the seam allowances of the side openings of the body to the inside.

3. Cut a piece of cord to the required length for the bag handle. Stitch the cord ends to the ends of the zipper, then tuck all the ends inside the bag. Slip stitch the side openings closed to conceal the ends.

4. Stitch buttons or beads to the points on the thorax, as marked, for eyes.

Lining

With right sides facing, stitch the bag lining pieces together around the lower outside edge, leaving open above the points as marked. Tack the seam allowances of the top edges to the inside. Insert the lining inside the bag; slip stitch the top curved edge to the back of the zipper tape to compete the bag.

'Forgiven', the story of Alexander Beetle, is a favourite childhood poem. It would be fun to work a stumpwork Alexander (the handsome Ground Beetle, Carabus cancellatus, *is ideal), and mount him in a matchbox. Together with a copy of the book* Now We Are Six, *by A.A. Milne, it would make a very special gift for a child (or adult!).*

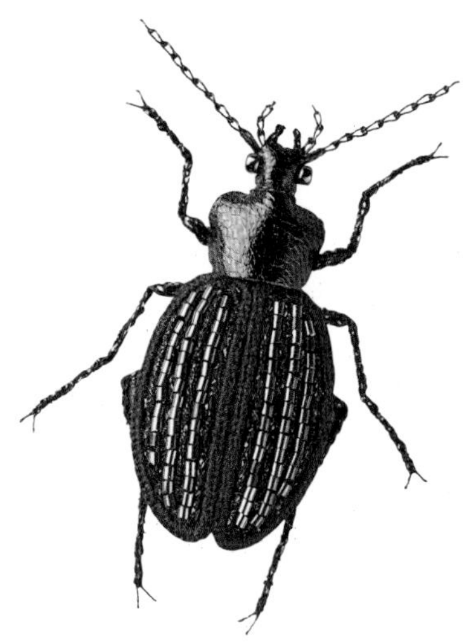

Part 9:

Techniques and Equipment

This section contains general information about the techniques and equipment that are referred to throughout the book. The bibliography contains a list of specialised reference books which provide more detailed instructions.

Transferring a Design to Fabric

There are several ways to transfer a design to fabric; choose the most appropriate method for your project.

You will need

- tracing paper (I use GLAD Bake baking parchment)
- fine HB lead pencil (0.5 mm clutch/mechanical pencil)
- stylus or empty ball-point pen (to trace a fine line)
- masking tape (to stop tracing paper from slipping)
- tracing board or small, circular lid (use inside the back of the hoop for support when tracing a design on to the front)

Preparation

Mount the main fabric and a backing fabric (quilter's muslin or calico), into a hoop or square frame. The fabrics need to be kept very taut—do not remove from the hoop until the embroidery is finished, unless instructed otherwise. To prevent distortion, transfer the design *after* the fabrics have been mounted into the hoop.

Tracing the design on to the front

The easiest method for working; use when the lines will be completely covered by the embroidery. Trace a skeleton outline of the design with the minimum amount of lead.

1. Trace a skeleton outline of the design onto tracing paper with lead pencil. Flip the paper over and draw over the outline on the back.

2. Tape the tracing, right side up, to the fabric in the hoop, place a tracing board (or lid) inside the back of the hoop for support, then transfer the design using a stylus, empty ball-point pen or a pencil.

Tracing the design onto the back

Use this method when the embroidery may not cover the design lines, if they were on the front, or when the fabric is coloured, patterned or textured. Work by referring to the outline on the back as you stitch. The design lines may be thread-traced through to the front, if required.

To ensure that your design is the 'right way up' on the main fabric, transfer the skeleton outline to the backing fabric as follows:

1. Trace a skeleton outline of the design onto tracing paper with lead pencil.

2. Tape the tracing, right (pencil) side down, over the muslin backing. Draw over all the traced lines with a stylus or empty ball-point pen, thus transferring a pencil outline onto the backing fabric. *Optional*: Draw over the pencil lines with a fine marking pen, as they tend to fade.

Thread-tracing the design

As this method does not permanently mark the fabric, it offers greater flexibility; however, it is difficult to accurately reproduce fine details of design.

1. Trace the design on to tissue paper with lead pencil. Attach the tracing to the edges of your frame or hoop with masking tape.

2. Work small running stitches over the traced lines, through the fabric, with fine silk or machine thread. Score the lines with a needle, then carefully tear the paper away.

3. Remove the tracing threads as you embroider.

Transferring the design with a paper template

Use this method to achieve very accurate outlines or shapes on the front, when pencil lines can not be used.

1. Trace the shape on to paper, clear tape, or 'post-it' paper. Cut out the template and hold in place on the front of the fabric with tacking stitches, if necessary.

2. Work around the template to achieve the desired shape or outline, removing the paper when necessary.

Working with Vliesofix

Vliesofix (also known as Bondaweb) is a paper-backed fusible web which is used to fuse or bond one material to another by applying heat with an iron. Use a layer of baking parchment (GLAD Bake) on either side of the fabrics to be fused to protect your iron and the ironing board. I use Vliesofix to obtain a precise design outline on felt—it is very difficult to trace a small shape onto felt and to cut it out accurately!

To fuse a design outline to felt

Trace the shape on to the paper side of Vliesofix then fuse to the felt (fusible web side down!) with a medium-hot dry iron. Cut out the shape along the outlines. Remove the paper before stitching the felt shape to the background fabric (e.g. beetle abdomen).

To fuse a design outline to organza and felt

Use the following method if internal design lines are required on a felt shape.

Fuse a layer of Vliesofix to organza. Trace the design outlines onto the *organza* side of the bonded materials. Remove the paper and fuse the organza onto the felt. Cut out the felt shape and stitch to the background fabric, organza side up.

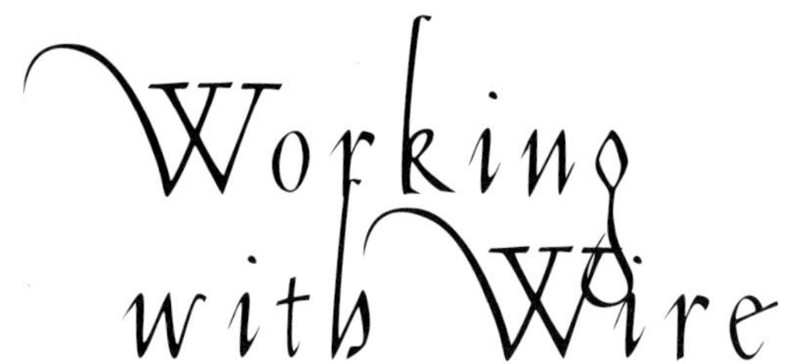

Working with Wire

Cake decorator's wire is used to form the detached, wired and embroidered shapes characteristic to stumpwork.

30-GAUGE COVERED WIRE

This sturdy wire has a tightly-wrapped, thin paper covering and is available in green and white (which can be coloured). It is a strong wire which maintains its shape when bent—use it for detached elements such as a beetle's elytra and legs, and larger leaves.

FINE FLOWER WIRE

This fine wire is covered with a layer of artificial silk which can be readily dyed—use a waterproof ink or paint to colour the silk, if desired. Flower wire is used for small, detailed detached shapes, such as flower petals and fine leaves.

28-GAUGE UNCOVERED WIRE

Uncovered wire, silver in colour, is used when a finer edge is required—use it for small or detailed detached shapes, antennae and grape tendrils. It can be used to replace flower wire. Select the 28-gauge weight as the 30-gauge is a little too thin to retain its shape when stitched.

To stitch wire to fabric

- When stitching wire to fabric, either with overcast stitch or buttonhole stitch, make sure that the needle enters the fabric at right angles, very close to the wire (not angled under the wire). The stitches need to be worked very close together, with an up-and-down stabbing motion, using a firm and even tension.

- If you need to renew a thread while stitching wire to fabric, secure the thread tails inside the wired shape. Do not use a knot as it may be cut when cutting out the shape.
- Using very sharp scissors with fine points, cut out the wired shape as close to the stitching as possible (stroke the cut edge with your fingernail to reveal any stray threads). If you happen to cut a stitch, use the point of a pin to apply a minute amount of PVA glue to the cut thread. This will dry matt and clear.

To attach wired shapes to a background fabric

Detached wire shapes are applied to a background fabric by inserting the wire tails through a 'tunnel' formed by the eye of a large (size 14) yarn darner needle.

1. Pierce the background fabric at the required point with the yarn darner and push it through until the eye is half-way through the fabric.

2. Insert the wire tails into the tunnel formed by the eye of the darner, through to the back of the fabric.

3. Gently pull the darner all the way through, leaving the wire tails in the hole.

4. Stitch the wire tails to the backing fabric, preferably behind an embroidered area, then trim. Do not let any wire protrude past the embroidered area.

5. Use tweezers to bend the wired shape as required.

Working with Leather

Leather is available in a wide range of colours, thicknesses and finishes—fine kid, thicker leather, suede and snakeskin—and is used in stumpwork, goldwork and other areas of embroidery to provide a contrast in texture and colour.

To cut a leather shape

To cut a shape out of leather, either trace an outline onto the back, or use a template of paper or clear adhesive tape. Using small, sharp scissors cut the leather with a long cutting motion (short cuts can cause an uneven edge or damage to the fine metallic coating of some leathers). If the leather is thick, it may be necessary to bevel the edges at the back. Do this with a sharp craft knife or scissors. The edges of the leather may be coloured with a matching waterproof ink.

To pad a leather shape

Leather is usually applied over padding. For a beetle's elytra, one layer of felt is used; in goldwork, many layers of felt may be applied to give a smooth, domed shape. If more than one layer of felt is required to pad a shape, cut one piece the actual size, and one or more successively smaller shapes. Attach each layer of felt with small stab stitches (coming out of the background fabric and stabbing into the felt), applying the smallest shape first, with the largest layer on top.

To stitch leather

Using a small needle (size 12 sharps) and clear nylon thread, or fine silk thread in a matching colour, apply the leather with small stab stitches, bringing the needle out just under the edge of the leather, and stab stitching into the leather (not too close to the edge or the leather may tear). The stitches should be worked fairly close together, at 1.5–2 mm ($^1/_{16}$ in) to avoid 'bulges' between the stitches, and need to be fairly firm to pull the sides of the leather down to hide the cut edge.

When applying leather inside a wired shape (as for the beetle elytra), stroke the edge of the leather (in the ditch next to the wire) with a blunt needle, or fingernail, causing the centre of the leather to curve into a smooth mound. Tweezers, or a nail file, can be used to smooth and ease the leather into shape after it has been applied.

To Mount Stumpwork Into a Paperweight

You will need

- glass paperweight—Framecraft 6 or 9 cm ($2^3/_4$ or $3^1/_2$ in) diameter
- recessed wooden base of the appropriate size (available from Jane Nicholas)
- circle of acid-free cardboard (1.5 mm)
- strong thread
- PVA adhesive
- clear silicone glue (Selleys Window and Glass Sealant)

1. Cut a circle of cardboard to fit inside the recess of the wooden base. Gather the embroidery firmly over this circle, then lace, using strong thread (gather the muslin backing and the satin separately for a smoother finish).

2. Using PVA adhesive, glue the embroidery-covered cardboard into the recessed wooden base, pressing gently until it is secure.

3. Gently brush (or vacuum) the surface to remove any dust or stray threads, then arrange the detached elements (e.g. wings) as desired, using tweezers.

4. Attach the glass paperweight to the wooden base with a thin layer of clear silicone glue (take care not to use too much). Leave under a weight until the sealant has cured.

5. Apply a circle of self-adhesive suede (or felt) to the base of the paperweight.

Equipment

The embroiderer's workbox should contain the following equipment:

- Good quality embroidery hoops: 10, 15 and 23 cm (4, 6 and 9 in); bind the inner ring to prevent slipping
- Slate frames in various sizes for goldwork and larger embroideries
- Needles (detailed information below)
- Fine glass-headed pins
- Thimble
- Embroidery scissors—small, with fine sharp points
- Goldwork scissors—small and strong with sharp points
- Paper scissors
- Small wire cutters or old scissors for cutting wire
- Mellor or old metal nailfile (for nudging threads or padding into place)
- Assortment of tweezers (from surgical suppliers)
- Eyebrow comb (for Turkey knots)
- Screwdriver (for tightening the embroidery hoop)
- Tracing paper (I use GLAD Bake baking parchment)
- Fine (0.5 mm) HB lead pencil (mechanical)
- Stylus or empty ball-point pen (for tracing)
- Masking tape
- Ruler and tape measure
- Ideas notebook

Needles

An assortment of needles is required. When selecting a needle, make sure that it is the appropriate type to suit the purpose. The thread should pass easily through the eye, and the needle should make a hole in the fabric large enough for the double thickness of the thread to pass through easily (without damaging the thread).

Crewel/embroidery sizes 3–10

Crewel needles are used with embroidery silks and cottons. They have a sharp point and long eye to take one or more strands of thread. Use a size 10 needle for one strand of thread, a size 9 for two strands (the more strands of thread, the larger the needle required).

Straw/milliners sizes 1–9

Straw needles have a round eye and a long shaft that does not vary in diameter from its eye until it tapers at the point. They are ideal for working French and bullion knots, and for stitching with metallic embroidery threads (make sure the needle is thicker than the thread). A size 9 is used with one strand of fine metallic thread; a size 1 with a thick metallic braid.

Tapestry sizes 24–28

Tapestry needles have an elongated eye and a blunt point which makes them ideal for working needlepoint, needlelace, surface darning, raised stem band and whipped spider web stitch.

SHARPS SIZES 8–12

These are sharp needles with a round eye. Size 12 is ideal for stitching with fine machine threads, silk and nylon monofilament, and to apply leather and beads. Use the larger sizes when stitching with metallic thread—the thicker the thread the larger the needle.

CHENILLE SIZES 18–24

Chenille needles are thick and sharp and have an elongated eye. Use when stitching with thick thread (e.g. soft cotton), and for sinking some metallic threads through to the back.

YARN DARNERS SIZES 14–18

Yarn darners are sharp and thick with a long eye. Use to insert detached wired shapes (e.g. beetle elytra) and for stitching very thick threads and chenille. Use the largest darner (size 14) as a stiletto, and for sinking metal threads through to the back.

Glossary of product names

This list gives equivalent names for products used throughout this book which may not be available under the same name in every country.

biro	ball-point pen
calico	muslin
clutch pencil	mechanical pencil
GLAD Bake	baking parchment
quilter's muslin	finely woven calico or cotton homespun
Vliesofix	paper-backed fusible web, Bondaweb

Thread Conversion Chart

DMC stranded cottons and Au Ver à Soie d'Alger stranded silks have been used to embroider most of the projects. When a finer, shiny thread has been required, Cifonda Art Silk (similar to Rajmahal) has been used. As some of these threads may not be available in other countries, a thread conversion chart has been provided to enable substitutions to be made. The colours suggested are as close a match as possible.

DMC	*Soie d'Alger*	*Cifonda*	*Finca*	*Anchor*	*Madeira*
154	3326	-	-	-	-
300	-	-	7656	352	2304
301	-	64	7740	1049	2306
309	2934	-	1661	42	0507
310	Noir	Black	0007	403	Black
321	916	-	1902	9046	0510
349	914	254A	1490	13	0212
350	913	-	1485	11	0213
351	912	-	1485	10	0214
400	-	-	7656	351	2305
469	514	-	4817	267	1503
470	522	523	4817	267	1502
471	-	522	4885	266	1501
472	-	521	4799	253	1414
498	-	-	1906	1005	0511
500	-	-	4323	683	1705
505	-	-	-	-	-
543	-	496	8140	933	1909
550	3316	125	2635	101	0714
552	3315	-	2627	99	0713
553	3314	-	2615	98	0712
580	2145	-	4817	281	1608
581	2144	-	4812	280	1609
606	-	-	1163	335	0209
680	524	-	7155	901	2210
700	-	-	4652	228	1304

DMC	Soie d'Alger	Cifonda	Finca	Anchor	Madeira
701	-	-	4643	227	1305
720	615	-	7574	326	0309
721	614	-	7567	324	0308
729	-	48	7155	890	2209
730	2215	-	5236	845	1614
741	-	-	1152	304	0201
743	-	-	1062	303	0113
778	4643	-	-	968	0808
780	4214	-	8072	310	2214
791	-	-	3324	178	0904
796	-	184	3405	133	0913
797	-	989B	3405	132	0912
814	-	-	-	45	0514
815	2926	-	1915	43	0513
817	915	-	1490	13	0211
823	163	-	3327	152	1008
829	526	50	7073	906	2113
830	525	-	7066	277	2114
833	2533	-	7046	907	2203
869	-	-	7408	944	2105
890	1846	495	4323	683	1314
895	-	-	4485	1044	1405
900	646	-	1344	333	0208
909	215	-	4402	923	1302
918	2636	-	-	341	0314
919	616	105A	7580	340	0313
920	-	64	7580	1004	0312
921	-	103	7644	884	0311
924	-	-	3745	851	1706
927	545	-	3721	848	1708
930	-	214	3151	1035	1712
934	2216	-	-	862	1506
936	2215	-	4823	846	1507
937	516	-	4823	268	1504
938	4136	-	8080	381	2005
939	3326	-	3327	152	1009
991	-	7	-	189	1204
995	-	-	3822	410	1102
3023	-	-	8567	899	1902
3047	2131	-	-	852	2205
3341	911	-	1307	328	0302
3345	2126	525	4565	268	1406
3346	2125	523A	4565	267	1407
3347	-	-	4885	266	1408
3371	4136	225A	8083	382	2004
3726	4635	-	2110	-	-
3750	-	215	3151	-	-

DMC	Soie d'Alger	Cifonda	Finca	Anchor	Madeira
3752	-	212	3139	-	-
3765	-	685	3574	-	-
3777	2926	-	1996	-	-
3799	-	-	8756	-	-
3802	4636	-	2123	-	-
3808	135	-	3670	-	-
3809	134	-	3670	-	-
3818	216	-	4402	-	-
3829	-	49	7155	-	-
3832	2933	-	-	-	-
3842	-	-	-	-	-
3847	1826	-	-	-	-
3853	612	-	-	-	-
3857	4626	-	-	-	-
3858	4615	-	-	-	-
3862	-	498	-	-	-
3864	-	497	-	-	-

Part 10:
Stitch Glossary

This glossary contains most the stitches used in this book, in alphabetical order.

For ease of explanation, some of the stitches have been illustrated with the needle entering and leaving the fabric in the same movement. When working in a hoop this is difficult (or *should* be if your fabric is tight enough), so the stitches have to be worked with a stabbing motion, in several stages.

Back stitch

A useful stitch for outlining a shape. Bring the needle out at 1, insert at 2 (in the hole made by the preceding stitch) and out again at 3. Keep the stitches small and even.

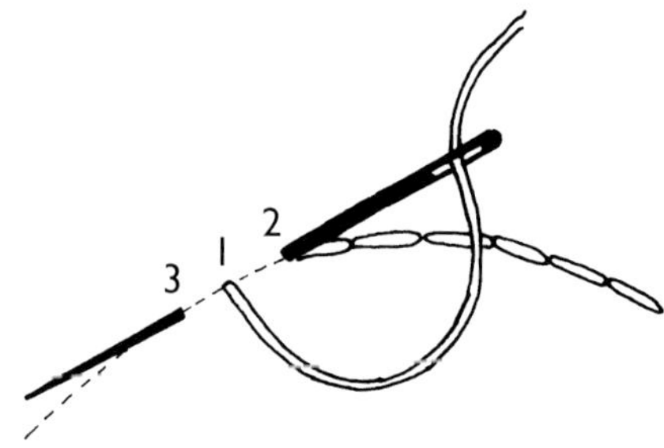

Back stitch—split

An easier version of split stitch, especially when using one strand of thread. Commence with a back stitch. Bring the needle out at 1, insert at 2 (splitting the preceding stitch) and out again at 3. This results in a fine, smooth line, ideal for stitching intricate curves.

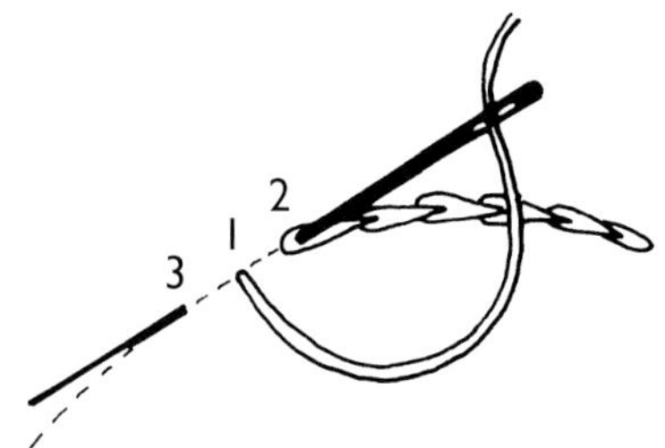

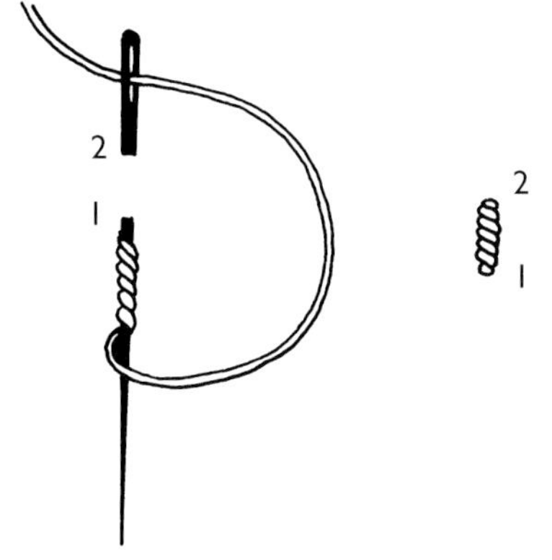

Bullion knots

These require some practice to work in a hoop. Use a straw needle of the appropriate size, with the number of wraps depending on the length of the knot required. Bring the needle out at 1, insert at 2 leaving a long loop. Emerge at 1 again (not pulling the needle through yet) and wrap the thread around the needle the required number of times. Hold the wraps gently between the thumb and index finger of the left hand while pulling the needle through with the right hand. Pull quite firmly and insert again at 2, stroking the wraps into place.

Burden stitch

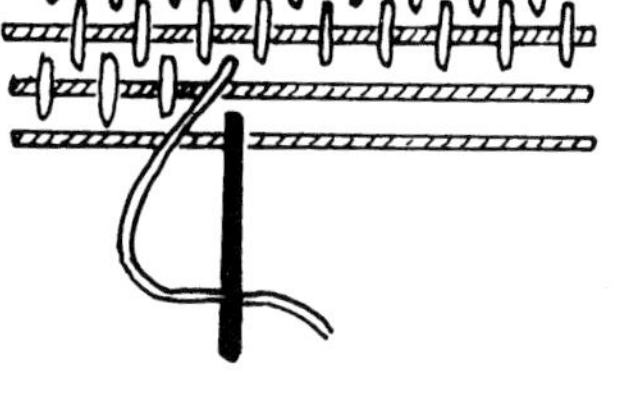

Burden stitch is a type of couching worked in a brick-like pattern. Firstly cover the shape with horizontal, evenly spaced long stitches (the size of the space between the rows can vary). Secure these stitches to the fabric with rows of vertical couching stitches—these can be arranged in a variety of brick-like patterns. The couching stitches can be worked in different colours to produce shading.

Buttonhole stitch

These stitches can be worked close together or slightly apart. Working from left to right, bring the needle out on the line to be worked at 1 and insert at 2, holding the loop of thread with the left thumb. Bring the needle up on the line to be worked at 3 (directly below 2), over the thread loop and pull through to form a looped edge. If the stitch is shortened and worked close together over wire, it forms a secure edge for cut shapes, e.g. a detached leaf.

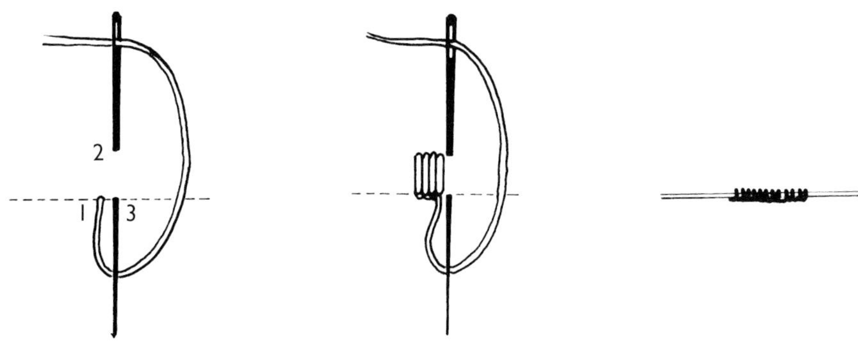

Buttonhole stitch—long and short

In long and short buttonhole stitch, each alternate stitch is shorter. Bring the needle out at 1, insert at 2 and up again at 3 (like an open detached chain stitch). When embroidering a shape like a petal, angle the stitches towards the centre of the flower.

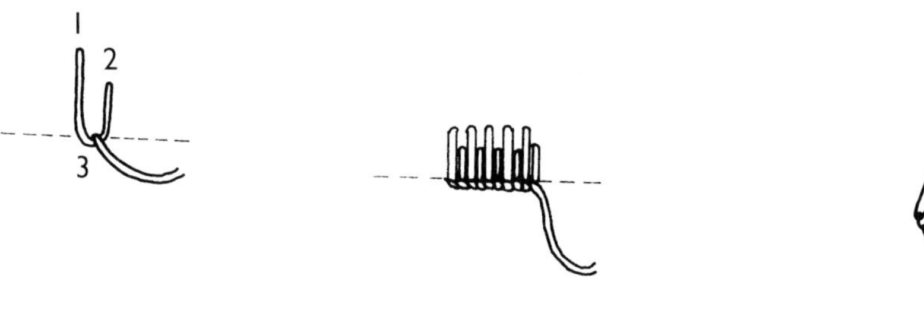

Buttonhole stitch—detached

Buttonhole stitch can be worked as a detached filling, attached only to the background material at the edges of the shape. First work a row of back stitches around the shape to be filled. Change to a fine tapestry needle. Bring the needle out at 1, work buttonhole stitches in to the top row of back stitches then insert the needle at 2. Come up again at 3 and work a buttonhole stitch into each loop of the preceding row. Insert the needle at 4. Quite different effects can be achieved when these stitches are worked close together or spaced apart.

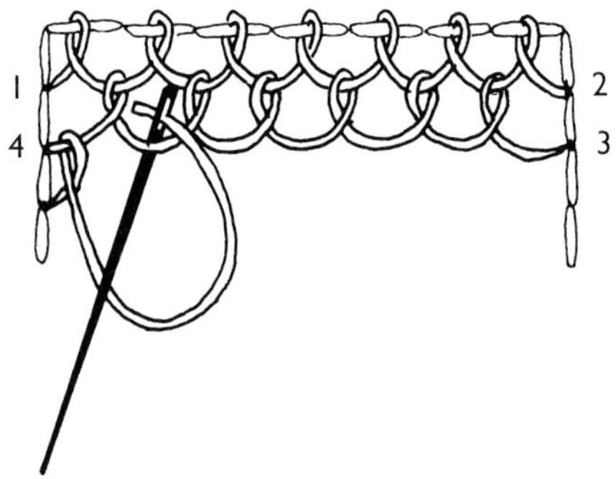

Buttonhole stitch—corded detached

Detached buttonhole stitch can be worked over a laid thread. Outline the shape to be filled with back stitches (or couch a wire frame to a buttonhole pad). Using a tapestry needle, come up at 1 and work the first row of buttonhole stitches into the top row of back stitches (or over the wire frame). Slip the needle under the back stitch at 2 (or around the wire). Take the needle straight back to the left side and slip under the back stitch at 3. Work another row of buttonhole stitches, this time taking the needle into the previous loops and under the straight thread at the same time. Slip the needle under the back stitch at 4 and continue as above. A contrasting thread (or gold thread), worked in another needle, can replace the straight thread, with interesting results.

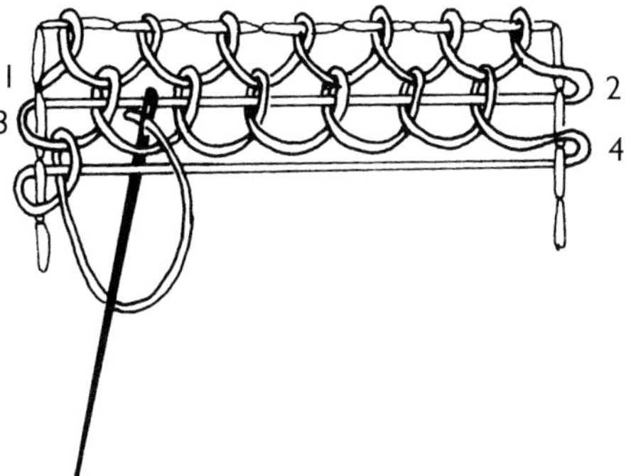

Chain stitch

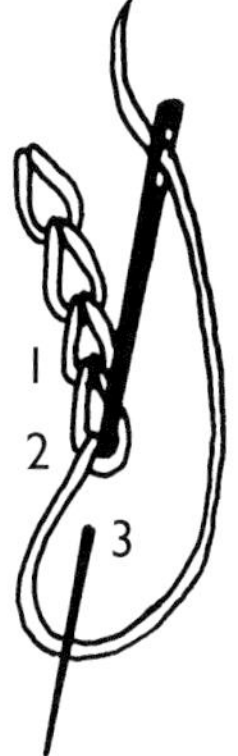

Bring the needle through at 1 and insert it again through the same hole, holding the loop of thread with the left thumb. Bring the needle up a short distance along at 2, through the loop, and pull the thread through. Insert the needle into the same hole at 2 (inside the loop) and make a second loop, hold, and come up at 3. Repeat to work a row of chain stitch, securing the final loop with a small straight stitch.

Chain stitch—open

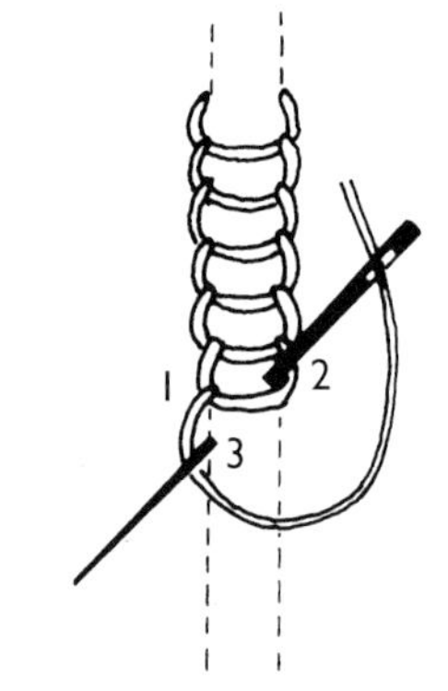

Open chain stitch is a wide variation of basic chain stitch. It can be worked between two parallel lines, or used to couch a narrow ribbon or bundle of threads. The stitch is worked in the same way as chain stitch; however, the needle is inserted to the right at 2, and brought out diagonally to the left at 3.

Chain stitch—whipped

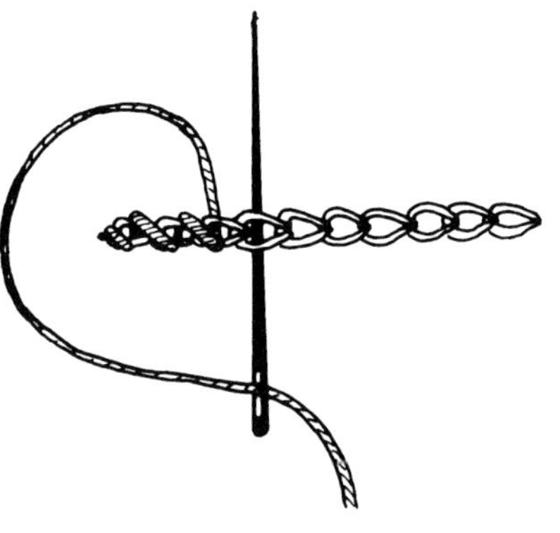

This is a useful method for working slightly raised outlines. Work a row of chain stitch then bring the needle out slightly to one side of the final securing stitch. Using either the eye of the needle or a tapestry needle, whip the chain stitches by passing the needle under each chain loop from right to left, back to the beginning of the row. When whipped chain stitch is used for stems, the thickness of the outline can be varied by the number of threads used.

Couching

Couching is used to attach a thread, or bundle of threads, to a background fabric by means of small, vertical stitches worked at regular intervals. The laid thread is usually thicker or more fragile (e.g. gold metallic or chenille) than the one used for stitching. Couching stitches are also used for attaching wire to the base fabric before embroidering detached shapes.

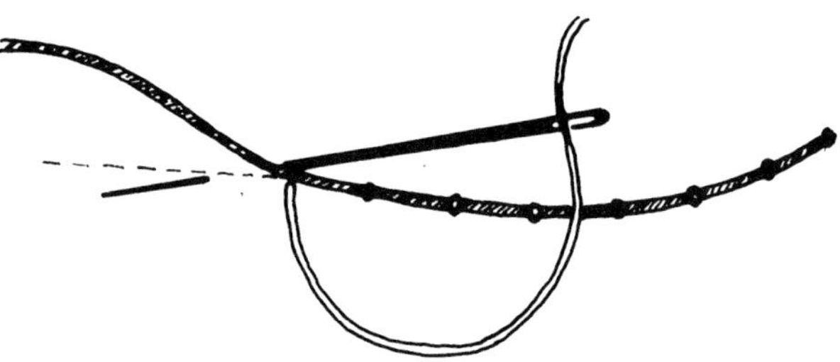

Couching—lattice

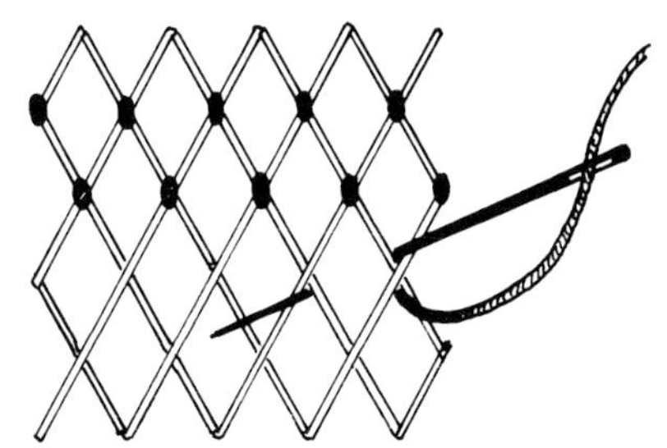

Lattice couching is one of the endless variations of couched fillings. The design area is filled with a network of laid, parallel, evenly spaced threads. Where two threads cross, they are secured to the background with a small straight stitch.

Fishbone stitch

This stitch is useful for filling small leaf shapes. Bring the thread out at the tip of the leaf at 1, and make a small straight stitch along the centre line (vein). Bring the needle out at 2, make a slanted stitch and go down on the right of the centre line. Bring the needle out at 3, make a slanted stitch and go down on the left of the centre line, overlapping the base of the previous stitch. Continue working slanted stitches alternately from the left and the right, close together, until the shape is filled.

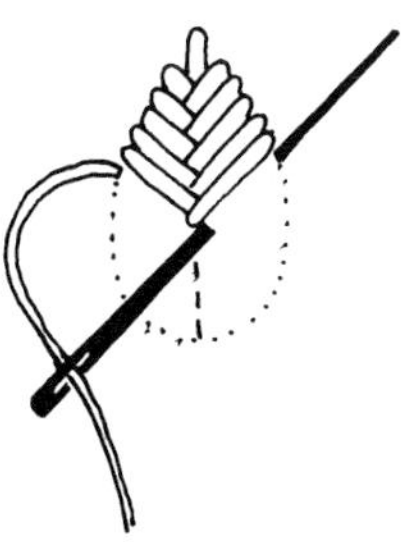

Flat stitch

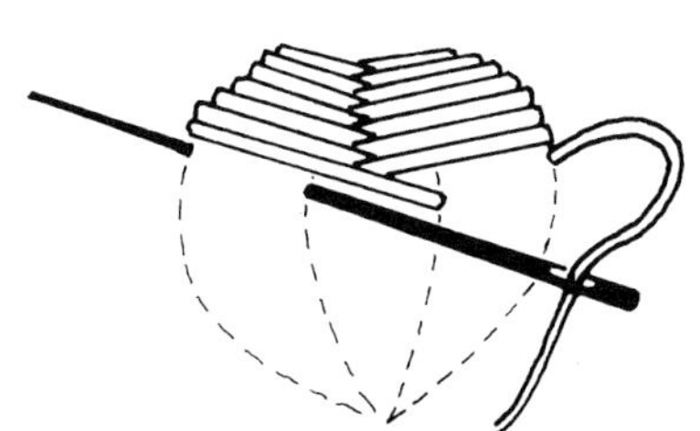

Flat stitch is used to fill small shapes, such as a ladybird's elytra. The stitches are worked close together to create a flat, smooth surface. Starting at a top corner, work slightly slanting straight stitches from side to side of the shape to be filled, inserting the needle inside the shape so that each stitch crosses over the base of the preceding stitch. A neater result is obtained if the shape is first outlined in split stitch, working flat stitch over the outline.

Fly stitch

Fly stitch is actually an open detached chain stitch. Bring the needle out at 1 and insert at 2, holding the working thread with the left thumb. Bring up again at 3 and pull through over the loop. Secure the loop with an anchoring stitch, which can be varied in length to produce different effects.

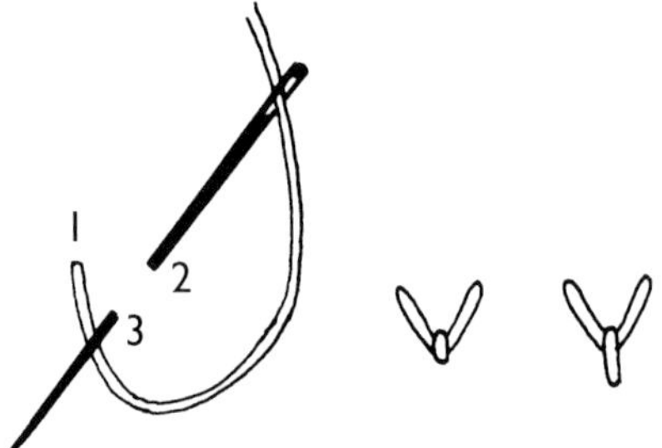

French knots

Using a straw needle, bring the thread through at the desired place, wrap the thread once around the point of the needle and re-insert the needle. Tighten the thread and *hold taut* while pulling the needle through. To increase the size of the knot use more strands of thread, although more wraps can be made if desired.

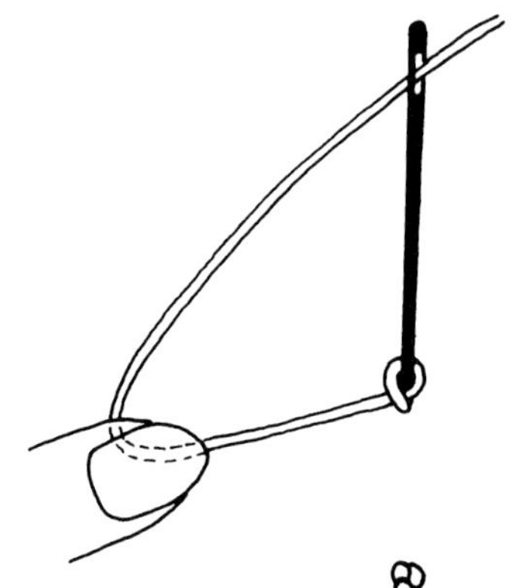

Long and short stitch

This stitch can be used to fill areas too large or irregular for satin stitch, or where shading is required. The first row, worked around the outline, consists of alternating long and short satin stitches. In the subsequent rows, the stitches are all of similar length, and fit into the spaces left by the preceding row. For a more realistic result when working petals, direct the stitches towards the centre of the flower. The surface will look smoother if the needle either pierces the stitches of the preceding row or enters at an angle between the stitches.

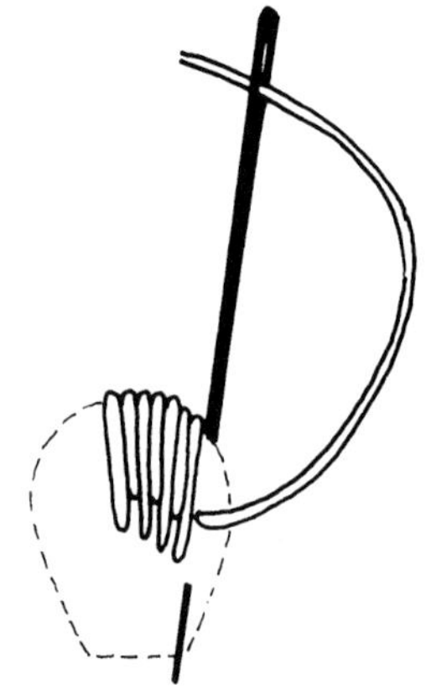

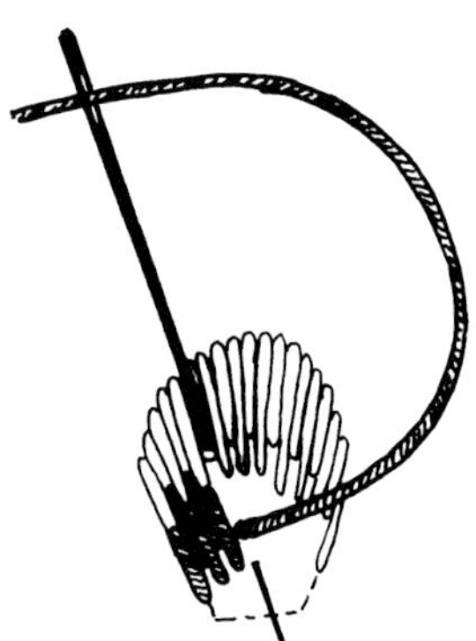

Outline stitch

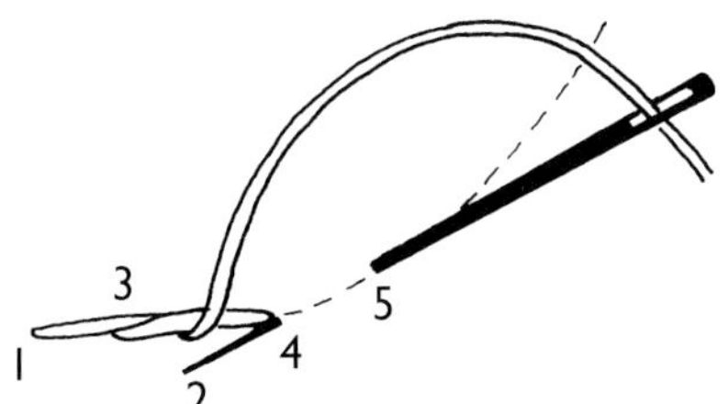

Worked from left to right, this stitch is perfect for working both simple and complicated outlines. Worked in the same way as stem stitch, the only difference is that the working thread is kept to the left of the line being worked. To start, bring the needle out at 1 on the line to be worked. Go down at 2, come up at 3 (to the right of the stitch) and pull the thread through. Insert the needle at 4, holding the thread above the line with the left thumb, and come up again at 2 (in the same hole made by the previous stitch) then pull the thread through. Go down at 5, hold the loop and come up again at 4, then pull the thread through. Repeat to work a narrow line.

Overcast stitch

This stitch is made up of tiny, vertical satin stitches, worked very close together over a laid thread or wire, resulting in a firm raised line. When worked over wire it gives a smooth, secure edge for cut shapes, e.g. petals. Place the wire along the line to be covered. Working from left to right with a stabbing motion, cover the wire with small straight stitches, pulling the thread firmly so that there are no loose stitches which may be cut when the shape is cut out.

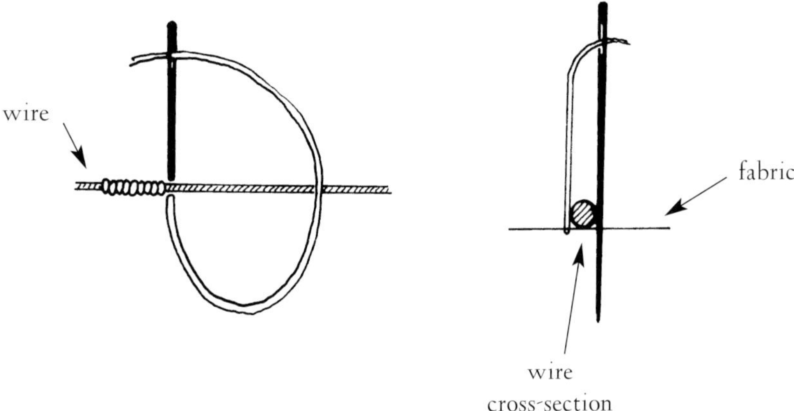

Pad stitch

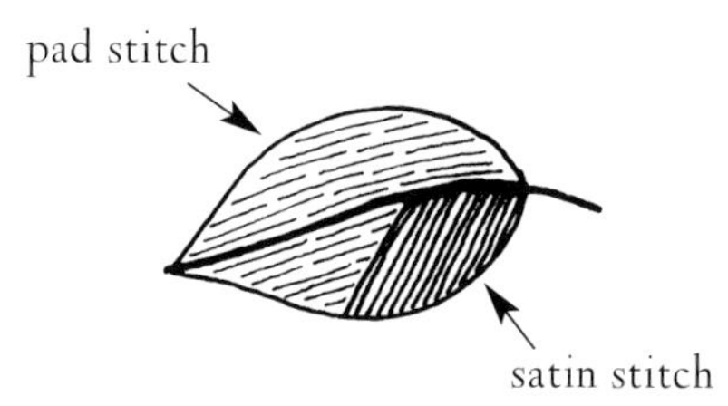

Pad stitch is used as a foundation under satin stitch when a smooth, *slightly raised* surface is required. Padding stitches can be either straight stitches or chain stitches, worked in the opposite direction to the satin stitches. Felt can replace pad stitch for a more raised effect.

Plaited stitch

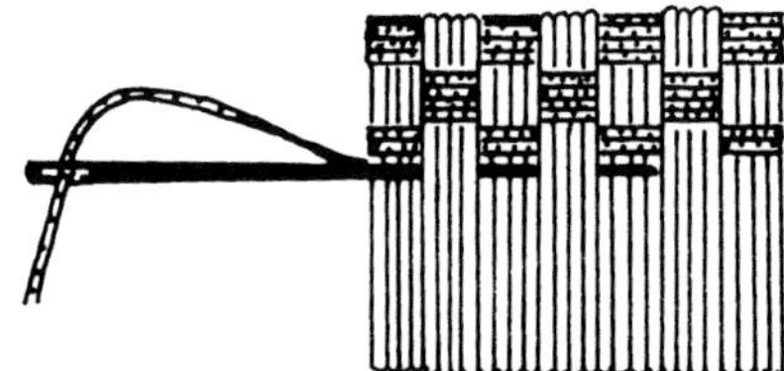

Plaited stitch, a variation of surface darning, produces an effective chequerboard pattern when worked in two colours of thread. First work a foundation of close satin stitches over the shape to be filled. Weave a second thread, in a contrasting colour, regularly in and out of the foundation stitches; going over four and under four satin stitches alternately (the number of stitches woven depends on the desired check size). Work four rows, then reverse the sequence of unders and overs for the next four rows. Continue until the shape is filled with a woven chequerboard pattern. Use a fine tapestry needle for the second thread and pierce the fabric only at the sides of the shape.

Roumanian couching

This form of couching is useful for filling in large spaces. Bring the needle out on the left, take a long stitch across the space to be filled, then insert the needle on the right. This laid thread is then caught down with loose, slanting, couching stitches going from right to left. Traditionally the couching was worked with the same thread; however, a contrasting thread in another needle is very effective.

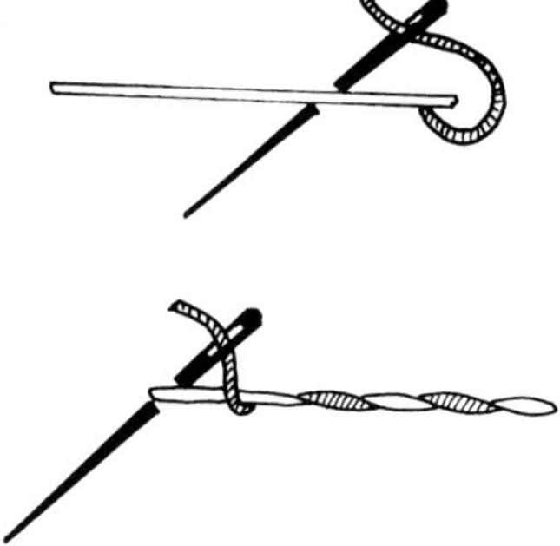

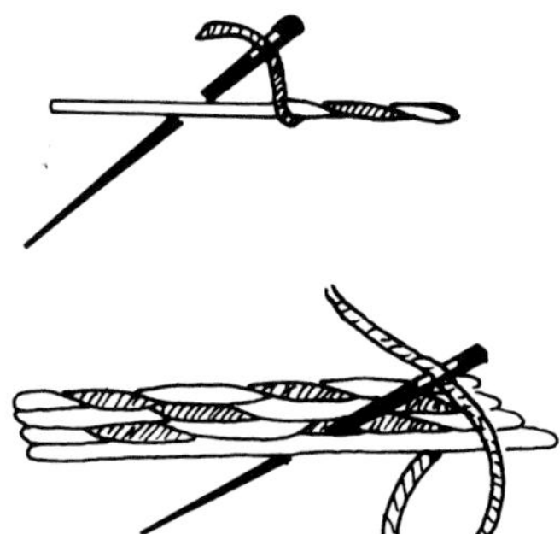

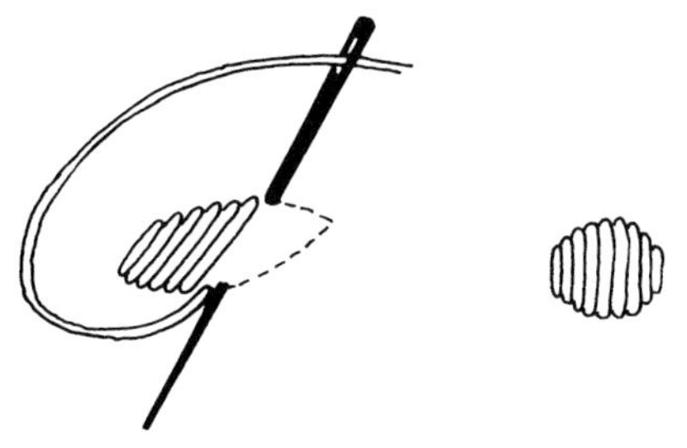

Satin stitch

Satin stitch is used to fill shapes. It consists of horizontal or vertical straight stitches, worked close enough together that no fabric shows through, yet not overlapping each other. Satin stitch can be worked over a padding of felt or pad stitches. Smooth edges are easier to achieve if the shape is first outlined with split stitch.

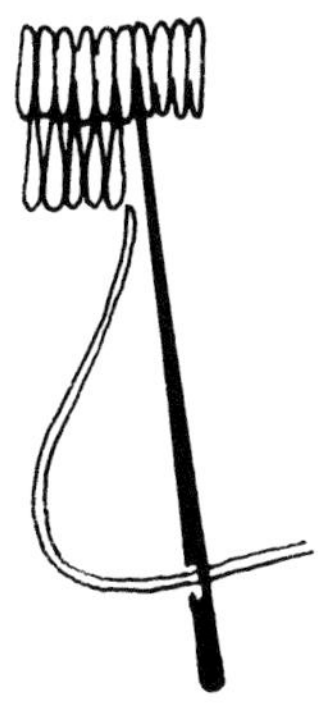

Satin stitch—encroaching

Encroaching satin stitch is a useful method of shading. First work a row of regular satin stitch; in the second, and all subsequent rows, the head of each satin stitch is taken *between* the base of two stitches in the row above, so that the rows blend softly into each other, e.g. the peacock (page 187). Vary the length of the stitches to achieve more subtle shading.

Slip stitch

Slip stitch is a dressmaking stitch, used to join two folds of fabric together, invisibly, with small running stitches. The stitches are of equal length and enter and leave each fold of fabric directly opposite each other. Come out at 1, enter at 2, slide the needle through the fold and come out at 3, enter at 4 and so on, pulling the thread to bring the folds of fabric together.

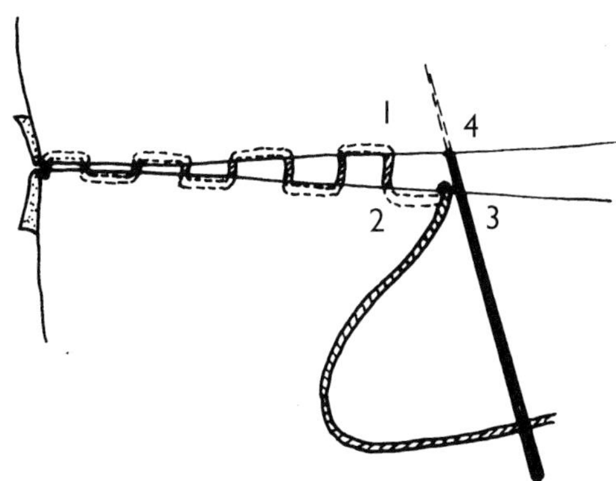

Split stitch

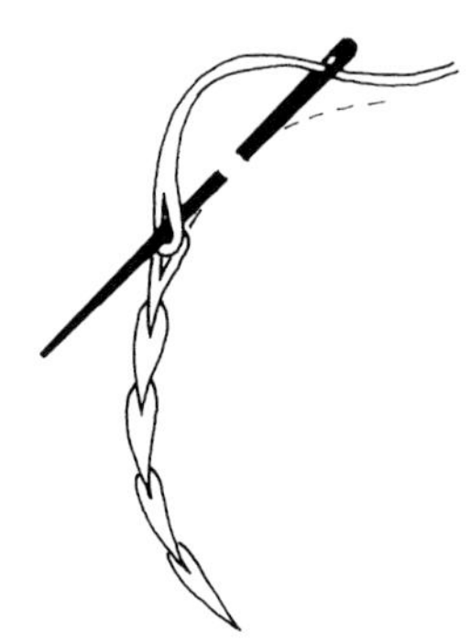

Split stitch can be used either as an outline stitch or for smooth, solid fillings. In the Middle Ages, split stitch was used to work most of the silk embroidery, e.g. the faces, hands and feet of human figures, on ecclesiastical vestments. Split stitch is worked in a similar way to stem stitch; however the point of the needle splits the preceding stitch as it is brought out of the fabric. To start, make a straight stitch along the line to be worked. Bring the needle through to the front, splitting the straight stitch with the point of the needle. Insert the needle along the line then bring through to the front, again to pierce the preceding stitch. Repeat to work a narrow line of stitching, resembling fine chain stitch.

Stab stitch

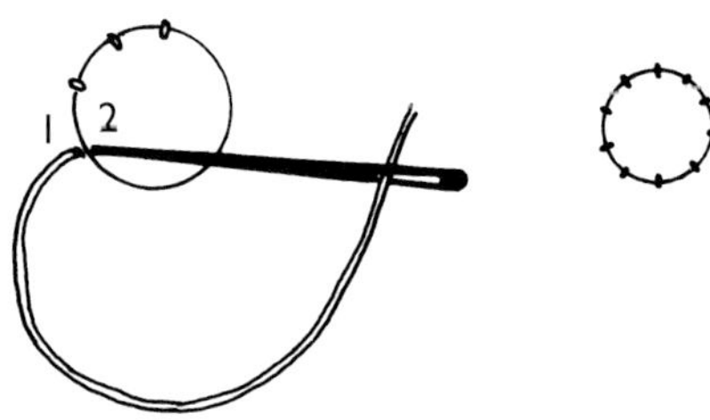

Stab stitch is used to apply leather or felt shapes to a background fabric. It consists of small straight stitches made from the background fabric over the edge of the applied shape, e.g. the felt padding of a beetle's abdomen. Bring the needle out at 1, and insert at 2, catching in the edge of the applied piece.

Stem stitch

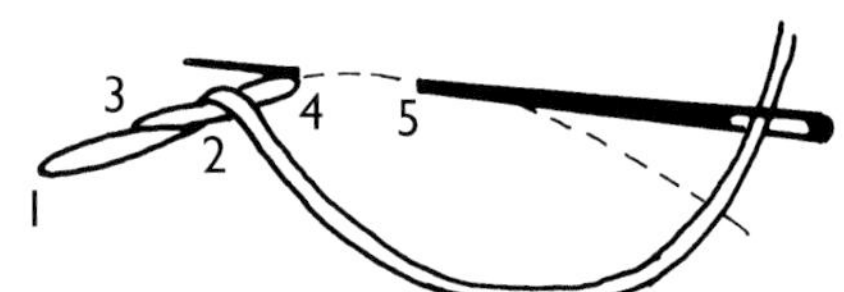

Worked from left to right, the stitches in stem stitch overlap each other to form a fine line suitable for outlines and stems. To start, bring the needle out at 1 on the line to be worked. Go down at 2, come up at 3 and pull the thread through. Insert the needle at 4, holding the thread underneath the line with the left thumb, and come up again at 2 (in the same hole made by the previous stitch), then pull the thread through. Go down at 5, hold the loop and come up again at 4, then pull the thread through. Repeat to work a narrow line.

Stem stitch band—raised

Stem stitch can be worked over a foundation of couched padding thread to produce a raised, smooth, stem stitch band, ideal for insect bodies. Lay a preliminary foundation of padding stitches worked with soft cotton thread. Across this padding, at fairly regular intervals, work straight (couching) stitches at right angles to the padding thread (do not make these stitches too tight). Then proceed to cover the padding by working rows of stem stitch over these straight stitches, using a tapestry needle so as not to pierce the padding thread. All the rows of stem stitch are worked in the same direction, close together and ending either at the same point, e.g. A, or spaced as in satin stitch, e.g. B.

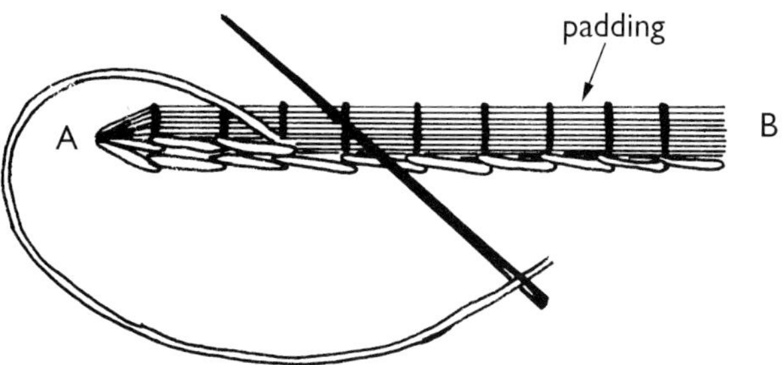

Straight stitch

Individual straight stitches, of equal or varying length, can be stitched with a variety of threads to achieve interesting effects, e.g. a beetle's legs in metallic thread.

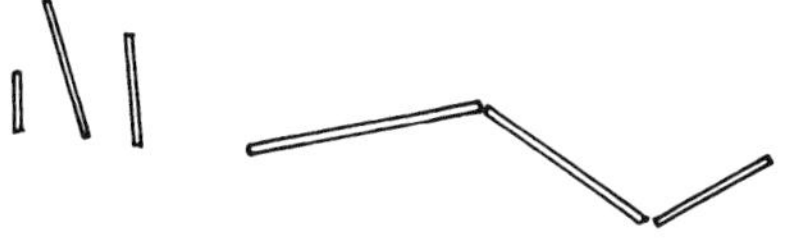

Striped woven band

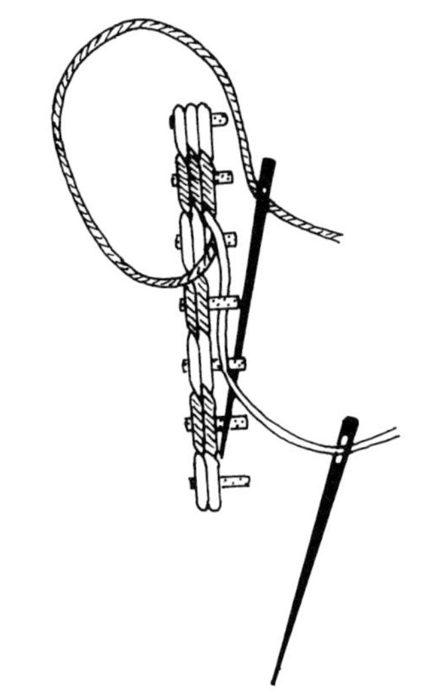

Striped woven band is worked in two colours to produce a solidly stitched, striped band. Work a foundation of evenly spaced horizontal stitches (if a raised effect is required, work some long padding stitches under the foundation bars). Thread two needles with threads of contrasting colours (A and B), and bring both through the fabric at the top left-hand corner of the foundation row. Working downwards, weave alternate threads over and under the foundation bars, always taking thread A over the odd numbered bars, and thread B over the even numbered bars to produce stripes. Each row of weaving starts again at the top, beginning each row of weaving with the same thread colour (A). Work the rows of weaving close together so that they completely cover the foundation bars and the padding.

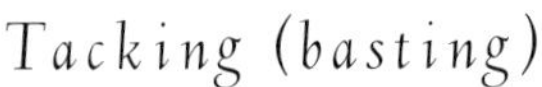

Tacking (basting)

Tacking, a dressmaking term, is a row of running stitches, longer on the top of the fabric, used to temporarily mark an outline or to hold two pieces of fabric together.

Tent stitch

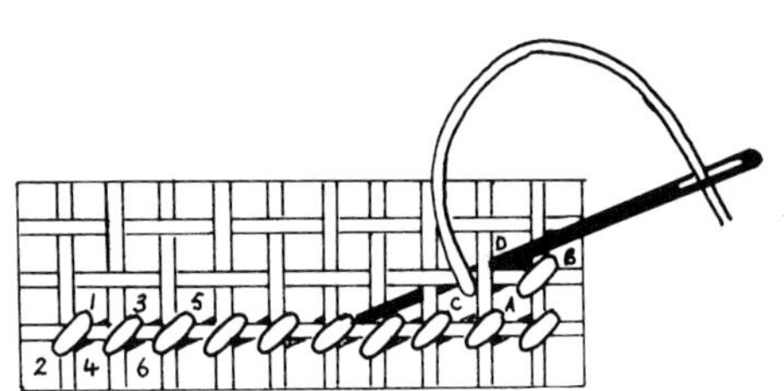

Tent stitch is a canvas-work stitch, worked over single thread of canvas or silk mesh. The stitch, which resembles a half cross-stitch, when correctly worked is longer on the reverse side than on the front. This has a padding effect and gives better coverage than half cross-stitch. The stitch is worked from left to right. Bring the needle out at 1, insert at 2, out again at 3, down at 4, and so on, making a horizontal row of slanting stitches. At the end of the line, turn the canvas and work a row of identical stitches, coming up at A, down at B, up at C, and so on. By turning the canvas around at the end of each line, the rows may always be worked from left to right, which is easier, and ensures that the stitches are alike on both sides of the canvas.

Trellis stitch

Trellis stitch, popular in the seventeenth century, is a needlelace filling stitch, attached only at the edges, and is most easily worked with a twisted silk thread. The first row of trellis stitch is worked into a foundation of back stitches, the size depending on the effect desired—close together and the trellis stitches resemble tent stitches in canvas work, further apart and an open 'trellis' is the result.

Bring the needle out at 1, slip it under the first back stitch (forming a T—a good way to remember this stitch) and pull the thread through, holding the resulting loop with the left thumb. Slip the needle through this loop (2), then pull the thread down, forming a firm knot. Repeat, to work a row of firm knots with loops in between. Insert the needle into the fabric at the end of the row.

To work a second row, bring the needle out at 3, slip the needle through the loop between two knots and pull the thread through, holding the resulting loop with the left thumb. Slip the needle through this loop (4), then pull the thread down, forming a firm knot. Repeat to the end of the row, insert the needle and continue as above.

The rows can be worked in alternate directions as described, or in one direction only.

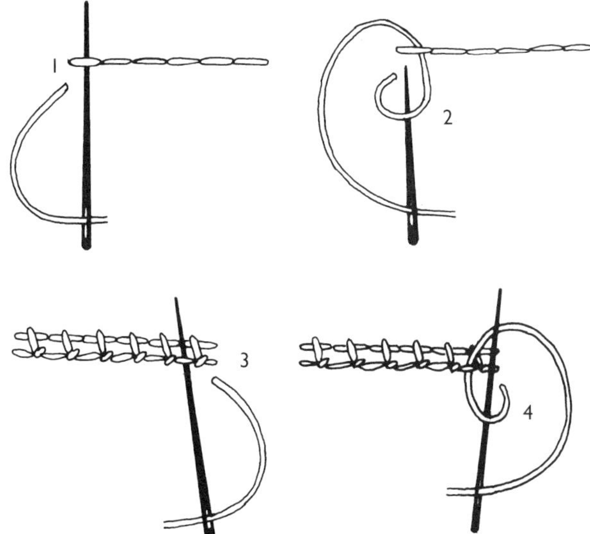

Turkey knots

Turkey knots are worked, then cut to produce a soft velvety pile. Although there are several ways to work Turkey knots, the following method works well for small areas. Use two strands of thread in a number 9 crewel or straw needle.

Insert the needle into the fabric at 1, holding the tail of thread with the left thumb. Come out at 2 and go down at 3 to make a *small* securing stitch. Bring the needle out again at 1 (piercing the securing stitch), pull the thread down and also hold with the left thumb.

For the next Turkey knot, insert the needle at 4 (still holding the tails of thread). Come out at 5 and go down at 2 to make a small securing stitch. Bring the needle out again at 4 (piercing the securing stitch), pull the thread down and hold with the left thumb as before. Repeat to work a row.

Work each successive row directly above the previous row, holding all the resulting tails with the left thumb. To complete, cut all the loops, comb with an eyebrow comb, and cut the pile to the desired length. The more the pile is combed the fluffier it becomes.

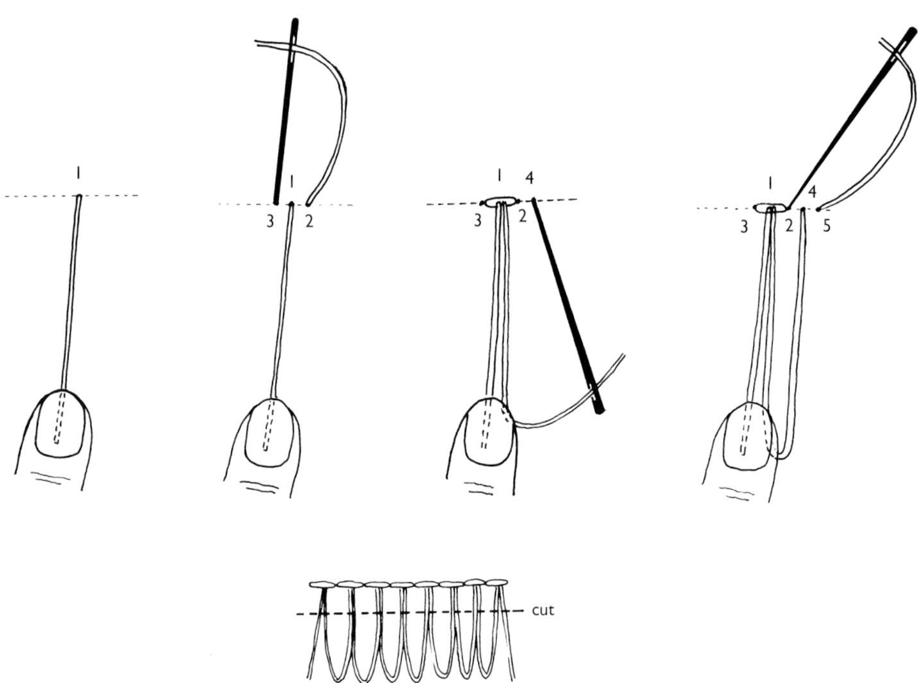

Whipped spider web stitch

Whipped spider web stitch is a form of needleweaving worked over a grid of foundation threads, which can be used to fill many different shapes, e.g. a beetle's elytra. First work the foundation stitches, often in a heavier thread, over the shape to be filled. Working from right to left, each of the foundation threads is whipped, as in back stitch, using a tapestry needle to avoid piercing the threads or the background fabric. To start, bring the needle out at the edge of the shape and slide under thread 1. Work a 'back stitch' over 1, then slide the needle under thread 2. Work a 'back stitch' over 2, then slide the needle under thread 3. Work a 'back stitch' over 3, then insert the needle at the edge of the shape. Repeat, always working in the same direction, until the shape is filled, resulting in whipped 'ribs' on the surface.

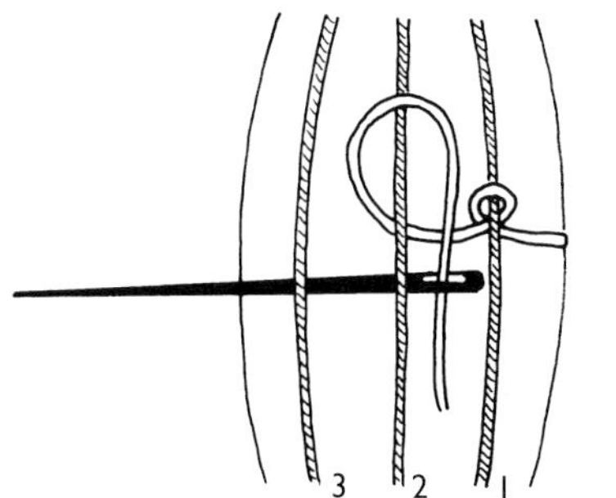

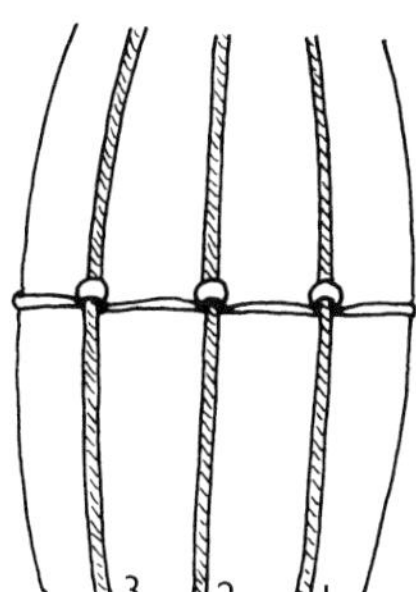

Bibliography and Further Reading

I gain an immense amount of pleasure from my books and can always justify the addition of another volume to the collection! I have referred to the following for information and inspiration.

INSECTS

Beckmann, Poul. *Living Jewels*. Prestel-Verlag, London, New York, 2001.

Cave, Ronald D. 'Jewel Scarabs,' *National Geographic*, February 2001.

Dierl, Wolfgang. *Insekten*. BLV, Munich, 1997.

Evans, Arthur, and Bellamy, Charles. *An Inordinate Fondness for Beetles*. Henry Holt, New York, 1996.

Field Guide to the Butterflies and other Insects of Britain. Reader's Digest, London, 1984.

Insects: An Illustrated Survey, Hamlyn, London, 1979.

Koch, Maryjo. *Dragonfly Beetle Butterfly Bee*. Smithmark, New York, 1998.

MacQuitty, Miranda. *Megabugs*. Carlton Books, London, 1995.

Mandahl-Barth, G. *Woodland Life*, Blandford Press, London, 1966.

Monteith, Geoff. *The Butterfly Man of Kuranda*. Queensland Museum, Brisbane, 1991.

Mound, Laurence. *Insect*. Dorling Kindersley, London, 1990.

Naumann, I.D. *Systematic and Applied Entomology*, Melbourne University Press, 1994.

Nuridsany, Claude, and Pérennou, Marie. *Microcosmos*. Stewart, Tabori & Chang, New York, 1996.

Urquhart, F. A. *Introducing the Insect*. F. Warne & Co., London, 1965.

Whitlock, Ralph. *Insects*. Macmillan, London, 1983.

Zahradnik, Jiri. *The Illustrated Book of Insects*. Treasure Press, London, 1991.

Zborowski, Paul, and Storey, Ross. *Field Guide to Insects in Australia*. Reed, Sydney, 1995.

GENERAL

Blunt, Wilfred and Stearn, William. *The Art of Botanical Illustration*. Antique Collector's Club, London, 1995.

Budden, Sue. *Floral Ornament*. BookKing International, Paris, 1995.

Cole, Herbert. *Heraldry Decoration and Floral Forms*. Crescent Books, New York, 1988.

Day, Lewis F. *Lettering in Ornament*, Batsford, London, 1902.

Durant, Stuart. *Ornament*. The Overlook Press, New York, 1986.

Epstein, Diana and Safro, Millicent. *Buttons*, Thames & Hudson, London, 1991.

Hodges, Sid G. *More Indoor and Community Games*. Methuen & Co., London, 1948.

Hoyle, Martin. *The Gardener's Perpetual Almanac*. Thames & Hudson, London, 1997.

Innes, Miranda and Perry, Clay. *Medieval Flowers*. Kyle Cathie Ltd, London, 1997.

MacQuitty, Miranda. *Megabugs*. Carlton Books, London, 1995.

Milne, A.A. *Now We Are Six*. Methuen Children's Books, London, 1989 edition.

Nahmad, Claire. *Garden Spells*. Pavilion Books, London, 1994.

Nissenson, Marilyn and Jonas, Susan. *Jeweled Bugs and Butterflies*, Harry N. Abrahams, New York, 2000.

Ruyak, Jacqueline. 'Japanese Chirimen Bags', *Piecework*, November/December, 1994.

Rivers, Victoria Z. *The Shining Cloth*. Thames & Hudson, London, 1999.

Robertson, Pamela. Charles Rennie Mackintosh: *Art is the Flower*. Pavilion Books, London, 1995.

Segal, Sam. *Flowers and Nature*. Hijink International, Amstelveen, 1990.

Seguy, Eugene A. *Seguy's Decorative Butterflies and Insects*. Dover, New York, 1977.

Sudo, Kumiko. *Omiyage*. Contemporary Books, Chicago, 2001.

Tolkien, T, and Wilkinson, H. *A Collector's Guide to Costume Jewelry*. Thames & Hudson, London, 1997.

Ware, Dora, and Stafford, Maureen. *An Illustrated Dictionary of Ornament*. Allen & Unwin, London, 1974.

EMBROIDERY

Anders, Nedda. *Appliqué Old and New*. Dover, New York, 1976.

Beany, Jan and Littlejohn, Jean. *Bonding and Beyond*. Double Trouble Enterprises, London, 1999.

Beck, Thomasina. *The Embroiderer's Flowers*. David & Charles, UK, 1992.

Caulfield, S. and Saward, B. *Encyclopedia of Victorian Needlework*, Vol. 2, Dover, New York, 1971

Christie, Grace. *Samplers and Stitches*, Batsford, London, 1920.

Clabburn, Pamela. *The Needleworker's Dictionary*. Macmillan, London, 1976.

Enthoven, Jacqueline. *The Stitches of Creative Embroidery*. Schiffer, USA, 1987.

Jarvis, Anthea. 'Beetle Wing Embroidery', *Embroidery*, Vol. 40, No. 3, 1989.

Levey, Santina. *Discovering Embroidery of the 19th Century*, Shire Publications, London, reprinted 1983.

Morris, Barbara. *Victorian Embroidery*, Herbert Jenkins, London (date unknown).

Snook, Barbara. *English Embroidery*, Bell & Hyman, London, 1985.

Thomas, Mary. *Dictionary of Embroidery Stitches*, Hodder & Stoughton, London, 1934.

Thomas, Mary. *Mary Thomas's Embroidery Book*, Hodder & Stoughton, London, reprinted 1989.

GOLDWORK

Dawson, Barbara. *The Technique of Metal Thread Embroidery*. Batsford, London, 1982.

Dean, Beryl. *Ecclesiastical Embroidery*. Batsford, London, 1968.

Franklin, Tracy A. *New Ideas in Goldwork*, Batsford, London, 2002.

Lemon, Jane. *Metal Thread Embroidery*, Batsford, London, 2002.

Saunders, Sally. *Royal School of Needlework Embroidery Techniques*. Batsford, London, 1998.

Zimmerman, Jane. *Techniques of Metal Thread Embroidery*. Self published, California, 1980.

STUMPWORK

Nicholas, Jane. *Stumpwork Embroidery: A Collection of Fruits, Flowers and Insects*. Milner, Australia, 1995.

Nicholas, Jane. *Stumpwork Embroidery Designs and Projects*. Milner, Australia, 1998.

Nicholas, Jane. *Stumpwork Dragonflies*. Milner, Australia, 2000.

Stumpwork Supplies and Kit Information

The threads, beads and needlework products referred to in this book (Au Ver à Soie, Cifonda, DMC, Framecraft, Kreinik, Madeira, Mill Hill) are available from specialist needlework shops.

A mail order service for embroidery and stumpwork supplies is available from Jane Nicholas Embroidery. All materials required for the projects may be obtained either in kit form or individually. Please write, telephone or fax for a catalogue and price list.

Jane Nicholas Embroidery
Chelsea Fabrics
PO Box 300
Bowral NSW 2576
Australia

Tel/fax: 61 2 4861 1175

Picture Credits

Page 14. Beetle anatomy (genus *Chrysochroa*) from *An Inordinate Fondness for Beetles* by A Evans & C Bellamy, 1996, p.126. Photograph by Lisa Charles Watson. Permission by Nevraumont Publishing Company, NYC, USA.

Page 24. Seguy's insects Plate 38 from *Seguy's Decorative Butterflies and Insects in Full Color*, E. A. Seguy, 1977. Courtesy Dover Publications, Inc.

Page 26. Seguy's insects Plate 33 from *Seguy's Decorative Butterflies and Insects in Full Color*, E. A. Seguy, 1977. Courtesy Dover Publications, Inc.

Page 27. Vauxhall Glass Beetle from *A Collector's Guide to Costume Jewelery*, T Tolkien & H Wilkinson, Thames & Hudson, London. © Michael Harvey/ Quarto Publishing plc.

Page 28. Lalique longhorn beetle ring. © MAK – Austrian Museum of Applied Arts/ Contemporary Art, Vienna

Page 28. Lalique blister beetle corsage ornament. © Calouste Gulbenkian Museum, Lisbon.

Page 30. Brooch and belt ornament. Cartier, London, 1924. Yellow gold, platinum, smoky quartz, cabochon emeralds, ancient blue faience scarab, diamonds, and enamel. Courtesy Cartier.

Page 31. John Paul Miller Beetle pendant/brooch. Courtesy John Paul Miller.

Page 33. Beetle button set on rock crystal from *Buttons* by Diana Epstein and Millicent Saffro, 1991. © Harry N. Abrams, Inc.

Page 33. Inlayed beetle on tortoiseshell from *Buttons* by Diana Epstein and Millicent Saffro, 1991. © Harry N. Abrams, Inc.

Page 34. Italian mosaic buttons from *Buttons* by Diana Epstein and Millicent Saffro, 1991. © Harry N. Abrams, Inc.

Page 35. *The Grand Parade*, c.1917, F.P. Dodd. Courtesy the Queensland Museum

Page 49. Buprestid Beetles. From the collection of and courtesy Victoria Z. Rivers, photography by Barbara Molloy

Page 51. Singing Shawl, Pwo Karen people, northern Thailand. From the collection of and courtesy Victoria Z. Rivers, photography by Barbara Molloy

Page 52. Detail of a Singing Shawl. From the collection of and courtesy Victoria Z. Rivers, photography by Barbara Molloy

Page 55. Black corded silk two-piece dress, trimmed with gold embroidery and beetles' wings (c. 1890). Courtesy Narryna, Tasmania.

Page 56. Detail trimming. Courtesy Narryna, Tasmania.

Page 57. Detail of all-over design of medallions. Courtesy Narryna, Tasmania.

Page 57. Trimming fabric. Courtesy Narryna, Tasmania.

Page 58. Trimming fabric. Courtesy Narryna, Tasmania.

Page 61. Pomegranate, piano or mantel slip end design. Courtesy Narryna, Tasmania.

Page 62. Pamela Spray, piano or mantel slip end design. Courtesy Narryna, Tasmania.

Page 63. Punica, piano or mantel slip end design. Courtesy Narryna, Tasmania.

Page 88. Jewel Beetles from *An Inordinate Fondness for Beetles* by A Evans & C Bellamy. 1996, p.23. Photograph by Lisa Charles Watson. Permission by Nevraumont Publishing Company, NYC, USA.

Page 96. Pill Beetle. © Frank Koehler

Page 100. Soldier Beetle © Frank Koehler

Page 104. Ground beetles from *An Inordinate Fondness for Beetles* by A Evans & C Bellamy. 1996, p.189. Photograph by Lisa Charles Watson. Permission by Nevraumont Publishing Company, NYC, USA

Page 113. Longhorn beetle (*Rosalia alpina*) from *An Inordinate Fondness for Beetles* by A Evans & C Bellamy, 1996, p.179. Photograph by Lisa Charles Watson. Permission by Nevraumont Publishing Company, NYC, USA.

Page 119. Ruby Longhorn Beetle © Hania and Hans Arentsen

Page 123. Leaf Beetles (*cassidine chrysomelids*) from *An Inordinate Fondness for Beetles* by A Evans & C Bellamy, 1996, p.143. Photograph by Lisa Charles Watson. Permission by Nevraumont Publishing Company, NYC, USA.

Page 130. Checkered Beetle. © Dr Stephan Roscher.

Page 134. Ladybird. © Hania and Hans Arentsen

Page 138. Weevil from *An Inordinate Fondness for Beetles* by A Evans & C Bellamy, 1996, p.8. Photograph by Lisa Charles Watson. Permission by Nevraumont Publishing Company, NYC, USA.

Page 142. Diving Beetle. © and courtesy Gerard H. Visser.

Page 147. Click Beetles from *An Inordinate Fondness for Beetles* by A Evans & C Bellamy, 1996, p.21. Photograph by Lisa Charles Watson. Photograph by Lisa Charles Watson. Permission by Nevraumont Publishing Company, NYC, USA.

Page 156. Fungus Beetle from *An Inordinate Fondness for Beetles* by A Evans & C Bellamy, 1996, p.110. Photograph by Lisa Charles Watson. Permission by Nevraumont Publishing Company, NYC, USA.

Page 159. Net-winged beetle. © Dr Stephan Roscher

Page 164 and 230. Gold & Silver Scarab Beetles (Plusiotis) from *An Inordinate Fondness for Beetles* by A Evans & C Bellamy, 1996, p.162. Photograph by Lisa Charles Watson. Permission by Nevraumont Publishing Company, NYC, USA.

Page 172. Rove Beetle. © Hania and Hans Arentsen

Page 176. The Entomologist. Courtesy Narryna, Tasmania.

Page 194. Passe, Crispijn van de. Hortus floridus ... Arnhem, Johannus Janssoon, 1614-1616.— Part 3, Autumnus, plate 23, "Crocus sativus et Montanus primus". © 2003 Hunt Institute for Botanical Documentation. All rights reserved.

Page 211. Charles Rennie Mackintosh, Fritillaria, 1915. © Hunterian Art Gallery, University of Glasgow, Mackintosh Collection

Page 230. Scarabs from *An Inordinate Fondness for Beetles* by A Evans & C Bellamy. Photograph by Lisa Charles Watson. Permission by Nevraumont Publishing Company, NYC, USA.

Page 271. Italian Mosaic Button from *Buttons* by Diana Epstein and Millicent Saffro, 1991. © Harry N. Abrams, Inc.

Page 290. Hand coloured print.Courtesy Narryna, Tasmania.

Page 293. Embroidered ivory satin waistcoat, c.1780. Courtesy Thomasina Beck.

Page 339. Detail from the quilt Redwork Garden Maze, c.1880. Courtesy Cindy Brick

Page 346. Ladybirds card. © James Ellis Stevens.

Index

Note: Page numbers shown in **bold** refer to illustrations

A

acknowledgements, 416
Alexander Beetle, 376
alphabet, 260, 285-286
Amazon, 47, 50, 89
  Shuar people, 50
America, 345
American beetle jewellery, 31
anthracite, 20
applied embroidery *see* Appliqué
Appliqué, 345-346
Appliqué beetles, 345-360
  how to, 347
  in fabric, 348-350
  in felt, 356-359
  Click Beetle, 351
  Diving Beetle, 352
  Ground Beetle, 353
  Longhorn Beetle, 354
  Scarab Beetle, 355
Art et Décoration, 23
Art Nouveau, 9, 28-30, **29-30**
Asia, 345
Assyrians, 227

B

Babylonians, 227
bags, 361-375
Bangkok, 64
beaded beetles, 36-45
  blue-green beaded beetle, 41-45
    beading diagram, **42**
    working the beetle, 41-42
  medallion borders, 43-45, **45**
    diagram, **44**
  red-orange beaded beetle, 37-40
    beading diagram, **40**
    working the beetle, 38-40
Bee-wolves *see* Checkered Beetle
beetle
  anatomy, 15-17, **15**
  abdomen, 17
  antennae, 16
  eyes, 16
  legs, 17
  mesothorax, 17
  metathorax, 17
  mouth parts, 16
  prothorax, 16-17
  size, 12-13
  thorax, 16-17
Beetle bags, 361-375
  Beetle Evening Bag, 369-375
  materials, 362
  Scarab Beetle Pouch, 363-368
  shape as inspiration, 362
beetle buttons, 32-34, **33-34**
beetle as design source, 22-26
beetle as embellishment, 20-45
Beetle families, 12, **85**, 87-175
  Buprestidae, 49, 50, 87, 89-95
  Byrrhidae, 87, 96-99
  Cantharidae, 87, 100-103
  Carabidae, 87, **104**, 105-112
  Cerambycidae, 87, 114-122
  Chrysomelidae, 87, 124-129
  Cleridae, 87, 131-133
  Coccinelidae, 87, 134-136
  Curculionidae, 87, 137-141
  Dytiscidae, 87, 142-147
  Elateridae, 87, 148-155
  Erotylidae, 87, 156-158
  Lycidae, 87, 159-162
  Scarabaeidae, 87, 163-171
  Staphylinidae, 87, 172-175
beetle jewellery, 27-31
beetle parts to embroider, 296
Beetle Species
  Agrypnus murinas see Skipjack Beetle
  Amber Soldier Beetle, surface embroidery, 302-303
  Amethyst Click Beetle, surface embroidery, 324-325
  Aqua Tortoise Beetle, surface embroidery, 315-316
  Aubergine Pill Beetle, surface embroidery, 300-301
  Bronze Ground Beetle, surface embroidery, 308-309
  Burnt-orange Scarab Beetle, surface embroidery, 332-333
  Campsosternus gemma see Click Beetle
  Cantharis fusca see Soldier Beetle
  Carabus cancellatus see Ground Beetle
  Cassida viridis see Green Tortoise Beetle
  Catoxantha gratiosa, **26**
  Catoxantha ocellata see Jewel Beetle

Catoxantha opulenta, **26**
Cetoniinae see Flower Chafer Beetle
Chafer Beetle, 163
surface embroidery, 334-335
Chartreuse Longhorn Beetle, surface embroidery, 312-313
Checkered Beetle, 77, 84, 85, **130**, **131**
goldwork, 259-261
Redwork, 342-344
stumpwork, 131-133
surface embroidery, 317-318
Chocolate Diving Beetle, surface embroidery, 322-323
Christmas Beetle, 163
Chrysobothris affinis see Metallic Woodboring Beetle
Chrysochroa fulgidissima, 89
Chrysomela aenea see leaf beetle
Click Beetle, 77, 84, 85, **147**, 148
appliqué, 351
stumpwork, 149-151
surface embroidery, 324-325
Coccinella quinquepunctata see Ladybird
Cockshafer Beetle drawings, 23
Copper Rove Beetle, surface embroidery, 336-337
Coral Net-winged Beetle, surface embroidery, 330-331
Crimson Skipjack Beetle, surface embroidery, 326-327
Cypherotylus guatemalae see Fungus Beetle
Cytilus sericeus see Pill Beetle
Diving Beetle
appliqué, 352
goldwork, 242-243
surface embroidery, 322-323
Dung Beetle, 163
Dytiscus marginalis see Great Diving Beetle
Emerald Click Beetle, surface embroidery, 324-325
Euchroma giganta, 50
Eupholus linnei see Weevil
Flower Chafer Beetle, 163
Fungus Beetle, 77, 84, 85, 156, **156**
Redwork, 342-344
stumpwork, 157-158
surface embroidery, 328-329
Garden Chafer, 77, 84, 85, 163
stumpwork, 168-171
surface embroidery, 334-335
Garnet Net-winged Beetle, surface embroidery, 330-331
Ghost-walker beetle *see* Violin Beetle
Giraffe Beetle, 137
Golden Chafer Beetle, 163
Great Diving Beetle, 76, 84, 85, **142**, 143
stumpwork, 144-146
Green Ground Beetle, surface embroidery, 306-307
Green Tortoise Beetle, 77, 84, 85, 124
stumpwork, 127-129, **127**
Ground Beetle, 77, 84, 85, **104**, 105
Appliqué, 353
beaded, **36**
goldwork, 240-241
Redwork, 342-344
stumpwork, 106-108
surface embroidery, 306-309
Honey Pill Beetle, surface embroidery, 300-301
Jewel Beetle, 77, 84, 85, **88**, 89-95
gold stumpwork, 282
goldwork, 247-249
Redwork, 342-344
stumpwork, 90-92, 205
surface embroidery, 298-299
wings used in embroidery, 64-66
Kelly Green Leaf Beetle, surface embroidery, 314-315
Khaki Diving Beetle, surface embroidery, 322-323
Ladybird, 77, 84, 85, **134**, 135
stumpwork, 135-136
surface embroidery, 319-320
Ladybird Notebook Cover, 338
Lampropepla rothschildii, **26**
Lasiorrhynchus barbicornis see Giraffe Beetle
Leaf Beetle, 77, 84, 85, **123**, 124
gold stumpwork, 283
jewellery, 29-30, **29-30**
stumpwork, 124-127
surface embroidery, 314-315
Leptura rubra see Ruby Longhorn Beetle
Lime Green Garden Chafer, surface embroidery, 334-335
Longhorn Beetle, 12-13, 77, 84, 85, **113**, 114, **115**
appliqué, 354
goldwork, 244-245
stumpwork, 115-118
surface embroidery, 310-313
Lyoreus alluaudi, **26**
Mahogany Scarab Beetle, surface embroidery, 332-333
Marine Tortoise Beetle, surface embroidery, 315-316
Metallic Woodboring Beetle, 77, 84, 85, **88**
stumpwork, 93-95
Metriorrhynchus rhipidius see Net-winged Beetle
Mormolyce phyllodes see Violin Beetle
Mustard Longhorn Beetle, surface embroidery, 310-311
Navy-green Fungus Beetle, surface embroidery, 328-329
Net-winged Beetle, 77, 84, 85, 159, **159**, 178
gold stumpwork, 281

stumpwork, 160-162, 192
surface embroidery, 330-331
Old Gold Garden Chafer, surface embroidery, 334-335
Orange Jewel Beetle, surface embroidery, 298-299
Paederus riparius see Rove Beetle
Peacock Longhorn Beetle, surface embroidery, 312-313
Pewter Rove Beetle, surface embroidery, 336-337
Phyllopertha horticola see Garden Chafer
Pill Beetle, **36**, 77, 84, 85, 96, **96**, 97-99
Redwork, 342-344
surface embroidery, 300-301
Plagiodera versicolora see Leaf Beetle
Plusiotis chrysargyrea see Scarab Beetle
Polyphylla petiti, **26**
Pumpkin Weevil, surface embroidery, 320-321
Purple Longhorn Beetle, surface embroidery, 310-311
Red Ladybird, surface embroidery, 319-320
Rosalia alpina see Longhorn Beetle
Rouge Soldier Beetle, surface embroidery, 302-303
Rove Beetle, 76, 84, 85, 86, 172, **172**
gold stumpwork, 279
stumpwork, 173-175
surface embroidery, 336-337
Ruby Longhorn Beetle, 76, 84, 85
stumpwork, 119-122
Rust-purple Fungus Beetle, surface embroidery, 328-329
Scarab Beetle, 20-21, 30, 33, 77, 84, 85, 163, **163**, **164**
appliqué, 355
gold stumpwork, 278
goldwork, 245-247
stumpwork, 165-168, 218, 222, 223-226
surface embroidery, 332-333
Skipjack Beetle, 78, 84, 85, 148
gold stumpwork, 280
stumpwork, 152-155
surface embroidery, 326-327
Soldier Beetle, 76, 84, 85, 100, **100**
stumpwork, 101-103
surface embroidery, 302-303
Steel Ground Beetle, surface embroidery, 308-309
Sternocera aquisignata, 50, 64
Tan Violin Beetle, surface embroidery, 304-305
Tangerine Skipjack Beetle, surface embroidery, 326-327
Teal Checkered Beetle, surface embroidery, 317-318
Titanus giganteus see Longhorn Beetle
Tortoise Beetle, surface embroidery, 315-316
Trichodes apiarius see Checkered Beetle
Turquoise Weevil, surface embroidery, 320-321
Violet Jewel Beetle, surface embroidery, 298-299
Violin Beetle, 77, 84, 85, 86, 105, **108**, **109**
goldwork, 262-270
skeleton, **263**
stumpwork, 108-112
surface embroidery, 304-305
Weevil, 76, 84, 85, 137, **138**
stumpwork, 139-141
surface embroidery, 320-321
Wine Checkered Beetle, surface embroidery, 317-318
Yellow Ladybird, surface embroidery, 319-320
Beetle Specimen Box, 83-175, **84**
identification chart, **85**, 87
see also stumpwork beetles
Beetle Wing Evening Bag, **65**, 66, 67-72
beetle wings
as adornment, 49-54
alternatives, 67
attaching, 64-66, **64**, **66**
as embellishment, 9
size, 64
steaming, 64
used in embroidery, 64-72
working with, 64-66
Bibliography, 412-414
Bone Room, 47, 48, 67
borders
goldwork, 269-270
medallion borders, 43-45
Boysenberries, stumpwork, 220-222
brooches, 30, 37
mounting, 226
Scarab Beetle Brooch, stumpwork, 223-226
Burma, 50, 52
Butterfly Man of Kuranda, 35
buttons, 32-34, 271

C

Cartier, 30
Chesterfield Coat of Arms, 253
Chile, 292, 294
China, 186
Cisterna, Miguel, 292, 294
Clover, 204
stumpwork, 204-205
Coleoptera, 12, 31, 83
crocus, 193-194, **194**
stumpwork, 195-203
Crocus sativus see crocus

D

Darwin, Charles, 59
Dodd, Frederick P, 35
Dresser, Christopher, 23, **23**
Dys, Habert, 23, **23**, **24**

E

East India company, 53
ecclesiastical embroideries, 262
Egypt, 20-21, 27, 30, 163, 227, 345
Elizabethan era, 228, 250, 292
elytra
 used in embroidery, 64-72
 see also beetle wings
embroidery catalogue (Narryna), 60-63
England, 47-48, 52, 291-292
English buttons, 33
English Work, 228
Entomologist, 176
equipment *see* techniques and equipment
Europe, 53, 194, 228

F

Fabre, John-Henri, 114
Fennel, 208
 stumpwork, 209
flowers
 clover, 204
 crocus, 195-203
 detached bud petals, 199-200, 214, 216
 detached flower petals, 200-202, 213
 detached leaves, 203, 217-218
 detached middle petals, 214
 detached side petals, 214
 fennel, 209
 fritillary, 207, 210-218
 pomegranate, 252-257
 sepals, 222, 257
 stamens, 213
 stigmas, 199
 surface bud petals, 198, 213
 surface flower petals, 199, 212-213
 surface leaves, 210-211, 254
 surface stems, 204
 surface stems and leaves, 197-198, 204, 209, 210, 221
Fritillaria meleagris see Fritillary
Fritillary, stumpwork, **207**, 210-218
fusing, 239, 381

G

gilded silver, 228
glass beads, 36
glass paperweight, 37, 221, 222, 386-387
glossary of product names, 390
Gold Stumpwork Beetles, 275-289
 elytra suggestions, 277
 embroidered initial and beetle, 284-289
 how to embroider, 276-277
 Jewel Beetle, 282
 Leaf Beetle, 283
 Net-winged Beetle, 281
 Rove Beetle, 279
 Scarab Beetle, 278
 Skipjack Beetle, 280
Goldwork
 borders, 269-270
 definition, 229
 initial, 259, 260
 stitches, burden stitch, 262, 265
 threads, 234-237
  broad plate, 235
  couched gilt passing thread, 234
  couched gold threads, 234
  couching thread, 235
  history, 227-229
  Jap gold (Japanese gold), 234
  milliary, 235
  passing thread, 235
  pearl purl, 235-236
  Rococo (Check) thread, 235
  sewing threads, 234
  twists, 235
 threads, cut gold, 236
  bright check purl, 236
  pearl purl, 236
  rough purl, 236
  smooth purl, 236
 threads, synthetic metallic embroidery, 236
 tools, 231-233
  beeswax, 232, 254
  cutting board, 232
  frames and hoops, 231
  mellor, 233
  nailfile, 233
  needles, 232
  scissors, 232
  tweezers, 232
Goldwork beetle, 227-289
 embroidering, 230-237
 materials, 233
  background fabric, 233
  backing fabric, 233
  leather, 233
  padding, 233
  spangles and beads, 233
 Or Nué Beetle, 271-274
 order of work, 231
Goldwork Beetle Sampler, 237-248
 beetle skeletons, **238**
 preparation, 239-240
Goldwork Beetles
 Checkered Beetle, 259-261
 Diving Beetle, 242-243

Ground Beetle, 240-241
Jewel Beetle, 247-249
Longhorn Beetle, 244-245
Pomegranate, Snail and Gold Beetle, 249-261
Scarab Beetle, 245-247
Violin Beetle, 262-270
grapevine, stumpwork, 179-184
Greeks, 12, 187, 250

I

India, 47, 51, 52, 53, 54-55, 64, 89
Naga women, 50
Indochina, 26
Indonesia, 105
initials, goldwork, 259, 260, 284
insects in jewellery, 28
Irish buttons, 33
ironing, 239
Italy, mosaic buttons, 34-35, 271

J

Japan, 27-28, 89, 363
jewellery, 27-31, 223-226

L

Ladybird Notebook Cover, 338
Lalique, R, 28-29, **28**
Langdon family, Tasmania, 176
laundering, 29, 296

M

Madagascar, 26
Malacca, 26
medallion borders, 43-35
Mediterranean, 194, 250
metal thread embroidery, 228-228
methods *see* techniques and equipment
Mexico, 26
Middle Ages, 194, 228, 262, 345
Miller, John Paul, 31
mounting stumpwork
brooch, 226
glass paperweight, 386-387
Murghal era, 51
museums, 9, 48, 54-58
music box, 37, 222

N

Napoleon, 28
Narryna Heritage Museum, Hobart, Tasmania, 48, 54-58
embroidery catalogue, 60-63
natural history, 12-17
Nepal, 32
net, beetle wing embroidery, 54-58
netsuke, 27
New Guinea *see* Papua New Guinea
New Zealand, 137

O

Omaha, Nebraska, 9
Or Nué Beetle, 36-37
goldwork, 271-274
history, 271

P

Pamela Spray, embroidery catalogue (Narryna), 61
paperweight, 37, 221, 222, 386-387
Papua New Guinea, 50
Waugi Valley people, 50, 165
Peacock, **180**, **185-186**
feathers, 154, 184, 191
stumpwork, 187-191
Peru, 89
Phillips, George, 22
Phoenicians, 250
plants *see* boysenberries; flowers; grapevine; pomegranate
Pomegranate
diagrams, 251
embroidery catalogue (Narryna), 61
goldwork, 251-257
Pomegranate and banana salad, 252
postage stamp beetles, 24
prints, 290
product names, 390
Punica, embroidery catalogue (Narryna), 61
Punica granatum see Pomegranate

Q

Queen, 59-60

R

Red clover *see* clover
Redwork, 340
Redwork Beetle Bag, 341-344
Redwork Beetles, 339-344
Checkered Beetle, 342-344
Fungus Beetle, 342-344
Ground Beetle, 342-344
Jewel Beetle, 342-344
Pill Beetle, 342-344
Romans, 114, 208, 250
Rutelinae subfamily, 163

S

saffron, 194, 195
Saffron Crocus *see* crocus
Scarab Beetle, 218, 222
Brooch, stumpwork, 223-226
buttons, 33

decoration, 20-21
jewellery, 30, **30**
Seguy, Eugene, 23, 25, **25, 26**
singing shawls, 50-51, **51-52**
snail, stumpwork, 257-258
Snake's head Fritillary *see* Fritillary
South Africa, 114
South America, 49, 89
Southeast Asia, 49, 64, 89
Stitches, 395-411
back stitch, 396
back stitch – split, 396
bullion knot, 397
burden stitch, 262, 265, 397
buttonhole stitch, 397
buttonhole stitch – corded detached, 399
buttonhole stitch – detached, 398
buttonhole stitch – long and short, 398
chain stitch, 399
chain stitch – open, 400
chain stitch – whipped, 400
couching, 400
couching – lattice, 401
fishbone stitch, 401
flat stitch, 401
fly stitch, 402
French knot, 402
long and short stitch, 402
outline stitch, 403
overcast stitch, 403
pad stitch, 404
plaited stitch, 211-212, 404
Roumanian couching, 404
satin stitch, 405
satin stitch – encroaching, 405
slip stitch, 405
split stitch, 406
stab stitch, 406
stem stitch, 406
stem stitch band – raised, 407
straight stitch, 407
striped woven band, 408
tacking (basting), 408
tent stitch, 408
trellis stitch, 409
Turkey knots, 410
whipped spider stitch, 411
Stumpwork Beetle Species
Checkered Beetle, 131-133
Click Beetle, 149-151
Fungus Beetle, 157-158
Garden Chafer, 168-171
Great Diving Beetle, 144-146
Green Tortoise Beetle, 127-129, **127**
Ground Beetle, 106-108
Jewel Beetle, 90-92, 205
Ladybird, 135-136
Leaf Beetle, 124-127
Longhorn Beetle, 115-118
Metallic Woodboring Beetle, 93-95
Net-winged Beetle, 160-162, 192
Rove Beetle, 173-175
Ruby Longhorn Beetle, 119-122
Scarab Beetle, 165-168, 218, 222, 223-226
Skipjack Beetle, 152-155
Soldier Beetle, 101-103
Violin Beetle, 108-112
Weevil, 139-141
stumpwork beetles, 73-225, **84-85**
background, 74, 86
body parts, **75**
abdomen, working, 75-76
antennae, 81
elytra
applied decoration, 77, 150-151, 166-167, 169-170
couched, 77, 91-92, 94-95, 98, 107, 126, 161-162
embroidered, 77, 116, 133, 136, 158
exotic fabric, 76, 102, 121, 144, 175
fused fabric, 76-77, 111, 128-129, 140
needlelace, 78, 153-154
working, 75-79
head and eyes, 79-82
legs, 82
embroidered, 82
wrapped wire legs, 82
thorax
embroidered, 81
leather, 79-80
wired fabric, 80-81
diagrams and skeletons, 85
embroidering, 74-82
mounting, 74
order of work, 74
padding, 75-76
preparation, 74
shaping, 82
size, 86
tracing, 74
Stumpwork projects, 177-226
Beetle and Boysenberries, 219-222
Crocus, Clover and Jewel Beetle, 193-205
Fritillary, Fennel and Scarab Beetle, 206-218
Peacock, Grapevine and Beetle, 178-192
Scarab Beetle Brooch, 223-226
stumpwork supplies and kits, 415
supplies and kits, 415
surface embroidery
background fabric, 295-296
how to embroider beetles, 295-96
suggested uses, 295
threads, 296

surface embroidery beetles, 291-343
Amber Soldier Beetle, 302-303
Amethyst Click Beetle, 324-325
Aqua Tortoise Beetle, 315-316
Aubergine Pill Beetle, 300-301
Bronze Ground Beetle, 308-309
Burnt-orange Scarab Beetle, 332-333
Chartreuse Longhorn Beetle, 312-313
Chocolate Diving Beetle, 322-323
Copper Rove Beetle, 336-337
Coral Net-winged Beetle, 330-331
Crimson Skipjack Beetle, 326-327
Emerald Click Beetle, 324-325
Garnet Net-winged Beetle, 330-331
Green Ground Beetle, 306-307
Honey Pill Beetle, 300-301
Kelly Green Leaf Beetle, 314-315
Khaki Diving Beetle, 322-323
Ladybird Notebook Cover, 338
Lime Green Garden Chafer, 334-335
Mahogany Scarab Beetle, 332-333
Marine Tortoise Beetle, 315-316
Mustard Longhorn Beetle, 310-311
Navy-green Fungus Beetle, 328-329
Old Gold Garden Chafer, 334-335
Orange Jewel Beetle, 298-299
Peacock Longhorn Beetle, 312-313
Pewter Rove Beetle, 336-337
Pumpkin Weevil, 320-321
Purple Longhorn Beetle, 310-311
Red Ladybird, 319-320
Rouge Soldier Beetle, 302-303
Rust-purple Fungus Beetle, 328-329
Steel Ground Beetle, 308-309
Tan Violin Beetle, 304-305
Tangerine Skipjack Beetle, 326-327
Teal Checkered Beetle, 317-318
Turquoise Weevil, 320-321
Violet Jewel Beetle, 298-299
Wine Checkered Beetle, 317-318
Yellow Ladybird, 319-320
Sykes, Godfrey, 260

T

Tasmania, 176
techniques and equipment, 377-393
Bondaweb *see* techniques and equipment, Vliesofix
equipment, 388
fusing, 239, 381
glossary of product names, 390
leather
cutting, 384
padding, 384
stitching, 385
mounting stumpwork glass paperweight, 386-387
needles, 389-390
product names, 390
thread conversion chart, 391-393
transferring design to fabric, 378-380
preparation, 378
requirements, 378
thread tracing design, 379-380
tracing design on back, 379
tracing design on front, 378-379
tracing design with paper template, 380
Vliesofix, 239, 381
fusing to felt, 381
fusing to organza and felt, 381
wire, 382-383
attaching to background fabric, 383
stitching to fabric, 382-383
Thailand, 50, 52
Thailand/Burma
Pwo Karen hill tribe, 50, 51, 52
thread conversion chart, 391-393
Trifolium pratense see Clover

V

Victorian dress, 47-48
Victorian Dress (c. 1890), 54-58, **55-58**
Victorian jewel embroidery, 59-63
Victorian jewellery, **27**
vines, stumpwork, 179-184

W

waistcoat, surface embroidery, 292, **293**
Weldon's Practical Needlework, 59
Worth, Jean-Philippe, 53

About the author

From Australia, Jane Nicholas is an experienced embroiderer in goldwork, crewel and ethnic embroidery but specialises in stumpwork. She has been researching this technique for nearly twenty years, has authored three books on raised embroidery, and was awarded a Churchill Fellowship to further her studies in the UK in 1999. She teaches regularly in Australia and New Zealand, and has taught for the Embroiderers' Guilds of the USA and Canada. Jane has a passion for books and is an avid collector of old textiles, needlework tools and insect specimens—to embroider in stumpwork. She is married, has three grown children and lives in Bowral, New South Wales, Australia.

Acknowledgements

Preparing this book has been a long and fascinating journey. Along the way I have received unfailing encouragement and support from my family—John, Katie, Joanna and David. Without their love and understanding, I would not have realised this 'beetle' passion.

I am indebted to the following for their willing assistance in my quest:

Joyce Mackey, Christopher Eden and the Trustees of Narryna Heritage Museum in Hobart, for allowing me unrestricted access to their beautiful beetle wing dress and the accompanying fabrics and patterns.

To all those involved in the production of this book at Sally Milner Publishing—your expertise, and belief in my work, is sincerely appreciated.

Finally, special thanks to my dear 'sewing friends', for their support and enthusiasm, and the opportunity to share ideas and cherished stitching time.